KU-166-204

1.00

35

HARRODS BOOK OF FINE WINE

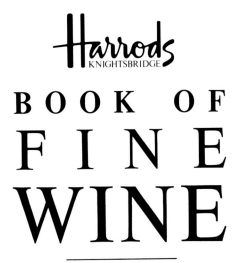

BOOK OF
FINE
WINE

EDITED BY JOANNA SIMON

**WITH CONTRIBUTIONS FROM THE
WORLD'S LEADING WINE WRITERS**

MITCHELL BEAZLEY

HARRODS BOOK OF FINE WINE

Edited and designed by
Mitchell Beazley International Limited,
Artists House, 14/15 Manette Street,
London W1V 5LB

Copyright © Mitchell Beazley Publishers 1990
All rights reserved

No part of this work may be reproduced or utilized
in any form by any means, electronic or mechanical,
including photocopying, recording or by any
information storage and retrieval system, without the
prior written permission of the publishers.

A CIP catalogue record for this book is available from
the British Library.

ISBN 0 85533 788 5

The author and publishers will be grateful for any
information that will assist them in keeping
future editions up to date. Although all reasonable
care has been taken in the preparation of this book,
neither the publishers nor the author can accept any
liability for any consequences arising from the use
thereof or from the information contained therein.

Editors Diane Pengelly, Rupert Joy
Senior Art Editor Tim Foster
Picture Research Brigitte Arora
Maps Pam Williams
Inputting Alison Franks, Kirsty Seymour-Ure
Indexer Anne Barratt
Production Ted Timberlake
Managing Editor Chris Foulkes

Typeset in Garamond by Servis Filmsetting Ltd,
Manchester, England
Colour Reproduction by Scantrans Pte Ltd, Singapore
Printed in West Germany by Mohndruck GmbH, Gütersloh

Contents

Introduction

Pursuing Excellence in Wine

THE WORLD OF FINE WINE is getting larger – and smaller. Each vintage brings into the fold both producers who attain new heights and new vine-growing areas. Every decade new countries and continents add their signatures to the viticultural map. Yet the wine world is also shrinking, as winemakers travel across countries, continents and hemispheres to exchange ideas and glasses of wine, to muddy their boots in each others' vineyards and, increasingly, to invest in joint wine-producing ventures.

At the same time, the fruits of their labours, the wines themselves, are party to more globe-trotting than ever before. It is possible to buy just about any kind of wine in London and New York today. Even the capitals of the traditional wine-producing countries which invariably favour their own wines – and, equally inevitably, protect their own industries spiritedly – now sport shops and restaurants with truly international wine lists. It is possible to buy wine *en primeur*, when it is still only partly made, and wine at auction that is literally hundreds of years old (see pages 243-45). And the more fine wine there is, the more there is to find out about the subject: about the vineyards, wineries and cellars where excellence is pursued; and about the people who dedicate a large part of their time and livelihood to its pursuit.

That is what this book does, by focusing on the wines, philosophies and practices of a series of leading producers in the context of his or her region. It does not aim to perform the role of atlas or encyclopaedia; nor is it a comprehensive survey of all the great wine producers. It would take more than one volume to do that these days. But, through individual profiles of leading producers, it investigates all the main areas of quality wine production – the long-established and the newly-rising stars, the expansive and the very limited. And it is the world's leading wine writers who investigate them. I wonder whether so many international authorities have ever before been gathered together to contribute to a single book.

In most cases the spotlight falls on a proprietor and his or her estate, but the formula is not rigid: in South Australia it would have been negligent to have passed over Max Schubert simply because he is a winemaker but not an owner, and Grange Hermitage, the wine he created, because it is a wine but not an individual estate. It would also have deprived readers of an arresting "fairy tale on a grand scale", as our storyteller James Halliday aptly describes it (see pages 214-18). In the case of sherry and Champagne, the archetypal blended wines, "estate" is also perhaps something of a misnomer – although, as Serena Sutcliffe explains, the house of Krug does boast one of the very few single-vineyard Champagnes, Clos du Mesnil (see page 60).

Some may be surprised at the choice of subjects, or at perceived omissions. Where, for example, are the profiles of the Médoc and Sauternes first growths?. The obvious answer is that they – and many other winemakers, vineyards and wines – make their appearance in other profiles or here in this first chapter. The quintessence of Châteaux Lafite-Rothschild and d'Yquem, for example, is captured in Michael Broadbent's exposition of some of this

8

Château Mouton Rothschild glories in the world's finest collection of wine art, including this Bacchus.

century's great tastings (see pages 239-41). Nor could Bob Thompson have written of the Californian producer Robert Mondavi and his achievements without referring to the Rothschilds of Château Mouton-Rothschild (see pages 189-90). And in this introduction I do not confine my comments exclusively to those who are profiled.

But the obvious answer in isolation misses the point. Other books have striven to define, rank and profile the world's foremost wine estates. This book identifies a subtly but fundamentally different and more varied category. It homes in on those producers who are pursuing excellence – whether idiosyncratically, like Nicolas Joly of Le Clos de la Coulée de Serrant in the Loire (see pages 67-72) and Serge Hochar of Château Musar in the Lebanon (see pages 177-79), or as part of the mainstream – and who, by force of personality, have made a personal contribution to the wine world. Who could deny that the global vision of the gregarious Jean-Michel Cazes, proprietor of fifth-growth Château Lynch-Bages and other properties (see pages 24-29), has had a profound influence on other producers and on wine lovers? Who knows whether some of the ungarlanded estates profiled here may not claim *premier* or *grand cru* status, or their equivalents, in the future? And who would argue that Lynch-Bages is not already of second-growth standard?

IT IS AXIOMATIC that this growing fund of fine wine is appreciated by the current generation of consumers. If it were not, producers could hardly be expected to continue applying such effort. And certainly, the dedication and perseverance that is revealed in some of these pages would seem futile. The fact is, of course, that the trend in this increasingly industrialized age is to drink less wine, but better wine. Days spent working the land, punctuated by the odd litre of *rouge*, are fast slipping away (to the relief of both governments and the medical profession).

In their place, notwithstanding the anti-alcohol fanaticism of a small but vociferous group, is a growing awareness in non-producing (or largely so) countries such as Britain, and in "new" producing countries such as the United States, of the pleasures and fascination of wine. No other drink – and, I would say, food – is so infinitely varied, appealingly natural, intriguingly complex; and, for want of better expressions, no other is so unfathomable, so alive and so "clever". Wine may have been much "de-mystified" by writers in the 1980s and by the rise of supermarkets and wine warehouses in Britain, but the product remains a conundrum. We have scarcely begun to understand what actually happens to wine as it evolves and ages, and the more the scientists learn, the more they find there is to unravel.

But what is fine wine? Can it be defined as a wine that combines a wealth of flavour with finesse? Can its vital quality be expressed even more succinctly in the single word "balance"? Or is the ultimate test its potential to improve with age over a significant period? It is this attribute of Riesling, for example, that devotees claim makes it superior to all other white grape varieties, even to the generously-flavoured Chardonnay. The ability to age is also an attribute of Chenin Blanc, but this grape, writes Steven Spurrier, reveals its real qualities only with age. Graceful evolution is undoubtedly as indispensable a facet of a first-class wine as it is in the career of a prima ballerina. But, in the words of Peter Sichel of Châteaux Angludet and Palmer in the Médoc, "longevity is not an end in itself". Together with other factors such as flavour, finesse and balance, it is a means to an end – to a fine, noble, or excellent (call it what you will) bottle of wine.

Hugh Johnson, in his illuminating talk about tasting and assessing wine (see pages 231-38), explains, simply, that the higher the pedigree of the wine the greater should be the concentration of all the expected flavours. And he pinpoints two further criteria – the length of time the flavour lingers in the mouth and the way in which it finishes. The flavour must persist, he says (and by all means gauge it by counting the seconds), and when it ends it must do so cleanly and with a suggestion of sweetness. A fine wine, then, has a lingering flavour, a clean finish, finesse and balance; it also improves with age.

There is, though, one other point that needs to be taken into consideration, and that is local taste. Distinctive tastes in wine, which may seem odd or even distasteful to outsiders, are acquired and nurtured – usually in conjunction with particular regional cuisines. While these often involve fairly humble wines (rasping red Vinho Verde, for example), they are not the exclusive preserve of the humdrum. Barolo is the classic example. A good Barolo is undoubtedly a fine wine, but even in today's modernized style its characteristic astringency is often an acquired taste. It may be hard, at first, to perceive the finesse and the suggestion of sweetness on the finish, but with patience they will emerge.

In the end, however neat or unwieldy our definition, the exciting question – and the really critical one – is what exactly determines a fine wine. In terms of both quality and character, the answer is the same: place and people. You could have the most perfect vineyard location on Earth, but the wine would never reflect that if the vines were not cultivated and the processes of wine production performed with consummate skill.

STRANGE THOUGH IT MAY SEEM from our "Green" perspective of the 1990s, it was only in the second half of the 1980s that wine producers generally began to recognize just how important an influence on potential quality was the particular condition of their vines. And this is true both of long-established regions in western Europe and of the New World recruits, although for slightly different reasons.

The Old World had been caught out in some places – most notably in Chianti and Burgundy – where old, low-yielding vines were pulled up and replaced on a grand scale in order to increase production. The producers of the time failed to appreciate fully two key facts. One is that young vines give less complex and intense-flavoured fruit than mature

Beyond the vineyards at Château Margaux are meadows and woods on the low-lying land.
The estate has always been devoted to general agriculture as well as wine.

plants. Although previous generations had been aware that older vines gave superior-quality grapes, albeit fewer of them, the new generation was seduced into thinking that any such handicap could be conquered with a little modernity in the winery.

There are exceptions to the old vines rule, just as there are to any other. The most notable is the pre-phylloxera "Nacional" vineyard of the port house Quinta do Noval: in 1931, just six years after it had been planted, it produced port of such magnificence that it is still the most sought after in the world today. Another exception – only partial, but nonetheless significant – is Château Pétrus (see pages 30-36). As David Peppercorn points out, half this legendary vineyard had to be replanted after the infamous frost of February 1956. Yet, only five years later, in the outstanding 1961 vintage, Pétrus produced a wine that has more than lived up to the reputation of both the vintage and the property; and Pétrus continued in this winning vein with great wines from 1962, 1964, 1966 and 1967, when half of the vines were still juvenile.

The other viticultural problem, and the more damaging, was that the replacement vines were not of the same potential quality as their predecessors. They were the same varieties – Sangiovese in Chianti and Pinot Noir in Burgundy – but not the same clones, or strains. The new clones were chosen for their productivity, not for their quality, again on the precept that progress had been such that any problems could be overcome in the winery. How wrong the producers were. In Chianti, quality and prices plummeted with such haste that Chianti wine became synonymous in export markets with plonk and, for the Tuscan vine-growers, with poverty. Burgundy managed to maintain a reasonable market for its wines, but not its good name.

Ultimately it became clear here, as it did on a larger and even more convincing scale in California, Australia and New Zealand, that no winemaker – no matter how talented or how futuristic his winery – can make a first-division wine out of second-division grapes. The extent to which the pendulum has swung away from blind faith in the combined power of machinery, laboratories and oenology degrees in favour of vineyards and viticulturalists (the new college- or university-qualified growers) can be gleaned from the sort of high-flyer of today who estimates that the grapes alone are responsible for about 50 per cent of quality in a white wine and as much as 80 per cent in a red.

Roughly speaking, the era of modern winemaking was heralded in during the late 1960s in California and during the next decade in Australia. What established its success in both areas was advanced technology of a kind not previously applied to wine. Today, fast-moving crushers and presses, temperature-controlled fermentation units, stainless steel, sterile filtration and fully automated bottling lines are all taken for granted (although not everyone chooses to have them). But they were revolutionary in the 1960s and still a novelty in the 1970s.

More importantly, the new machinery and procedures were effective. They eliminated from winemaking the hit-and-miss element that was such a part of the tradition of the traditional European regions. Their reliability inspired confidence – over-confidence. New World producers assumed that all they had to do was plant the noble French grape varieties to make wines as noble as their French models. Indeed, their warmer, more reliable climates seemed to promise greater consistency from vintage to vintage than is possible in any of Europe's fine wine regions; and surely, they felt, with such sugar-rich, sun-ripened grapes, they ought to be able to produce even better wines.

By the mid-1970s California was making some splendid wines – dark, rich Cabernet Sauvignons and ripe, exotically fruity and oaky Chardonnays – and before long the Cabernets were beginning to knock spots off fabled red Bordeaux when they were pitched in blind-tasting battle. The French regarded with disdain such stunts (which were organized by those who had no reputation to lose and therefore everything to gain). Their peevish riposte when challenged about the success of these upstarts was simply that the exuberant, ripe flavours of the California wines overwhelmed the subtler, more elegant Bordeaux: "tasting" wines, not "drinking" wines, they said.

And they were right. California's wine style was big, fruity, alcoholic, oaky (because of the quantity of new oak barrels they used) – and it was in many cases bruisingly upfront. Underneath there was seldom much complexity: finesse was a foreign word; with low acidity, balance was a precarious claim; and few wines had much ageing potential, although the 1974 Cabernets were certainly an exception.

So it was true, the wines were not much like classic Bordeaux. But the French made a great mistake in not taking the opposition seriously and in failing to see how seriously the opposition was taking itself. The Californians listened to what the French said (even if, frequently, they thought them outmoded and wrong); they studied French wines and other European classics; and they brought science to bear. Gradually, by experimenting, they came up with a series of theories and formulas on almost every conceivable aspect of wine production and every type of wine.

The new tenets were applied not only in California, but in other wine regions of the New World. More significantly, because the New World producers were such inveterate travellers, visiting the classic European regions and jumping at any opportunity to take part in a vintage, winemakers in the Old World started quietly to absorb and adapt some of the new measures. They also began to embark on ambitious field work and laboratory research of their own.

*Gérard Chave with an ancient bottle of Hermitage from his ancestral cellars and, right,
Jean-Michel Cazes in studious mood at a tasting at Château Lynch-Bages.*

Suddenly it was not sufficient to do things in the vineyard or winery simply because that
was what had been done by previous generations. Young producers wanted to know why
stems were left on the grapes, why fermentation temperatures were allowed to rise so high,
why sulphur dioxide was added at several stages of the winemaking process, why the
malolactic (second and acid-softening) fermentation was allowed to happen at random,
why wines were aged in old barrels, and so on. The whole world of wine began to progress
at a much faster pace than it had ever done before – with the result, as we know, that more
fine wines and fewer bad ones are produced, even than ten years ago.

It is hard to say which has been the single most important development in the quarter of
a century since the New World began to make its dramatic impact on the wine scene.
Certainly in the traditional regions, from Burgundy and Bordeaux to Barolo, the ability to
control fermentation temperatures was nothing short of revolutionary, as Jean-Michel
Cazes' experience demonstrates. After a series of difficulties with vintages throughout the
1970s, he installed 25 large stainless steel vats at Château Lynch-Bages in 1980 and, as
Robert Parker explains, he has produced since 1981 a succession of highly successful wines.
Freeing producers from the tyranny of all sorts of fermentation problems, whether caused
by excess heat or sudden cold, raised quality, ensured much greater consistency, and saved
many a wine from complete disaster. Not that control of fermentation invariably means
cold fermentation. Gérard Chave (see pages 73-77) has always allowed the temperature
of his fermenting red Hermitage to reach 90°F (32° C), and his superlative wine lasts for 30
or 40 years.

Being masters of temperature had another advantage: it allowed grapes to be picked
riper. Previously, to prevent a fermentation from getting stuck part-way through the
process, grapes had to be harvested before they were too rich in sugar. Later harvests were
a particularly beneficial stay of execution for Bordeaux, because they allowed more time for

the tannins in Cabernet Sauvignon to ripen and soften, resulting in wines less hard and aggressive in youth and therefore ready for drinking sooner. What we do not know yet is whether these rounder clarets with their soft tannins will be as long-lived. We can of course hope, and it is interesting to hear from Burton Anderson that Angelo Gaja in Piedmont believes his modern Barbaresco and Barolo, vinified to extract soft tannins from the grape-skins and limit hard ones, will be just as long-lived as the old-style wines (see pages 102-107). In fact, says Gaja, their prime will last longer – because they are better balanced and the chance of defects appearing in the bottle is less.

Perhaps, though, improved hygiene – mundane as it sounds – has been even more far-reaching than temperature control, simply because no wine production in the world is unaffected by it. Earlier generations were, on the whole, blissfully unaware of how inextricably linked were grubby winemaking conditions with bacterial spoilage of their precious liquid. Again the Old World has the New to thank for the revelation.

Inevitably, in a wine world that never stands still, there has already been a backlash. A small number of Californians began around the mid-1980s to subscribe to what they call "the school of dirty winemaking". Although the name may not be altogether serious, the subscribers – producers such as Joel Peterson of Ravenswood – take their winemaking very seriously indeed. Theirs was a response to what they believed were the excesses of 1970s and 1980s "squeaky-clean winemaking" – uncritical enthusiasm for high technology which sometimes resulted in the baby being thrown out with the bathwater, in the replacement of distinctive flavour by clinical neutrality and homogenization.

Instead of relying on machines, laboratories, computers and chemicals, these producers have reverted to some of the traditional, more hand-made aspects of European wine production (though emphatically not to bacteria-rampant wineries). By New World standards, they take risks when they ferment at higher temperatures than average – using the naturally present yeasts rather than adding cultured ones, allowing the malolactic fermentation to take place in its own time, or filtering only very lightly. But they have today's science at their disposal should nature or instinct fail them. For powerful proof of the workability and rewards of this philosophy you have only to look to Ravenswood's rich characterful Zinfandel, a wine that also, incidentally, demonstrates what a wasted asset California's native red grape is when disposed of in bland "Blush" wine.

But I have digressed and leapt forward. We must rewind to the New World's great milestone – the realization of the importance of place, and more particularly of the importance of *terroir*, as the French refer to the complete package of climate, aspect, altitude, soil and substructure, or of microclimate, as the New World refers to the specific environmental conditions of a pocket of land. Little by little experience showed that no amount of technology or tender-loving-care can make up for a natural deficit in the form of inadequate climate, unfavourable aspect, poor drainage or unsuitable soil.

Looking at how the well-defined French wine regions have evolved, this now seems staggeringly obvious, but French *vignerons* were unable to explain why it should be so, save to say that vines "need to struggle" to give of their best and point to the bitter weather conditions in Champagne or Chablis. In the New World's cheerfully sunny climes the attitude that life should deliberately be made tough was alien and incomprehensible, and since there was no evidence that it was the critical key to quality the idea was widely dismissed as myth, mysticism or obfuscation.

There is no absolute consensus now that a vine which suffers to survive yields superior fruit, but both advocates of the theory and doubters may be swayed by instances in this book. To take one example, at an altitude of 2,600 feet (790 metres) in Spain's Ribera del Duero, summer days are searingly hot, nights are sharply cool, and in winter it freezes. But,

*Slate and clay: contrasting landscapes and soils at Château Pétrus in Pomerol, with its clay soil
and flat terrain, and the almost vertical slate cliffs of the Mosel.*

as Simon Loftus discovered (notwithstanding the frost that wiped out an entire crop in
1971), such a harsh environment suits the vine. The splendid wines of Vega Sicilia (see
pages 137-43) are the proof. On the other side of the coin, Château Musar's vines in the
Lebanon may suffer from their proximity to battle lines, but they do not struggle in the
Beka'a Valley's climate or soils.

Nor is there agreement on the importance or relevance of the soil type. The French
generally regard soil as pivotal. No discussion of Pomerol and its jewel, Château Pétrus, is
complete without mention of the complex and varied soils, including Pétrus' seam of rich
clay. Gérard Chave has ten individual vineyards (known as *lieux-dits* in France) on the hill
of Hermitage and he vinifies each separately because each has its own character; Les
Greffieux, for example, with its rich soil produces a lighter, more compellingly perfumed
wine than many of the others. And there could be no clearer demonstration of how high
feelings rise on the subject than the controversy that has raged across the Kimmeridgian
clay of Chablis intermittently during the last two decades (see pages 50-55). In Germany,
too, great emphasis is placed on the contribution of different soil types. In the Rheingau, no
fewer than 286 varieties have been identified. Along the Mosel, the slate soils are ideal for
Riesling and many a taster has described individual Mosel wines as having a distinctive
"slatey" character.

In contrast, the New World tends to see soil, as long as it is well-drained (the one point
on which there is universal accord), as secondary. If anything, there is a growing body of
opinion that, apart from drainage (a question of structure rather than chemical content),
what counts in soil and bedrock is temperature, just as it is important above ground.

Whether or not vines are defined as "struggling", though, there is no doubt that
relatively cool climates and localized cool microclimates within hotter areas produce the

finest wine, because they prolong the growing season, allowing the grapes to ripen more slowly and develop more intense aromas and more interesting fruit flavours. So the trend in California and Australia has been to seek out microclimates, with the differing requirements of each grape variety in mind. These varieties have been overwhelmingly the noble French vines for making into varietal (unblended) wines, but there is a discernible swing now, especially in California, to other French varieties for use in blended wines, and in a very small way to Italian varieties such as Nebbiolo, Dolcetto and Sangiovese.

As long ago as 1966, David Lett made his way north out of the Golden State to Oregon to find a suitable home for that most fastidious of French grapes, Pinot Noir (see pages 199-202). More recently, others in California (including French Champagne houses which decided to invest overseas in the 1980s) have headed to the southern end of the mainstream wine regions of Sonoma and Napa. Here, in the Carneros region, where the vines benefit from cooling sea breezes from San Pablo Bay, some excellent Carneros Chardonnays and Pinot Noirs, both still and sparkling, are already being made.

In Australia, James Halliday (a wine producer as well as a wine writer) is one of a number who pin their hopes on Victoria's Yarra Valley as the country's most promising new viticultural region. His "unashamedly Burgundian" Coldstream Hills Pinot Noir is world-class, as are the Yarra Yering wines (one blend based on Cabernet and another on Shiraz) of his near-neighbour, Yarra pioneer Bailey Carrodus. Likewise Brian Croser, one of Australia's foremost winemakers and a partner of Len Evans (see pages 209-13), has put his money into the Piccadilly region of the Adelaide Hills in South Australia. His impressive Petaluma Chardonnays and sparkling wine show that his conviction is well-founded.

Another Australian, David Hohnen, wanted to complement his top-class Cape Mentelle Cabernet Sauvignon with a white wine of the same calibre. He looked not only outside the Margaret River region of Western Australia, but beyond Australia altogether – finally choosing the Marlborough/Blenheim region of New Zealand's South Island as the best place to grow and make Sauvignon Blanc. The world-famous Cloudy Bay Sauvignon (see pages 223-26) is the result. And, in South Africa, Tim Hamilton-Russell spent ten years looking for the perfect Cape microclimate in which to grow Pinot Noir and Chardonnay before he found a sea-influenced valley in the Walker Bay area, an area not previously used for vine-growing (see pages 227-29).

Concern with microclimate is not limited to the New World (although near-obsession with it tends to be). Miguel Torres in Spain has increasingly bought vineyards high up in the Penedès hills where the climate is cooler than in Torres' hotter, traditionally-sited Penedès vineyards (see pages 132-36). In Israel, Shimshon Welner realized that the Golan Heights, unlike the sun-baked coastal vineyards, were sufficiently high and cool to produce fine-quality grapes (see pages 180-81). And, in the unlikely-sounding setting of Mediterranean Greece, John Carras discovered his ideal solution – planting French varieties on the cooler, higher slopes and heat-resistant indigenous grapes lower down (see pages 175-76). Along the Mosel, there are variations in microclimate even within the bounds of one site and that is why, as Ian Jamieson explains, Ernst Loosen (see pages 89-92) produces about 30 different bottlings a year from just 20 acres (8 hectares).

The other point on which opinion is uniform is yield: restricting the amount of fruit a vine produces enhances the quality of the fruit. Thus at Château de Beaucastel in Châteauneuf-du-Pape, the Perrin family's average yields are a mere 20-30 hectolitres per hectare, well within the permitted level for this *appellation* – and this in a region where other growers struggle to keep their yields within the confines of the law.

Yields can be limited by pruning at various stages, including summer thinning of the bunches, but if a vine is having to fight to survive it may not be necessary, because the plant

Former sheep pastures transformed into top-quality vineyards in the Carneros district of California.

will invariably produce less fruit. Similarly, old vines are less productive, as are most of the best-quality clones. That is not to say you cannot have a crop that is handsome in both size and quality. You can – 1970, 1982 and even 1986 in Bordeaux, for example – but the perfect weather conditions that produced these vintages simply do not occur frequently.

Another successful method was discovered by the unceasingly-innovative Miguel Torres who found that planting vines closer together decreased the yield per vine (and improved the flavour of the grapes) because it forced the vines to compete harder for the nutrients in the soil. This makes for strong, healthy roots, but an otherwise less vigorous plant. And in fact, although the amount of fruit per vine is reduced, yields per hectare can be maintained because of the greater density of plants. At first, producers in other warm climates, where heavy yielding and thickly foliaged plants were a problem, were reluctant to follow Torres' lead – not because they doubted the evidence but because their machinery could not be manoeuvred through the narrow rows of vines. Technology has since caught up and the fashion for high-density cultivation has spread widely. In Chile, for example, where irrigation can result in very hefty yields, Viña Santa Rita (see pages 203-205) has planted densely, a measure which, combined with severe pruning and a reduction in fertilizers, has made the vines "struggle".

For similar reasons, cultivating vines organically, or biodynamically – without synthetic chemical fertilizers, herbicides, insecticides or pesticides – reduces quantities and tends to improve grape flavour. Château de Beaucastel's low yields illustrate the point. So do those of many of the leading Rheingau growers, including Bernhard Breuer (see pages 93-97), although Bernhard is not alone in disdaining the "organic" tag. Ernst Loosen is satisfied to achieve yields of 55 hectolitres per hectare (very low for the Mosel) in his organically worked vineyards, and Nicolas Joly – who not only practises biodynamism but links the life cycle of the vine with the movements of the planets – obtains probably the lowest yields of any dry white wine in France.

New World wineries bring impressive scale and state-of-the-art technology to wine, be it through
stainless steel vats (as at Mondavi in California) or new oak casks, at Rothbury in Australia.

Inevitably, organic viticulture has lately become something of a vogue, although, in a
reversal of the usual roles, it is catching on more slowly in the New World than it is in
western Europe. Resistance is not hard to understand. Organic growing is largely
unmechanized, labour-intensive and risky, especially in the early stages before the vines
have built up resistance to disease and inclement weather. Labour costs and low yields
make it expensive, in spite of the savings on chemical treatments. Because it is artisanal it
does not adapt readily on a large scale, although Château de Beaucastel's 325 acres (131
hectares) show that it can be done. And for it to be done scrupulously there need to be
natural barriers (such as woods or water) surrounding organic vineyards to protect them
from their non-organic brethren. Organic viticultural philosophy and practice thus go full
tilt against the major technological developments and enlarging tendencies of the last 25
years, amounting to as much of a backlash as the "school of dirty winemaking".

Yet it is a trend that is certain to continue. Its natural corollary, organic winemaking,
will also increase, although the tendency here is to reduce chemical usage in wineries as far
as seems practicable – stopping before quality seems threatened by instability, rather than
cutting out all chemical treatments and finishing with an undrinkable wine. The substantial
decrease in the use of sulphur dioxide (the most important antiseptic and preservative in
winemaking) in the last five years is a happy sign that there is a wider awareness of the
desirability of keeping wine as "natural" as possible.

Of course some Old World producers have never seen fit to change, so they have not had
cause to revive more "natural" traditional techniques nor to join the organic bandwagon.
Gérard Chave's innate curiosity has led him to California several times, but, as Robert
Parker explains, he continues to make his wines as his forefathers made them. He ferments
the wines in concrete vats or primitive large wooden *foudres* and uses no chemicals to

Horse power and old vines at Coulée de Serrant in the Loire: survivals from bygone days which now gain approval as an organic, environmentally sound approach to growing grapes.

clarify or stabilize any of them, simply because he believes that such modern methods denude wines of their flavour and character.

Similarly, although Jean-Michel Cazes has travelled the viticultural world and invested in stainless steel fermentation tanks, the general philosophy of making wine at Château Lynch-Bages remains intrinsically traditional. After vinification, the wine is put into *barriques* (small French casks) – a substantial proportion of them new – of the sort that have been copied the world over. During this crucial ageing period the wine absorbs flavour and tannin from the oak and also begins to mellow as it very slowly oxidizes via the pores of the wood. After 16-18 months, it is fined in the traditional way with egg whites and filtered lightly before bottling. Apart from the stainless steel, all that is "modern" is the higher proportion of *barriques* used since 1983 and the attention paid to the whole subject of oak. But Jean-Michel is not alone in this. In fact few, if any, wine regions have been untouched in the last 20 years by the fashion for oak – at times an obsession – as a provider of flavour, depth and complexity, and as a factor influencing the way individual wines age.

The interest started in California, where winemakers were trying to emulate French wines. Led by the indefatigable Robert Mondavi, they not only began experimenting with oak from different sources – from different French forests as well as from other countries and a variety of coopers – but they also began experimenting with different "toasts" (the degree to which the wood is charred). In this atmosphere of excitement the Old World could not fail to become intrigued and absorbed by the subject or, in the case of Piedmont's Angelo Gaja, as embroiled in its controversies as the New World.

Again, the wheel of wine had turned full circle – a revolution in every sense. And it is the story of this book, the quest for perfection which is as old as wine itself and which will continue as long as wine is made.   **JOANNA SIMON**

19

France

IT IS THE GOOD FORTUNE of wine lovers of the late 20th century that fine wines are now made all around the globe – from Oregon to New South Wales. France, we can safely say, no longer has a monopoly of excellence; yet France, indubitably, is still the leader, the world's foremost producer of fine wine. A glance at a map of the country will be sufficient to dispel any doubts. Bordeaux, Burgundy, Champagne, Alsace, Hermitage, Châteauneuf-du-Pape and the rest unfold in rapid succession. And these revered names owe their continued pre-eminence as much to the recognition of their unique qualities by the world's other winemakers as they do to the appreciation and loyalty of wine drinkers. France, quite simply, has been mentor to every other wine-producing country at one time or other – and looks set to continue playing the star role well into the next century.

There is no single reason that explains the greatness of France for making wines. Climate and microclimate, soil and aspect, grape varieties and a 2,000-year history of vine-growing – these have all combined in ways both obvious and subtle to produce an astonishing diversity of fine wines. But it is all too easy to assume, from the apparent richness of resources and the litany of famous, sometimes fabulous, names and *appellations*, that splendid vineyards cover almost every inch of the country. That is not the case at all. The whole northern sweep of France is without vineyards and large expanses in the centre are relatively vine-free. Equally, though most of the south often appears to be awash with vines, they are, with a few honourable exceptions, responsible for very ordinary wine – basic *vin de table* and humble, though sometimes interesting, *vin de pays* – all of it a far cry from the noble châteaux of the major *appellations contrôllées*.

Of all these regions, Bordeaux must take pride of place. It is not only the largest fine wine region in France with the most extensive and imposing wine estates, it is the largest fine wine-producing area in the world and has long been the mainstay of the international wine trade. The wines of some châteaux have been sought after by wine drinkers for 300 years or more, and the classification that ranks in groups from one to five (*premier grand cru classé* through to *cinquième cru*) the wines of the 61 leading Médoc and Graves châteaux was drawn up by the powerful Bordeaux wine merchants 135 years ago. Only one property, Château

Carthorses are still used to plough the steep vineyard at La Coulée de Serrant
in Savennières, one of France's miraculous microclimates.

Mouton-Rothschild, has ever succeeded in changing its position: it was elevated from second to first growth in 1973.

Such is its importance, Bordeaux can be a thorn in the side of other wine areas. The success of a Bordeaux vintage can, quite wrongly, determine the reception given to wines of the same year from other regions – Burgundy and Champagne, for example – even from other countries. There are vintages that are almost universally good in France (1989 is an example) and some that are broadly miserable (such as 1977), but more often than not there are divergences, which is hardly surprising in view of the country's geography.

Bordeaux, in the south-west, occupies a gently undulating stretch of land reaching almost to the sea. The climate, though cool by New World standards, is even and maritime, with a long, mild growing season which is ideal for the Cabernet Sauvignon grape, especially when combined with the well-drained gravelly soils of the Haut-Médoc. To the east, on Bordeaux's so-called Right Bank, the earlier-ripening Merlot thrives in the cooler, damper clay-and-limestone soils of Pomerol. While further south, on the Left Bank, Sémillon flourishes in the unusual misty microclimate of the Sauternes-Barsac district.

In many more ways than mere meteorology, conditions could not be less similar in Burgundy – or in Champagne, Alsace, the Loire or the Rhône. The Burgundian climate is harsher and more continental, and in Burgundy an estate of 20 acres (eight hectares) is regarded as substantial; there are few self-contained estates compared with the number of tiny vineyard holdings anyway. In such a different set of conditions one would expect different grapes, appropriately different winemaking traditions and trading practices. In Burgundy there are just two main varieties (three if you count the Gamay grown in the far south of the region in Beaujolais): the fashionable and easy-going Chardonnay for white wine and the chic but devastatingly difficult Pinot Noir for red.

If Burgundy is a northerly, often marginal climate, Champagne, north-east of Paris, is still more so. The same grapes are grown as in Burgundy, together with Pinot Meunier, but they ripen less, so the Champenois created a wine – multi-blended and sparkling – that was all the better for being made from lean, light, acid grapes, and matured for some time in cool, underground chalk cellars. Around this distinctive production process evolved a very particular trade structure, involving growers, "houses" and co-operatives.

The Loire, which flows for more than 600 miles (965 kilometres) from the interior to the sea at Nantes, is inevitably different. It has so many wines – white, red and rosé, dry, medium and sweet, still and sparkling – that variety rather than coherence is its hallmark. It is not generally considered one of the world's great fine wine areas (it is not really one area), but alongside household names such as Muscadet and Sancerre it hides some glorious gems, among them Savennières, one of the longest-lived of all dry white wines.

In its abundance of diverse wines, the Rhône Valley shares some similarities with the Loire. But whereas the Loire veers towards light reds and white wines, the Rhône, in the warmer south, is reputed for its rich, majestic reds – especially those of Hermitage and Châteauneuf-du-Pape. At the opposite end of the spectrum, the wines from Alsace are some of the most aromatic, spicy white wines in the world, borne of one of those miraculous French microclimates – and, of course, borne of century upon century of winemaking experience, for which the technology of the late 20th-century is a complement but not a straight substitute.

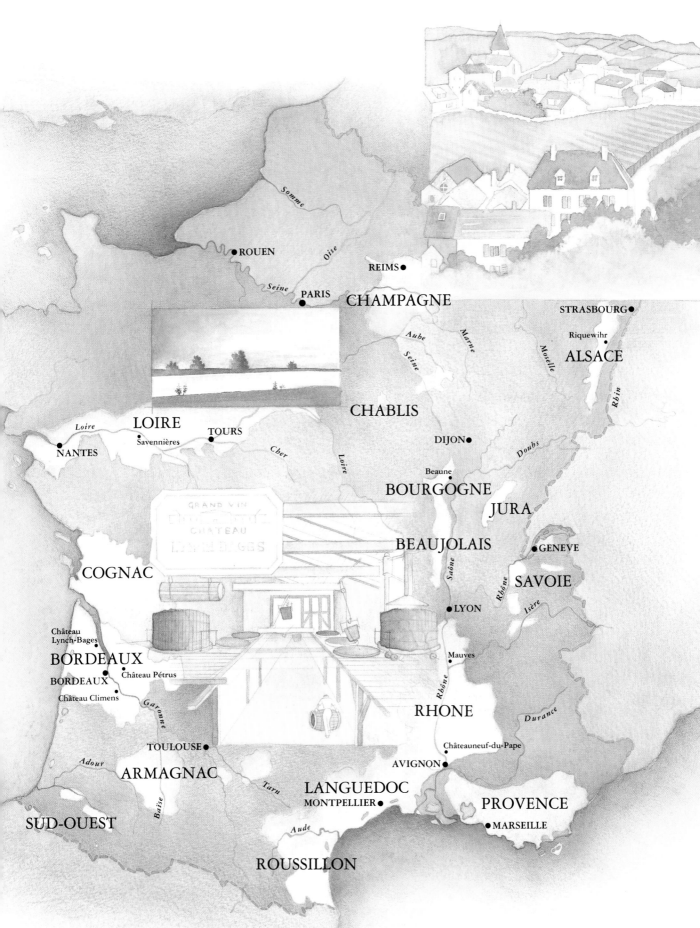

ROUEN

REIMS

Somme

Oise

Seine

PARIS

CHAMPAGNE

STRASBOURG

Aube

Marne

Riquewihr

Seine

Moselle

ALSACE

Rhin

CHABLIS

LOIRE

Loire

Savennières

TOURS

Cher

Loire

DIJON

Doubs

Beaune

BOURGOGNE

JURA

BEAUJOLAIS

GENEVE

Saône

Rhône

SAVOIE

NANTES

COGNAC

GRAND VIN

CHÂTEAU

LYNCH BAGES

LYON

Isère

Château
Lynch-Bages

BORDEAUX

Mauves

BORDEAUX

Château Pétrus

Château Climens

Garonne

Rhône

RHONE

Durance

Adour

TOULOUSE

ARMAGNAC

Tarn

Châteauneuf-du-Pape

AVIGNON

LANGUEDOC

MONTPELLIER

PROVENCE

Baïse

SUD-OUEST

Aude

MARSEILLE

ROUSSILLON

THE MEDOC

Jean-Michel Cazes of Château Lynch-Bages

In the 1855 Classification of Médoc châteaux, Château Lynch-Bages was placed well down in the pecking order, but this has not held it back. Lynch-Bages has become one of the best-loved of all Pauillacs – taking its place alongside such revered neighbours as Lafite, Latour and Mouton – for the simple reason that it is so generously flavoured, so pleasurable a wine. The architect of its more recent triumphs, as **Robert M Parker Jr** explains, is Jean-Michel Cazes, a man as open and charming as his wines.

If Bordeaux is the world's most famous fine wine region, Pauillac is certainly Bordeaux's most famous *appellation*. While the commune of Margaux may have a more lyrical and romantic name, as well as a famous first-growth château of the same name, it is Pauillac that can lay claim to three of the Médoc's four first-growth châteaux – Lafite-Rothschild, Mouton-Rothschild and Latour. Yet, despite the prestige and world acclaim these three first-growths bring to the *appellation*, a strong argument can be made that Pauillac's most internationally popular and best-loved wine is none of these, but the fifth growth, Château Lynch-Bages.

A textbook Pauillac could be described as a rich wine with a medium- to full-bodied texture and a compelling bouquet of blackcurrants and cedary scents. Lynch-Bages not only possesses all these characteristics, but takes them almost to the point of excess, offering what is perhaps Pauillac's most obvious yet generously flavoured, pleasurable wine. There are critics who deplore the fact that a Bordeaux wine should flaunt such lushness so early in its life, but their complaints usually fall on deaf ears. After all, wine is surely a beverage of pleasure, and Lynch-Bages' popularity derives from the simple fact that whether it is five, ten or 20 years old, it provides great pleasure.

The château itself is located just west of Bordeaux's Route du Vin, as one approaches the dull, commercial town of Pauillac. It is situated on the Bages plateau, the small ridge rising above the town and the adjacent River Gironde from which the château takes the second half of its name. Until recently, the kindest thing that could be said about the château buildings was that they were utilitarian. However, Lynch-Bages has benefited enormously from a major facelift and renovation. The château now sports a new façade, new cellars with large stainless steel tanks, and a state-of-the-art tasting room.

Apart for these recent changes, this large estate has remained essentially intact since the 16th century. The first half of its name is derived from its 75-year ownership during the

The château and working buildings at Lynch-Bages have both been completely renovated by Jean-Michel Cazes (left) since he took control of the business from his father André (right) in 1973.

17th and 18th centuries by Thomas Lynch, the son of an Irish immigrant whose family ran the property. After Lynch-Bages was sold by Thomas Lynch, it passed through the hands of several wine merchants before being purchased in 1937 by Jean-Charles Cazes, the grandfather of the present owner, Jean-Michel Cazes. In his time, Jean-Charles Cazes was a prominent château proprietor and renowned winemaker, having directed the fortunes of one of the leading *cru bourgeois* of St-Estèphe, Château Les-Ormes-de-Pez.

Jean-Charles Cazes continued to direct both châteaux until 1966, when his son André, a prominent politician and long-standing Mayor of Pauillac for nearly two decades, took charge of the family concerns. In 1973, control of the two châteaux and the insurance business passed in turn to André's son, Jean-Michel, who returned to Bordeaux after 18 years of working as an engineer in Texas and Paris. During his years in America, Jean-Michel had not only learned to speak English like a native; he had also developed an international perspective on business. He made perhaps the smartest decision of his business career in 1976 when he hired the brilliant Daniel Lose as director of Lynch-Bages and Les-Ormes-de-Pez.

However, after the great success Lynch-Bages enjoyed in the 1950s (when the 1952, 1953, 1955, 1957 and 1959 were all among the top wines of the decade) and 1960s (with wines such as the 1961, 1962 and 1966), Jean-Michel's early years were somewhat difficult. His inheritance consisted of a disappointing 1972 still in cask, and his first vintage, the 1973, was largely a wash-out. This was followed by the collapse of the international wine market, hard on the heels of the oil crisis, and another disappointing year in 1974. Even 1975 was no great success for Lynch-Bages: the wine from this sometimes troublesome vintage was less than exhilarating.

Besides Lynch-Bages itself, Jean-Michel Cazes also produces an excellent second wine, Château Haut-Bages Averous, and directs the fortunes of Château Les-Ormes-de-Pez, a leading cru bourgeois.

During the late 1970s, Jean-Michel recognized that the old wooden vats were creating sanitation problems, and also that they made it difficult to control the proper fermentation temperature in both hot and cold years. At the same time he began to flirt with a newer style, producing several vintages of Lynch-Bages that were lighter and more elegant. Long-time fans and supporters of Lynch-Bages were dismayed. Thankfully, after he installed 25 large stainless steel vats in 1980, the slump in quality between 1971 and 1979 came to an abrupt end. Lynch-Bages produced a very good 1981 and it has continued to build on that success with highly successful wines in nearly every vintage since.

The vineyard itself is located midway between Mouton-Rothschild and Lafite-Rothschild to the north, and Latour, Pichon-Longueville Comtesse de Lalande and Pichon-Longueville Baron to the south. There are 175 acres (71 hectares) here, 70 per cent of which is planted to Cabernet Sauvignon, 15 per cent to Merlot, ten per cent to Cabernet Franc and five per cent to Petit Verdot (the latter a much-uprooted variety nowadays, but one that Jean-Michel Cazes finds useful in good years, when "it gives colour, body and flavour"). The average age of the vines has been admirably maintained at 35 years.

In spite of all the modernization and rebuilding that has taken place at Lynch-Bages, the general philosophy of making wine is quite traditional. Since 1980, the vinification has taken place in new steel tanks. After the vinification, the wine is transferred directly into small French oak casks. The percentage of new casks increased from 25 per cent in the 1982 vintage to 60 per cent in later vintages such as 1987 and 1988. Lynch-Bages spends an average of 16-18 months in these oak casks; it is then fined with egg whites and lightly filtered prior to bottling. With the vineyards fully planted, production soared from an

Racking the wine off the sediment at Lynch-Bages. Facilities have been transformed over the last two decades, but the thrust of Daniel Lose's winemaking is still largely traditional.

average of 20,000-25,000 cases in the 1970s to an average of nearly 45,000 cases in the abundant years of the 1980s. In addition, 20-30 per cent of the harvest is relegated to the second wine of Lynch-Bages, Haut-Bages Averous.

In the famous 1855 Classification of the 61 top châteaux of the Gironde (the Médoc and Graves), Lynch-Bages was placed in the last tier as a fifth growth. I know of no professional in the field today who would not argue that its present-day quality is more akin to a second growth. The writer Oz Clarke has lightheartedly argued that those responsible for the 1855 Classification must have been Puritans, because they "couldn't bear to admit that a wine as open-heartedly lovely could really be as important as other less generous growths".

Just as it is difficult not to enjoy a bottle of Lynch-Bages, so is it difficult not to appreciate the affable, open and gregarious Jean-Michel Cazes. With his global vision, he has been the architect behind Lynch-Bages' more recent stratospheric rise to international prominence. Anyone who talks with him knows that he wants his wines to be lusty, open and direct, yet also to reflect the class and character of a top Pauillac. For that reason he always prefers vintages such as the 1985 and 1982 to more tannic and severe years such as the 1988 and 1986. Jean-Michel is an untiring ambassador not only for his own wines but for the wines of the entire Bordeaux region. There rarely seems to be a conference, symposium or international tasting of Bordeaux wines where one does not encounter him. There is no other producer in Pauillac (with the possible exception of Madame Lencquesaing of Pichon-Lalande) who travels so extensively, and who pleads his case so eloquently.

Cazes does have his critics – or are they cynics? – who largely resent his success. There is no doubting the fact that he has created something of an empire, expanding his sphere of

Picking grapes is hard work – but good food is one of the rewards at Lynch-Bages.
A welcoming fire and a hearty lunch await the pickers in the cuisine des vendanges.

influence more than any other single proprietor over the last decade. In 1987, for example, he assumed control over the management and winemaking of the slightly run-down second growth Château Pichon-Longueville Baron, which had been sold by the Bouteiller family to the large French insurance company Axa. To his credit, Cazes quickly recognized that this famed second growth was one of Pauillac's perennial under-achievers. He instituted a second wine called Tourelles de Pichon-Longueville Baron, abolished the use of mechanical harvesters, changed the system of racking and vinification to minimize oxidation, and enlarged the winemaking facilities. Over 30 acres (12 hectares) of unplanted land on the estate were planted with vines to increase the production of Pichon-Longueville Baron. The results were a very good 1987 and an 1988 that may well equal or surpass the Pichon that has been attracting all the rave reviews lately, Pichon-Longueville Comtesse de Lalande.

Jean-Michel Cazes has also assumed control of the winemaking at Château Pibran, a well-placed *cru bourgeois* property on the plateau of Bages between Châteaux Mouton-Rothschild and Pontet-Canet. As well as running this estate and Château Franc-Mayne in St-Emilion, he recently opened his own wine school, Château de Cordeillan, immediately adjacent to Lynch-Bages. And, realizing that the northern Médoc had no good hotel or eating establishment, he decided to build a fine hotel and decent restaurant there too, which he uses as a reception centre for visiting Bordeaux wine enthusiasts.

Of course, the bottom line in any empire-building of this sort is to continue to provide high quality. And in that, no one seems to fault Jean-Michel Cazes. Ever since the shaky period in the mid- to late 1970s when he and his talented winemaker Daniel Lose were experiencing some painful birth pangs, Lynch-Bages has taken a steady course. Among the great vintages of the 1960s, there remains the colossal but now slightly tiring 1961, the now faded (though once elegant and sumptuous) 1962 and the still firm and austere, yet very Pauillac-like, 1966. There is only one classic vintage from the 1970s – the profound, compelling, massively proportioned 1970, a wine that may ultimately turn out to be the longest-lived Lynch-Bages made in the last three decades. Of the others, the 1975 has always performed inconsistently: while I have had good bottles that displayed a chocolaty, ripe, blackcurrant and cedar aroma, too many bottles seem slightly old and out of balance. Both the 1978 and the 1979 are soft, relatively commercial yet pleasurable examples of Lynch-Bages, but it was not until the 1980s that Lynch-Bages began its return to fame.

The 1981, while fully mature, is showing a precocious, curranty, cedary, herbaceous-scented bouquet, good ripeness, a nice touch of acidity and medium body. It is fully mature and should drink well until the late 1990s. The heroic vintage of 1982 produced a wine that should light up the eyes of those who have always enjoyed the robust, opulent, fleshy, deeply concentrated style of Lynch-Bages. This is a quintessential Lynch-Bages with immense body, extract and a chewy texture. Although it will never possess great elegance and finesse, it makes up for these shortcomings with a furious display of concentration, power and pure hedonism. The 1982 was followed by another excellent wine. Less brawny and massive than the 1982, and perhaps more to the liking of those who prefer their claret reserved and austere, the 1983 is no wimpish wine, showing a full-blown, big, ripe, gutsy, cedary, blackcurrant bouquet and deep, rich, briary flavours. It is drinking just as well as the 1982, but will probably not last as long.

Like most other producers, Jean-Michel Cazes made a light yet adequate wine in 1984 that should be consumed by 1995-96. His 1985, however, rivals many of the first growths, and he is convinced it will eventually surpass his 1982. I disagree, but whatever the truth, this opulent, supple wine can be drunk with great pleasure today. Although it does not have the size of the 1982, it does possess an aromatic dimension that provides a degree of exhilaration yet to be matched by any other vintage in the 1980s. Whether it will ultimately make old bones is debatable, but for drinking over the next 15 or more years, the 1985 provides immense pleasure. The 1986 is extremely tannic, hard, full-bodied and powerful – as are so many wines of this vintage – but it will undoubtedly reward those who have patience. It is perhaps not up to the quality of the flamboyant 1982 or the complex 1985, but nevertheless it is a superb Pauillac. The 1987 is an unequivocal success for the vintage, showing fleshy, ripe, soft fruit, a good meaty texture and five to seven years of ageing potential. The 1988, finally, is stern, tannic and tough; though not at the level of the 1982, 1983, 1985 or 1986, it will age for 15-20 years, and may well resemble the 1966.

All things considered, Lynch-Bages has had a remarkably consistent and favourable track record in the 1980s. The estate's second wine, Haut-Bages Averous, is also excellent value, and was particularly successful in 1985 and 1988; it is a wine that should be consumed within its first seven or eight years of life.

One wonders where Jean-Michel Cazes intends to go next. Certainly, he is committed to restoring the reputation of the great second growth of Pauillac, Pichon-Longueville Baron, and there is no doubt that he would love to see his restaurant/hotel turn into a mecca for visiting wine enthusiasts and scholars. There has also been talk of investing in a winemaking operation in California. One thing is certain about Jean-Michel Cazes – he will never be content with the status quo.

POMEROL

Christian Moueix of Château Pétrus

At the heart of the Moueix family achievement is the small, highly fragmented *appellation* of Pomerol on Bordeaux's Right Bank, and at the heart of both Pomerol and the Moueix empire is Château Pétrus, home of the world's great Merlot wine. Christian Moueix began work there 20 years ago and, from the first, his boots were caked in mud; not for him the New World belief in the supremacy of the press-house. As **David Peppercorn MW** explains, Christian Moueix's starting point was the heavy clay soil of the vineyard.

The burden of being the son of a great father is not easily borne: it can be a challenge; it can equally be smothering. It is Christian Moueix's achievement that he has been able to emerge from his father's shadow to create his own distinctive niche, not only in Bordeaux, but in the wider world of wine.

When peace broke out in 1945, Jean-Pierre Moueix was picking up the pieces of a small family business in Libourne. He and his family belonged to that group, disparagingly referred to by the Bordeaux *noblesse du vin* of the Chartrons as "les petits Corrèziens", who, since the early years of the century (but especially since the First World War) had made their way from the impoverished region of Corrèze to find a better future in wine. As a group they were, and are, conspicuous for their energy and enterprise and, even during the long years of depression, they prospered.

Over the next 20 years, Jean-Pierre Moueix patiently pieced together, from his modest offices on the Quai du Priourat in Libourne, an intricate web of exclusivities (the sole right to sell the wines of a particular château), management of properties and outright proprietorship. Right at the beginning, in 1945, he obtained the exclusive selling rights for Château Pétrus, then the least known of all the great Bordeaux. When Madame Loubat, the legendary owner of Pétrus, died, he succeeded in buying a half-share of the property from one of her heirs, thus sharing the ownership with Madame Loubat's niece, Madame Lacoste-Loubat. This has remained the situation ever since, and the Moueix family are always meticulous in emphasizing their partnership in Château Pétrus with Madame Lacoste-Loubat.

Today, Christian Moueix can look back on 20 years of endeavour in the family business. It is characteristic of the difference between the Old World and the New that his starting point should have been in the vineyard, and not in the press-house. When he began work at Pétrus in 1970, after a short spell in England to perfect his English, it was down to basics.

The pretty but unimposing château belies the international status of Christian Moueix's great wine.
Demand is intense: only 3,000 cases of Pétrus are produced each year.

In those days, he did everything that needed to be done in the vineyard, and enjoyed driving the tractor. He still gets mud on his boots.

The family now farms 395 acres (160 hectares) of vineyards in the Libournais, encompassing the *appellations* of Pomerol, St-Emilion, Canon-Fronsac and Fronsac. This may not sound like very much when compared to the Médoc, where Lafite has 222 acres (90 hectares) and where 124 acres (50 hectares) is an average-sized *cru classé*, but here it is divided among no fewer than 17 properties, eight of them in Pomerol. And it is Pomerol that lies at the heart of the Moueix achievement.

It must be realized that Pomerol is a very small and highly fragmented *appellation*. Its production averages less than 400,000 cases annually, and its 1,930 acres (780 hectares) of vineyards are divided among 124 principal growths – an average of only just over 15 acres (six hectares) per property. Compare this with St-Julien where, out of 1,850 acres (750 hectares), some 1,680 acres (680 hectares) are owned by 11 *crus classés*, giving an average vineyard size of about 150 acres (60 hectares)! Yet the Moueix have turned this apparent handicap into an advantage. Today, not only is Pétrus itself far more expensive than any of the first growths of Médoc, but both Lafleur (a Moueix exclusivity) and Trotanoy (a Moueix property) also fetch prices well in excess of those obtained by the Médoc's super seconds. The wines of Pomerol are now the most expensive in Bordeaux.

How has it been done? With such small quantities of any one wine available, the Moueix have worked with a series of exclusivities to distribute wines for which they themselves have, for the most part, been either proprietors or exclusive distributors. They established the reputation of Pétrus in this way. Until International Distillers & Vintners, through its Gilbey-Loudenne company, began selling the 1962 vintage, the wine was known in

The magic of Pétrus lies in the heavy clay soils which dominate the vineyard.

England more by hearsay than by experience. By the end of the decade, the château's reputation was firmly established and, soon after Corney & Barrow took over sales in the mid-1970s, prices swept past the Médoc first growths, and rapidly went out of sight.

But it would be entirely wrong to suppose that this success has been built simply on clever marketing. Rather, it has been based firmly on producing the best possible wines, and then finding the right people to sell them and talk about them. And the best possible wines begin in the vineyard. To a Frenchman, the Californian concept of the winemaker, in the context of making fine wines, is almost incomprehensible. Christian Moueix and company oenologist Jean-Claude Berrouet work as a team. Christian's training began in the vineyard and Jean-Claude's in the laboratory, but neither has been confined or limited by this original training because they are part of a culture that emphasizes a wholeness of approach, to which a narrow departmentalism would be quite foreign. From the beginning, Jean-Pierre Moueix had a complete understanding of the inherent potential of the varied and complex soils of Pomerol, and laid his plans accordingly. He knew precisely which properties he wished to own and which proprietors to court and persuade to entrust their sales to him. His analysis of Pomerol began in the vineyard, and that was where he wanted his son Christian to start.

He also wanted him to possess that command of the English language he has never had, so a stay in England preceded Christian's apprenticeship. This has since stood him in good stead as a world-wide ambassador for both Moueix and Pomerol. For one of the astonishing feats of Jean-Pierre Moueix is that he achieved so much simply by sitting in Libourne and getting people to come to him. The almost studied and unchanging decrepitude of his office on the Quai du Priourat contrasts with the Aladdin's cave of artistic treasures at his house on the banks of the Dordogne. Now, Christian visits his

The château salon reflects the traditional Bordeaux taste – solid, even and solemn.

principal markets and spreads the gospel far and wide. Favoured visitors to Libourne may also be received at his house – only a short distance from his father's, and also on the river. Something about the house, its Victorian chalet style, painted yellow and grey, reminds me of Louisiana and the Deep South of the United States. Art is an abiding passion for both father and son, and Christian has followed his father's interest in the avant-garde.

So what has Christian Moueix made of his inheritance? When he arrived at Pétrus in 1970, it was to find a vineyard still marked by the infamous frost of February 1956, when the temperature fell to -18°F (-28°C), so that vines exploded like rifle-shots as the sap froze and burst the wood of the vine asunder. In the event, half the vineyard had to be replanted, so it was just 13 years old in 1970. The Merlot vine is supposed to die at -9°F (-23°C), so the survival of just half the old vineyard was in itself something of a miracle. How astonishing, then, were the great vintages of the 1960s – 1961, 1962, 1964, 1966 and 1967 – produced with so many young vines.

Rotation in a vineyard is vital for good management. Old vines give concentration and high quality but also lower yields, and these are still further depleted by those that die – around one per cent per year. While it is possible to replace dead vines in a young vineyard, Christian – in common with most viticulturists in Bordeaux – is against the practice in mature vineyards. It makes good management too difficult. The result is that, in plots with vines of over 40 years old, depletions of 35 per cent or more are the norm. So, to allow a vineyard to grow old *en bloc* would clearly be disastrous. Yet it is hard to rotate such a small vineyard as Pétrus.

In the event, Christian drew up a rotation of replanting for Pétrus which extends into the middle of the 21st century. On average, 2.5 acres (one hectare) are replanted every eight or nine years which means that, at any one time, a little under ten per cent of the vineyard is out of production as far as the *Grand Vin* is concerned, and so disruption is kept to a minimum and a good average age maintained. One hectare was replanted in 1972, and the same in 1981 and 1989. So, the hectare of 1981 vineyard will be included in the 1989 vintage Pétrus for the first time and was pruned very short to produce the best possible quality. The oldest vines in the vineyard are 70-75 years old, and the producing vineyard has an average age of 40 years. January 1985 produced temperatures as low as -9°F, but fortunately without causing serious damage.

Another important improvement to the Pétrus vineyard, introduced by Christian, has been a new drainage system, consisting of a huge central ditch filled with gravel. This has greatly assisted the working of the heavy clay soils which dominate the vineyard. It is not always realized how important such drainage schemes have been in the development of the great Bordeaux vineyards; nature does not always provide everything. So, the great reputation of Cheval Blanc – not far away, at the extremity of the St-Emilion *appellation* – really only began after an extensive drainage system was installed in the 1850s.

One of Bordeaux's main problems of the 1980s has been high yields, the legacy of healthier vines and better rotation in the vineyards. Christian Moueix believes in tight pruning, but also knows that this alone cannot solve the problems of high yields, since the actual situation can only be assessed after the fruit has set, usually in July. He has been one of the pioneers of the new concept of crop-thinning, which he carries out in early July. His instinct was that July thinning was much more effective than August thinning, but his recent field tests seem to show no discernible difference in the end results. Such thinning is especially important in regulating the yields of the Merlot – the backbone of Pomerol vineyards, and also prominent in neighbouring St-Emilion. The effect of unchecked yields can be seen in many 1982 St-Emilions, now brown in colour and showing their age, in contrast to the Moueix properties, whose 1982s are deep in colour and still youthful.

I asked Christian Moueix for his personal assessment of the Pétrus vintages since 1970. As can be seen, his judgements tend to be cautious and understated, and expressed with his customary diffidence – a refreshing change from the hype we are increasingly subjected to!

1970: good to very good
1971: wonderful, silky
1972: difficult, slightly vegetal, but a touch of class
1973: pleasant in a light style
1974: good, but austere
1975: still closed, outstanding potential
1976: charming, slightly over-matured; excellent in magnums
1977: herbaceous; can be enjoyed with a light meal
1978: good and characteristic
1979: dense, good after decanting

1980: pleasant, with good balance
1981: still closed, good promise
1982: still closed, excellent promise
1983: good to very good, with lighter tannins
1984: well balanced, good for the vintage
1985: great classic wine
1986: rich and exotic
1987: surprisingly balanced and pleasant
1988: great classic wine with strong tannic structure
1989: probably outstanding

A sidelight on the fame of Pétrus, and the problems this brings in its wake, is amusingly illustrated by the château's visitors' book. One volume lasted from 1947 until 1970. Since then, it has got through three more volumes! In a property as small as Pétrus, the presence of visitors creates obvious disruption, and the Moueix are now anxious to enforce stricter criteria on those requesting visits.

However, one advantage of such a small property is that its wines can literally be "handmade". The winemaking has long been meticulous, as the roll-call of great vintages testifies. But now there is more space in the *chais*, which has been expanded, and the equipment to control temperatures is installed. The fine-tuning today has more to do with picking at precisely the right moment, and in the right conditions. When there are morning dews or mists, Christian picks only in the afternoon – the best time of the day in autumn conditions. One year, he even used a helicopter to blow the water off the vines after a sudden downpour. As he commands a large team of pickers, who make the rounds of the vineyards he farms, it is always possible to pull in as many pickers as are needed to harvest Pétrus at exactly the optimum moment. Nowadays, it is usually all picked in two or three days, something only possible on such a pocket-handkerchief estate.

So far, we have talked almost exclusively about Pétrus, because this is inevitably the Moueix flagship – even though it is only part-owned. But the same meticulous care goes into the other properties owned and farmed by the Moueix, and it has been one of the features of recent years that Christian has steadily extended the scale and quality of the care given to each of their wines. One of his earliest ventures outside Pomerol was the

Although the wine itself has risen from near-obscurity to stardom, the château at Pétrus, usually uninhabited, remains simple and unadorned.

acquisition of the tiny Canon vineyard in Fronsac. More recently, this led to the purchase of three other important vineyards in that district: La Dauphine, Canon-Moueix (the only one of all the family's properties to bear their name) and Canon de Brem. The resuscitation of this once-famous district is now firmly under way.

In St-Emilion, the great Moueix vineyard is Magdelaine, one of the 11 *premiers grands crus classés*, on the plateau and *côtes* just a few minutes' walk from the medieval ramparts of the town. It has, for years, been consistently one of the best wines of this *appellation*, a wine of great refinement and rare delight. Other Moueix *grands crus classés* are: La Clotte, a tiny vineyard producing a little pearl of a wine; Fonroque, the longest-held of the family properties, producing a strong-flavoured robust wine that has shown a marked improvement since 1981; and Moulin du Cadet, adjoining Fonroque, but making a wine which is lighter, with the emphasis on elegance rather than power. The latter two *crus* have recently been upgraded, with some new oak introduced into their cask maturation.

In Pomerol, pride of place among the Moueix wines, after Pétrus, belongs to Trotanoy – home of Christian's cousin, Jean-Jacques, who heads the commercial side of the company, yet is also responsible for Fonroque. Trotanoy is a wine of sumptuous power and originality. Then comes La Fleur-Pétrus, lighter in texture but wonderfully perfumed and elegant. Latour à Pomerol, which belongs to Madame Lacoste-Loubat, the Pétrus partner, but is farmed by the Moueix, is a wine that has made great strides in the last decade and really shows the sure hand of Christian Moueix and Jean-Claude Bérrouet at work. Lagrange, a Moueix property since 1959, needs time to show its undoubted breed and charm. Christian's own property, La Grave (formerly known as La Grave-Trigant-de-Boisset), was acquired in 1971. It is an excellent second-tier Pomerol, with stylish richness, but not opulence; the 1985 here was outstanding. Two slightly less well-placed vineyards, La Fleur Gazin and Feytit-Clinet, have been most successfully improved in the 1980s.

Christian Moueix was the first Bordelais to try his hand in California, a field well marked out by a number of the great Champagne houses. But, inevitably, the concept of Dominus is totally different from that of Opus One (see page 190), the joint-venture wine produced by Robert Mondavi and Mouton-Rothschild, with the largest input coming from the California side. Christian characteristically began with a vineyard, when the opportunity came to buy one that was once part of Inglenook and responsible for its historic vintages. These were some of the first outstanding wines made in California. He believes this to be one of the three best vineyards in Napa Valley. The vineyard was a mature one, which Christian is still working on and judiciously replanting. In recent vintages, he has been obtaining around 3.5 tonnes to the hectare, the equivalent of about 53 hectolitres per hectare. He uses the same 16 pickers each year, and pays them a bonus of five dollars a tonne for picking cleanly, removing unripe or imperfect grapes from the bunches, and ensuring that the loads are free of leaves, which impart a bitter taste to the wine.

It is still early days for Dominus, and Christian is typically hesitant as to just how good a wine he can make, or how long it will take him to do it. But, at a blind tasting of 1984 California Cabernet Sauvignons recently given by German collector Hardy Rodenstock in Bavaria, Dominus performed with distinction among the top names of the Valley.

And what of the man himself? Like a great wine, the longer you know him, the more you are aware of the complexities, nuances and subtleties of the man. As one who has had the privilege of knowing both his parents, the fascinating blend of physical, mental and psychological elements from both sides is intriguing. There are the gracious manners, the assurance tempered by diffidence, the humour, the restlessly-questing intellect, the impatience of the perfectionist, the sensitivity of the artist, the broad, many-faceted culture and the wisdom that knows there may not be answers to all the questions – at least not yet; and then, behind all this, there is a deeply private man, who has the courage to know that he has embarked on a task that will encompass a lifetime, and that there are no short cuts.

SAUTERNES-BARSAC

Lucien Lurton of Château Climens

The bucolic twin *appellations* of Sauternes and Barsac are at last experiencing a deserved renaissance, with wine drinkers once again appreciating their fragrant, sweet, unctuous white wines. Without question the most concentrated and expensive is Château d'Yquem – but another estate, writes **Robert M Parker Jr**, makes wines that are more complex and compelling, and more companionable with food. It is Château Climens which, sitting on the highest plateau in Barsac, is presided over by Lucien Lurton.

The communes of Sauternes and Barsac, famous for the production of sweet white wines, are located a short 40-minute drive south of down-town Bordeaux. Yet, in this relatively short distance, something dramatic happens to the climate. Just south of Barsac, the tiny River Ciron flows into the warmer Garonne, and in the autumn this conjunction of rivers creates a mist which encourages the development of the *Botrytis cinerea* fungus. Providing the weather is warm and dry, the fungus attacks the vineyards, dehydrating and concentrating the grapes. The result is shrivelled, but sugar-rich, grapes that make opulent sweet wines.

For much of this century, the wines produced here were the dinosaurs of Bordeaux, labour-intensive and expensive to make. Producers here have had huge problems of climate and manpower to overcome almost every year. Even when Mother Nature smiles on the region, only three vintages a decade are likely to bring outstanding quality; another three are good to very good. The rest are usually wash-outs. When one considers the capriciousness of Mother Nature and the lamentable dwindling of demand for these luscious, sweet, sometimes decadently rich and exotic wines, it is not surprising that so many producers entering the 1980s were increasingly pessimistic about their future – feeling, with much justification, that their time had passed. Many even began to produce dry white wines to enhance their cash flow.

However, after decades of neglect by both consumers and owners, the bucolic *appellations* of Sauternes and Barsac are at last experiencing a degree of success unparalleled this century. During the second half of the 1980s, châteaux owners here made significant investments in newer barrels and winemaking equipment, and consumers began to recognize that these remain France's most under-valued and under-appreciated great wines. For who can contest the unique pleasure of a glass of unctuous, fragrant, sweet wine at the conclusion of a meal?

Mist rising from the River Garonne swathes the vineyards of Barsac until the sun breaks through in the early afternoon. The warm dampness promotes Botrytis, the secret of Sauternes.

The most famous château of the region is, without question, the Sauternes estate of Château d'Yquem, which makes the most concentrated and expensive sweet white wine in France. But the wine I find most companionable with food, and most complex and compelling to drink, is that of Château Climens in Barsac. Climens has been owned since 1971 by Lucien Lurton, who presides over a considerable empire of Bordeaux estates, including the famous Margaux properties of Châteaux Brane-Cantenac, Durfort-Vivens and Desmirail, as well as the reputable Graves estate of Château Bouscaut. All of these properties produce very good wine, but none of them has quite the standing in its respective commune that Château Climens has in Barsac.

For much of the last two centuries, Climens has been considered one of the two leading estates in the commune of Barsac. The 75-acre (30-hectare) vineyard and modest one-storey château – its only physical distinction being two slate-roofed towers at each end – is located just north of the tiny village of La Pinesse, sitting on the highest plateau of the Barsac region, a full 70 feet (21 metres) above sea level. Most observers claim that this elevation has contributed to the vineyard's excellent drainage, giving Climens a distinct advantage over lower-lying properties in wet years.

While the names of most châteaux here can be traced back to former owners, no one is quite sure how Climens acquired its name. For most of the 19th century the château was owned by the Lacoste family, who produced a wine they called Château Climenz-Lacoste. At that time the vineyard's 70 acres (28 hectares) achieved an annual production of 6,000 cases, but the devastating effects of phylloxera in the late 19th century destroyed most of the vineyards in Bordeaux, including that of Climens. (Today, at a time when most major wine-producing estates are doubling the yields from their vineyards, Climens commendably maintains an average annual production of only 6,000 cases, from a vineyard area 17 acres (seven hectares) larger than it was in the mid-19th century.) In 1871, Climens was sold

The stark, angular manor house at Château Climens dates back to the English rule of Aquitaine, but the exact origin of the château's name remains a mystery.

to Alfred Ribet, the owner of another estate called Château Pexoto which was subsequently absorbed into what is today known as Château Sigalas-Rabaud.

In 1885, Ribet sold the property to Henri Gounouilhou, whose family managed Climens until its current proprietor, the dynamic Lucien Lurton, purchased it in 1971. It was Henri Gounouilhou, director of Bordeaux's most famous daily newspaper, *Sud-Ouest*, and his successors who raised not only the level of quality at Climens, but also the public's awareness of this great estate. The legendary vintages of 1929, 1937 and 1947 enabled Climens to surpass the reputation of its larger neighbour, Château Coutet, and rival even that of the great Château d'Yquem.

Lurton has merely enhanced the extraordinary reputation of this outstanding property. His only change has been the removal of the small quantities of Muscatel planted in the gravel, red sand and clay-like soil of the vineyard. The current plantings, which he believes produce the best wine from the *terroir* of Château Climens, are a blend of 98 per cent Sémillon and two per cent Sauvignon Blanc. Lurton eschews a larger proportion of Sauvignon in the blend because it has a tendency to lose its aroma after several years. The average age of the vines is maintained at an impressive 35-38 years, as Lurton believes in replanting only three to four per cent of his vineyard per year. In addition, his yield of 12 hectolitres per hectare remains one of the smallest of all the estates in the Sauternes-Barsac region. No doubt this statistic alone accounts for the exceptional concentration and quality of the wine produced.

Lurton is aided by his daughter Brigette in the operation of Château Climens, and also, in no small measure, by the Janin family who have looked after this estate as *régisseurs* for nearly a century. Once this brain trust has determined the proper picking date, usually not before mid-October, the vines of Climens are harvested on four, five or even six separate occasions. Only grapes that are undamaged and have been attacked by the "noble" *Botrytis*

Once affected by "noble rot", the grapes of Sauternes produce only a quarter of their former potential volume of juice. The result is a concentrated, unctuous, honey-gold nectar.

rot are selected. *Botrytis* causes a profound change in the Sémillon grape. It shrivels the skin, consumes up to 50 per cent of the sugar content, forms glycerol and decomposes the tartaric acids. The result is a grape capable of rendering only one-fourth of its volume of juice prior to the *Botrytis* attack – an unctuous, concentrated, aromatic, sweet nectar. The wine is fermented in cask and aged for two years in 55-gallon (250-litre) barrels before being bottled. In most vintages, 45-50 per cent new oak is used; this is believed to develop the proper marriage of honeyed, pineapple- and apricot-flavoured fruit with the vanillin toastiness of new oak barrels. The wines are fined with egg whites and filtered lightly through cellulose pads prior to bottling.

What makes Climens so precious is that it produces the region's most compellingly elegant wine. There is no doubt that for sheer power, viscosity, and opulence Climens will never rival Château d'Yquem, nor even Château Rieussec, Château Suduiraut and the luxurious, rare "Cuvée Madame" of Château Coutet. However, if one measures the greatness of a wine by its extraordinary balance and finesse, Climens not only has no peers, but deserves its reputation as the most quintessentially elegant wine of the region. Many Sauternes can border on the cloying, but in the top vintages Climens seems to combine a rich, luscious, exotic character of honeyed pineapple fruit with a remarkable inner core of lemony acidity – giving the wine zestiness, precision to its flavours and a profound, hauntingly pleasurable bouquet.

Notwithstanding the legendary vintages of 1929, 1937, 1947 (though I have only seen disappointing bottles of the 1947 – the result of poor storage – it enjoys a phenomenal reputation among those who have tasted it) and 1949, it seems to me that Climens has never been stronger in terms of both greatness and consistency than it is now, some two decades after Lucien Lurton assumed control. Of the 1950s vintages, only the 1959 stands out as memorable. Of the 1960s wines, there is much to admire about the pleasant 1964 and 1969, and they are, no doubt, successes given the horrendous weather conditions that afflicted the producers of Sauternes and Barsac, but I do not believe there was an exciting Climens made that decade. It was in the 1970s that Climens began to produce really great wines.

While the 1970 is fully mature and a foursquare, uninspiring wine by Climens standards, the 1971 is undeniably a great Climens. It has drunk well since the late 1970s, becoming seemingly richer and more profound as it matures. It is a classic Climens, powerful yet restrained, rich and opulent yet delicate. The wine's superb balance is a result of its crisp acidity: this gives not only remarkable penetration and clarity to its bouquet, but also precision to its flavours. Climens produced a surprisingly good wine in the dreadful vintage of 1972, an attractive, lightweight wine in 1973, and two excellent, nearly exceptional wines in 1975 and 1976. The 1975 has remained slow to mature (a characteristic of most of the wines of Sauternes and Barsac), displaying a light golden colour, a tight bouquet of coconuts and flowers, and a ripe, honeyed, pineapple fruit. In the mouth it displays the crisp acidity that is so characteristic of Climens, with plenty of power and length. It will last for several decades into the next century. In contrast, the 1976 is much more advanced – already charming and evolved with a more unctuous texture, lower acidity and a plump, honeyed, tropical fruit-scented and -flavoured character, wrapped judiciously in a glove of toasty oak. In 1977, Climens again produced a very respectable wine from a poor vintage, making me wonder if this is not the best property in Sauternes-Barsac to search out in the off-years. Both the 1978 and the 1979 are competent, successful wines, although drier, lighter and lacking the *Botrytis* of the great years.

As for the 1980s, Climens has produced three legendary wines – the 1983, 1986 and 1988; one outstanding wine – the 1980; and very good wines in 1981, 1982 and 1985. The last three vintages are not particularly well-regarded in the Sauternes-Barsac region, but Climens certainly succeeded in producing admirable wines. One can imagine how much fun collectors and enthusiasts of Climens will have ten or 20 years hence in comparing the three legendary wines of 1983, 1986 and 1988. I terribly underestimated the 1983 when I first tasted it from cask. It appeared flabby and unstructured, both uncharacteristic traits of Climens. However, after it was bottled it seemed to develop more and more structure, and, in my view, has turned out to be the finest vintage of Climens since the glorious 1971. Extremely concentrated, with stunning ripeness and a gorgeous bouquet of honeysuckle, pineapples and other tropical fruits, this full-bodied, rich, impeccably made, well-structured Climens should drink well for another 15-20 years.

However inconceivable it may seem, the 1983 has been surpassed in quality by the 1986. The latter vintage of Climens manifests a bouquet that seems to roar from the glass, displaying scents of honey, tropical fruits (principally pineapple) and spicy, vanillin-scented new oak. On the palate, the wine is extraordinarily deep and sensationally concentrated, with great precision and clarity to its flavours. It has a finish that must last for several minutes. What is so admirable is that its crisp acidity makes the wine taste refreshing rather than heavy or cloying. As profound as the 1986 has turned out to be, the 1988 may well be a Climens to surpass everything produced at the château in the last four decades. Perhaps one will have to go back to the legendary 1929 to find another Climens so sublime. What makes it so very special is that it has everything the 1986 has, but even greater length, greater intensity to its bouquet, and a balance that is nearly perfect.

Of course, none of this would be possible were it not for the remarkable attention to detail exhibited at this property, the strikingly low yields, and the overall commitment to producing as fine a wine as man, and the vineyard's soils, are capable of achieving. For that, we must thank Lucien Lurton.

THE COTE D'OR

Robert Drouhin of Maison Joseph Drouhin

Burgundy is a complex and capricious wine region: its northerly climate, the treacherous Pinot Noir grape, the fragmentation of its vineyards, and the relationship between grower and *négociant* all make it a minefield – as much for the Burgundian vine-grower or wine merchant as for the unwary wine drinker. In this highly complicated scene, explains **_Serena Sutcliffe MW_**, the perfectionist Robert Drouhin has a foot firmly in all camps, as domain owner, *négociant*, farmer, winemaker and businessman.

Burgundy is the great conundrum of the wine world, the area we cannot quite crack. We know there is splendour lurking there somewhere, perhaps just a little out of reach, but we cannot quite find the key to the treasure trove. Instead of learning more about the region and unlocking the door to its remarkable wines, we shy away from the challenge and give up the chase. But we do so at our peril, for Burgundy can provide some of the most exotic, hedonistic and show-stopping tastes ever found in wine.

That, in itself, is extraordinary. Burgundy, in winemaking terms, is a northern area, with a capricious climate to match. And red and white Burgundy are each mono-grape wines, the whites made from the ubiquitous (and currently globally popular) Chardonnay, the reds from the mercurial, elusive Pinot Noir. Many other great red wines are a brilliant blend of several grape varieties, leaving much scope for intelligent *assemblage* if one variety is not so successful in any one vintage; Bordeaux is the classic example of this flexibility. But red Burgundy stands, and in some cases falls, by the Pinot Noir. If it rains at the wrong time, if late summer is not warm enough, producers still have to make wine from that one grape. It is a hard taskmaster, but when the winemaker rises to the occasion, it can dazzle.

I choose my words carefully for, to make good Burgundy, the human hand should guide the grapes, never tame them. The essence of the art is to draw out all the incomparable flavours of the Pinot Noir, and then give them rein. The trick is to do less, and not more, in the cellar; to adopt a "hands-off" or, wherever possible, non-intervention policy. For the Pinot Noir is fragile: manipulate it excessively, and it will become boring. The Chardonnay is altogether more robust and forgiving, although here again it is often better for it to find its own way rather than forcing it to behave in too refined a manner.

The heart of Burgundy is, of course, the Côte d'Or, that amalgam of the Côte de Nuits and the Côte de Beaune, running southwards from Dijon to below Beaune. Then there is Chablis, a vinous island equidistant between Dijon and Paris, logically and geologically

Robert Drouhin's wines are full-bodied and long-lived, with grands crus earning accolades world-wide.
His 1989 vintage, maturing in the Drouhin caves, promises to be impressive.

more part of Champagne than Burgundy. South of Beaune, there is the Côte Chalonnaise,
producing very respectable "B-film" Burgundies of both colours. Around Mâcon, there is
the Mâconnais, renowned for quaffable whites, and this area runs into the Beaujolais, about
which we all think we know quite a bit. Actually, we do not, as there is an immense amount
of somewhat beguiling wine made here, and we have to keep our heads in order to judge it
accurately. Suffice it to say that an individual domain wine from one of the ten *crus* (Moulin-
à-Vent, Morgon, Chénas, Juliénas, Chiroubles, Fleurie, Brouilly, Côte de Brouilly, Saint-
Amour and Régnié) is very likely to please.

The special feature of Burgundy, what causes it to be fascinating, or impenetrable,
depending on how you see it, is the fragmentation of its vineyards. Each area is divided into
many hundreds of domains, which vary in both size and quality – one man's Gevrey-
Chambertin is very definitely not another's. While this undoubtedly gives us a great
diversity of tastes, it is also a trap: we might have been favourably impressed with a Nuits-
St-Georges of a given year, but we will not necessarily be as enchanted with another from
the same vintage. So, to be sure of repeating pleasurable drinking experiences, we must
retain not just the name of the *appellation* and the *climat* (the Burgundian term for an
individual vineyard), but also that of the grower or producer.

This is complicated by the fact that properties are so much smaller in Burgundy than in,
say, Bordeaux. Whereas down in the south-west of France, a château might consist of 75-
100 acres (30-40 hectares) – some of the Médoc first growths own double that quantity –
where one château wine will be made, a Burgundian grower might own 25 acres (ten
hectares) and make ten different *appellations*. This is both a logistical exercise for him and a
challenge for the consumer seeking his way amongst the myriad names of the region.

Perhaps such a complex state of affairs requires a complex man to understand them. Such a person is Robert Drouhin, the universally respected head of the house of Joseph Drouhin in Beaune. Robert Drouhin is not an easy man to know, somewhat reserved and sober, especially in the rollicking ambience of Burgundy. He is deeply serious, utterly committed both to his own wines and to his area, and a perfectionist who is as demanding of himself as of others. If he is a tough critic, both of what he produces and of what is produced by the region as a whole, it is because he is intent on setting high standards.

But Robert Drouhin, in his quietly-spoken and incisive way, is also one of the most frank and open of all inside commentators on the Burgundian scene. He is ready to admit any kind of change or modern technical development if it is proved to be good, and to revert to traditional mores if they are proved to be better. It is typical of the man that he is also utterly unchauvinistic in his social and professional relationships. What matters to Robert Drouhin is that you are good at your job, and it is for this reason that he employed a woman oenologist, Laurence Jobard, to run the operational winemaking side of the business. This was at a time when the technical end of the Burgundian wine world was exclusively male, but Robert Drouhin is not a man to bow to custom for its own sake.

It is hardly surprising that in such a family milieu Véronique, Robert Drouhin's daughter, became an oenologist and immediately joined the winemaking team. But she has a very special responsibility of her own. She went to Oregon (see pages 199-202) to increase her experience with the Pinot Noir and was so impressed by what she saw that she was instrumental in persuading her father to buy land there. Now she supervises the Oregon Drouhin domain, and divides her time between the New World and the Old.

Robert Drouhin is ideally placed to understand the entire Burgundian wine scene, as he and his firm fulfil many roles. First of all, they are vineyard owners, with 59 acres (24 hectares) on the Côte d'Or and 89 acres (36 hectares) in Chablis. Then, they run the estate of the Marquis de Laguiche, a connection which goes back to the war when Robert's uncle and adoptive father, Maurice Drouhin, began buying the wines, taking over the exclusivity in 1947. The house of Drouhin now vinifies an enormous amount of wine in its *cuverie* in Beaune – 1,300 barrels of red and 1,800 barrels of white in 1989 – while it oversees fermentations taking place elsewhere. It gives advice where it has contracts for buying in grapes or wine, so as to ensure optimum quality. So Robert Drouhin and his firm are domain owners and *négociants*, farmers, winemakers and businessmen, intimately linked with their product from planting to when the bottle is put on the table.

Robert Drouhin and I decided that the best way to trace the history of both the house and the man was through a retrospective tasting, with each year both a professional and a personal milestone. At the same time, the climatic differences between the Burgundian vintages would be revealed, as well as the multifarious flavours of a range of red and white wines stretching from Dijon to Beaujolais.

We began with the oldest wine and worked our way up to the great 1989 vintage, which had just been made. Robert has been steeped in Burgundy (in the best possible way, of course!) since childhood: Maurice Drouhin was very much of an older generation, so the wines drunk round the family table were from the first three decades of the century. Meanwhile, Robert was listening and learning. He joined the firm in January 1957, when the 1955s and the very poor 1956s were in the cellar. The first vintage he made was 1957, and he drew on the expert advice of Monsieur Michel from the *station oenologique* for help, particularly with the malolactic fermentations.

Véronique Drouhin, a trained oenologist, has a special interest in the difficult Pinot Noir grape. She divides her time between the family's Burgundy and Oregon estates.

Any tasting that starts with the Corton-Charlemagne 1955 shows distinct promise. This wine was bottled, but not made, by Robert Drouhin, and fully justified the vintage's fine reputation for white Burgundy. The colour was of deep gold brocade, with a nose of walnuts, honey and camphor wood. Corton-Charlemagne, especially in youth, does not have the fat of Montrachet and frequently begins its life quite austere. Now, this wine has a vanillin flavour, a real satiny texture and, later in the glass, wonderful exotic notes of coffee. One kept going back to it.

Next, we essayed a Gevrey-Chambertin 1957, Robert Drouhin's first vintage. This clearly illustrated that a straight *village* wine, as opposed to a *premier* or *grand cru*, has to be quite exceptional to stay the course for over 30 years. 1957 was a good year, but this wine would have been better 15-20 years ago. The colour was still pretty, but there was definitely a mushroomy element in the wine that comes with old age. Robert himself is weathering the decades a great deal better, being tall, upright and distinguished-looking, an imposing figure in any setting.

We had to have a wine from the great 1959 vintage, which was especially astounding for reds. The grapes were beautifully healthy, the key to success in any vine-growing area. Robert Drouhin remembered that his Montrachet fermented out to 15.2 per cent alcohol, it was so rich! But we sampled Drouhin's Moulin-à-Vent 1959, and very remarkable it was too, every bit as good as some of the fabled 1947s. Drouhin's source of supply for Moulin-à-Vent is the same now as it was for this wine – a real sign of the strength of continuity. It had been matured in barrel and bottled after a year. As with most old, top Beaujolais *crus* from great years, the nose resembles the Pinot Noir more than the Gamay, from which all Beaujolais is made. Only in the aftertaste did one detect the true grape variety, but it would have fooled most of us at a dinner table. The colour was still very blue and young – astonishing – and the overwhelming impression was one of richness and ripeness. There was a whiff of roses on the nose and a delicious sweetness – a piece of history in the glass. Drouhin remains highly regarded for its Beaujolais, whether Beaujolais-Villages or one of the *crus*, and many only drink Nouveau if it is from this house. However, although Robert Drouhin is involved in all types of wine from what could be called Greater Burgundy, he refuses to deal in any *appellation* outside the area, or in *vin de table*, eschewing the creation of a *marque*, or brand, of basic quality that he could promote across the globe.

The following year, 1960, was a difficult time for Robert as Maurice Drouhin died. It was also a difficult year for Burgundy, with many of the wines unripe or rotten. But the Charmes-Chambertin that we tried was unexpectedly attractive, with a good, deep colour and a nose of what the French call *cerises anglaises*, and from which they make jam. There was also a vegetal influence and the fruit was drying up, but it was most respectable. The beginning of the 1960s was a turning point for Burgundy, as it was for many other wine regions in France. From now onwards, tractors, fertilizers and pesticides were in use, and there was much new planting. Then, the first oenologists were appearing. The degree was only created in 1955, so they started being taken on by the larger firms from 1960. They had no immediate "feel" for wine and they abruptly changed many time-worn methods, without reflecting whether it was necessary. Traditionally, in Burgundy, the cellar masters were also coopers and they really knew their barrels. There was a golden rule they followed: that when they transferred the wine to *fûts* after fermentation, it should be in its elementary, cloudy state, still warm from the fermentation vats. The oenologists preferred to work with cold, clear wine. Some character disappeared in the changeover, when the *chefs de caves* lost their status to the oenologists.

However, from the wines that followed, it was evident that Robert Drouhin was keeping an eagle eye on the situation *chez lui*. 1961 was truly felicitous, both for him and the

*The house of Drouhin vinifies an enormous amount of red and white wine in its cuverie in Beaune,
and Robert Drouhin is intimately linked with the product from planting to sale.*

vintage. Robert married, and his first son, Philippe, was also born this year. Philippe, after
completing a business training, is now working in the firm, providing totally different
talents from his sister, Véronique. 1961 and 1962 were reference points for Burgundy,
which still had a quantity of old vines. Robert feels that, by this time, he had enough
experience to draw the maximum from the fine grapes grown in these vintages.

Certainly, these two examples were memorable – paradigms for paradise. The
Chambertin Clos-de-Bèze 1961 had a very young, dark colour and a nose of roasted
cherries. This was high-extract wine, almost resembling a liqueur. There was a softening
touch of violets, often found in this part of the Côte de Nuits, but with all the body and
structure of the year. Clos-de-Bèze like this is grand, tight-packed and complex, coating the
mouth and becoming softer in the glass. We wished we were eating grouse with it!

As 1962 was Véronique's birth year, Robert wanted to show his Chambolle-Musigny
Amoureuses. Anyone meeting the delightful Véronique would understand why. She was
born on December 1st, which was also the Sunday of the Hospices de Beaune Sale (see page
243), an exceptional deviation from the rule of holding it on the third Sunday in
November. In 1961, Robert had bought vines in Chambolle, so he both cultivated and
made this 1962. It was one of the best red Burgundies of my life, and it is the archetype of
what Robert Drouhin aims to make, combining finesse and complexity in a magical whole.
But you cannot do this every year in the climate of Burgundy; many Burgundians think
1962 produced the apotheosis of quality. The silky texture and constancy in the glass
reminded me of La Tâche 1962, but there is also the raspberry side to Chambolle, linked to
the breed of Les Amoureuses, which could so easily be *grand* and not *premier cru*. This must
be the epitome both of Burgundy and of the Pinot Noir.

Ageing in new oak barrels imparts a distinctive flavour to the wine, giving great red Burgundies much of their tannic backbone. Barrels are periodically topped up to prevent the wine from oxidizing.

We passed over, but paid homage to, 1964 and 1966, both good vintages – the 1964s a mite more austere than the 1966s, which were not real keepers and sometimes resembled the 1953s. Laurent Drouhin was born in 1966, and he had more luck than Frédéric, who was born in 1968, an unredeemingly poor vintage. But the red Beaune Clos des Mouches 1968 we tasted was produced from old vines which must have contributed to its survival. The unripeness of the year gave the impression of a Pinot Noir that could have come from Switzerland, but the wine was good, if short. There were many fine wines from the 1969 vintage, but we took it on trust this time.

Our next landmark was 1971, a sad one for Robert Drouhin, as he lost his adoptive mother. Our tasting also showed a sad aspect of this otherwise opulent vintage, as this was a wine affected by the widespread hail of the year, an affliction that hits Burgundy more often than Bordeaux. The Clos de la Roche had a real nose of class, but the taste showed the drying influence of wounded grapes.

The first half of the 1970s proved to be very trying for the house of Drouhin, as in February 1973 there was a fire that destroyed 250,000 bottles of wine and some wines in vat. The worst result of the catastrophe was that Robert then had to hire premises and bottling facilities and so could not exercise the control he normally insists upon. Everything changed in 1976, a good, if rather extraordinary year. Now Robert had the cellars and bottling lines to face with confidence what nature had given him. He compares the vintage with 1937, hard at first and taking time to develop. Certainly, the tannins of 1976 astonish; Drouhin recommends decanting the wines, normally not a Burgundian practice. The red Beaune Clos des Mouches 1976 is a powerful wine; Robert wanted it that way and left all the stems, as he did in 1989, while in other vintages he removes half. There is the familiar nose of prunes recognizable in many 1976s, and tannin and freshness on the palate.

Then we exercised our palates on a superb Grands-Echézeaux 1978, a great year for Burgundy, and one in which Drouhin took full advantage of what was on offer. The dark colour leads to an incredible bouquet of slightly *sauvage* fruit, which in turn will become more like hung game. There are brambles in there too, great glycerol, and a terrific explosion of mouth-filling truffles. Who could wish for more?

The next year, 1979, was perhaps better for white than for red; certainly Drouhin's Montrachet is a monument to the former. The reds can be a bit diluted on the Côte d'Or, as in 1970 and 1982, when large quantities were produced. But 1980 was another situation altogether – prematurely misjudged, but with some fine reds, especially on the Côte de Nuits. However, we tested our theories on the Clos des Mouches, which had a seductive nose of warm, soft earth and was very sweet and delicious on the palate, with volumes of utterly desirable fruit – perfect now. In 1980, Drouhin celebrated its centenary, and so Robert and his team made the famous Clos des Mouches on their old press. It was a huge success, but when they did the same thing in 1981, the results were not so happy. Robert says, only half jokingly, that good wines are sometimes made "by accident"!

The 1983 vintage, which can be dramatic or disappointing, produced long-term laying-down wines *chez* Drouhin. Some of the 1984 *grands crus* confound the generally modest reputation of this vintage, while the splendid 1985s are a credit to the house and flagships for the region. 1986 was extraordinary for white Burgundy, and Drouhin's Clos des Mouches is a honey of a wine, with great potential and just the right amount of oak. Drouhin never exaggerates new oak; the formula, for example, for the magnificent Montrachet 1987 was 40 per cent new barrels, with the rest put into one-year-old *fûts*. This wine was bottled in January 1989, and is all acacia and discretion, apricots and mocha. Robert says that it will be at its apogee in seven or eight years' time. He makes white wines that will age well, but are not designed to flatter and overwhelm in young tastings; precocity can sometimes deceive.

The 1988 vintage has confirmed that Robert Drouhin has a place reserved for him in the firmament. In extensive tastings from cask, the reds look majestic, none more so than one of Drouhin's signature wines, Griotte-Chambertin, with its crushed-cherries character that is more than just auto-suggestion. Griotte is to Gevrey what Amoureuses is to Chambolle – and once tasted, never forgotten. The white 1988s at Drouhin surpass the overall level. I have particularly admired the Chablis – the *grand cru* Vaudésir has a lovely, warm, hay-like nose, with enormous fruit and a great follow-through. At Drouhin, Chablis *grands crus* are bottled at nine months, after maturing in *fûts*, but with a small proportion of new wood; *premiers crus* are bottled earlier to keep their lively Chablis character. I respect Robert Drouhin for wanting to keep that typical Chablis verve – these wines should not be made like mini-Côte d'Or whites.

With the 1989s, Robert Drouhin has come into his own. He says, with characteristic reserve, that he expected to make another 1929, but the yields precluded that. Most of us will not be able to make the comparison. Suffice it to say that the reds look like being on a par with the very fine 1985s and 1988s, and the whites could be very great. Certainly, a sneak preview of the Clos des Mouches was impressive.

But, then, Robert Drouhin is himself impressive, and perhaps wines are made in their master's image. To make classic Burgundy, you need both integrity and intelligence. Robert Drouhin has both, with an extra *je ne sais quoi*. I think, with my nose in a glass of his wine, I would call it flair.

CHABLIS

Jean-Marie Raveneau of François Raveneau

The holdings of the Raveneau family are diminutive by comparison with those of most other vine-growers in Chablis, but size is by no means all. The key to quality in the vineyards of this frosty northern region is the lie of the land: its exposure to the ripening sun and its Kimmeridgian soil. But nor are the vineyards all; simple, natural, hygienic winemaking, loyalty to tradition, and an awareness of what is going on elsewhere are the crucial adjuncts to Jean-Marie Raveneau's success, as **Anthony Rose** explains.

On a sunny morning, you can walk out of the town of Chablis – or run if you're feeling energetic – and before you can say white Burgundy you will find yourself surrounded by vineyards. Before the sun burns the rolling mists off the folds in the hills, delicate spiders' webs strung from plant to plant along the roadside glisten like a collection of fabulous silver necklaces. The dew dries and in an instant the spiders and their webs are gone, rendered invisible by a miracle of nature – like the wine itself, as finely poised and delicate as a spider's web.

The town itself, mind you, is not much to write home about. In fact it has little to commend it except for the fleshpot cuisine of Michel Vignaud at L'Hostellerie des Clos and the pepperpot towers of the Porte Noël, remnants of a prosperous bygone era when Paris was accessible to Chablis and the extensive vineyards of the River Yonne via the waterways. Chablis is theoretically part of Burgundy. But, at 86 miles (138 kilometres) from Beaune, the region is almost as far north of Burgundy's heartland as it is south-east of Paris. So nondescript is the little town that when I arrived there, having unintentionally taken the scenic route from Beaune, I found that I had driven through it and out the other side without realizing. "Without wine, Chablis would be totally dead," said Jean-Marie Raveneau, and I knew just what he meant.

I was visiting Jean-Marie Raveneau shortly after the harvest of 1989. It was a historic harvest, the earliest in his memory and the earliest since 1947 according to his father François, who has now handed over the reins of the business to Jean-Marie. I had wanted to visit at harvest time to pick a few grapes – not too many mind you, but just enough to soak up a bit of local colour, as it were.

Unfortunately, it was not to be. When I met Jean-Marie's wife Bernadette in London for a wine tasting, she had politely but firmly refused my offer of a free hand. Somewhat miffed at this rejection, I asked Anthony Hanson, Raveneau's importer, to intercede on my behalf.

Jean-Marie Raveneau eschews quantity in his all-out quest for top-quality Chablis.

This cut no ice either. "It's no use," he said. "Don't get the wrong idea. It's not a question of hiding illicit sacks of sugar from prying journalistic eyes. They just want to be able to receive you at their best. And harvest isn't the best time."

Mollified by this kindly ego massage, I began to wonder just how much of a public relations exercise my visit was going to turn out to be. I needn't have worried. When I turned up at the narrow doorway in the rue de Chichée in Chablis, Bernadette told me they had forgotten I was coming. No standing on ceremony here. As it happened, Jean-Marie was at home. But then he usually is: home is where the wine is made, aged and consumed; and if he's not at home, he's only a stone's throw away in the vineyards. Young, lean and tanned, with a handsome, angular face that wouldn't look out of place on the silver screen, Jean-Marie has a semi-perpetual Gauloise dangling from his lips, which adds to the general impression of nonchalance.

The Côte des Grands Crus, site of the greatest vineyards, above the little town of Chablis.

We were soon standing at the top of a pine-clad hill, overlooking the seven greatest vineyards – the *grands crus* – of Chablis: Les Clos, Valmur, Vaudésir, Les Preuses, Grenouilles, Blanchot and Bougros. At the bottom of the hill lies the town of Chablis in the bowl of the Serein Valley, and up the opposite hillside are many of the *premier cru* vineyards, one rung down in the hierarchy from *grand cru*, and the lesser sites entitled simply to the *appellation* Chablis.

The poplar-lined river lives up to its name. Serene it certainly is, almost eerily so. Nothing moved: not a car, not an animal, not even a bird. As we stood there, Jean-Marie gave a discourse on exposition. The best vineyards, the seven *grands crus* and the 17 *premiers crus*, are on undulating slopes facing south-west or occasionally south-east; between them they account for only 13 per cent of the total vineyard area. These choice sites nestle next to the less favourably sited vineyards of straight Chablis and Petit Chablis.

"My father always said to me you can tell the best sites by the snow," said Jean-Marie. "The great vineyards are all on slopes and the best plots are the ones that melt first in the sun." As we looked, he pointed to part of Valmur, one of the *grand cru* vineyards, in a north-facing dip in the hill, demonstrating that even in the *grands crus* not every plot is equally favoured. He didn't think much of Bougros either: "it's a heresy that it's a *grand cru*". Chablis growers are not slow to express an opinion, gratis, on the relative merits of these great vineyards. As often as not, the answer is determined by the particular interest or lack of it vested in that vineyard. In the case of Bougros, however, there is a general consensus that the site does not reach the heights of the other *grands crus*.

Raveneau has 18 acres (seven hectares) of vineyards, a tiny acreage compared to the 212 acres (86 hectares) owned by the great Chablis firm of Laroche or the Beaune firm of Joseph Drouhin (see pages 42-49) with its 89 acres (36 hectares). Next to the giant co-operative of

A strict pruning policy helps to reduce yields, increasing the wine's concentration.

La Chablisienne, which handles 1,225 acres (496 hectares), the Raveneau holdings are diminutive. But size isn't everything; the lie of the land is the key to quality. With only choice *grand cru* vineyards, distributed between Les Clos, Valmur and Blanchot, and *premiers crus* at Montée de Tonnerre, Chapelot, Butteaux and Vaillons, the Raveneau family vineyards are well placed to deliver top-quality grapes.

The expansion of the Chablis vineyards in recent times remains a controversial issue. A century ago, the extensive vineyards of the Yonne were devastated by the twin blights of phylloxera and competition from Midi wines. By the mid-1950s, the vineyards had dwindled to a mere 1,200 acres (486 hectares). In recent times, Chablis has expanded once more to over 6,000 acres (2,430 hectares) and, thanks to crop-enhancing practices in the vineyards, yields are now four times as large as they were in the 1960s. Despite – or perhaps because of – the increase, there is pressure within Chablis itself to expand vineyards even further. Producers are divided on the issue, with one group in favour of a strict delimitation of the existing vineyards and the other for expansion.

Jean-Marie stands firmly in the former camp: "Between 1970 and 1981 there has been an explosion. Expanding the vineyard area is asking for trouble. The fact is that the best vineyards are already planted." He believes that expansion can only further dilute the good name for which many have fought for so long; his own concern is with quality, not quantity. As systematic re-planting becomes necessary due to the age of the vines or destruction by frost (a constant problem in this northerly latitude), Jean-Marie is looking for new clones of the Chardonnay grape. With a good trellising system in the vineyard, he is aiming for lower yields per acre: "I'm down to yields of 60-70 hectolitres per hectare, but I want to reduce the yields still further for extra concentration". This sacrifice of quantity over quality distinguishes Raveneau's wines from run-of-the-mill Chablis.

Walking back through the picnic area of the pine-clad Bois du Taillis, Jean-Marie stooped to pick up a big clump of crumbly grey-white stone, picking out the tiny clusters of comma-shaped fossilized oyster shells (*ostrea virgula*) from which it is constituted. The bigger lumps of Kimmeridgian limestone like this one have been removed from the vineyard slopes below and thrown onto the hilltops to make the land easier to work. Named after the Dorset village of Kimmeridge where this kind of soil is also found, the thick underlying limestone substratum is a special feature of Chablis. "Kimmeridgian soil," said Jean-Marie, "together with the favourable microclimate of the valley, is the key to the secret of Chablis. The wine is higher in acidity and more minerally – with a smell of acacia and *noisette* – than the white wines of the Côte d'Or."

As a name Chablis is so well-known that, like Burgundy, port and Champagne, it is widely used as a synonym for dry white wine. In its campaign against the misuse of such generic names, the INAO (Institut National des Appellations d'Origine) has calculated that only one in 20 bottles sold as Chablis world-wide actually comes from the region. Most

Summer serenity reflected – by the banks of the Serein.

of these imitations don't even pretend to capture the character of Chablis. Yet, while the fashion for Chardonnay continues with no sign of abatement, the elusive yet distinctive character of Chablis remains the hardest of all white Burgundies to imitate. It is one of the few white wines made from the Chardonnay grape whose character is instantly recognizable, sometimes from a whiff alone. Its lively bite, purity of fruit flavour and minerally character all help to distinguish it from other full-bodied dry white wines.

Jean-Marie Raveneau, a fourth generation grower and winemaker, was born in Chablis. His great-grandfather was involved in the battle against the phylloxera louse, one of the few growers far-sighted enough to realize that some form of inoculation against the bug – in fact the grafting of American rootstock – was the answer to the problem. After his grandfather sold most of the family's holdings, his father François bought half the vineyards the family now own. The other half came from his mother's side, she being the sister of René Dauvissat, another owner of *grand* and *premier cru* vineyards here.

Jean-Marie studied wine first at Beaune and then at Dijon, over a period of five years, with apprenticeships in Champagne, Beaujolais, Provence and the Côte d'Or. "Studies opened my mind," he admits, yet so devoid is he of academic pretension and technical mumbo-jumbo that it comes almost as a surprise to hear that he learned about wine at college at all. When he says "I prefer empiricism to technicality", he means that academic techniques are subservient to the practicalities of winemaking that he has learnt with his father since he started making wine jointly with him in 1978.

He believes that winemaking ought to be as simple, natural and hygienic a process as possible. Although 80 per cent of Chablis grapes are picked by machine, he still prefers to harvest by hand – not, he suggested, because the wine is better as a result, but rather because "hand-picking is traditional, part of 'le folklore'. When we sell our wine, we're also selling part of a dream." The concept of selling "le folklore" crops up again and again in conversation. In the video of the harvest he showed me – seeing the film was my consolation for having missed it – a Canadian picker is himself picked up and hurled like an oversized grape into the cart, doing no good at all to the rather expensive grapes inside. "It's all part of 'le folklore'," laughs Jean-Marie.

The harvested grapes are brought in by cart to the backyard, where they are immediately destalked, crushed and pumped into a press in the ivy-clad *chais*. After a gentle pressing, the juice is left to settle in preparation for its metamorphosis into precious alcohol. Jean-Marie doesn't add sulphur if he can help it but if the weather is hot – as it was in 1989 – a judicious dose of sulphur is essential to avoid oxidation. The juice is fermented at a cool temperature in enamel-lined tanks, where it remains until its transfer in March into oak barrels.

Cleanliness, for Jean-Marie, is close to godliness. "In making a quality product," he says, "the main thing is the quality of the raw material. Hygiene plays a vital role. Everyone has the opportunity to bring in the same product: 80 per cent of people can bring in good, healthy grapes, but hygiene is the key – not always easy when there's so much going on at harvest time. Maybe it's just a pipe. There are people who will say they're tired, so they'll leave it until the morning: that attitude's fatal. Cleanliness is the start of good winemaking, but you mustn't get obsessed. A wine shouldn't be smothered with kindness; it should be tested a bit to allow it to struggle."

Small casks of new and used oak fill a tiny, three-part barrel-vaulted cellar beneath the street, its walls thick with ancient black mould which thrives on evaporated alcohol. There the wine remains, protected from fluctuations in temperature, for 12-18 months before bottling. Here we tasted Chablis 1988s straight from the barrel – hard to judge, as shockingly refreshing as a cold shower first thing in the morning. First it was Chapelot, peachy and well-rounded; then Montée de Tonnerre, delicious with its spicy aromas, intense fruitiness and bite. "Good Chablis must have bite," commented Jean-Marie. From there we moved on to Blanchot, more closed, but richer and rounded; and then to Valmur with its new oak "à la limite" – as Jean-Marie described it. Finally we tasted Les Clos, a wine of exceptional finesse and bite, but barely in its stride yet.

If the question of oak barrels is a live issue throughout the winemaking world, in Chablis it is virtually a matter of life and death. This is because one of Chablis' principal attractions is its very particular, unusual purity of fruit flavour and steely acidity, untrammelled by the taste of oak. In too-high doses, the vanilla character of oak can flatter to deceive. Yet new oak is fashionable and attractive; as an aid to fermentation, it can enhance a great wine, giving it structure for the long haul. As is the way in these debates, heated arguments rage on both sides of the oak divide. Jean-Marie's approach is practical and undogmatic: "California is largely responsible for the trend towards ageing wine in cask. Ten years ago I was a defender of the tank; now I'm coming round to the cask. But the wood must add something to the wine, not vice versa. What's important is to hang on to tradition, to remain true to type without closing your eyes to what's going on."

Like his father before him, Jean-Marie believes strongly in the need to nurture the product from the cradle to the grave. "Being a grower is an all-year-round job," he explains. Even holidays at la Rochelle at the home of Bernadette's family involve selling the product. Until they met Jean-Marie, they were confirmed red wine drinkers. Now – and it does go rather well with oysters – they're sold on a rather special Chablis.

CHAMPAGNE

Henri and Rémi Krug

It is the second fermentation that puts the fizz into Champagne, but the blending of the wine behind the scenes that gives it quality. No one understands this better than Henri and Rémi Krug. Their non-vintage Grande Cuvée may have as many as 47 different wines from eight vintages in it, their vintage Krug as many as 29 wines. And that is not all that is exceptional about the two brothers. *Serena Sutcliffe MW* describes the illustrious house of Krug.

In almost any language, Champagne is a trigger word. The very sound of it is exciting. It stimulates imagination as well as appetite, creating a mood of anticipation in a way that no other wine can.

For we must not forget – it is a wine! As the bubbles dance in the glass weaving their spell over us, we might be forgiven for thinking that Champagne is the plaything of the vinous world. In fact, it is one of the most difficult and challenging of all wines to make, demanding skill, knowledge, experience and investment. Only people as talented and resourceful as the Champenois would have attempted it, let alone taken it to the very pinnacle of winemaking achievement.

The region of Champagne would not seem the obvious birthplace of the bubble. But what might appear as disadvantages are, in reality, ideal conditions for producing the wine that will ultimately become Champagne. The climate might be harsh in winter, but sunnier climes would result in wines too heavy to be made into sparkling wine of any finesse. The austere sweep of the chalky hills might look forbidding when the vines are bare of leaves, but that chalk contributes to the delicacy and breed of Champagne.

The trick, as always, is to marry climate and soil with grape variety, and here the Champenois have centuries on their side. They juggle with a *palette* of three grapes which combine to give Champagne its inimitable taste. They know exactly where each variety should be planted within the region so as to give of its best. Broadly speaking, that means the red Pinot Noir is grown on the Montagne de Reims to the east of Ludes, and the red Pinot Meunier on the "petite montagne" to the west. The white Chardonnay is grown on the Côte des Blancs, running south from Epernay. Along the Vallée de la Marne, the Pinot Noir is grown in certain *grands crus* such as Aÿ, Mareuil, Cumières and Hautvillers, and the Meunier in most of the other areas as well as in the adjacent valleys such as at Leuvrigny. This is the stuff of which Champagne is made.

All Krug wine is fermented in cask and Henri, like his brother Rémi, is fanatical about detail.

The Champagne Method is the vital process that puts the bubble in the bottle. You start off with a still, light white wine, and then you rebottle it with a judicious mixture of wine, sugar and selected yeast culture. This induces a secondary fermentation in the bottle, which performs the necessary service of transforming what would be a rather dull little wine into something altogether more vivacious.

But the secondary fermentation does not give the *quality* to Champagne. That comes directly from the blending, or *assemblage*, of all the component parts – the different grapes, vineyards and sites, together with a blend of years if non-vintage Champagne is being made. This is the catalyst, this is what crowns Champagne with complexity, what makes it the prima ballerina among the dancing girls.

And this is where the house of Krug should come in, for no one understands the art of blending better than the Krug family. They have been doing it for a long time, since the firm was founded in 1843 by Jean-Joseph Krug. Now it is Henri and Rémi Krug who shape the course of their Champagne and of their illustrious house. They themselves are a blend of many qualities, taking their responsibilities as inheritors of an awe-inspiring tradition very seriously, but with an almost impish sense of humour lurking near the surface.

They are immensely proud of what Krug is, but modest enough to know in their work that the grape is master and they are there to mould it. They are staunchly conservative where their methods are concerned, but sufficiently intellectually curious to make experiments. It was not, for example, enough for the Krugs to be convinced that fermenting their grapes in small wooden barrels gave their Champagne something "extra". Was the use of wood really necessary, or was it just the Krug way? So they tried fermenting small quantities of wine in other materials and in containers of other sizes, and then compared the results. They found that the wines fermented in their 45-gallon (205-litre) Argonne oak casks of an average age of 35 years were fuller, more complex and just a little more profound than the others in the experiment. When the wines were analyzed, it appeared that the balance between the alcohols was different, with the small casks giving alcohol that better "fixed" the bouquet and aromas, and adding extra length on the palate; maybe the wine breathed better in these small *fûts*.

Krug Champagne is immunized against oxidation in the future, as the wine has already been under the influence of oxidation while fermenting in cask. This might well explain the particular longevity of Krug Champagne; it might also be at the heart of the mystery of the tiny Krug bubbles. In any case, Krug will continue to ferment all its wines in cask, unlike nearly all other great houses – and I will not be the one to complain.

Of course, if you make wines meant for ageing, you have to hold more stock. At the moment, there are seven years of stock in the Krug cellars. Certainly, the Krugs seem to begin where the rest stop. They own nearly 40 acres (16 hectares) of vineyard, all rated 100 per cent (the top crust of the Champagne vineyard sites), which supply about 20 per cent of their requirements. The rest they buy on contract or on long-term understandings: for instance, at Ambonnay on the Montagne de Reims they have bought from the same family for three generations.

The *assemblage*, or blending of the still wines, takes place in the early part of the year following the harvest. The Krugs disappear into their laboratory and sniff and taste and pour wines into each other with glass funnels. They are creating the Krug style, the Krug character that its devotees demand. Before them they have a mass of villages and sites to choose from. At Krug, they always use the three grape varieties, respecting the soft, fragrant qualities that the Pinot Meunier can bestow on a blend. The Grande Cuvée may have no less than 47 different wines in it, from eight vintages. Vintage Krug may have 29 different growths in the blend, but the proportion of each grape variety will vary slightly each year, in order to enhance the inherent character of the wine.

Listening to the Krugs talk about the villages is like hearing a fond father describing the characteristics of his children. Pinot Noir from Ambonnay, they say, is solid and structured, austere and severe – like the people there. It is the point of departure, on which one can build a blend. Aÿ, facing full south, is round, extrovert, smiling and fruity – always more forward than other villages. On the Côte des Blancs, Chardonnay from Le Mesnil is flinty, with a little hardness, while Avize and Oger are elegant and more flattering. Put them together, and they merge in the most delightful way. Leuvrigny, in the Marne Valley, gives grapes of a redcurrant, fruity character; these Pinot Meuniers can also have a touch of cassis. You need even more *crus* to make up your "lot" of Pinot Meunier than you do for

*The walled Clos du Mesnil in Le Mesnil-sur-Oger. Once owned and worked by a
Benedictine monastery, the Clos has belonged to Krug since 1971.*

your Pinot Noir or your Chardonnay, although the latter two grape varieties are more
important overall in the blend.

The logistics of it all seem too complicated for a mere taster, but the Krugs are imbued
with the Krug style and they know what they are looking for. A touch of Meunier, for
instance, can bring out the tastes of the other component parts. It is like a Tuscan
Renaissance painting, where the background falls away in layers, unfolding, revealing,
opening out. Henri and Rémi work instinctively. Their father Paul taught them, and his
father taught him. It is this continuity that is the rock-firm guarantee of Krug quality.

So what are they like, these Krug brothers? Do they have a sense of importance, of being
guardians of a grail to be worshipped, rather than drunk. Heaven forbid! Glasses clink
merrily when the Krugs are around, conversation buzzes and decibels escalate. One minute
they are earnestly explaining how they made a particular vintage, or how the flowering is
developing in the Champagne vineyards, the next they are enthusing about a concert they
have been to, or a meal they have experienced. For both Henri and Rémi are committed
gastronomes, passionate about good food and the wines that go with it. Rémi orchestrates
the fabulous dinners for "Krugistes" around the world, but to hear Henri questioning
Gérard Boyer at Les Crayères, the famous three-star restaurant in Reims, is to understand
how he is so exacting with his wines. Henri is the technician, while Rémi displays the flair. I
have been at a few of these occasions – and survived the course! They have given me some
of my greatest gastronomic memories.

If ever there were a Champagne to go with food, it is Krug. Raymond Blanc at Le
Manoir aux Quat' Saisons, the illustrious restaurant near Oxford, obviously feels the same,
for he created an autumn dinner fusing an array of Krug Champagnes with some of his
most inventive food. We started with Grande Cuvée, always elegant yet plump, mouth-
filling yet taut. You can drink Grande Cuvée wherever and whenever you find it, but it also

keeps beautifully, becoming increasingly grand with age. At Le Manoir, we were not in the mood for patience, and consumed quantities of it with a dish as intricate as aubergines, sun-dried tomatoes and artichoke hearts soused in sweet vinegar, served with lobster and *langoustine* tails dressed with basil-scented vinaigrette. Only a Champagne such as Krug would take this in its stride, and come sailing through.

Then we had the somewhat cutely-named Assiette de Mon Ami Spartaco, three variations on the theme of pasta. It was the perfect opportunity to launch Krug 1982, very aptly as it turns out, for Krug is much loved in Italy. Immediately you meet a great vintage such as this, you appreciate the sheer complexity of the bouquet. Here we found walnuts, with notes of caramel, hawthorn and vanilla – multi-dimensional Champagne and total Krug. The family considers that the 1982 bears some resemblance to the renowned 1964, or even the 1953.

With the fillet of Cornish turbot, poached in Champagne served with *cèpes* and wild mushrooms, we delved into the Krug Clos du Mesnil 1982. The 4.6-acre (1.9-hectare) walled Clos has existed in Le Mesnil-sur-Oger since 1698 and it was bought by the Krugs in 1971. The unique position and history of the Clos persuaded the family to depart from their fundamental belief in the art of blending in order to produce great Champagne. Essentially, it is more Krug in character than typically Blanc de Blancs. Pure Chardonnay, the bouquet is less complex than a black and white grape blend: the 1982 smells of clean laundered cotton! The taste is fresh and crisp and crammed full of fruit. I have a feeling that a slice of ripe white peach in a glass of Clos du Mesnil would be paradise discovered.

Next we experienced a *coup de théâtre*, roasted wild young partridge served with a Champagne sauce, fresh grapes and autumn vegetables, washed down with Krug Rosé. The colour is not pink at all, but pale and tawny, teasingly subtle. There is a marvellously wild and exuberant bouquet, coming straight from the contact with the black grape skins that also give that tantalizing colour. The Krugs always use Pinot Noir from Aÿ to make their rosé, as the fruit is supple and forward in this village, positively come-hither. But the taste is surprisingly full and weighty and imposing, belying the pale colour; it was sublime with the partridge. This is a rosé Champagne that defies you not to notice it. But always let all Krug Champagnes air in the glass for their full beauty to develop; and use quite a wide tulip glass, with a base tapering to a point, so that the wine can breathe and expand.

For many years I was under the mistaken impression that no Champagne went with cheese; Krug taught me otherwise. We were very daring at Le Manoir, marrying the strong, pungent Maroilles Fromage des Vendanges with the magnificent Krug Collection 1959. This was exotic, powerful fare, a heady combination which none of us will forget for a long time. The nose is of vanilla pods and, believe it or not, autumn days. The freshness of the wine, at 30 years old, was astounding. It reduced me to silence, the senses were so occupied trying to identify all the mysteries of aroma and flavour. To drink the 1959 is to comprehend what is Krug – and be grateful.

Another shibboleth shattered was that of Champagne and pudding. *Bien sûr*, an ordinary *brut* Champagne is completely eclipsed by sweet-nothings, but put a magnum of Krug Collection 1964 with Raymond Blanc's Assiette aux Parfums de Caramel et Epices – *et voilà*, fascination. The 1964 has an ethereal quality, more austere and with more finesse than the 1959, and very classic. It is drier than the rich 1959, with a toffee tail to it – perfect with the caramel. The trick was to know that the 1964 would have been drowned by the Maroilles cheese, while the splendour of the 1959 would have been lost on the dessert.

Old Krugs are almost a fetish for some collectors. They spend happy hours comparing the 1961 with the 1962, Henri's first vintage. Then there are the two giants: the nutty, complex 1945, and the legendary, honeyed 1928. Krugistes are just limbering up for the

The old casks or pièces are a valuable commodity: new barrels must be aged before
use to prevent the taste of oak tainting the delicate wine.

enormously graceful 1973, while waiting for the sensual, fleshy 1976. Others are still savouring the 1981, a year when there was more Chardonnay in the blend than usual, so the hazelnut tastes become bolder as the wine stays in the glass. I last drank this – "tasted" would be inaccurate in this instance – with one of the most innovative dishes in France: Joël Robuchon's Gelée au Caviar à la Crème de Choufleur, a shellfish jelly, infinitely delicate, enhanced by a layer of the finest caviar and then covered with a cream of cauliflower, white flecked with green. Between 1928 and 1982 inclusive, Krug produced only 25 vintages, so the appearance of a single-year Champagne from its headquarters in Reims is always an event rather than a regular fixture. *Chez* Krug, "pairs" of successive vintage years are rare: 1928/1929, 1952/1953, 1961/1962, and now 1981/1982.

It would be a travesty to suggest that Krug can only be drunk in the grandest of gastronomic contexts. I have taken bottles of Grande Cuvée with me to far-flung Far Eastern islands, where it went down a treat with fish hauled straight out of the water and cooked over a beach fire. The Krugs themselves are fond of drinking it with cheese soufflé, and my own preferred brunch is Krug and kedgeree. Plain roast chicken, and even cold pheasant, takes very kindly to Krug. Rémi informs me that his rosé is delicious with bread and butter pudding, and I have enjoyed Grande Cuvée at the races with scones, cream and strawberry jam! The possibilities are endless.

What of the future *chez* Krug? First, the vintages. The 1982 will be followed, in good time (for Krug never hurries anything, least of all ageing in bottle), by the 1985. And perhaps, at the turn of the century, we will be drinking Krug 1989. The family tells me that this was the first year they have ever dared to prophesy quality at the time of picking. Normally, they reserve all judgement until the time of the *assemblage*, but in 1989 they came out with a resounding pronouncement of "superb". It was a very early vintage: they started picking in the Clos du Mesnil on September 6th. Henri could not contain his excitement, and telephoned Rémi in the office in Reims from the vineyards to announce that it "could be another 1928!". Krug makes one want to live longer.

The sixth generation is now ready to be indoctrinated. Olivier, the oldest son of Henri, began his in-house training on September 1st 1989, plunging into the *vendanges* in the Krug commando, and then going on to sales. His business school training will be invaluable in today's tough commercial world, as will that of Caroline, Rémi's oldest daughter, who will start work *chez* Krug in two years. There are others waiting in the wings, so that vital continuity is assured.

A symbiosis such as that between Henri and Rémi Krug is the perfect alchemy for making majestic Champagne. For what is this endlessly intriguing wine if not a blend of technical discipline and unbridled inspiration? The Krugs say that if you are a small house you have to be fanatical about detail. They are. They are fanatical about the condition of their grapes, about how they press them – using only the first 450 gallons (2,050 litres) that come out of the hand-operated vertical presses – and about how they ferment them. They do not mind if their wines, after bottling for the secondary fermentation, have quite a high acidity reading, as they know they will remain for years in their cellars. They like to keep their reserve wines, which give the *gravitas* to Grande Cuvée, in 40-hectolitre stainless steel vats to preserve their freshness. They do not wish to produce more than about 500,000 bottles a year, as this gives them total control over their production and bestows that hand-made quality. They are maddeningly obstinate about releasing their wine; even if the shelves are empty, they insist on ageing their bottles for the time they need.

But, we forgive them – because they are right. We forgive them because they continue to show us what magisterial Champagne is all about, what depth and profundity can be coaxed out of this northerly region of France. And we have confidence in them, because we know that whatever the market force or prevailing fashion, Krug will always be Krug. When Henri and Rémi Krug taste, when they mould the elements to their vision of what Champagne should be, they are working with the combined palate memory of five generations. Making Krug is like owning a stately home: they are the caretakers of part of France's glorious heritage.

ALSACE

Jean Hugel of Hugel & Fils

With a 350-year tradition of vine-growing and winemaking in the village of Riquewihr, the Hugel family is well placed to understand the intricacies of the Alsace region as a whole, and to contribute its own top-class wines to the melting pot. In fact it was Jean Hugel, one of a trio of brothers currently running the famous company of Hugel & Fils who, with his father, devised the beautifully simple classification for late harvest wines. *Ian Jamieson MW* explains.

"The vine is a Mediterranean artist, and all artists do their best work when they suffer. If life is too easy for them, they become lazy." Like many of Jean Hugel's *ex cathedra* statements, this is imaginative and based on fact. Where the vine is as well-fed as a favourite household pet, its roots have no need to search for nourishment. They lounge in the feeding zone near the surface of the soil, utterly dependent on their unvarying diet, and their wines taste like a vinous equivalent of battery-fed chicken. "Free-range" vines, on the other hand, planted in land where little else will prosper, produce grapes with a complexity that makes the difference between wine that has character and wine that is merely specious.

The Hugel family has reason to understand this, for vine-growing and winemaking has kept it in the Alsatian village of Riquewihr, overlooking the plain that stretches across to the River Rhine, since the 17th century. Today the company is run by three brothers, Georges, Jean and André, all in their sixties; and the next generation is already well-established. Jean, or "Johnny" as he is widely known, trained as a winemaker at the viticultural school in Montpellier. Ebullient and energetic, he has for many years been an ambassador both for Hugel & Fils and for Alsatian winemaking as a whole.

Life over 350 years in one of Europe's bloodiest battlegrounds must have been as hard for the inhabitants of Riquewihr as it has been for their vines. Perhaps that is why, for Jean Hugel, the establishment of the European Community meant above all an absence of war, rather than the creation of a free-trade zone. Looking beyond the village boundary has long been a Hugel pastime. Early in 1789, Jean-Michel Ortlieb, a relative of the family, produced a treatise on agricultural improvement, a plan to improve *les biens de la terre*, the produce of the soil, the first edition of which was dedicated to the King of France. (A second edition, swiftly printed later in the same year and addressed to the States-General, showed that Ortlieb was not going to let the fall of a monarch get in the way of a good idea.)

Vines rise above the steep-pitched roofs of Riquewihr where "Johnny", Georges and André are the present proprietors of Hugel & Fils. The business has been in the family since 1637.

In his *Plan*, Ortlieb urged his contemporaries to "carefully observe the agriculture of neighbouring countries, in order to hasten the adoption of whatever could be most useful and advantageous to ourselves". Today, the Hugel family still keeps a close eye on viticultural progress in the outside world. Though aware of his own company's value, Jean is in touch with other great winemakers around the world and his attitude is non-parochial. The finest white wine that he has ever tasted, he says, was a *feinste Beerenauslese* 1949 from J J Prüm on the Mosel.

With such an unpartisan outlook, the Hugels are, not surprisingly, very successful in the export market, where they now sell over 80 per cent of their wine. The standard range of Hugel wines, produced in a typical Alsatian arrangement from grapes supplied by growers under long-term contracts, is made up of Pinot Blanc, Silvaner, Riesling, Tokay-Pinot Gris, Gewürztraminer and Pinot Noir. It is by these wines, which should lead the drinker onto the higher-quality bottles, that Jean Hugel would like his company to be judged.

The hierarchy of Hugel wines is based on the sugar content of the grape juice. In order to maintain continuity of style, each rung in the Hugel wine ladder is directly related to potential alcohol, determined by vine variety. Thus, the unfermented grape juice of Gewürztraminer in Hugel's regular range holds up to 11.5 degrees of potential alcohol, while the next rung up in quality, the Cuvée Tradition, varies from 11.6 to 12.9 degrees, and the Jubilee range (formerly known as Réserve Personelle) has a minimum of 13 degrees. These classifications remain the same, regardless of vintage variations, so in indifferent years when the grapes may not be fully ripe, wines of the top categories will be missing. In some years, a higher-quality wine may be added to a young wine in the regular range if it is a little light after being transferred from the deposit left by fermentation. Apart from this, the route that leads from grape to bottle is noticeably free of deviations.

All "handling", including where necessary chaptalization (the addition of sugar to increase the alcohol content), takes place before fermentation is complete. If a must is sweet enough to generate 12 degrees of alcohol, no sugar is added. The Hugels adopt a pragmatic approach to the relative merits of keeping wine in vat or in cask. The greatest wines mature in wood, simply because the casks happen to be the right size for the limited amount of wine available. The venerable Sainte Caterine cask, built in 1715, holds the equivalent of a little less than 12,000 bottles. Accordingly, it is only in the greatest years that sufficient quantities of any one top-flight are made to fill Sainte Caterine's girth, and since 1976 the old lady has had to associate with somewhat less than aristocratic wines. In fact, living with the middle classes must often have been her lot over the centuries, for great vintages occur seldom. The climatic pattern usually allows for two "off" vintages in a decade. Recent years (1983, 1988 and perhaps 1989) have produced some wines that might be called "great", but quantities have been too small for any vintage as a whole to be so described.

The strength of Alsace wines, since the region was returned to France after the First World War, has lain both in the simplicity of their varietal nomenclature and in an increasing concern for better quality. Compared to the average production figures across the Rhine, the yield per hectare is low here, reaching a peak of 120.5 hectolitres per hectare in the abundant vintage of 1982. The best German producers also achieve relatively low yields, even in large vintages, for it is a generally accepted rule that an over-large crop produces wine that is less concentrated and therefore less good. Hugel has long understood this, but continues to experiment. In six rows of Riesling, the potential alcohol content of the grapes was increased in 1989 by over two degrees, by reducing the number of bunches on the vine by 20 per cent.

Of wider interest, however, is the success of the classification devised by Hugel for late-picked and selected wines, which is now established in the law of the land. Until 1959,

Hugel would occasionally produce late-picked wines when conditions were suitable, which were made to their own specification and sold as *Spätlesen*. In the same way, until 1967, high-grade wines from selected *Botrytis*-affected grapes were occasionally harvested and sold as *Beerenauslesen*. Jean Hugel *père*, head of the family until 1980, and his son, the current Jean, drafted a law for the production of *Vendage Tardive* (late-picked) and *Sélection des Grains Nobles* (or *Beerenauslese*) wine which was accepted in its entirety and came into force in 1984. Today Jean Hugel points out with satisfaction that this was the first wine law in France written by producers and not by civil servants.

The successful application of this law has been deeply gratifying to the Hugels, whose aim is to promote the prestige of Alsatian wines and to increase the income of all growers who strive for the finest possible quality. The controls on production of *Vendange Tardive* and *Sélection des Grains Nobles* wines are strict and effective, even though the official tasting panel rejects a proportion (up to 35 per cent in some years) for failing to meet the required standard. These speciality wines are unique in France, according to Jean Hugel, in that they cannot under any circumstances have sugar added to increase their alcoholic strength. Commercially, much of Hugel's own success with these wines has been in the best restaurants. Previously, some had been reluctant to list Alsatian wine, but the arrival of the *Vendanges Tardives* has enabled Hugel to obtain listings for its drier Jubilee range of white wines made from the classic varieties and its red Pinot Noir.

Hugel winemaking may be described as traditional, individual and expensive. All wines undergo a malolactic fermentation in years when the acidity is high enough to make it necessary. Temperature, an important element in the control of this process, can be adjusted in the fermentation vats as required. The installation costs of such a system are large but, as Jean puts it, "they can be paid off in two years by the mistakes you do not make". Some of the Pinot Noir wines spend a period in new oak but by the time the almost-mature wine is released for sale, any additional flavour is hardly noticeable. "We sell wine, not oak," observes Jean, and advises his customers to decant his Jubilee Pinot Noir because the sight of the tall Alsatian bottle, associated with white wine, might prevent them from judging the wine for what it is – well-structured and true to the grape variety.

The Hugels' reputation throughout the world has been built around their holdings in important vineyard sites at Riquewihr, Schoenenbourg and Sporen. But success over three centuries has been assured not only by the quality of their vineyards, but by their personalities. In each generation of a family business, says Jean, only the best should be employed: "It is not a rest place for the incompetent, who cannot hold down a job elsewhere". At Hugel the energy and intelligence that have kept the family trading since the 17th century are still apparent.

THE LOIRE

Nicolas Joly of Le Clos de la Coulée de Serrant

Such is the jewel-like reputation of the distinctive dry white wine of Le Clos de la Coulée de Serrant that this compact estate, planted with vines continuously for six centuries, has its own individual *appellation* above that of regional Savennières. At times during this long history, its fortunes have floundered, but today the future looks secure – if idiosyncratic – in the hands of the inimitable Nicolas Joly, a devoted disciple of biodynamism. ***Steven Spurrier*** examines the wine, the man and his theories.

The white wine produced at Le Clos de la Coulée de Serrant in the Loire Valley is one of the most famous in the world. The renowned French gastronome, Curnonsky, placed it among the five greatest white wines that he had tasted. The London wine merchants that I joined in 1965 spoke of it in the same tones they reserved for wines of the Domaine de la Romanée-Conti, the Montrachet of Le Comte de Moucheron (shortly to be acquired by the Domaine) and the magical Rosé des Riceys. This 17-acre (seven-hectare) vineyard, planted without a break for six centuries, with its special *appellation* above that of the regional Savennières, thus has quite a reputation to live up to – a reputation of which Nicolas Joly was well aware, when, 12 years ago, he gave up merchant banking to help his mother manage the estate.

La Coulée de Serrant, like the other wines of Savennières, is made solely from the Chenin Blanc grape, a variety vastly superior to the more popular Sauvignon Blanc, but whose real qualities show only with age. This characteristic of the grape has created problems for the area since the Second World War. For two generations, the growers of Savennières, whose splendid houses and parks bear witness to better times in the distant past, have battled to keep their *appellations* alive. The steep, slate-dominated slopes here, first planted in the 12th century, produced wines that were famous at the court of Louis XIV. Post-war difficulties were exacerbated in 1952 by the *appellation* laws, which changed Savennières from being a sweet wine made with botrytized grapes to a dry wine, but kept the draconian low yields and high minimum alcohol. The oldest bottles of La Coulée de Serrant I have drunk, the 1947 and 1949 (both still available at Chez Point in Vienne) were fully sweet – rivals to the finest wines of Sauternes.

Before the current growth of interest in high-quality hand-made wines, running a property in Savennières was considered by the owners to be "like keeping a mistress, only more moral". It took Nicolas' mother and her husband 20 years from the purchase of the

First planted on this site in the 12th century, vines have been cultivated at La Coulée de Serrant ever since – and working methods remain much as they must have been for centuries.

ravishing but dilapidated estate in 1959 to put it onto a proper commercial footing. Now, although there is some difference of opinion as to the style of Savennières, the *appellation* is secure. Le Clos de la Coulée de Serrant remains the jewel, unequalled by the others; and Nicolas Joly, in his singular approach to viticulture, is far in advance of his neighbours.

This singular approach is based around the theory of biodynamism, a programme to reverse the effects of years of artificial fertilizers and pesticides in the vineyard by allowing the soil to regenerate its natural energy, thereby assuring the growth of healthy, sturdy vines. Add to this Joly's conviction that the position of the planets throughout the year provides a firm guide to when vineyard work should be carried out, together with his intention to return to non-grafted vines, and you have a very special approach indeed.

Nicolas Joly, a handsome man in his mid-forties, laughingly admits that many people think he is quite mad. With the benefits of a world-renowned vineyard, a fine product and buoyant sales, why should he wish to return to what his detractors regard as "the dark ages"? Joly's answer is simple: to protect the *appellation*, the individuality of its soil and microclimate, against the stifling uniformity that modern viticulture can impose on winemaking. Lazy agriculture, he maintains, ends up destroying all but the topsoil, which is artificially nourished by constant fertilizing; careful agriculture, on the other hand, will reinforce the intrinsic character of the wine. To use a biblical analogy, it is a question of building your house on rock rather than sand.

There is an almost religious fervour in Joly's quest for quality. At a time when the individual characteristics of races and creeds are, at least in the West, giving way to an

Nicolas Joly's highly individual approach to winemaking bemuses some of his critics, but the distinctive dry white wine of La Coulée more than vindicates his faith in biodynamic viticulture.

internationalism, when regionalism is almost akin to eccentricity, French vineyards are as much under threat as any aspect of European culture. Joly regards "progressive" viticultural aids, such as artificial weedkillers, insecticides and fertilizers, as a slow death for the soil. Similarly, he regards much "progressive" cellar work – the precipitation of tartrates through flash-freezing, centrifuges, sterile filtration – as an immediate death for the wine. His aim is that his wine should speak for itself.

To this end, he has chosen the more difficult route of good husbandry (whose principles were unquestioned only a few decades ago), almost doubling labour costs at Coulée de Serrant: two fine cart-horses are used to plough the vineyard; wines are cellared in 131-gallon (600-litre) oak barrels, with no trace of easy-to-clean stainless steel; and he has banished fining – "why should I put eggs into my wine?" – in favour of racking by gravity and a light filtration before bottling.

Joly rightly insists that fine wine is the product of vineyards, not laboratories. Although magnificent progress has been made recently in many aspects of vinification – especially in attitudes to cleanliness – refrigerated tanks and rows of new barrels are less responsible for the quality and potential of a wine than healthy, ripe grapes. And the grapes should not only look nice; they should contain everything to make well-balanced wine, more or less intense depending on the vintage. If the soil has been asphyxiated by weedkillers and then artificially nourished by fertilizers, the vine slips into the easy "fix" of finding its nourishment in the topsoil. In a few years, the vine's roots become too enfeebled to dig deep into the subsoil for proper nourishment and support – and in many cases there is no nourishment left there anyway. This vicious circle lays the vine open to numerous diseases, which have to be "cured" by regular treatment with artificial sprays. It is not surprising, then, that such vines – cut off from the mineral force of the soil, reacting more to this or that treatment than to the changeability of the seasons – collapse after two decades of semi-natural life.

Joly goes further, and risks being thought a charlatan by insisting on the links between the position of the planets *vis-à-vis* the earth and the life cycle of the vine. The passage of the moon through the different constellations, he maintains, shows four distinct elemental influences on the vineyard. These favour either the growth of the leaves (water signs: Cancer, Scorpio, Pisces), the strengthening of the roots (earth signs: Taurus, Capricorn, Virgo), the emergence of the flowers (air signs: Gemini, Libra, Aquarius) or the ripening of the fruit (fire signs: Aries, Leo, Sagittarius). Each of the four elements has its particular influence, and it is the dates of the fire signs that are most appropriate for working in the vineyards. Why, asks Joly, ignore such influences that afford natural growth, and replace them by chemical or empirical aids to growth, which we now realize can only lead to an ecological dead-end?

Such influences must be allied to the revitalization of the soil, and this is attained slowly. Joly considers that it takes seven years to bring a vineyard back to full health, by treatments using vegetable and animal extracts, "dynamized" by dilution in vast quantities of water, and applied at cosmically auspicious moments. A vine so treated in a healthy soil will become strong and resistant, and have less, or no need for, artificial pesticides. To take an example: the red spider, long thought to be an enemy of apparently healthy vines, is prevalent in Le Clos de la Coulée de Serrant to no ill effect; the negative effect of the red spider elsewhere is an indication of the actual weakened state of the vineyard.

On top of everything else, Joly has come out forcibly against clonal selection. Until the 1970s, to replant a vineyard or part of it, one selected wood from the 300 or 400 most sturdy vines, and multiplied these, thus creating an improved population in the vineyard. Clones, on the other hand, are all taken from one single vine, as often as not chosen for its productivity rather than the quality of its grapes. This is likely to condemn the next generation of vines to over-production, which will exhaust them quickly, especially if they are planted in a deficient soil. It is the variety of vines in a vineyard that contributes to making a great wine, each bringing its own character to the whole. A clonal selection, a single vine multiplied many thousand times, will not have the same effect, and even less effect if it is planted in ill-adapted soil. The old system – *massale* rather than *clonale* – produced a family of vines that were slower to produce fruit, but that reached full maturity at a time when their clonal cousins were ready for the compost heap.

La Coulée de Serrant is produced from what are, with yields of 25-30 hectolitres per hectare, probably the lowest-yielding vines in France for a dry white wine. And the resulting quality is obvious in its integrity and length of flavour. Such is the demand for his wines that Joly has been able to keep very little in reserve, though he intends to keep back the 1988 which he considers climatically a perfect vintage.

Depending on the vintage, the wine should be drunk between ten and 30 years after bottling. In its first year, the wine presents a fine medium-yellow colour with greenish tints, an aroma more floral (reminiscent of honeysuckle) than fruity, and a ripeness of flavour backed by firm acidity. After two or three years, it loses its first fruit to begin a long evolution during which mineral aspects will begin to dominate. Even old vintages, those

Early-morning mist, rising from the Loire, hovers over La Coulée de Serrant – a scene little changed since monks chose this outstanding site over 800 years ago.

*The splendid estates of Savennières bear witness to more prosperous times. It took Nicolas Joly
20 years to put his beautiful but dilapidated estate onto a proper commercial footing.*

made from pre-biodynamic vines, bear out La Coulée's incredible ageing qualities; a 1968, a meagre year of crushing acidity, left unnoticed in my cellar in Paris, showed an intensity of fruit and harmony when opened in 1989 despite the terrible vintage conditions.

Around the end of the century, Joly's theories will begin to be vindicated. At a time when one-year-old bottles of Montrachet are on sale, and some producers of *cru classé* Médoc admit that their wines are drinkable at four to five years due to the softer tannins now extracted by modern vinification, it is certain that varietal flavour and new oak will dominate. La Coulée, on the other hand, should find its way onto an end-of-millennium dinner table, to precede the Hermitage 1978 of Gérard Chave (see pages 73-77), Château d'Yquem 1975 and Taylor's 1963 port (see pages 150-56).

Joly's final bet, and one that he is convinced his vineyard will weather, is to return Le Clos de la Coulée de Serrant to non-grafted vines, like those that existed in Europe for thousands of years on their original rootstocks before the scourge of phylloxera at the end of the 19th century. By bringing his vineyard back to full vigour, in harmony with nature, will he be able to achieve the final step towards the originality, the inimitability of a really great wine?

The relevance of Nicolas Joly's work is not limited to his own vineyard, but serves as an example to wine producers everywhere. His vision and his work so far is a brilliant lesson to us all.

THE NORTHERN RHONE

Gérard Chave of J L Chave

Born into a remarkable family winemaking tradition stretching back some five centuries, Gérard Chave has been to California several times and has wondered at the technological razzle-dazzle of the wineries there. But, returning to his drab cellars in the northern Rhône Valley, he has continued to make wine just as before, and just as his father and grandfather before him. As **Robert M Parker Jr** explains, one of the world's greatest winemakers finds he has no more need of modern trappings than previous generations.

There would be no reason to stop in the dreary village of Mauves, which lines the busy N-86 highway on the western bank of the River Rhône, were it not for the fact that one of the world's greatest winemakers lives there. The cellars of J L Chave, behind and beneath the Chave family's unassuming house, are as understated as the village. There is no brash display, merely a metal sign much in need of repainting, to mark the spot.

The Chave family have been growers and wine producers on the Hermitage Hill since 1481. This remarkable 500-year tradition must be unparalleled in the Rhône Valley and equalled by few in France. The current proprietor of the family firm is Gérard Chave, a man of vigour and energy, sympathy and warmth. His winemaking alone provides much to admire, but he himself, in spite of his remarkable achievements and family tradition, remains an unassuming man with one goal – to make wine using the same techniques as his father and grandfather before him, wine in the traditional mode, which the buyer must cellar until it is mature. He has brought up his two children, 21-year-old Jean-Louis and 16-year-old Géraldine, to continue the Chave tradition.

It is tempting to compare Gérard Chave with his better-known neighbour and dear friend, Gérard Jaboulet, who runs the famous *négociant* firm of Paul Jaboulet-Aîné. The two Gérards produce the two greatest wines of Hermitage: Jaboulet's is called La Chapelle and Chave's is estate-bottled under his own name. While Jaboulet is a jet-setting promoter of Rhône wines, Chave has been construed by some as parochial.

This is far from the truth: Chave does not follow the old ways blindly and he has an enquiring mind. He has made several trips to California, and he has seen there both the advantages and the dangers of the centrifuges and filters that can remove so much uncertainty from winemaking. He will tell you that these machines also remove most of the wine's flavour and character, killing the wine before it has ever been bottled. Chave will use none of these methods, which he calls "the tragedy of modern winemaking".

Technological advances have not impressed Gérard Chave, who prefers to rely on traditional methods.

Visitors to Chave's Mauves cellars are usually greeted by his wife Monique and then taken to the waiting room which looks out over the back yard of the house. Beneath this yard are the damp cellars where more than 500 vintages of the family's Hermitage have been made and stored in much the same way for generations. Gérard Chave, crediting his visitor with a degree of passion for these compelling wines equal to his own, is swift to arrive. A quick jaunt across the yard takes the visitor into the deep catacombs beneath, where there awaits an education in winemaking, in blending and in a faithful but studied adherence to a tradition that has produced some of the world's greatest and most interesting wines.

The major drawback of Chave's wines is that they are simply not made in large enough quantity to satisfy world-wide demand. Not only are all of France's greatest restaurants beating on his door, but he is besieged by private clients eager to buy his wine direct and importers from all over the world begging for additional cases of his rare red and white Hermitage. After acquiring the holdings of the Domaine L'Hermite (previously owned by the well-known British Egyptologist Terence Gray), Chave now owns 27 acres (11 hectares) on the renowned dome of granite known as Hermitage hill that looms over the small town of Tain L'Hermitage. This has allowed him to augment his production of red and white Hermitage slightly, but even now annual output rarely exceeds 3,000 cases – a minute quantity of wine given the global demand. Chave also owns a 2.4-acre (1-hectare) parcel of very old vines in St-Joseph, where he makes what is probably the best wine of the *appellation*; but the quantities are again so small (less than 300 cases) that the wine is largely unknown. It remains the great secret of this cellar, and anyone who has the opportunity to try or purchase a bottle should not hesitate to do so.

The vinification technique practised by Chave – and by his father, grandfather and great-grandfather before him – is totally traditional. He crushes and ferments the grapes from his ten acres (four hectares) of white vines (90 per cent Marsanne and ten per cent Roussanne) in both old wooden *foudres* and vats for 14-18 months. His white Hermitage is encouraged to go through a malolactic fermentation, for he believes that when the grapes are picked at the correct time they have enough natural acidity for balance, and that the malolactic provides a creamy richness and additional ageing potential. His white Hermitage is, along with that from the *négociant* firm of Chapoutier, the longest-lived of the *appellation*.

After ageing, the wine is blended and bottled naturally without filtration, a rarity today. It behaves curiously in the bottle and is often seductive when young, displaying a bouquet of pineapples, wet stones and spring flowers, with a honeyed, broadly flavoured, lush palate. Yet, after several years the wine seems to lose its baby fat, close up, and often reveals little character or charm for another five or six years, only to re-emerge thereafter with even more nuances and subtleties to its bouquet. If you should neglect to drink this wine within its first four or five years of life, you will need the patience to wait a decade or 15 years until it re-emerges in full maturity. Top recent vintages such as 1988, 1986, 1985 and 1983 have the potential to last 20 more years.

One of the most memorable bottles of wine I ever tasted was the white Hermitage 1929, taken directly from Chave's underground library of vintages that have been maintained by the family for generations. In accordance with family practice, this wine had never been re-corked. Chave served it with *foie gras*, which turned out to be an ideal marriage. Initially there was a slight mustiness and a hint of oxidation. As the wine developed in the glass, it seemed to take on an aroma and character not unlike that of a very old vintage of Château d'Yquem. Its bouquet was dominated by the scent of toasty hazelnuts, and in the mouth it was dry, rich, relatively heavy and intense, while still possessing fruit. Drunk in 1986, at the grand age of 57, this wine was a revelation.

One of the ancient traditions in Hermitage is the production of *vin de paille*, a dessert wine made from white grapes harvested late and allowed to dry out on beds of straw until late December. This causes the grapes to dehydrate and take on a raisiny, super-concentrated character. The dry grapes are then crushed and fermented, creating one of the most individualistic and nectar-like sweet wines in the world. In 1974, Chave made a *vin de paille* that I have had the good fortune to taste several times. He has never sold it commercially, and apparently he has only a limited interest in producing it again. This is sad, given the extraordinary quality and complexity of the wine.

Chave is among the latest of all the growers in Hermitage to harvest his red grapes, pushing them to their optimum maturity. This provides the ripeness and richness that he regards as an essential starting-point for a great wine. Delaying the harvest is a risky business because of the heavy rain that frequently plagues the Rhône Valley in October, but Chave insists that his harvesters only bring in healthy bunches of grapes, leaving any diseased grapes on the vine or discarding them.

Red wine fermentation takes place in concrete vats and primitive wooden *foudres*. Chave is not a practitioner of cold fermentation, and will permit the fermentation temperature of his red Hermitage to reach 90°F (32°C). During the harvest he rarely sleeps, punching down the *chapeau* (the mass of skins, stalks and pips that rise to the surface of the fermenting juice) at least twice a day to assist the process of extracting colour and the wine's lifeline, its tannins. The maceration period depends on the style of the vintage. When presented with grapes that have little pulp and thick skins, Chave is often concerned about extracting too much tannin, which creates an unbalanced wine that is hard and charmless. Confronted with this scenario, he shortens the usual *cuvaison* (or maceration of juice and grape skins) of two or three weeks to ten days. When there is better balance and Chave feels the wine will not become too tannic or hard, the period is extended to upwards of three weeks.

Defying the frequent October rains, Chave harvests his red grapes as late as possible to ensure that they achieve their ripest and richest potential.

One of the main differences between Chave's cellars and those of other major Hermitage producers is that Chave keeps the wine from each of his vineyards (or, as the French say, *lieux-dits*) separate for almost a year. His wines come from ten separate vineyards on the hill of Hermitage and each, according to Chave, has its own characteristics. Tasting through these separate *cuvées* with Chave is like obtaining a doctorate in Hermitage.

Among the most famous of Chave's vineyards is Le Méal. It is one of the greatest vineyards on the hill, and is renowned for producing very fragrant, supple, intensely fruity red Hermitage. Les Bessards, reputedly the finest vineyard for red Hermitage, produces the deepest-coloured, most intensely flavoured, fullest-bodied wines with a great deal of tannin. It is always one of the most important components of Chave's Hermitage, as well as the dominant component of Jaboulet's Hermitage La Chapelle. Les Beaumes is known for its stylish, elegant, lighter-framed, austere, almost Bordeaux-like red wine. Les Greffieux, with its rich soil, is known for producing lighter, more perfumed, aromatically pleasing red wine; it is also one of the great locations for white Hermitage. Les Diognières, located on the lower flank of the Hermitage hill, produces wines that are less compellingly aromatic, but dense, powerful and tannic; it lacks the complexity of the other vineyards. Les Rocoules is an outstanding source for both red and white wines; its perfumed, quite concentrated reds are often blockbusters. L'Hermite, the vineyard with the highest elevation, turns out wine that is often the richest and most concentrated; it is the component of Chave's Hermitage that provides the intense, peppery, cassis-scented bouquet. There is also Peléat, which produces lighter yet well-structured wines, and several other parcels that do not figure so prominently in Chave's Hermitage.

Chave lets these wines sit and mature for at least one year before deciding how he will fashion his blend. It is in this painstaking process of following all the different *cuvées* over the course of a year that his formidable tasting skills are best demonstrated. Once the blend is made, the wine spends another eight to ten months in wood before being bottled; it is not filtered. Chave's extraordinary talent makes tasting his vintages enthralling; each reflects his great skill, his personality and, above all, the signature of the vintage.

Chave's red Hermitage is a long-lived wine in the top vintages. It is hard to predict how long it will take to peak – 15, 20 or 30 years. Less opulent and less dramatic than Jaboulet's La Chapelle, it starts life slowly and is rarely impressive when young, often needing seven or eight years in bottle to reveal its fine class. In the great vintages, such as 1978, 1983 and 1985, there are probably less than a dozen producers in France who have produced as noteworthy wines.

Chave's success during the 1980s was nothing short of spectacular, let down only by the mediocre red wines of 1980 and 1981 – but then he had plenty of company in those difficult years. For those with patience, Chave's longest-lived red wines will no doubt include: his excellent 1988, certainly the best Hermitage he has produced since the more opulent 1985; the stunning, potentially monumental 1983; and his flirtation with perfection, the glorious 1978. Those lucky enough to get hold of a bottle of Chave's powerful yet harmonious, staggeringly rich, deep red Hermitage 1978 should count their blessings, for this is a wine for celebrating the turn of the century. It will no doubt have a lifespan of over 40 years, and should certainly prove to be Gérard Chave's legacy to future generations of Chaves.

All of these wines should last 30 or more years. For more current drinking, the 1985 should drink well in the mid-1990s as it avoids the over-supple style of many red wines from this vintage. Its closest companion is Chave's ripe, succulent, intensely perfumed, silky 1982. Though these wines have less structure, tannin and sheer potential than the 1978, 1983 or 1988, they are glorious for drinking over the next decade. The same can be said for the 1979 and the quickly maturing 1984 and 1986.

As for the white wines, the greatest recent vintages include the quite astonishing 1985, with its huge aroma of pineapple and honeysuckle, and its long, amply-endowed flavours; and the 1983, which produced a more structured wine that gracefully balances power and finesse. With the Hermitage 1982 I have noticed definite bottle variation, which Chave is unable to explain. Some bottles exhibit superb richness and a very heady, honeyed, pineapple fruitiness; other bottles are dominated by the alcohol, which seems to be poking its head through the fruit in a rather annoying and unflattering fashion. Other top white wines from Chave include the very good 1986 and 1988, but for sheer sensational flavours and extract the 1985 will be hard to match for a least the next ten to 15 years.

It is unfortunate that today's wine world is not sprinkled with more individuals who are driven – as is Gérard Chave – to achieve a level of quality, if not perfection, far and above what is required.

SOUTHERN FRANCE

François Perrin of Château de Beaucastel

With its famous papal past and a massive output of 12 million bottles each year, Châteauneuf-du-Pape is as well known as any French wine. But all is not as it should be: there is an excess of heavy, charmless wines and a dearth of serious fine wine producers. The Perrin family of Château de Beaucastel is one of the honourable exceptions. **Robert M Parker Jr** shows how tiny yields, meticulous husbandry and old vines combine at this large estate to produce distinctive wines of a rare excellence.

The *appellation* of Châteauneuf-du-Pape begins less than 12 miles (19 kilometres) north of the hallowed, historic walled city of Avignon, continuing northwards along the east bank of the River Rhône to Orange. It is one of France's most privileged *appellations* – as well-known in the global wine market as that country's more glamorous viticultural regions of Bordeaux, Burgundy and Champagne – and it can produce some of the world's finest and longest-lived red wines. Yet, in spite of its fame and potential, the huge production (in excess of one million cases a year) and the dearth of serious producers committed to achieving long-lived, multi-dimensional wines has far too often resulted in excessively alcoholic, unbalanced wines of no style or charm.

One of the most notable exceptions is the estate of Château de Beaucastel, in the north-eastern corner of the *appellation* near Courthezon, within view of the A-7 super-highway. Until his death in 1978, the estate was run by Jacques Perrin, considered by many to be among the most brilliant and philosophical of the Rhône Valley's winemakers. Jacques Perrin lived by three principles: that a wine must be made as naturally as possible, with minimal intervention from the winemaker; that the percentage of Mourvèdre in the blend of Châteauneuf-du-Pape must be significant; and, that the wine's character and intrinsic qualities should never be compromised by concessions to modern technology. "Do not search in a wine for the reflection of an exact science," he once said. "The formulas of scientific oenology are only a thin competition which does not know how to respect the mysteries of the eternal creation."

Jacques Perrin brought up his two sons, François and Jean-Pierre, in this artisanal philosophy of winemaking and, since 1978, they have followed in his footsteps. François Perrin, an articulate, studious and highly confident winemaker, has assumed increasing responsibility for the wines of Château de Beaucastel as well as those of Cru de Coudoulet, the neighbouring Côtes du Rhône estate of 74 acres (30 hectares) across the road. His

*François Perrin believes that a wine should be made with as little interference as possible.
A true craftsman, he is dedicated to preserving the tradition of naturally made, expressive wine.*

handsome brother Jean-Pierre continues to help with the making of Beaucastel, but is more involved with his highly successful *négociant* business, La Vieille Ferme, which stresses the production of high-quality, inexpensive wines from *appellations* such as the Côtes du Ventoux, Côtes du Lubéron, and the Côtes du Rhône.

The first thing a visitor notices when visiting Châteauneuf-du-Pape is the blanket of rounded quartzite pebbles, *cailloux roules*, that are strewn all over the area. The most spectacular layer of these stones (which range in size from a tennis ball to a fair-sized beach ball) is on the plateau behind the congested, yet photogenic, village of Châteauneuf-du-Pape. These stones are not, as many have speculated, the result of alluvial deposits from the River Rhône, but the residue of deposits left by the ancient Alpine glaciers that worked their way across southern France. As one moves toward Château de Beaucastel in the north-eastern corner of the *appellation*, the soils are more dominated by sand and clay mixtures. The carpet of stones is still the visual highlight, but Beaucastel's vineyards are not as strikingly stony as those of Domaine de Mont-Redon or Château de Cabrières.

Château de Beaucastel's estate of 325 acres (131 hectares) is one of the largest in the *appellation*, yet its yields per hectare are among the very lowest; only the idiosyncratic Château Rayas and its eccentric proprietor Jacques Reynaud produce yields lower than Beaucastel's average of 20-30 hectolitres per hectare. No herbicides, insecticides or other chemicals are used, but each year over 500 tons of manure from local farmers are dumped on the vineyards. The vines, through a meticulously organized rotational replanting formula, maintain an average age of 50 years – a remarkably impressive statistic. The tiny yields and careful management of the vineyards here translate into wines that are among the Rhône Valley's greatest and most distinctive.

What makes François and Jean-Pierre Perrin so impressive is that they represent the consummate craftsmen of their profession – lamentably a dwindling number of men and women – committed to preserving the tradition and the grandeur of naturally made, expressive wine. They refuse to make any concession to the commercial demand for polished, ready-to-drink, zealously filtered wines that are incapable of evolution, and that shamefully lack the character of their place of origin. For example, Château de Beaucastel is one of the very few estates in Châteauneuf-du-Pape to grow all 13 permitted grape varieties. Its preferred blend for the red wine consists of 30 per cent Grenache, 30 per cent Mourvèdre, ten per cent Syrah and five per cent Cinsault, with the remaining 25 per cent divided among Counoise, Muscardin, and Vaccarèse, though this formula varies from year to year depending on the harvest.

One of the most fascinating times to visit Beaucastel is during the first eight or nine months after the vintage, before the assembly of the master blend. At this time the component parts can all be tasted, and it is a rare chance to try these unusual varietals on their own. I vividly remember tasting through the different *cuvées* that were due to be blended to create the opulent, seductive, mouth-filling Beaucastel 1985. In that year, the *cuvée* of Cinsault tasted relatively light and fruity, simple and straightforward. Counoise, on the other hand, which the Perrins feel has as great a potential as any of the southern Rhône Valley grapes, had an extraordinary deep, dark colour, and a rich, blackberry perfume intermingled with the aromas of smoked meat, flowers, and toasted nuts. Grenache, the preferred grape of the *appellation*, which usually represents 80 per cent or more of most other Châteauneuf-du-Pape blends, was the most alcoholic *cuvée*, with an intense bouquet of kirsch, roasted peanuts, pepper, and liquorice.

Mourvèdre, Beaucastel's signature grape, frequently comprises one-third of the blend. In 1985, it manifested an excellent colour and an eccentric bouquet of fresh mushrooms, tree bark, leather and even white truffles. Muscardin tended to be among the most perfumed of the different *cuvées*, with good strength and richness in the mouth. Syrah did not have the depth and length that one would expect from it in the northern Rhône, but it exhibited the blackest colour and a rich cassis and coffee-scented bouquet. Lastly, Vaccarèse seemed to offer more aromatic complexity than flavour dimension. It flaunted a bouquet reminiscent of tobacco, hot tar, liquorice and black pepper. I have always been fascinated by the fact that the sum of these component parts is superior to any one.

Over the last several decades there has been no shortage of profound wines from Château de Beaucastel, which, in complexity, concentration and character, rival most of the world's finest red wines. In off-years, such as 1980 and 1984, Beaucastel will age well for ten to 15 years. In soft, precocious years, such as 1973, 1979, 1983 and 1985, 15-20 years of ageing is normal. In great years, such as 1966, 1970, 1978 and 1981, 20-35 years is not unrealistic. The reason for this extraordinary ageing potential has much to do with the fact that the wine contains a high percentage of grapes such as Mourvèdre, Syrah, and Counoise, which protect it from oxidation.

François Perrin has continued his father's controversial vinification *à la chaud*. This process, inaugurated by the late Jacques Perrin with the 1964 vintage, involves heating the incoming grapes at high temperatures and then immediately cooling them down as they go into the fermentation tank. It is believed to achieve two critical results: halting any oxidation in the grapes by killing the harmful enzyme polyphenoloxidase, and extracting tremendous colour and tannin from the skins of the grapes. Critics argue that it is a form of

Châteauneuf-du-Pape's famous layer of smooth, oval stones absorb the sun's heat during the day and radiate it at night, helping the grapes to achieve their full, luscious potential.

The cool cellars under the ruined Papal palace are still used by the town's winemaking fraternity.

flash-pasteurization, but anyone who has tasted pasteurized wines knows that they have little character to their bouquets; that is never the case with a Beaucastel. Another positive benefit of this vinification is that no sulphur dioxide is used, which is in keeping with the organic principles that the Perrins follow in the vineyards.

After fermentation the wine is macerated for just over two weeks, with all of the different *cépages* kept separately until blending in the following spring. The different *cuvées* are then aged for 18-22 months in huge 110-gallon (500-litre) oak casks. They are fined only with egg whites and never filtered. Filtration, the process of running wine through either a diatomaceous earth filtering system or through cellulose filter pads, can often eviscerate a wine of its bouquet, body, flavour and ageing potential. François Perrin, no backward-thinking provincial, conducted filtration trials with one vintage and was appalled by the negative effect it had on the wine's bouquet and richness. Both Perrin brothers acknowledge that a filtered wine is more stable and less vulnerable to going bad or developing "off" aromas in the bottle if exposed to extremes of heat, but they still prefer to bottle the essence of what their remarkable vineyards are capable of producing, hoping that consumers will be intelligent enough to treat the wine as a fragile, evolving thing. Beaucastel, after only a few years in the bottle, will often throw a heavy sediment that cakes the inside of the bottle in the great vintages, making decanting absolutely essential.

The commitment to quality at Beaucastel is not only shown in the meticulous care of the vineyards and in the winemaking, but also in the investment the Perrins have made in their cellars. One of the problems with buying Châteauneuf-du-Pape is that many large estates bottle the wine as it is sold. Certain vintages may require three to four years to sell out completely. This unfortunate practice often results in extreme bottle variation, since the wines bottled after 18 months are likely to be totally different from those bottled after three

Beaucastel's signature grape is Mourvèdre, but François uses all 13 authorized varieties.

or four years. Until 1980 this was also the practice at Beaucastel, but in that year the Perrins constructed a new underground wine cellar that permitted them to bottle the entire crop, à la Bordeaux, at the same time. Since then, there has been only one *mise en bouteille* each year, and this has resulted in a much more uniform quality of wine in the marketplace.

Production of red wine at Beaucastel has varied in recent years from 11,000 cases in 1982 (when the Perrins sold off more than half of their production to *négociants*, as they were dissatisfied with the general quality) to 22,000 cases in the super-abundant vintages of 1985 and 1986. Tiny quantities of a white Châteauneuf-du-Pape are also produced – about 1,000 cases in an abundant year. Like Beaucastel's red blend, this wine is the longest-lived white Châteauneuf-du-Pape of the *appellation*, and undoubtedly the most age-worthy white wine of the southern Rhône Valley.

Due to its eccentric ageing pattern, white Beaucastel is frequently misjudged by first-time drinkers. It is delicious to drink for the first two or three years after it is bottled; then it closes up and reveals little bouquet or fruit for three to five years. Only after that, depending on the style of the vintage, does the wine blossom fully, revealing smoky, buttery, hazelnut aromas, intermixed with flavours of honeyed, pineapple fruit. The Perrins are the only producers who put their white Châteauneuf-du-Pape through a full malolactic fermentation to give it a creamy richness and additional complexity. They have also begun to age 15 per cent of the white wine in new oak barrels, fermenting and ageing the other 85 per cent in stainless steel tanks. The blend is unique in comprising 80 per cent Roussanne and 20 per cent Grenache Blanc. Roussanne was the basis for the great reputation of the long-lived, luscious white wines of Hermitage in the northern Rhône Valley, but I know of no other estate in Châteauneuf-du-Pape that makes use of this fickle, low-yielding, though potentially superb, white wine grape.

The vines, which maintain a remarkable average age of 50 years, are kept low and bush-like by careful pruning to maximize exposure to the summer sun.

Not content to produce the finest white Châteauneuf-du-Pape of the *appellation*, François Perrin introduced an astonishing wine in 1986 called Roussanne-Cuvée Vieilles Vignes, made from vines over 50 years old. This wine has established a new benchmark for how complex and brilliant a white wine from the southern Rhône can be. The 1986 and 1988 both exhibited smoky, hazelnut- and pineapple-scented bouquets, honeyed, lush fruit and extraordinary length. It is quite conceivable that both will be capable of lasting ten to 15 years, outliving many white Burgundies that sell for twice the price.

Of the red wines produced during the 1980s, the outstanding 1988 represents a structured, elegant and tannic example – somewhat reminiscent of the estate's 1979; ready to drink around 1993, it is capable of lasting 15-20 years thereafter. The 1987, the most difficult vintage of the decade in the southern Rhône, is a fruity, soft, straightforward Beaucastel, but it manifests more ripeness, body and character than most wines from this justifiably maligned vintage. The 1986, one of the more backward, tannic examples of Perrin's wines, should only be purchased by those who are willing to invest the time and patience it so desperately requires. Very full-bodied, with excellent balance and depth, it should not be approached before 1994-96.

Although François Perrin has always considered it too soft to be a classic, the Beaucastel 1985 may well be the best current vintage to appreciate this estate's style, because it can be drunk at such an early age. Drinkable when released by the Perrins in 1987, the wine is full-bodied, chewy and opulent, with an accessible but exciting *mélange* of berry, smoky, animal-like flavours. I have no doubts that this wine will drink beautifully for at least another ten to 12 years. 1984 was another successful off-year for Beaucastel. The Beaucastel 1984 displays plenty of black-cherry, smoky fruit, with good body and tannin; though lighter and more acidic, the wine is generally well-balanced and should last through the mid-1990s. The 1983, meanwhile, is beginning to reach its plateau of maturity, where it will last for another 15 years. An aromatic wine, which reflects the relatively high proportion of Mourvèdre to Grenache in the final blend, it has an intense bouquet of raspberries, leather and truffles, and is admirably concentrated.

Much of the 1982 was sold off to *négociants*, but the remaining wine – the most alcoholic (14.5 per cent) Beaucastel made this decade – has drunk well from its release. It is perhaps the best wine produced in Châteauneuf-du-Pape from this troublesome vintage. The 1981 has turned out to be the great classic of this decade, a blockbuster of a wine that defines in bold terms the style of Beaucastel. From its extraordinarily sublime bouquet of leather, truffles, cedar wood, liquorice and blackberry fruit to its powerful, dense, concentrated, gamey flavours, this wine is crammed with character, and roars from the glass when poured. With time, it may even surpass the great 1978 and become the finest Beaucastel since the legendary 1970.

As for older vintages, the 1980 has drunk beautifully since its release. It continues to do so, but holding it any longer would be risky. The 1979, although obviously overshadowed by the 1978 and 1981, is excellent, very Beaucastel-like with its tarry, peppery, damp, woody aroma and rich, full-bodied flavours; it should drink well for another ten to 15 years. Although 1978 was Châteauneuf-du-Pape's greatest vintage since 1970, the 1978 remains a wine filled with more potential than current appeal. Enormously proportioned and forbiddingly tannic, it was absolutely astonishing when tasted numerous times from cask, but has since gone into a tannic shell and seems dumb and nowhere close to maturity. It is extremely concentrated, still ruby-purple in colour, and has colouring matter caked inside the bottle much like that of a vintage port. This should turn out to be an extraordinary wine, lasting into the first two or three decades of the next century. For those lucky enough to find any old Beaucastels that might appear in the marketplace, do not hesitate to try the 1970, 1966, 1964 or 1959.

I would be remiss in not mentioning the rich, intense, long-lived wine that Perrin makes from his Cru de Coudoulet estate – probably the best wine made in the Côtes du Rhône *appellation*. Made from a blend of 40 per cent Grenache, 30 per cent Mourvèdre, 20 per cent Syrah and ten per cent Cinsault, it often surpasses many of the wines of Châteauneuf-du-Pape and is capable of lasting for ten to 15 years. The 1978, for example, is just now coming into maturity at the beginning of the 1990s, and the exceptional wines of 1981, 1983 and 1985 are all capable of lasting for up to a decade. This wine is made in exactly the same manner as Beaucastel, and consequently, it will deposit a very heavy sediment. It usually sells for about half the price of Beaucastel, and shares much of the same character as its more famous sibling.

There is much to admire about François and Jean-Pierre Perrin. They have never been content with their record of impressive accomplishments, and are always aspiring to higher levels of quality. The Perrins are now hoping to purchase a large tract of property in the Paso Robles area of California's central coast, where they plan to start a vineyard dedicated to Rhône Valley varietals. The thought of a California Beaucastel or Cru de Coudoulet is indeed an exciting possibility. The Perrins are among the world's most gifted winemakers, and their commitment to naturally made, artisanal wines produced by organic methods is an example that increasing numbers of other winemakers will follow.

Germany

THE OTHER GREAT WINE-PRODUCING NATIONS find strength in diversity and sharp contrasts, in making red wines and white, varietals and blends, still wines and sparkling, oak-influenced and unoaked wines. But the essence of Germany's strength is a white wine from a single grape variety – Riesling. There are other vines and other wines – there is a great deal more Müller-Thurgau than Riesling and there are even some red wines – but it is Riesling that makes Germany stand out.

It is, without doubt, one of the world's finest grape varieties, perhaps the greatest of all the whites – superior to the other serious contender, Chardonnay, because of its potential for ageing and because it is so complete in itself. Riesling has no need of new oak barrels, extended skin contact, lees contact, or of any other tricks of the winemaker's trade, to give it depth and complexity; indeed, adding anything simply sullies it.

No other country can match the stylishness and purity of taste of German Riesling. Alsace produces marvellous Rieslings in a fuller, more alcoholic style; Australia provides delightful, exuberant, lime-flavoured examples. But from the chilly German vineyards come wines of an almost diaphanous lightness and at the same time of a penetrating, lingering intensity – wines of sharp acidity but great delicacy. And it is the pursuit and achievement of a perfect balance between these seemingly contradictory elements that marks out Germany's top estates.

With quality so much more dependent on the grape than on the technical wizardry of the winemaker, vineyards assume an inestimable importance. And, because Germany is the most northerly of the world's principal vine-growing countries, location is absolutely fundamental: it does not matter how well the vines are tended, if the site is not right they will not yield good raw material.

Latitude, however, is not the only consideration; France's northernmost vineyards are on the same latitude as Germany's most southerly, but, significantly, these are not Germany's finest. What counts, as so often, is microclimate. To counteract the inhospitable climate, most of Germany's vineyards flank the Rhine, the Mosel, or one of their major tributaries, where they benefit from the moderating influence of the water. The best vineyards cling to steep, sometimes terraced, south-oriented valley sides where they are most exposed to the sun. Even so, the ripening period is a nerve-racking time, especially on the Mosel and the Nahe and in the Rheingau and Rheinhessen. But if the climate is kind, as in 1988 and 1989, wine drinkers the world over have cause for celebration.

Bottling the wine was a once a three-man job, as depicted in this 19th-century barrel-carving in the Rheingau cellars of Weingut Georg Breuer.

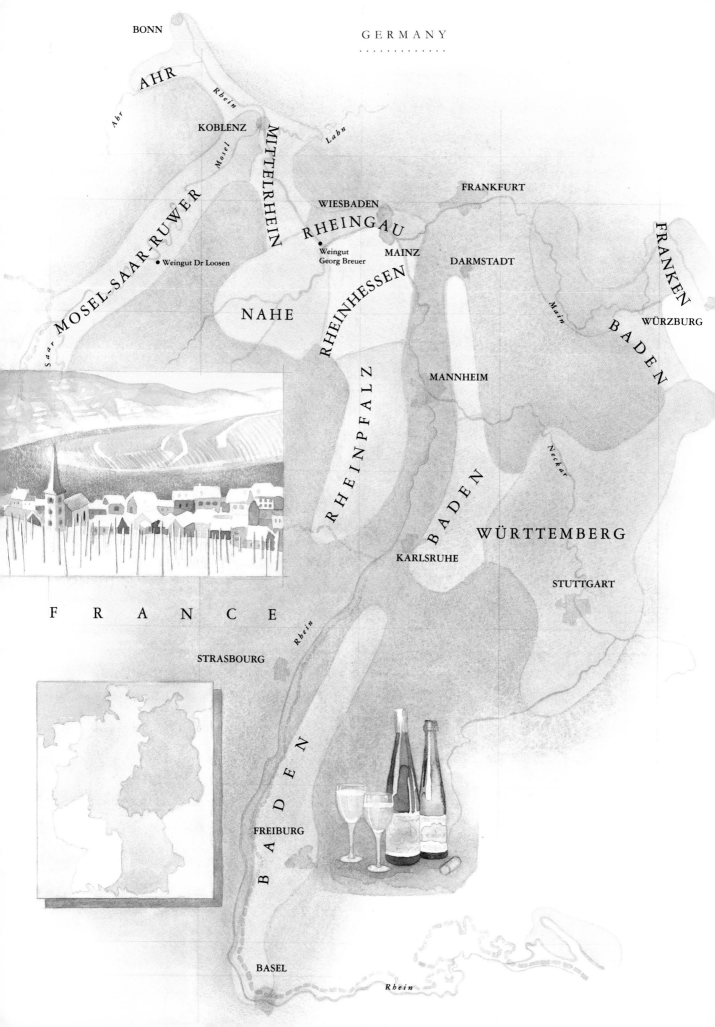

GERMANY
· · · · · · · · · · · ·

BONN

AHR

Ahr

KOBLENZ

Rhein

Mosel

MITTELRHEIN

Labn

FRANKFURT

WIESBADEN

RHEINGAU

Weingut
Georg Breuer

MAINZ

DARMSTADT

FRANKEN

WÜRZBURG

MOSEL-SAAR-RUWER

• Weingut Dr Loosen

Saar

NAHE

RHEINHESSEN

Main

BADEN

MANNHEIM

RHEINPFALZ

Neckar

BADEN

WÜRTTEMBERG

KARLSRUHE

STUTTGART

FRANCE

Rbein

STRASBOURG

BADEN

FREIBURG

BASEL

Rhein

THE MOSEL

Ernst Loosen of Weingut Dr Loosen

The individuality of their Riesling wines is the hallmark of the best estates on the steeply-sloping slate-covered vineyards of the Mosel. Across Ernst Loosen's 20 acres (eight hectares) of vines, there are so many variations in microclimate that he produces some 30 different bottlings a year. But he is, after all, a perfectionist determined to make great, not merely good, wines. *Ian Jamieson MW* describes how Loosen is realizing these ambitions.

Ernst Loosen of Weingut Dr Loosen is obsessed with wine. While other 32-year-old bachelors are enjoying the Mediterranean beaches in summer, he visits vineyards elsewhere in Europe. As he expresses it, making good Mosel wine is relatively straightforward, but producing the finest possible needs an added effort. Eighty per cent of the work is routine, but the remaining 20 per cent reveals the skill and dedication of the winemaker. It is the sum of the little refinements, from the selection of the grapes to the work in the cellar, that can make a wine great, and Ernst Loosen a happy man.

Because of his father's declining health Loosen, or Ernst, as so many of his overseas customers have come to know him, was summoned home to look after the 1985 vintage. He had already achieved the highest qualification of "Weinbauingenieur" after seven terms at the Geisenheim Viticultural School, and had followed this up with practical experience in Switzerland and France. He had just begun to study archaeology at Mainz University. His passion for the past might well have taken him away from wine, had it not been for the call from the family estate.

Ernst's father, Dr Loosen, was much involved in political life, and as a result often away from home, leaving matters of the estate to a manager. The return of young Ernst brought with it not just a new family face to a long-established scene, but a change to "hands-on" management of the most intense sort. Inevitably, feathers were ruffled. Relations between father and son became strained, and only one of the six full-time workers showed any enthusiasm for following the new chief's instructions to the letter.

Just before the 1987 vintage, the staff rebelled. A difficult harvest with many unripe grapes would require particularly selective picking if high-quality wine was to be made. Ernst had to dismiss his soured and uncooperative labour force. One faithful follower remained, to whom was added a team of young grape pickers from America, Japan, New Zealand, Australia, and Great Britain. Whilst Ernst spent his days in the vineyards, his old

Some of Loosen's most important decisions are made in the cellars, when the first sample of Mosel is drawn off and the winemakers gather to appraise the vintage.

school friend, Bernard Schuck, took charge of the pressing. Today, Ernst cannot speak highly enough of Herr Schuck. With a degree in agriculture, but no formal training in winemaking, Bernie is as much a zealot as Ernst.

The Loosen team is now smaller than it was in the early 1980s, and with Ernst leading from the front, it is a happy and well-integrated force, producing wine from 20 acres (eight hectares) of vineyard. The holdings are at Bernkastel, Wehlen and Graach, with others at Erden and Uerzig, a few miles down the Mosel. The vineyards are slate-covered, ideal for Riesling, but steep and time-consuming to work. Even within the confines of one individual site there are variations in the microclimate, and that is why from his eight hectares Ernst Loosen produces some 30 bottlings per year, each of an average size of just under 200 dozen bottles. He reflects a little enviously on the big blends in Bordeaux, which lead to one or two wines per château per vintage, but on the best Mosel estates it is the individuality of the wines that is their hallmark, and this would be lost by a more rationalized bottling programme.

Much has been said and written recently about ways of improving the range of German wine sold on the world's export markets. The great commercial success of the cheapest wines has made us forget the stunning quality of the best. Some, perhaps with a certain amount of reason, blame the German Wine Law of 1971, which is said to be more concerned with the semblance of quality as shown in the analysis of a wine than in quality itself. Ernst Loosen does not spend time on such thoughts, but goes on making wine to his estate's own high standards. This means a low average yield of 55 hectolitres per hectare, encouraged by organic viticulture, with more concentrated wines as a result.

The Müller-Thurgau wine from the picturesque Bernkasteler Schlossberg vineyard is an excellent example of what this often over-produced vine can do when suitably restrained. In the district (*Bereich*) of Bernkastel in 1988 the average yield of the Müller-Thurgau vine

Ernst Loosen aims to ensure that all his wines excel in their category. He refuses to compromise, scrutinizing every detail of the process in his quest for perfection.

was 126 hectolitres per hectare, but from his Bernkasteler Schlossberg holding Loosen cropped 33 hectolitres per hectare which, after fermentation, he stored for six months in *barriques* of 49.5 gallons (225 litres). These second-hand casks had already been used for one year in Chablis so that the initial aggressive tannin flavour of new wood had been reduced. Low yields produce wine with a high mineral content which takes well to *barrique*-ageing, and Loosen's strongly flavoured Müller-Thurgau 1988 is remarkable. It seems more akin to a Pinot Gris from further south in Germany than a Mosel, and, according to Ernst, it has gained in fruitiness through its time in *barrique*. In spite of its quality, it is not a wine upon which Ernst would wish to build his reputation. For him, as for all good producers of Mosel, Riesling is the preferred vine and covers over 90 per cent of his vineyards.

The Müller-Thurgau is the only wine that Ernst ages in young casks. An attempt in 1986 to age Riesling in *barrique* was a disaster, and the loss of 225 litres of Wehlener Sonnenuhr Riesling Spätlese still hurts. Not all experiments succeed, and in relation to the main part of the Loosen operation they are relatively unimportant. Perhaps Ernst's best wine-making achievement so far is the 1987 vintage, for it was with that wine that the discipline of severe pruning and careful grape selection showed its value.

In 1987, 86 per cent of the harvest in the Bereich Bernkastel fell into the simple quality wine category (QbA), and six per cent was potentially better quality wine (QmP) – *Kabinett* or *Spätlese*. Sixty-five per cent of Loosen's crop, on the other hand, could legally be sold as QmP. Although QmP commands higher prices than QbA, the difference is not always sufficient to offset the loss of liquid that occurs as a result of Loosen's pruning methods. Another reason why Ernst strives to ensure that every one of his wines shines in its own category is so that his mainly private customers in Germany will be happy to pay a premium for all Weingut Dr Loosen wines. It is a finely-balanced exercise and reflects the long-term approach to developing the estate's reputation.

Ernst admits that his cellar is too small, even for the low yields that he allows the vines. Perhaps one day, when the money is available, a larger cellar will be found but, in the meantime, Bernard Schuck and Loosen must give as much thought to the use of space as they give to everything else.

In outline, the vinification is conventional, but the difference lies in the detail. Experiments are taking place in which grapes are not crushed before they are put into the press. This idea, borrowed from Alsace, could be useful when handling grapes damaged by hail. Only those that are ripe release their juice; any unripe grapes remain intact.

Many producers today lay great weight on harvesting their grapes when the acid levels are still quite high, for it is the good acidity that gives fine German wine its backbone. In the potentially over-acidic 1987 vintage, some winemakers preferred to use chemical means to reduce acid levels, but Weingut Dr Loosen allowed its wines to undergo a biological reduction of acid (a malolactic fermentation) and, as a result, did not finish bottling the vintage until some seven months later than usual – in December 1988. Although their acidity is still high (about 10 grams per litre), the wines now taste ripe and, of course, full of the flavour that comes from the low yield.

In spite of the working principle that all Loosen wines receive the same care, the additional variables of microclimate and soil ensure that not all are born equal. The star vineyard, the jewel in the crown, is the small piece of land known as the Erdener Prälat, whose total area is just over five acres (two hectares). From the decomposed slate of this steep site, Loosen coaxes concentrated, beautiful wines of real class, with sometimes, as he says, a touch of almond flavour. Wines that fall within the legal parameters for *Spätlesen* are automatically "downgraded" to *Kabinett* quality. Riesling *Auslesen* on the Mosel must reach a minimum of 11.1 per cent of potential alcohol, but Loosen will not sell an Erdener Prälat Riesling Auslese unless it has at least 12 per cent.

Ernst reveres tradition but is unorthodox in his attitude to the much-discussed topic of wine with food. In his view, not every German wine has to be able to accompany a meal, and he drinks Erdener Prälat Riesling Auslese as an aperitif or digestif. The same doubtless applies to his Riesling *Auslese* wines from the Wehlener Sonnenuhr. Here a remarkable, weighty 1988 *Auslese* was picked in five tours through the vineyard, at two- or three-day intervals in the course of November. *Botrytis cinerea*, or noble rot, had spread among the grapes at the upper reaches of the vine, where the wind blows most easily. The grape juice contained over 13 per cent of potential alcohol. A slow fermentation came to a natural halt later than usual in the following March, and left the wine with 42 grams per litre of sugar, a restrained but balanced sweetness.

When considering wines as serious as those of Ernst Loosen, the question inevitably arises as to how long they should be matured. His reply is that they may be drunk within three years of the vintage – or ten years after it. In between, the wines seem to pass through a dull stage, as was the case with the 1983-1986 vintages at the start of 1990. With very sweet wines from rotted grapes, or wines from years with high acidity (1987 or 1984), this period of dullness is reduced: it is the average good vintages, such as 1983, 1985 and 1986, that seem to sulk the longest.

Ernst Loosen is advancing quickly. He is typical of a younger generation whose interest in wine – unlike that of their parents – goes far beyond the German frontier. Ernst regularly meets a group of enthusiasts in Bernkastel to taste the wines of Bordeaux and his visits abroad have inspired new ideas, some of which have already been put into effect. The flow of information and critical appreciation among the new young winemakers is producing fascinating wines in a number of cellars. The happy thought is that with Ernst Loosen and Bernard Schuck, the best is yet to come.

THE RHINE

Bernhard Breuer of Weingut Georg Breuer

The enviable reputation enjoyed from Victorian times by the noble dry wines of the Rheingau was dragged down during the 1960s and 1970s by its mediocre semi-sweet outpourings and, even more, by those of Germany's larger regions. And when Bernhard Breuer inherited his family wine business in 1975, the image of German fine wines was at a low ebb. But Breuer is not a man to be beaten by circumstances. He set about raising the quality of his own wines, and, by example, of those of neighbouring winemakers in the Rheingau, as *Joanna Simon* explains.

It cannot be easy to inherit a great wine-producing company or estate in peak form: you have to maintain the high standards and, if you are to make your mark, strive to improve upon them. But it must be infinitely harder to inherit a producer of rather dowdy wines, to transform it within the space of ten years into two successful companies with wines that range from good to world-class, and to gain the recognition for your achievements and your wines that you, and they, undoubtedly deserve.

That Bernhard Breuer of Weingut Georg Breuer had done all this by the time he was 40, after an "authoritarian upbringing" which brooked no opposition, would have been a considerable achievement in any wine region. To have done it since 1975 in the Rheingau region of West Germany is a still greater accomplishment, because Rheingau wines, like all German fine wines, have suffered from the lowly image associated with Liebfraumilch and its down-market companions over the last 15 or so years.

Historically, Rheingau wines have always been Germany's most highly-prized. And, although they come from one of the country's smallest wine regions – a picturesque stretch on the north bank of the Rhine between Rüdesheim and Wiesbaden – they have always been exported. Britons above all, right up until the 1960s, used to value them as great, long-lived wines and Queen Victoria herself had a well-documented affection for "Hock" (the traditional English name for Rhine wines, derived from the town of Hochheim).

Hard though it is to imagine nowadays, Britons were prepared to pay more for Hock than for any other wine. Thus, in 1896, the London wine merchant Berry Bros & Rudd could ask 120 shillings per dozen for Rüdesheimer Rottland Cabinet 1886 and 200 shillings per dozen for Rüdesheimer Hinterhaus 1862 – and this on a list that asked only 144 shillings per dozen for its most expensive claret, a celebrated vintage of the highest-ranked of all Bordeaux wines, Château Lafite 1870. As for Champagne, the most expensive could only muster 100 shillings per dozen, half the price of the Hinterhaus.

Even as recently as 1966, German wines still formed an important fine wine ingredient of any London merchant's list. Norton Langridge (a now defunct City merchant) listed as many Hocks as clarets, and at comparable prices: a Rüdesheimer Berg Riesling Spätlese 1964 was priced at 27 shillings and sixpence a bottle, while Château Léoville-Poyferré 1962 was 24 shillings and sixpence; only Château Lynch-Bages (see pages 24-29) from the great 1961 vintage was, at 35 shillings, more expensive than the Rüdesheimer.

But things had begun to go wrong for German wines after the Second World War – it is said, because of the war. When sugar returned to the market place in quantity, it was ladled into everything, with the result that both Germans and Britons developed a notably sweeter tooth. The thousands of American GIs posted to Germany after the war may also have exerted an influence. Either way, producers perceived the demand for sweeter wines and began to accommodate it. Whereas previously they had fermented to dryness all save the small amounts of specially late-harvested grapes, they now began to halt fermentation before it had finished so that sugar still remained in the wine. The result, says Bernhard Breuer, by the end of the 1950s, was a plethora of styles that confused the consumer. Once that had happened, German wines began to lose their reputation and value.

"Producers neglected their wines – they lost their successful formula," he says of the 1960s and 1970s. The German Wine Law of 1971 only made matters worse: "It took away a lot of traditional village names, like Nierstein and Piesport, and that made consumers drift away". Still more damaging was the way in which the law "aimed to be watertight against fraud, but took away responsibility from the individual grower and gave it to the state. The grower should have the authority and privilege to make and sell good wines. It is based on sweetness and on analytical content, when it should be based on quality. The inner values of a wine are just not measurable by *oeschle* [potential sugar] levels in the lab." He gives the example of two Rüdesheimer wines from different vineyards, Kirchenpfad and Berg Schlossberg, which have almost identical analyses, yet Kirchenpfad is always fruitier and quicker to develop. "A hierarchy based on sweetness brings everything down to the lowest common denominator."

The problem was compounded by the introduction of many new grape varieties, bred simply to give steadier yields and higher *oeschle*. None of these has approached Riesling for quality and longevity, and this is hardly surprising when you consider that Riesling is one of the world's most noble varieties – perhaps the greatest of all white wine varieties.

Bernhard believes the ideal solution to Germany's problem would be a classification of wines from one to five, drawn up by the trade (not the bureaucrats) and based on what the consumer is prepared to pay, like the system in Bordeaux. "At the end of the day, price is a long-term indication of quality." But the law, he says matter-of-factly, will not change, so German producers "must forget about the wine laws". This statement, arresting though it is from a German, is entirely in keeping with the philosophies Bernhard Breuer has expounded and acted upon since he assumed control of the merchant firm Scholl & Hillebrand and, with his brother Heinrich, founded the estate of Weingut Georg Breuer. Today his most expensive wine – and it is expensive – is mere *Deutscher Tafelwein* (basic table wine) in the eyes of the law, yet it is much sought after, and others will follow.

But these are the 1990s and, though Bernhard can now look back on the 1980s as a decade during which his wines were sought by connoisseurs, his opinions canvassed, his innovations imitated, it was not always so – and none of it could have been achieved without his very considerable resources of determination, energy and intelligence.

He joined Scholl & Hillebrand, then run by his father Georg, as a clerk in 1969 at the age of 22, having spent a number of years in Switzerland, France and the United States, including a year as a guest student of oenology at Montpellier. It may sound like the Grand

Bernhard Breuer, leading by example, has persuaded other top producers in the region to join him in restoring the tarnished reputation of the Rheingau's once highly-prized wines.

Tour of a fancy-free youth but, according to Bernhard, "there was never any question but that I would do these things and then go into the family company. I would like to have done the full course at Montpellier, but I had no choice." It was not ideal for him: "I wouldn't advise it to anyone. You haven't any experience and you pay for all your mistakes because it's your company."

It is hard to see where Bernhard made those mistakes. It is equally clear, though, that errors were being made at Scholl & Hillebrand up until 1975, errors that culminated in the sale of the firm. It was then that, in desperation, Bernhard finally went to his father and said, "either we change, or I go". He fully expected to go. But, to his father's credit, it was he who came in the next day and said, simply, "OK, I quit". With this brief showdown came the end of an era of financial mismanagement and of selling to the wrong people. "We were selling to supermarkets. They bought on price, so there was just no motivation." But even today Bernhard and his brother still do not have a majority share in the business.

Decisively – and bravely – Bernhard began by closing the doors on these existing customers, at the same time creating the Georg Breuer label for estate wines from the vineyards the family had deliberately retained after the Scholl & Hillebrand sale. It was a painful process: "We were an unknown quantity except for those who knew us from our supermarket days". But the family restaurant in their home town of Rüdesheim, which Heinrich runs today, sustained the wine businesses through the years it took Bernhard to prove that the name Breuer was one of the Rheingau's most serious and not that of some gimmicky young producer. Even in 1980, his creativity was still mistrusted: when he launched the Georg Breuer Rüdesheimer Berg Schlossberg, with a label bearing a specially commissioned painting (à la Mouton-Rothschild, he is the first to admit), it did not sell at all. Now it is the first of his Rieslings to sell out each year.

By 1984, however, Bernhard Breuer's standing was beyond doubt. He was elected the first president of the Charta Association, a new group of top Rheingau estates dedicated to restoring the region's wines to their former glory, and he has since been re-elected to the position. As the Charta members see it, this former glory was based on dry and off-dry wines with relatively high acidity, which could be drunk as an accompaniment to food all the way through a meal and were capable of ageing for many years. This was precisely the direction in which Bernhard had been moving since 1980. Yet, for all his apparent innovation and invention, it was a step back in time to the pre-1950s style of Rheingau wines. "The region, the soil, the grape variety have not changed," he says – only the successful formula.

Today, Bernhard's methods (which are in principle shared with all Charta producers) lay a heavy emphasis on the vineyard: on particularly favoured sunny sites, higher up the slopes away from the river, where the soils – of which there are no fewer than 286 varieties in the Rheingau – are well-endowed with minerals; and on careful husbandry, using "green" fertilizer and a minimum of chemical herbicides and pesticides. Such measures limit yields and so concentrate the flavour elements in the grapes. Bernhard insists that all 37 acres (15 hectares) of Breuer vineyards are hand-picked, because he believes that selection in the vineyards is vital. He is also beginning to re-introduce a certain amount of polyculture, and has planted 140 trees in the last two years. With polyculture, many pests will be eliminated by predators and other natural phenomena, or so the theory goes.

Such practices smack of organic winemaking, but Bernhard has a simple answer: "From the philosophical point of view, I am against it. But if you go for quality in the vineyards, you will be behaving almost like a so-called organic producer – you don't have to join an association." It is certainly true that wherever fine wine is made there is a now an awareness of the disadvantages inherent in the lavish application of chemicals, in wineries as well as vineyards. Chemicals increase quantities, no doubt, but if their use is unchecked they have an adverse effect on quality.

While many of the methods used in the Breuer vineyards are similar in principle to what one might expect at a leading estate anywhere in the world, the philosophies that guide the cellarmasters of the Rheingau (and other German regions that concentrate on the Riesling grape) are somewhat different. The term "cellarmaster" is used advisedly – for that is what they are, insists Bernhard, not winemakers. The Riesling grape, when ripe and healthy, contains all the ingredients to make fine wine; there is no need for the flavours of new oak casks, for extended lees contact or for malolactic fermentation. In fact, the less the grape is manhandled the purer and finer an expression of quality it is likely to be. "We do as little as possible in the cellar. For that you have to know what you're working against and you have to have first-class material."

This can all come as a bit of a shock to those from other wine cultures. The young American winemaker who joined Breuer for two years in the late 1980s was astounded by the instructions of his new boss: "Just sit there, keep everything clean, and watch it". He wanted to do all sorts of treatments, says Bernhard, and at one point turned to Bernhard and said despairingly, "but you guys just don't do anything". This, of course, was music to Bernhard's ears – but only as far as Riesling is concerned.

With other grape varieties, there is no end to the creativity and activity in the Breuer cellars. In spite of Riesling's rightful dominance in the Rheingau, there have always been odd rows and parcels of other vines. Over 80 per cent of the Breuer holdings are Riesling and the figure is set to rise to 90 per cent during the course of the 1990s, but in the last few years Bernhard has begun to take a greater interest in his Pinot Blanc and Pinot Gris. So far he has used them together with Riesling in a sparkling wine which, in the same manner as

Bottles of 1983 Riesling should be safe enough behind this plaque until they reach maturity in 1993.

Champagne, will be released after it has spent three years absorbing flavours from its lees. The Pinot Gris, some of which is aged in oak to give an extra dimension, contributes a creamy taste, the Pinot Blanc fragrance and the Riesling acidity; Bernhard did not want to make "just another German *Sekt*".

One of Bernhard's other great creations has already come to fruition in the form of the "Trius" label. This is the result of a highly unusual joint venture with two estate owners in the Palatinate region – Bernd Philippi (whom Bernhard regards as Germany's greatest winemaker) and Walter Henniger. Each provides some of his finest Pinot Blanc to go into a tripartite blend with Breuer's. It is then aged in new Limousin oak to make a wine that in "style and quality is very near that of a great white Burgundy". It is indeed rich, buttery, complex and oaky, although it has an acidity structure that is not Burgundian. Yet it is this acidity that will allow it to age in the manner of the best traditional Rheingau wines.

Yet another experimental wine is aged in Limousin oak. A dessert wine, but not a typical German *Beerenauslese* or *Trockenbeerenauslese*, it is modelled on Château d'Yquem, the great Sauternes wine, in all but grape variety. Instead of Sémillon, it is a blend of Riesling and Huxelrebe – the latter variety chosen because, like Sémillon, it is susceptible to *Botrytis* and because Bernhard is not (or at least not yet) prepared to use non-Germanic grape varieties.

It is tempting to wonder whether these sometimes outlandish-seeming experiments are not diluting Bernhard's traditional efforts with Rheingau Riesling. Not at all, he counters, "you learn a lot of things that you can use in your ordinary winemaking. You need experimentation to go forward. There's always room for improvement. We can probably make a 20-30 per cent improvement in our wines in the next five years."

And that probably sums up Bernhard Breuer better than anything. He is always seeking for better ways to achieve better wines. He is one of the wine world's most creative people, in a region that has never seen the need to be creative. It is impossible to predict what he will have achieved in ten years' time, but one thing is certain: his name will be even better known than it is today – and deservedly so.

Italy

It is impossible to be bored by Italian wines: bemused, exasperated, sometimes bitterly disappointed, undoubtedly; excited and delighted, most certainly; but never reduced to a state of boredom. There are of course many dull and some extremely poor mass-produced "industrial" Italian wines, abusing such names as Soave and Valpolicella. But there is also the most remarkable and inspiring diversity.

The country hums with vines. From the foothills of the Alps to the hot Mediterranean south and islands, vineyards cloak rugged mountain slopes, envelope gentle hills, carpet featureless plains and surround the great cities. The vine, of course, has had many years in which to establish its hold: the Greeks bestowed the first, the Aglianico variety, on Basilicata when they arrived in the south of Italy nearly 3,000 years ago; and Italian viticulture has never looked back.

The vine and the Italian *terroir* – as much because of the infinite variety of climate, landscape and soil as despite it – are natural partners. Today there are around 1,000 grape varieties – not that anyone can be quite sure. It is not, though, this unequalled total so much as the unrivalled number of indigenous varieties that makes Italy such a treasure trove of rare and original wine tastes. Some, grapes such as the Nebbiolo of Barolo and Barbaresco, the Sangiovese of Chianti and a host of other Italian reds, are famous; others – Pagadebit, Favorita, Arneis – are almost as unfamiliar. Only Portugal has a comparable individuality, but Portugal has far fewer native varieties.

While Italian viticulture did not look back, for a very long time it did not seem to look forward either. It was not until the 1960s that rapid, often revolutionary change began, as post-war industrialization and mechanization started to make an impact. And yet even this intended progress was not always a step in the right direction. There was widespread replanting to raze unproductive old vines and to introduce new, more practical training and cultivation methods. Tuscany, homeland of Brunello di Montalcino, Vino Nobile di Montepulciano and, of course, Chianti, took centre-stage in all this vineyard activity. Intentions were largely good; results, unfortunately, sometimes less so.

The go-ahead replanters made one simple but crucial mistake. They failed to see that particular clones, or strains, of the same vine produced wine of different quality and that the clones that yielded the largest crops also yielded the poorest-quality fruit. So they planted

Brilliant colours lend a spectacular autumnal beauty to the vineyards of Piedmont, whose golden-leaved Nebbiolo vine takes its name from the fog (nebbia) that characterizes the season there.

inferior but higher-yielding Sangiovese clones, and Chianti rapidly became synonymous with cheap, cheerless plonk. The rest, of course, is history, because in the 1970s realization slowly dawned. Dispirited and financially distressed growers sold their vineyards and energetic new owners brought much needed money to the region. They replanted with the right clones; they even dabbled with Cabernet Sauvignon and tried new oak barrels. By the end of the 1980s Chianti had been revitalized.

As important as all this was for Tuscany, its effect was national. By showing that the intrinsic character and quality of Italian wines need not be compromised in the absorbing of external influences – indeed, could benefit from them – Tuscany acted as catalyst to other areas such as Piedmont in the north-west and Valpolicella in the north-east, where quantity had taken priority over quality. These areas have set about producing both classic Italian wines and newer styles with a renewed vigour and a sense of excitement as great as any to be found in the developing regions of the New World.

Barbaresco's gently sloping hills provide the ideal vine-growing environment. Sheltered, well-drained soil combines with sunshine and humidity to maximize the grapes' tannin, concentration and alcohol.

TRENTINO
ALTO-ADIGE

FRIULI-VENEZIA
GIULIA

VALLE
D'AOSTA

LOMBARDIA

VENETO

MILANO

L. Garda

Quintarelli

VENEZIA

Po

Po

TORINO

PIEMONTE

Gaja

EMILIA-ROMAGNA

LIGURIA

GENOVA

BOLOGNA

TOSCANA

FIRENZE

Castello di Volpaia

MARCHE

UMBRIA

LAZIO

ABRUZZO

MOLISE

ROMA

PUGLIA

CAMPANIA

NAPOLI

Fratelli D'Angelo

BASILICATA

SARDEGNA

CALABRIA

CAGLIARI

PALERMO

SICILIA

PIEDMONT

Angelo Gaja

The man who aroused and withstood deep controversy when he introduced Cabernet and Chardonnay and French oak barrels to the ultra-traditional region of Piedmont in north-eastern Italy is now equally adamant that Barolo and Barbaresco, the region's famed Nebbiolo-based wines, will flourish only if producers build upon traditions within the confines of the country's wine laws. Yet Angelo Gaja, one of the world's great winemakers, insists that this is no volte-face on his part, as **Burton Anderson** explains.

Angelo Gaja, the reformist who led the winemakers of Alba into the modern era, seems out of character defending the staid heritage of Barolo and Barbaresco, and the disputed wine laws that grant them a guarantee. But the man who brought Cabernet and Chardonnay to southern Piedmont's Langhe Hills, along with the equally controversial French barrels for ageing them, insists that his views do not represent a change of heart. Rather, he explains, his experience with the world's recognized great wines has reinforced his conviction that Alba's venerable reds deserve a more prominent place among them. But that status can be achieved only if producers build upon the Barolo and Barbaresco traditions within the limits of the wine laws.

Gaja's words flowed with customary momentum as we tasted recent vintages at his cellars in the village of Barbaresco during the 1989 harvest. He admitted that his view of tradition differed from that of many other producers in a wine zone long regarded as Italy's most parochial. But he denied accusations that he had changed the typology of Barbaresco, which his family has made for decades, or that he aimed to do so with Barolo, which he resumed making in 1988. "A concept that is not well understood here yet is that you can maintain a wine's basic character and give it more appealing style," he said. And, indeed, his wines are balanced and supple, with early signs of the power and glory of Nebbiolo, but with none of that raw, biting extract or those tongue-numbing tannins and acids that typified the young wines of the old school.

He talks about Alba's wine industry in tones that convey as much concern as approval. "There has been remarkable progress here, both in large houses and in small estates. I believe the general quality level of our red wines is now the highest in Italy again, after a time when Tuscany seemed to be pulling ahead. But, unfortunately, some producers have been caught up by the vogue so popular in Tuscany and elsewhere to make up-market table wines. So they are using their best Nebbiolo for *barrique* wines with fantasy names, rather

A portrait of dynamism: Angelo Gaja's spirited pursuit of excellence continues to gain momentum.

than for Barolo and Barbaresco. I can understand the temptation, but if the trend spreads it could damage one of Italy's few great wine traditions. This is a favourable moment for the wines of Alba, but it's a time to plan for the future and to proceed with caution."

Proceed with caution? Can this be the Angelo Gaja described by Hugh Johnson a few years ago as "the fanatic, the powerful, the Young Turk of Piedmont"? Or has he been mellowed by success, by the international acclaim that allows him to sell bottles of single-vineyard Barbaresco at prices equivalent to the great châteaux of Bordeaux? Certainly, his travels have made him more worldly, more aware of Piedmont's place in wine's universal scheme and, even more acutely, of his own status. So now, as he passes his 50th birthday, maybe he reckons it is time to slow down and reap the fruits of his labours.

Nothing of the sort. My autumn visit to Gaja indicated that if anything he was stepping up the pace. He was excited about the 1989 harvest, rated the fourth excellent vintage in eight years in the Langhe. "It's incredible," he exclaimed: "It's never happened before." Even Guido Rivella, the in-house oenologist whose steady hand keeps this dashing family winemaking operation on an even keel, voiced a superlative or two about the small but vital crop that was harvested that year.

We were tasting in a room off the courtyard, concealed at one end from the street by an immense sliding door and, at the other, giving onto a balcony with sweeping views over the vine-draped moors of the Langhe. It was a busy afternoon. Tractors arrived with crates of the season's first Nebbiolo grapes. Builders operating power-drills and cranes were working to complete yet another addition to the winery, its five levels carved into a steep hillside. Lucia, Angelo's wife, business partner and *alter ego*, interrupted us from time to time, gracious and shy with apologies, bringing papers to sign, more tasting glasses, reminders of things to do. The phone rang with menacing frequency. Unannounced visitors showed up and were politely turned away. Even Gaja, who has a juggler's knack for keeping several things going at once, seemed to have trouble concentrating.

Finally, to escape the commotion, we drove off to inspect his vineyards, scattered through the communes of Barbaresco and Treiso in medium-sized to small plots. At Costa Russi and Sorì Tildin we admired flawless bunches of blue-violet Nebbiolo grapes amid vines whose summer greens had just begun to turn to auburn. When dusk fell, we drove to dinner at a restaurant in the hills high above Alba, reached by a series of tortuous roads which Gaja negotiated like a rally driver. Most of all, we talked, or rather, he talked; and, as always, he had a lot on his mind.

Gaja's aspirations for the Langhe and its wines seemed foremost in his mind. "This is one of those places where the soil and climate and the human element have combined to create an environment that is practically ideal for wines ... yes, great wines – and not only Barolo and Barbaresco. But even if Cabernet and Chardonnay and – who knows? – maybe Merlot and Pinot Noir can do magnificently here, Nebbiolo is our strong point. It gives us a unique chance to distinguish ourselves on the international market, because consumers are getting tired of the standardized tastes. But, so far, we have not taken full advantage of this. We have not given our wines the modern image they deserve."

He pointed out that Barolo and Barbaresco are misunderstood: "They are known as big, heavy wines that need long ageing and a dish of braised beef or game to bring out their true character. Labels will tell you to open bottles hours ahead of time and serve the wine at 68-72°F (20-22°C), like soup. Producers who support these myths are either too stubborn or too naive to realize that people don't want those wines any more. Most Italians are afraid of Barolo. They will save it for certain occasions and then sip it, but only a glassful, like Marsala. Now, how can you build a market that way?"

Said to have one of the most astute marketing minds in the business, Gaja has made his own name better known to the world's wine drinkers than the Barbaresco DOCG *appellation*, though that was not his aim. "If my wines appeal to the so-called international palate, it's because Guido [Rivella] and I have worked for years to make them that way." He attributes their class primarily to the quality of the grapes, which are rigidly selected from vines whose yields are held to about half the consented limits. But what polishes the Gaja style are the studied techniques used in his computerized cellars.

Fermentation is guided to extract the so-called soft or noble tannins from the grape skins and reduce the hard tannins. The final phase of ageing takes place in barrels of French oak, after a spell in the traditional large casks of Yugoslavian oak. Gaja's use of *barriques* was heavily criticized when he first introduced them, but now many progressive winemakers here rely on them. He insists that his Barolo and Barbaresco lack none of the basic size, structure or character of the old-style wines; and he scoffs at the often-repeated notion that

Gaja's prime vineyard land forms the starting point for his highly-prized Barbaresco wines.

they won't age as well. "They should have a much longer prime than the earlier wines, because balance and tone are superior and the chances of defects coming out in the bottle have been greatly reduced."

He admits that Barolo and Barbaresco have been justly criticized for defects in the past, though he blames human errors such as uncontrolled fermentation and excessive cask-ageing rather than poor-quality grapes. "Some interesting wines were made anyway," he says – perhaps recalling the work of his father Giovanni, whose Barbaresco from the 1960s can still be impressive – "but I am convinced that by sculpting the wines the way we do now, we have come up with something finer."

Experts seem to agree. Gaja once predicted that the success of premium wines, and their market values, would depend increasingly on critics' ratings and results in competitive tastings, rather than on time-worn classifications. If that is the case, recent releases of his single-vineyard Barbaresco Sorì Tildin, Sorì San Lorenzo and Costa Russi would rank among the world's *grands crus*. His regular Barbaresco, like the single-vineyard Alba DOC wines of Nebbiolo Vignaveja, Barbera Vignarey and Dolcetto Vignabajla, is regularly placed at the top of its category as well. And, though they are mere *vini da tavola*, his Chardonnay Gaia & Rey and Cabernet Sauvignon Darmagi have not only been compared with the élite of France and California but carry prices to match. Yet Gaja has a rule that the *cru* Barbarescos, like the eagerly awaited Barolo, should be priced at the top of the line.

When he moved smartly up-market in the late 1970s, foreigners were at first reluctant to pay dearly for wines from a country that hitherto had always offered bargains. But Gaja persisted, making regular forays abroad to tell wine drinkers why his bottles were worth it and to remind them that his name is pronounced *Guy-ah* (not *Gah-jah*). He carried out his mission with such drive and charisma that he became one of the wine world's most visible personalities. More than just the King of Barbaresco, as he is sometimes known around Alba, he has become the spiritual leader of the drive to have the wines of Italy recognized on an equal footing with France. He knows better than most of his peers what an uphill battle that is – but Gaja would not be Gaja if he did not have odds to defy.

He pursues his goals with unrelenting aplomb, an air of self-confidence that has been mistaken for a big ego; that, though, is one of many luxuries that this winemaker on the run doesn't have time for. Yet he can be sensitive to criticism of his prices: "Maybe people don't realize how much more it costs to make outstanding wine, in Piedmont as anywhere else. Reduced yields, increased personnel, the best in equipment, constant research – these are prime considerations. But also packaging, marketing, public relations have costs that are magnified in a small winery. Anyway, when my prices are criticized, I point out that no one is compelled to buy a bottle because it has the name Gaja on the label. There are less costly alternatives, good ones at that. Take the Produttori del Barbaresco [a nearby co-operative cellar]: their wines are first-rate, especially the *crus*, and so reasonable."

When Angelo Gaja entered the business in the early 1960s he convinced his father that grapes should come exclusively from family-owned vineyards to assure quality control. The new policy excluded Barolo, which had been made from purchased grapes. Total production was held to about 20,000 cases a year, roughly two-thirds of it Barbaresco. Besides developing the winery, he formed a company called Gaja Distribuzione to import wines and wine accessories. By offering choice bottles from Bordeaux (Châteaux d'Yquem, Margaux and Lafite) and from California (Robert Mondavi, Stag's Leap and Jordan) he enhanced sales of his own wines in Italy. But, wherever he went, he was asked for Barolo, whose reputation had kept it a notch above Barbaresco in prestige. Though he was reluctant to admit it, he knew something vital was missing from his product line.

In 1988, after years of secret searching, Gaja announced the purchase of a property at Serralunga d'Alba in the heart of Barolo. That transaction may have seemed routine to outsiders, but in the Langhe it was remembered as the wine event of the decade. Not that surprises from Gaja were anything new. In the late 1970s he had shocked local sensivities by planting Cabernet Sauvignon beneath his hilltop home in Barbaresco in a vineyard previously sanctioned for Nebbiolo. Even his father, then Mayor of Barbaresco, objected. In a tongue-in-cheek tribute, Angelo named the wine Darmagi (meaning "what a pity" in the Francophone patois of the Langhe) after his father's frequent lament.

Gaja went on to plant Chardonnay and Sauvignon Blanc in plots that had previously yielded the popular red Dolcetto and Barbera. Though branded as a heretic and worse, he held his ground and eventually came out with wines that won wide acclaim. "In working with new varieties, we have learned things that are useful for our own vines," he explains. "Not only that: the Cabernet and Chardonnay have convinced some foreign wine drinkers to try my Barbaresco."

So many other growers have planted new vines now that even Gaja questions whether things are not being overdone. "But, on the other hand," he continues, "we have no native white varieties of particular distinction in the Langhe, except for Moscato for sweet wines. So why not Chardonnay and Sauvignon? The natural conditions are right. If nothing else, making wines from them is good experience, a diversion." Today even the doubters would have to admit that what Angelo Gaja says and does will determine patterns of winemaking in the Langhe for years to come.

Gaja reflects on what he describes as the best decade ever for Piedmont's wines, with outstanding vintages in 1989, 1988, 1985 and 1982, and a better-than-average 1986. By the

Serralunga d'Alba, in the heart of Barolo, where Gaja outraged locals by planting French grape varieties.

1980s, techniques had improved to the point that fine wines were made even in such middling years as 1987, 1984 and 1983. This has helped build his faith in Piedmont's future: "I have come to realize that not only do we have stronger traditions than other Italian regions, but in Nebbiolo we have the native variety that has reached the greatest heights. Now, I don't mean to sound chauvinistic, but when our Barolos and Barbarescos from the 1980s reach their prime, we'll reassert our supremacy with reds. This is our chance to be recognized as one of the world's great wine areas, to establish the name Piedmont alongside Bordeaux and Burgundy.

"You know, until not long ago I was envious of Tuscany," he confesses. "They seemed to be moving ahead while we stood still. Well, I have since tasted many superb reds from there: Sangiovese, Cabernet, Merlot. But so many of them are wines invented yesterday, like their names. Some have made quite an impact individually, but there's no collective image behind them, no geographical identity. How can people be expected to remember all those names? Look at Chianti, it's still the best-known wine of Italy; it's even DOCG. But if producers there continue to produce table wines that are superior to it and more expensive, then the historical value of the name Chianti will be lost."

During his travels Gaja has noted that Italy's lack of faith in its wine laws has helped to erode consumer confidence abroad. "Instead of complaining about DOC or finding ways to get around it, we should be working to improve quality from within the system, because strong *appellations* will have a much greater chance of success on international markets." Though the prime wines of Alba are covered by DOC or DOCG, he believes that much more could be done to strengthen them, especially since Barolo and Barbaresco are among the few zones where *crus* can be classified on the basis of the time-proven market value of the wines. "It's inevitable that one way or another, officially or unofficially, our better vineyards are going to be rated, so we should be studying ways to make it systematic."

There is no need to ask where he thinks his own *crus* might end up on the scale, since Angelo Gaja always aims for the top, while proceeding, of course, with caution.

VALPOLICELLA

Giuseppe Quintarelli

High up in the hills north of Verona, a patchwork of terraced vineyards along the winding valleys marks out the heartland of Valpolicella Classico. Here, where autumn mists roll through the valleys prolonging the ripening of the grapes, intensifying their flavours and curbing yields, Giuseppe Quintarelli makes majestic, concentrated "meditation wines" that are faithful to classical traditions. **Simon Loftus** reveals the philosophy that lies behind true Valpolicella and its maestro, Quintarelli.

Giuseppe Quintarelli, maestro of Recioto and Amarone, is a diffident genius who works within a glorious tradition that survives from classical antiquity. His wines would be immediately familiar to Virgil, but the enthusiasts who now outbid each other for Pétrus (see pages 30–36) and Romanée-Conti are more likely to identify Quintarelli's region, Valpolicella, with the dreary mediocrities of modern industrialized production. For the most part they would be right, but the renown of this region survives from an earlier age and is based on "meditation wines" of unique grandeur – not the light, inoffensive and utterly nondescript stuff that is nowadays sold in two-litre bottles in the supermarkets.

Even so, the character of these superlative rarities is so alien to general expectations as to cause many critics to look askance. Recioto is mostly red but can be sweet or dry; it is often so strong as to taste like a fortified wine, though it is entirely unfortified; it frequently has rather high levels of volatile acidity; and it can be enjoyed equally well with roast beef or an almond tart. So explanations are called for before introducing the man.

The word is derived from *recie*, local dialect for "ears". These are the topmost grapes of each bunch which catch the sun longest, ripening most richly. For at least 2,000 years it has been the practice in Valpolicella to cut the ears off the ripest bunches and set them aside on bamboo racks to dry like raisons for three or four months before fermentation. Nowadays they tend to select entire bunches, rather than cutting off the ears, and Quintarelli stacks his grapes in second-hand tomato boxes, but the process is essentially unchanged.

As the grapes dry in the loft, the natural sugars are concentrated by evaporation and there is often some infection by *Botrytis cinerea*, the "noble rot" so essential to the production of Sauternes. Here in the Veneto it performs a similar function, enriching the juice and adding nutty complexities of flavour. Occasionally, in humid winters like 1982, the rot is of the ordinary grey sort and ruins the carefully preserved crop.

Quintarelli's extraordinary wines, fashioned in the classical tradition, begin life in old tomato boxes.

Fermentation of the crushed grapes is very slow, because of the cold winter temperature, and it takes a long time for the heroic local yeast strains to convert concentrated grape sugars into alcohol. After a few months, having achieved an alcoholic strength of between 14 and 15 degrees, the yeasts tend to give up, leaving a rich residual sweetness in the wine. The result is Recioto della Valpolicella.

Sometimes (particularly if the vines have been grown on the west-facing slopes which receive most light, thus photosynthesizing more nitrogenous substances to feed the yeasts) the fermentation continues until most of the sugars have been converted; the wine is then dry but immensely strong, with perhaps 17 degrees of natural alcohol. This too is Recioto, but the label will also bear the designation Amarone – "the bitter one". "For the first three or four years of its life this was a sweet wine," says Giuseppe Quintarelli as we taste his Amarone 1977. "Then *piano, piano, piano* it became itself, a dry wine but very rich." Some of the best examples come from a tiny valley called the Vaio Amaron. Was the place named for the wine, or vice versa? No one knows.

Such a time-consuming process is costly, partly because the dried grapes yield a fraction of the juice provided by a normal crop, partly because of the long ageing in cask which is necessary before the wine can be sold – at least two years for Recioto and four for Amarone. So these extraordinary wines have always been rarities, sought after by enthusiasts but beyond the reach of most consumers.

By far the largest part of the region's production is the much less expensive Valpolicella, made for daily consumption. Produced from the same vines that make Recioto (Corvina,

Rondinella, Molinara and a little Negrara), Valpolicella varies markedly in quality. At its best it can be a scaled-down version of Amarone, having been re-fermented in the spring following the harvest on the rich lees of Recioto. But only a handful of traditional producers like Quintarelli still use this *ripasso* technique. In general, Valpolicella is simpler stuff – light, refreshing and slightly bitter, perhaps with a hint of cherries. Much of it is indistinguishable from the most ordinary red table wine. At one industrial producer, I was quoted the same price for bulk consignments of "Valpo" (Valpolicella), "Bardo" (Bardolino) and Veronese *vino da tavola*. To his evident amazement I asked for a sample. The taste, like the price, was identical for all three wines.

The story is simply told in terms of yield. A rigorously pruned vineyard in the hills of Valpolicella Classico will produce about 35 hectolitres of wine per hectare each year. The DOC regulations permit 85 hectolitres, but in the most fertile, low-lying vineyards, planted with prolific clones of the traditional grape varieties, yields of 140 hectolitres are not uncommon. Such unsuitable land has been granted the right to the DOC as a result of an exchange of favours between the biggest producers and the legislators – a recipe for mediocrity that has parallels in most renowned wine regions of Italy. The effect has been to depress both reputation and price, making the task of serious growers doubly difficult.

Against this background of widespread indifference, Quintarelli's achievements seem all the more remarkable. One of a handful of producers dedicated to quality (many would say the best), he lives in the hills north of Verona and east of Lake Garda. This is the real heartland of Valpolicella Classico, a patchwork of terraced vineyards climbing up the sides of three twisted valleys that lie roughly parallel to each other, descending as they open towards the south. The altitude of 980 feet (300 metres) and upwards is close to the limits of viticulture and there is considerable variation in temperature between day and night, summer and winter. Mist fills the valleys in autumn and spring, modifying the heat of the sun and extending the ripening season. Such conditions are ideal for quality wine, producing a small harvest of grapes with intense concentration and complexity of flavour, invigorated by the high levels of fruit acidity that are essential for longevity.

Finding Quintarelli is a difficult business. He lives on a steep slope above the village of Negrar, but detailed directions become strangely confused as you wind through the tortuous terrain. His house, when you come to it, is unexpected. Modern and oddly suburban, it commands tremendous views across the vineyards, and its hillside position has facilitated the construction of a substantial cellar beneath the terrace. Quintarelli himself seems to regard the living quarters as a temporary perch, a place to pause for a moment between the attics where the grapes are dried and the cellars where the wine is matured and stored.

The son of a local winemaker, he has been building his own reputation for the best part of 40 years. In recent times his renown has spread abroad and he has been able to command high prices for his much-treasured wines. Hence the house, the stainless steel tanks in the fermentation room, the new *botte* (large casks of varying age and size in which his wine is matured) and the experimental French *barriques* in his cellars; hence the bottle of California Cabernet on his sideboard. Hence also the fact that this quiet countryman is liable to put on a pin-stripe suit when he is expecting visitors, over which his cheerfully protective wife Renata will drape a warm coat before he descends to the chilly cellars.

Follow him down to his lair and you enter a cave of treasures. Lines of *botte* surround apparently random clusters of glass demijohns, full of different vintages awaiting the moment of bottling. Only Quintarelli has any idea what lies in this labyrinth and even he tends to be forgetful, discovering from time to time that there remains a demijohn or two of some fabulous vintage supposedly long since sold. I tasted an Amarone 1971 with him

An invaluable curtain of moisture hangs over the winding valleys north of Verona, modifying the heat, prolonging the ripening and intensifying the flavour of the grapes.

once, still sitting in a large glass jar 15 years after the vintage; it was vigorous but past its best. Quintarelli remarked absent-mindedly that he had last tasted it three years earlier.

All the wine is from his own vineyards: 12 acres (five hectares) surrounding the house (the Monte Cà Paletta), another 2.5 acres (one hectare) on the hill opposite and a further seven acres (2.5 hectares) lower down the valley, towards Verona. Apart from the traditional red grape varieties of this region, he also grows a little Nebbiolo (the classic grape of Barolo in Piedmont), some Cabernet Franc and perhaps others which he won't admit to. Quintarelli makes his white wines from Garganega (the mainstay of nearby Soave), Saorin (a rarity he rates very highly), Trebbiano and Tocai.

Most of his production is red, and 70 per cent of that is Valpolicella, most of it made by the *ripasso* method (though he also makes a non-*ripasso* version from a single grape variety, Molinara, and a light *vino da tavola* called Primofiore). His production methods are indeed intensely traditional. The best grapes are dried for three and a half months, from the harvest until mid-January. There is no destalking of the grapes destined for Amarone wines. Fermentation for both Recioto and Amarone takes place initially in tank, until the wine is racked into cask in April, leaving a rich sediment onto which Quintarelli pumps his young Valpolicella. Once the wine is in cask, he interferes as little as possible: the bung-holes are sealed up with plaster of Paris to minimize oxidation and the wine is left to get on with its maturation, undisturbed save for the occasional topping up. It is only racked once, six months before bottling and there is no fining – "only the weather". Cold winter temperatures clarify these Reciotos and Amarones as they mature for up to five or six years in *botte*. When ready for bottling, the various casks of Valpolicella may be blended together but the grand wines are bottled cask by cask, entirely by hand. If there are insufficient orders on hand for a particular vintage, the contents will be transferred to glass demijohns, which slow the process of maturation to a snail's pace.

Quintarelli also makes a little white wine by similar methods. His simple Bianco Secco is a light wine for local consumption, but he really prides himself on his sweet whites, made from dried grapes. His Bianco Amabile is fermented for three months on the skins of the grapes, just like his reds, but he also makes tiny quantities of a white that does not have any skin contact, which is aged like the Vin Santo of Tuscany. Tiny casks are stored under the eaves, in the roof, to endure five years of fierce variations in temperature, baking in summer and freezing in winter. The result is the wine that Quintarelli calls Il Bandito ("the bandit") because it has lived at the extremes, in hiding.

Tasting with Quintarelli is both a challenge and an obstacle course, since there are liable to be small tests for the unwary. Surrounded by the clutter of casks and demijohns, a single dangling light bulb casting shadows into the corners of the cellar, Quintarelli hands you a

The vines' topmost grapes are sorted before being partially dried for Recioto.

glass of the first wine, the Valpolicella. He stands there expectantly, head cocked to the side, knowing the wine is good but pleased to hear an appreciative comment. It is indeed startling stuff: deep in colour, with a fresh but rich aroma of purple fruit and raisins; a lively acidity on the palate balanced by extraordinary depth and generosity of flavour. As we move to another corner of the cellar for the first Amarone I spot a couple of French *barriques* and ask what he's up to. Quintarelli explains that he's experimenting with *barrique*-ageing for two different grape varieties, but won't reveal more.

Quintarelli squats beside an unlabelled demijohn and starts sucking on a short tube to syphon a glassful out of the jar, a laborious process that he repeats patiently throughout the tasting, apparently oblivious to the advantages of a pipette. The Amarone echoes the Valpolicella, but on a much grander scale, with a tarry bitterness and suggestions of blackberries and elderberries. We move on to a ten-year-old Amarone Riserva (with 17 degrees of alcohol). Fractionally lighter in colour, this has a much more complex aroma, creating a series of impressions that follow each other in swift succession: black cherries, black chocolate, the sweet lees of *marc*. On the palate there is a velvety richness but the wine is dry, spicy, with extraordinary intensity and a suggestion of gunpowder tea at the end.

The Amarone Riserva 1971, announced as an unexpected treat, turns out to be disappointing, but we pass on to an experimental blend, an Amarone 1983 made half from the traditional grape varieties and half from Cabernet Franc. This is in cask and appears to be still fermenting, so we move on to the even more unusual wine that he calls Alzero – effectively an Amarone but made entirely from Cabernet Franc. The combination of the grassy freshness that you might expect from this grape when grown in the Loire with the rich intensity and depth of the Amarone process is sensational. We pause, and Quintarelli smiles quietly to himself at my evident satisfaction.

At the next wine, the Recioto Amandorlato 1980 – a sort of half-way stage between Amarone and Recioto – Quintarelli actually laughs with delight as he smells it. A mixture of all his red grape varieties including Cabernet and Nebbiolo, this wine is deep purple, with a rich *mélange* of fruits on the nose evoking elderberries and plums, figs and damsons; it gives an initial impression of richness, but has a surprisingly dry, elegant finish.

The fine Recioto 1980 is followed by the less fine 1979 and I allow myself a mildly disparaging comment. Quintarelli seems delighted, and I sense that I have passed a small test. Then it's on to the Riserva Tre Terre ("from the three vineyards"), a wine explosively

High-trained Molinara grapes are sheltered by a canopy of their own foliage.

alive with concentrated summer pudding, prunes and figs: rich, dense, luscious and magnificent; entirely natural, entirely unfortified, it makes vintage port look puny.

We go into a tiny room off the main cellars, the treasure house of Quintarelli's secrets, and taste from the penultimate demijohn of his Recioto 1978, made entirely from Nebbiolo. Perhaps Barolo was made this way hundreds of years ago: would that it were now. With its deep garnet colour, truffles, loganberries, mulberries and chocolate, this is one of the most extraordinary wines I have ever tasted, and one of the finest.

We end with three whites. The first is still fermenting and smells of shrimps in hot butter – bizarre and unexpectedly attractive. The second, an Amabile Tre Terre 1981, has an exhilarating quince-like character and a lingering succulence of flavour, a suggestion of apricots. Finally we come to the Bandito, a wine of burnished gold, greengages, a suggestion of Chardonnay that sets me wondering, and a level of acidity that balances its rich intensity, constantly pointing up the changing complexities of its flavour.

As we climb the stairs I realize that in the past two hours we have tasted no more than a dozen wines; it felt like 30, so demanding of concentration was each. The light, unemphatic voice of Quintarelli as he says goodbye breaks incongruously into my reflections and I turn to glance at him, blinking in the sun like a subterranean creature out of its natural habitat. He doesn't look like a hero and he is certainly not built on the scale of his majestic wines, but there is an air of subtlety, a sense that all is not revealed. This man is a magician.

TUSCANY

Giovanella Stianti and Carlo Mascheroni of
Castello di Volpaia

When Giovanella Stianti inherited it in the 1970s, Castello di Volpaia was one of many run-down Tuscan estates suffering from the dwindling reputation and price of Chianti. She and her husband Carlo Mascheroni set about revitalizing the estate – not by filling the beautiful medieval village with brash modern winery buildings, nor by attacking the vineyards with chemicals, but by restoring and improving upon the old Tuscan traditions of viticulture and winemaking, as *Simon Loftus* explains.

Volpaia is the dream of a Tuscan hill village – a cluster of tiled roofs around a medieval church, perched above a landscape of vineyards dotted with olive and cypress trees. Wine flows beneath the cobbled streets and if you open the door of one of Volpaia's 14th-century houses you may be confronted by a gleaming stainless steel fermentation tank rising to the rafters, or a horizontal wine press controlled by computer. Walk up the street, past lemon trees in enormous terracotta pots by the door of an office, a telex chattering under its ancient beams, past stone stairways and arches, geraniums and cats. You might find yourself doffing your hat to an old widow in black, or you could encounter Nuccia, her deep and harshly lovely voice ringing down the street as she calls Tullio from the winery to answer an urgent telephone query from Maurizio Castelli, the consultant oenologist. Or you could turn a corner and tumble over a couple of children playing hopscotch. For Volpaia is no village in decline, its houses empty or converted into tourist shops, but a community whose indigenous population continues to grow.

All this is typical of the new wave of winemaking that is revitalizing the old Tuscan traditions, and yet extraordinary, for Volpaia is the expression of two exceptional people: Giovanella Stianti and Carlo Mascheroni. She is the daughter of a Florentine printer who bought the estate, including most of the village, in 1966. He is one of eight brothers, members of a Milanese family of commercial lawyers. Giovanella studied gerontology before their marriage and Carlo sailed single-handedly across the Atlantic. Both have energy, enthusiasm for a host of connected projects, a love and sympathy for the place itself and an extraordinary, almost childlike generosity. Between them they have made Volpaia an earthly paradise.

As well as its excellent wine, the estate produces superlative vinegar, olive oil and honey; the landscape is cherished, and old buildings carefully restored to use; the Commenda di Sant'Enfrosino, the 15th-century church depicted on the labels of Volpaia Chianti, is the

Giovanella Stianti's energy has transformed a crumbling hill village into an earthly paradise. Volpaia now flourishes in a rich Tuscan tradition, producing superlative olive oil, vinegar, honey – and wine.

annual setting for exhibitions of Italian 20th-century art; and every year, in August, the community celebrates the village's rebirth. For months beforehand Nuccia the cook is busy making ice-cream and preserves. As the feast of San Lorenzo approaches, every kitchen is pressed into service. Finally, on the day itself, there is food and wine, music and fireworks in a spectacular display of Tuscan hospitality. At two concurrent parties, Giovanella and Carlo entertain the villagers, vineyard workers and cellarmen, wine lovers, friends from the nearby estates and guests from abroad; and the local priest, the roof of whose church was repaired in return for the use of its cellars.

These are startling achievements for a couple whose week is of necessity based in Milan, where Carlo works and the children are educated. They make the long drive to Tuscany most weekends and spend as much time as they can there during the school holidays. But Volpaia seems infused with their energy even when they are absent.

To begin with, after their marriage in the early 1970s, Giovanella and Carlo were confronted with problems that took all their determination (as well as the considerable financial strengths of the Stianti-Mascheroni alliance) to solve. The estate was far from self-supporting because the price of Chianti was so low: buildings and vineyards needed extensive renovation; there was no modern equipment or bottling plant; wine quality was at best variable, and the workforce was elderly. But its new proprietors did inherit some natural advantages, the most important of which was Volpaia's altitude, at between 1,640 and 1,970 feet (500-600 metres) above sea level. Because the vineyards are so much higher than most others in Tuscany, the vines benefit from the great difference in temperature between warm days and cool nights, resulting in an extended ripening season and a late harvest. These conditions are ideal for the development of aromatic delicacy, elegance, complexity and finesse. A less evident advantage was that much of the Volpaia estate was still planted with the traditional haphazard mixture of olive and fruit trees, vegetables and vines – "promiscuous cultivation", as it is called. This is no way to produce great wine, but it did provide a vital genetic reservoir for the propagation of the old local vine strains, which are far superior to the modern high-yielding versions of Sangiovese planted so widely elsewhere.

Carlo recognized that the estate was bound to lose money if they continued to sell all their wine in bulk. However, they could not afford the heavy investment of replanting the vineyards, re-equipping the cellars and installing new bottling plant unless the results were of a quality that could be sold at a premium price. In any case, neither he nor Giovanella were the type to settle for mediocrity. So they set to work. The vineyards were mapped in detail; every vine was counted. Nursery beds were established, and a programme of replanting and regrafting was initiated to improve quality. They bought a large flock of sheep and hired the services of a Sardinian shepherd, not simply for the pleasure of eating their own lamb and ricotta cheese but to provide a vital source of organic manure. They recruited and trained a team of young workers to prune the vines rigorously, spray them when necessary (not with modern systemic pesticides and other agrochemicals, but with the traditional Bordeaux mixture of copper sulphate) and eventually to harvest by hand, working four or five times through the vineyards to select only the ripest grapes.

Equally difficult was the work of installing a modern winery discreetly in the 14th-century fortified village. At the top of the cobbled lane which winds through the heart of the *castello* you may now see an unloading bay and reception hopper; otherwise all is invisible. Tiles were stripped from the medieval roofs so that stainless steel fermenters and sophisticated cooling equipment could be lowered into the irregular spaces between the ancient walls. Each stone on the lane was numbered and mapped on a plan before the cobbles were lifted to allow the laying of stainless steel pipes that would let wine flow by gravity into tanks, barrels and bottling plant. Then the stones were relaid as before, leaving no sign of disturbance except the occasional remains of a painted number. Traditional *botte* (large casks of Slovenian oak) were ranged neatly in the cool crypt of La Commenda and, somewhat more recently, a large number of smaller casks made of French oak from the forests of Limousin have filled the cellars of the parish church.

Giovanella took charge of the marketing, promoting her Chianti at wine fairs and tastings in Italy and abroad. Her smile, energy and idiosyncratic English, backed by the ever-increasing quality of Volpaia's wines, proved irresistible. But Carlo recognized that to achieve the full potential of the estate they needed a top oenologist. In 1980 he persuaded Maurizio Castelli (the Tuscan equivalent of Bordeaux's Professor Peynaud) to work as consultant, with the aim of improving still further the Chianti and developing new wines of superior quality. The results were impressive. Castelli continued Carlo and Giovanella's programme of improvements in vineyards and cellar, accelerating the pace of innovation. Using the experience he had gained studying in France to modify Tuscan traditions, he proved that it was quicker and more effective to regraft selected clones onto existing rootstocks than to replant from scratch.

Sangioveto, the best small-berried version of Sangiovese, and Mammolo, an ancient variety valued for its delicate perfume, were propagated from old vines on the estate to form the basis of a new wine, a grand *vino da tavola* called Coltassala. Matured for a year or so in French *barriques*, this proved to be a wine of striking concentration, which needed bottle-

Beneath the apparent rusticity of Volpaia lies the sophisticated mechanics of its economic success.

age to develop its attractive balance of lean elegance and almost smoky fruit: a suggestion of oak and blackberries.

Castelli's next brainwave was Balifico, named like Coltassala after a particular section of the Volpaia estate. Cabernet Sauvignon and Cabernet Franc were grafted onto rootstocks of the despised Cannaiolo and blended with 70 per cent Sangioveto. The Bordeaux grapes added their black fruit aromas to the roast chestnuts of Sangioveto, modified by Limousin oak. From the first vintage in 1985, it was evident that this was a wine of great promise.

Like so many of the best wines of modern Italy, Coltassala and Balifico fall outside the legal definitions governing their region of origin. Hence they can be sold at nearly double the price of bottles bearing the somewhat discredited denomination of Chianti. But their undoubted quality should not cause wine lovers to underrate their less expensive cousins, the Chianti Classico and Riserva which continue to represent the bulk of Volpaia's production. The relative lightness of these wines (blended from Sangiovese di Volpaia and Sangiovese di Lamole, with perhaps a tiny proportion of the other traditional grape varieties) can easily cause them to be overlooked in blind tastings. The real test is to enjoy them with food, which reveals their delicious elegance and chestnutty persistence of flavour. I once stayed for a week at Volpaia, drinking the current vintage of the basic Chianti Classico every day at lunch and dinner, and found myself reluctant to open a bottle of anything grander. The Volpaia Chianti is so appetizing, so simple, such an excellent foil to food and apparently so healthy that I could cheerfully drink nothing else.

Tuscany is never likely to make great white wines, but Volpaia stands a better chance than most Tuscan wineries thanks to its altitude. Traditional Vin Santo is made here as it has always been – fermented from dried grapes and matured in tiny casks stored in the attic

Crops other than the vine still proliferate in many of the vineyards. Promiscuous cultivation, as it is known, is not recommended for top vineyards but, in the regenerative spirit of Volpaia, it provides a vital reservoir for superior old strains.

– but Castelli has been busy improving the basic Volpaia Bianco, which is now vinified at low temperatures to preserve its freshness, and this wine has much more character than hitherto. Recognizing that there are limits to what even he can achieve with Trebbiano and Malvasia, essentially second-rate grapes, he has enlivened the blend with a touch of Sauvignon. It is this variety, unblended and matured in casks of Tronçais oak, that constitutes the new Torniello, a grand *vino da tavola*. The first vintage was 1986 and there is every expectation that the ripe fruit flavours, already evident, will be increasingly emphatic as the vines get older. A comparable experiment with Sémillon, however, proved less successful. Cuttings were imported from the vineyards of Château d'Yquem in Bordeaux, but showed no evidence of their aristocratic origins when planted at Volpaia: the yield was high and the wine was dull. Carlo seems much more excited about the red wine which he hopes to produce from a recently-planted patch of Pinot Noir.

Carlo has also enlisted Castelli in his latest enthusiasm, the production of an olive oil even more refined than that for which Volpaia is already renowned. The project had its origins in the winter of 1985/86, when a prolonged and fearful frost ravaged the olive groves of Tuscany, killing or stunting huge numbers of productive trees. Anticipating a drastic and long-lasting shortage of Tuscan olive oil, Carlo and Castelli took immediate steps to ensure continuity of supply for Volpaia by searching out the few sheltered patches of olive trees that had escaped the frost and doing immediate deals with the farmers to rent these precious survivors until full production had been restored on the estate. Carlo then planted 4,000 young trees at Volpaia, choosing the best varieties, and began to dream about the possibilities. Volpaia oil is already unusually elegant, like its wine. This is partly the result of climate, partly attention to detail at every stage of production from hand-harvesting to cold-pressing. But, for a perfectionist, this is not enough: Carlo has decided to experiment with making oil from individual varieties of olive tree, rather than the usual blend of different cultivars; he also plans to install a revolutionary machine to extract the oil without pressing, which he believes will result in higher yields of finer quality. Giovanella matches his enthusiasm with her own, talking as knowledgeably now about olive oil as she has always talked about wine.

This process of refinement is comparable to Carlo's earlier mastery of the production of wine vinegar. Unsatisfied with the old haphazard ways, Carlo invented his own method by trial and error, and has now patented it. The system involves the use of good-quality wines and selected bacteria, sprayed at a controlled temperature through successive trays of wood chips. The result is matured for six months in oak casks to produce the most delicious red and white wine vinegar that I have ever tasted. More recently he has developed a range of five aromatized vinegars, chosen from 178 trials.

Giovanella, not to be outdone, will offer you a choice of four different types of honey – Chestnut, Heather, Acacia or Thousand Flowers – produced by moving the hives about the estate according to the season. My favourite is the Chestnut honey, which has a particular affinity with the flavour of Volpaia's wines.

In the yard below the kitchen window a bad-tempered turkey gobbles away in grumpy monologue and occasionally charges at strangers, wings flapping. One day, I feel sure, he will be roasted, basted in olive oil and chestnut honey, freshened with a few tablespoons of wine vinegar and eaten by a cheerful company of friends, who will toast his demise in the wine of Volpaia. Few will pause to consider that turkeys were introduced to Europe from a distant continent named after Amerigo Vespucci, the great Tuscan navigator born a few miles away from Volpaia. The adventurous Amerigo was a true Renaissance man, impatient with the constraints of the medieval world, confident, curious and experimental. Giovanella and Carlo are his spiritual descendants.

SOUTHERN ITALY

Donato D'Angelo of Fratelli D'Angelo

The Greeks brought vines to Basilicata nearly 3,000 years ago, and it is tempting to speculate how slowly time has moved there since. Yet there are reasons, other than poverty, for the antiquated methods of vine cultivation used here on the volcanic soil of Monte Vulture. The vine is the Aglianico, one of Italy's great reds – but one of the most temperamental. Such is its sensitivity that there are many vine-growers but very few winemakers, and only one – Donato D'Angelo – who excels, as **David Gleave MW** relates.

The signs that welcome you into Ginestra, a small village in the shadow of Monte Vulture in northern Basilicata, are in two languages. One, of course, is Italian; the other is Albanian. The bilingual tradition, apparently attributable to the arrival of Albanian settlers centuries ago, is not shared by any of the neighbouring villages.

Basilicata (also known as Lucania) is Italy's poorest region, so it is something of a mystery that the Albanians should have chosen to settle here in the first place. Perhaps they were following in the footsteps of the Greeks who colonized this part of Italy almost 3,000 years ago, bringing with them, among other things, the vine and the olive tree. Both remain vital aspects of the agricultural economy upon which villages like Ginestra still depend for their livelihood.

Peasants in this part of Italy have always lived in hilltop villages, leaving early in the morning to work their tiny patches of olive trees, wheat or low-yielding, low-trained vines. As the sun sets over the western hills, you can still see shepherds and their dogs driving the sheep back into the villages, or peasants returning from their land on mules. At first sight, it is tempting to suggest that the peasants here would do well to discard their antiquated practices – to increase both yields and income by swapping their mules for tractors and training their vines higher. In Apulia, less than an hour's drive to the east, the high-trained vines come close to buckling under the weight of their crop.

There are, however, two very good reasons for the local approach to viticulture. One of these is the chill that descends at the end of the day. The hills that circle the region from Potenza in the south to the extinct volcano of Monte Vulture in the north bring some of the lowest winter temperatures in Italy, comparable with those of Bolzano in the South Tyrol. Even in summer, cool night temperatures give locals a respite from the hot sun.

The second factor is the sensitive temperament of the Aglianico, the unusual vine cultivated here. Introduced to northern Basilicata by the Greeks (its name is thought to be a

The low-trained Aglianico is grown up canes on the volcanic soil of Monte Vulture.
Temperamental and difficult to cultivate, in expert hands it becomes one of Italy's greatest vines.

corruption of Hellenic), the Aglianico is one of Italy's great vines. Late-ripening and low-yielding, it produces deep coloured, tannic wines that are characterized by a fairly high level of acidity and are capable of developing well in bottle over several years. Because of the difficulties it presents in the vineyard, it is not widely grown. It is planted in Campania, where it is the mainstay of Taurasi, but it reaches its greatest heights in the volcanic soil of Monte Vulture. Indeed, there are those who argue that the Greeks named Italy Enotria Tellus ("the land of vines") because of the affinity that the Aglianico displayed for the soil and climate here. The DOC for this small zone is Aglianico del Vulture and, with about 740 acres (300 hectares) under vine, there are only two producers of note: Paternoster and Fratelli D'Angelo.

Where Paternoster is good, Fratelli D'Angelo excels. Its wines are among the best produced in southern Italy, displaying a quality, value and concentration that is a frequent source of amazement to producers from the north. Fratelli D'Angelo was one of the first firms in the south to bottle its own wines, rather than selling them locally in bulk. The grandfather of Donato D'Angelo, present head of the family firm, started bottling in 1946 at the old cellars of Rionero in Vulture, the small town at the heart of the DOC zone.

Donato entered the business in 1972, after successfully completing his oenology degree at Conegliano in the Veneto. His father gradually ceded control to him, and over the years Donato has wrought a number of improvements in the quality of the wines. The Riserva 1977 was initially excellent, revealing the outstanding quality of the raw materials, but the excessive level of volatile acidity (a sign that wine is well down the road to becoming vinegar) that became evident in the mid-1980s indicated the need for modern production practices in the cellar.

Such levels of volatility are now a thing of the past. In order to extract less tannin, Donato has reduced the length of time that the skins are kept in contact with the fermenting must. This in turn means that the wines do not need to spend as long in cask in order to smooth out the rough edges prior to bottling. Temperature control during fermentation is not necessary in Rionero, in spite of its southerly latitude. The Aglianico is not usually harvested until the third week of October, making it the last vine in Italy to be picked. By that time, when the late-ripening Nebbiolo grape is safely in its fermenting vats in the cellars of Piedmont, the weather in Rionero is so cool that Donato can have trouble getting the yeasts to start fermentation.

Unusually among Italy's top producers, Fratelli D'Angelo owns no vineyards; the firm buys grapes to meet its requirements from about 20 growers. While Donato admits that he

The brothers D'Angelo. Unseduced by "easier" varieties, Donato (left) is dedicated to the Aglianico and determined to explore its full potential.

would one day like to buy vineyards, he does not expect to do so in the near future. The problem, he explains, is that the zone is divided between so many small growers. Each has his own few acres on which he cultivates wheat, vines, olives and other crops, creating a patchwork landscape of tiny holdings. Assembling even a modestly-sized vineyard at present would be next to impossible. But the situation may well change as the older generation dies out. The fields are currently worked by old farmers and, as in the rest of Italy, many of the young have abandoned the agricultural life to find work in the cities. With the ensuing changes in the social fabric, land is likely to become available for purchase, providing an opportunity for Fratelli D'Angelo to grow its own grapes.

Donato is already well aware of the problems involved in growing the extremely sensitive Aglianico vine. The system of training, the yield and the style of wine produced are all dictated by the altitude, which varies within the zone from 980 to 2,130 feet (300-650 metres). Lower down the slopes, vines are trained by the Guyot method, with the canes running along wires; further up, the *alberello* is used, with the vines trained low in a bush. On the upper slopes, you can still see old vines trained low and supported by three converging canes, a system traditional to the zone, called *cappanno*.

Yields vary from 40 to 50 hectolitres per hectare lower down on the slope to 20-30 from the older vines higher up. These yields, Donato stresses, are what the better growers obtain; if quantity is pushed any higher, the Aglianico loses its character. The style of wine made from lower-lying vineyards tends to be broad and sturdy, that produced at higher altitudes finer and more perfumed. Donato generally blends the wines from various parts of the zone to create all the elements he requires in his finished wine.

The grower is also presented with problems relating to climate. Being a late-ripening grape, the Aglianico needs a long, warm autumn to achieve full ripeness. When conditions are poor, as in 1980, 1983, 1984 and 1986, Donato does not bottle an Aglianico del Vulture. This is a considerable sacrifice, but it would be impossible to do otherwise. "When the Aglianico is good," he says, "it is exceptional. But when it doesn't ripen properly, it produces very unattractive wine."

Despite – or perhaps because of – its difficult nature, Donato is full of enthusiasm for the Aglianico. A lean and wiry figure, he darts from vine to vine, alternately admiring and scorning the quality of the grapes. His air of nervous energy is quickly dispelled when he sees a ripe, healthy bunch of grapes, but the sight of even one poor bunch sets him fretting again. He is determined to explore the grape's full potential, and for this reason remains uninterested in experimenting with other varieties such as Cabernet Sauvignon. "The Aglianico gives very complex wines, but I am certain that we have not yet produced the best wine that we can."

In an attempt to understand the grape variety better, he began experimenting with *barrique*-ageing in 1980. Although the Aglianico is traditionally aged in large, old oak barrels called *botte*, D'Angelo felt that it had sufficient tannin, acidity and strength of personality to withstand the spicy character lent it by new wood. "I wanted to augment the character of the grape with the oak," he says. After five years of experiment, he felt that he had struck the right balance with the oak. The result, released in 1988, was Canneto D'Angelo 1985, an Aglianico wine from old vineyards aged for a year in a mixture of used and new *barriques*. It is a stunning wine – rich, velvety and long – and the 1988 promises to be even better.

The Aglianico del Vulture and Riserva from 1985 were also both outstanding. The former is the better wine to drink in the five years following the vintage, as it has a wonderfully lively and tightly-knit fruit that shines through unhindered by oak. The Riserva, on the other hand, is aged for five years (two of them in wood) before being released and acquires a more complex character, becoming savoury and tarry after several years in bottle. As the Canneto ages, it seems likely that it will shed the oakiness of its youth and develop something of the cedariness that old claret acquires, while retaining the tannin of the Aglianico grape.

These three wines are different facets of this intriguing grape, each sculpted by a master craftsman. They are produced using the most modern of techniques, in a region whose vinicultural history can be traced back as far as any other in France or Italy. This welding of innovative energy to a traditional base, providing us with a strong link to our vinous past, is what makes Fratelli D'Angelo such an outstanding presence in the south.

Spain

It is tempting to think of Spain and Portugal together, as though the Iberian land mass were a coherent vine-growing entity. Iberia is, after all, responsible for the world's two greatest fortified wines – sherry and port – and even the third, Madeira, though scarcely Iberian, is truly Portuguese. Spain and its neighbour also share a similarly structured wine industry, a feature which has had enormous significance for the evolution of table wines in both countries. Landholdings are very small because growing vines is commonly a sideline or a weekend hobby, with the result that wine production is dominated by co-operatives and large commercial wineries. Individual estates are thus unusual and, although the situation has begun to change (starting earlier and with a little more vigour in Spain than in Portugal), the co-operative weight has tended to retard progress.

It is, moreover, customary in both countries to mature wines for a long time (too long, one might say), both before and after bottling. But there, really, the similarities end. While both are backward in winemaking compared with other EEC countries and the New World, Spain is more advanced and has absorbed more influences from outside.

Spain, indeed, was gleaning ideas from France prior to the 1870s, when the devastation by phylloxera of the French vineyards prompted an influx of Bordeaux vine growers into the Rioja region. The idea of maturing wine in small oak barrels was introduced at Marqués de Murrieta (as it was later named) in the 1840s. And, in the 1860s, Cabernet Sauvignon, Merlot and Malbec cuttings gathered from Bordeaux were being planted alongside the native varieties at Vega Sicilia's vineyards in the Ribera del Duero.

While Portugal is to be applauded for very largely resisting Cabernet Sauvignon and Chardonnay, it has been well worth Spain's while to carry on the experiments started by innovative winemakers in the 19th century – simply because Spain has less variety and quality among its indigenous vines. There are now some good Spanish Chardonnays and some excellent Cabernets in an increasing number of regions. Miguel Torres Junior in Penedès has been the outstanding pioneer.

What is most important, however, is that Spain's use of classic French grapes, especially Cabernet Sauvignon, is producing wines that are uniquely Spanish in character, because it is often blended with indigenous grape varieties. Around 15 per cent of Cabernet can produce a perfect marriage with the popular Tempranillo, and it is significant that several

The cellarmaster samples wine from the cask at Bodegas Miguel Torres in Penedès, where new techniques of vinification have been successfully introduced alongside age-old traditions.

of the finest Rioja producers, including Murrieta, have "experimental" vineyards of Cabernet, even though it is not a variety permitted in Rioja wine (not yet, anyway).

The one area that has remained entirely untouched by foreign grape varieties – though not by modern technology – is Jerez in the hot south. And that is as it should be. Sherry is unique and, try as they might in Australia, California and South Africa, no other wine region has quite been able to duplicate it.

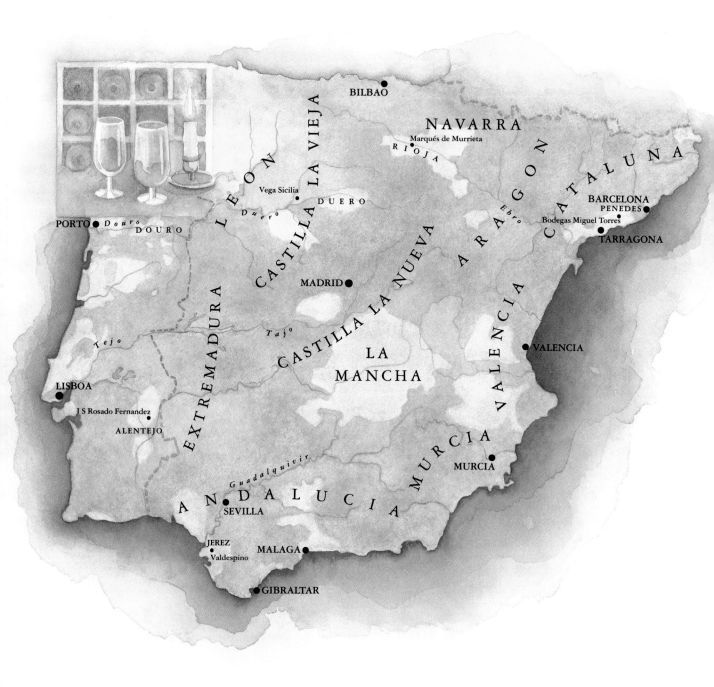

RIOJA

Marqués de Murrieta

Marqués de Murrieta is unique in Rioja not only because its red and white wines are both matured in oak barrels for an exceptionally long time, but because it is a large, self-contained estate. Upholding tradition and its long-established reputation is the Conde de Creixell, who bought the estate in the 1980s from the family who had cherished it for over a century. *Joanna Simon* explains how the new owner is maintaining past glory and planning a splendid future.

In winter the Castillo Ygay estate looks bleak, almost lunar: at 1,970 feet (600 metres) above sea level it is cold; the earth is bare, if occasionally snow-covered; the vines are denuded; a gnarled grey olive tree here and there relieves the foreground monotony; sombre snow-capped mountains form a distant backdrop. It is not the sort of place with which you could imagine yourself falling in love, although you might make a pilgrimage in homage to the wines of Marqués de Murrieta. For the Murrieta wines from Ygay, both red and white, are the most majestic of all Riojas. Matured in oak barrels for an extraordinarily long time, they live to a venerable age in bottle. True, not everyone actually likes these wines – for some the intense assertive flavours, particularly when encountered in the white, are just too shocking – but everyone respects them, some gradually acquire a taste for them, and many (like me) adore them.

The present owner first set eyes on the estate in late summer. Had he arrived about four months later, I really wonder whether the outcome would have been the same, because it was not the wine that appealed to his senses, but the place – the very place that looks so bleak in winter. Vicente Cebrian Sagarriga, Conde de Creixell, to give him his full title, simply fell in love with Castillo Ygay "at first sight" in 1983. Being a man who, from time to time, acts entirely on impulse, he bought it. "We make our life more difficult than it is. We complicate matters," he says, as though this explains everything.

Until then, he had never been involved with any aspect of the wine trade (although his father owned an estate in Galicia that produced a little white Albariño, which he has now begun restoring, too). Nor was he a native of the Rioja region. In fact, when he was "tipped off that Marqués de Murrieta might be for sale at a good price" in 1983, he was a Madrid-based construction tycoon and founder of a successful radio broadcasting company. On the spur of the moment he decided to take a look at the property, was hooked immediately and "more or less that next day" bought the two-thirds shareholding that was available.

Row upon row of low-cropped vines stretch out across the stony soil of the Ygay plateau.

The following year Vicente Cebrian became sole owner of Marqués de Murrieta, and he has been almost totally immersed in life and work there ever since.

For an outsider to buy a leading wine estate from the family that has built its fine reputation and in whose hands it has remained for 125 years requires considerable self-assurance. But this confidence needs to be tempered with a degree of humility in the running of the estate, because people will be quick to accuse you of arrogance if you make too many changes, too soon and too conspicuously. On the other hand, if you are over-diffident and do nothing, you will be accused of letting things go. It is a tightrope that the tall, strikingly heavyweight Vicente Cebrian has managed to negotiate with skill. He has initiated change in the last seven years, and for the better, but the greatest compliment you can pay him is to say that he has integrated the new with the old – which he has.

Marqués de Murrieta is the largest single, self-contained estate in Rioja, with over 740 acres (300 hectares). Nearly 618 acres (250 hectares) are now planted with vines, a substantial increase on the 494 acres (200 hectares) of vineyards planted in 1983. The estate is in a prime position, just north-east of the town of Logroño in the Rioja Alta, the most prized of the three Rioja areas.

Under its previous owners the estate provided about 65 per cent of the grapes needed for the wines, a uniquely high proportion for the Rioja region, where most grapes are grown by small farmers but most wine is made and marketed by co-operatives and large *bodegas*. Already, by gaining hard-won official permission to plant new vines and by replanting wherever necessary, the proportion of estate-grown grapes in Murrieta wines has been raised to nearly 90 per cent. Within a few years the estate will be fully self-sufficient – an objective that Vicente Cebrian believes will ensure quality in years to come. "The strength of Murrieta," he says simply, "is its vineyard."

128

Vicente Cebrian Sagarriga, Conde de Creixel, checks progress in the cellars at Marqués de Murrieta.

Together with the unequalled parcel of land came an old *bodega*. This, aside from the vast stocks of wine in more than 10,000 barrels, was sparsely and primitively equipped. The most recent press dated from 1940 and the loyal 1904 model was still in active service. There was a hotch-potch of fermentation vessels – wooden vats, glass-lined concrete, stainless steel. Wines were bottled by hand when an order was placed which, apart from being hopelessly impractical and well-nigh impossible at harvest time, meant that wine from the same vintage could vary widely from first to last bottling.

By modern winery standards, the *bodega* is still meagrely equipped, but a discreet programme of modernization has provided a new press and fermentation room, new ageing halls and a bottling line. The building containing these new facilities is on top of the old cellar, but it has been imposed with care using the same architectural vernacular.

As significant an inheritance – and surely a more daunting one than the mere three-dimensional elements – was Murrieta's starry reputation. Its distinguished, trail-blazing history dates back to the 1840s, when Luciano de Murrieta, a Peruvian-born winemaker who had studied in Bordeaux, introduced to Rioja the Bordelais technique of ageing wine in small oak casks. This soon established the superior quality and stability of the wines of Ygay, and during the later decades of the 19th century they began to win recognition overseas, notably in France. In the Paris World Expositions of 1878 and 1889, Bodegas Marqués de Murrieta (as the company had been named in 1872) clocked up a gold medal, two silvers and a commendation; several years later, in the Bordeaux Exposition of 1895, it took a further silver medal.

For another 88 years the estate survived and prospered in the same family, in spite of intermittent onslaughts on Rioja from such varied sources as phylloxera, war and, in the 1970s, the rapacious buying of long-established, family-owned *bodegas* by American multi-

Thick stone walls and tiny windows offer some protection against the fierce Rioja heat.

nationals, sherry companies and the (now defunct) Rumasa group. But then, in 1983, two of the three family shareholders decided to sell. Enter the Conde de Creixell.

If the Count was daunted by the prospect of taking over this unblemished reputation, he does not let on. He became obsessed (his word) with the quality of Murrieta and, in so doing, found there were ways in which the wines might be improved – so long as these things were instituted quietly. "A silent revolution," he says, although revolution seems too strong a word to me. Revolution or refinement, the important point is that he was not seduced by what was happening elsewhere in the wine world. He resisted the temptation to modernize the style of the wine and tended, rather, to lean the other way, emphasizing the traditional techniques and the originality of Murrieta Riojas.

Thus, although he has planted some experimental Cabernet Sauvignon at the request of the Rioja authorities (the Consejo Regulador), the grapes in Murrieta remain the same – predominantly Tempranillo for the red and Viura for the white. And, although there is a new press and fermentation room, the grapes, juice and wine are treated as before: grapes are de-stemmed; filtration is kept to an absolute minimum; and wine is moved by gravity, a much gentler method than pumping.

Similarly, far from reducing the idiosyncratic and expensive wood-ageing, he has increased it for the standard wines, both red and white. These now spend about two and a half years in oak and 18 months in bottle before they are released, the amount of time most *bodegas* allow their *Reservas*. Murrieta's *Reservas*, like other producers' *Gran Reservas*, stay in wood for four years, followed by two in bottle. And Castillo Ygay, which is made in tiny quantities only in the finest of years, is aged for anything from 15 to 35 years in barrel, with a further five or more in bottle. The most recent Castillo Ygay red, superseding the 1942, is the 1968. And all the wines, though they are ready to drink when they are finally released, continue to develop in bottle.

Below the newly-renovated bodega, dust and cobwebs gather in the ancient cellars.

Stepping up the ageing of the wines has meant that more barrels have had to be bought – 5,000 this year alone – and this has given the Count an excuse to dabble with different combinations and sources of oak. Locally produced American oak barrels are still the most important, together with some Spanish barrels which mature the wine much faster, but in recent years he has also bought second-hand barrels from Châteaux Lafite and Pavie for the red wines and Château d'Yquem for the white.

The fact that they are second-hand is crucial. New oak is used at Murrieta, but with extreme caution, because it is vital that none of the wines becomes overwhelmingly woody during such long sojourns in barrel. On average, the higher the quality of the wine, the longer it is to be aged and the older the wood, because these elderly casks (often 40 years old) will be lined with thick deposits of tartrate crystals which form a glass-like barrier between the wine and wood, and between the wine and any air that permeates from the outside. This barrier not only prevents old wines from being horribly oxidized, but preserves their fruit and gives them an astonishing, invigorating freshness.

Glass-like, and yet not exactly like glass. The Count has experimented with maturing Murrieta wines in bottle, but the result, he says, is Bordeaux, not Murrieta – and the last thing he wants is for his wine to be some sort of Spanish claret. "I want Murrieta to be totally different, as broad-shouldered as possible," he says a trifle enigmatically. And yet it is also a strangely evocative description. These are not light fresh fruity wines in the modern idiom. They have a freshness, they have perfume and fruit, but there is much more to them: penetrating spice and nut flavours, a vanilla richness, honey, oak, suggestions of dried fruit, plums and lemons, leather and liquorice. These are complex wines, yes, and broad-shouldered – why not?

PENEDES

Miguel Torres Junior of Bodegas Miguel Torres

Torres was already a successful Spanish wine company when Miguel Torres Junior returned to the family fold after three years of study in Dijon. Yet there was little to distinguish this *bodega*, apart from size, from others in Penedès. The young Miguel soon began to plant the French grape varieties he had come to appreciate and to experiment with new winemaking techniques. From there it was a short ride to fame. ***Charles Metcalfe*** traces Torres' inexorable rise.

At times, the clouds of dust raised by well-publicized family skirmishes within the Torres wine dynasty have threatened to obscure the achievements of the company itself. Bodegas Miguel Torres is the largest family-owned wine company in Spain, and Miguel Torres Junior one of the most highly regarded winemakers in the world – certainly the most innovative in the country. Yet the Penedès region south of Barcelona has often seemed too small an area to contain the outsize characters of the Torres family.

Miguel Torres Senior, president of the company for life and a "commercial genius" according to his son, restored the company after the Spanish Civil War had brought it to the brink of ruin. Miguel Torres Junior is a superstar winemaker whose wines have been applauded by the world, and whose strength of character has enabled him – when necessary – to oppose his father's iron will in matters of viticulture and winemaking. His sister Marimar had to emigrate to the United States in order to escape the prospect of "a good marriage" – all that she was offered or expected to achieve in Catalonia. She married an American wine writer and moved to California: now she is acknowledged throughout the States as a great ambassadress for the family wines.

Miguel Junior studied winemaking for three years at Dijon between 1959 and 1961, and then returned to Vilafranca del Penedès to apply what he had learned. But working within the family was not easy and by the mid-1970s the strain was beginning to tell. He found some respite by turning his attention to the new Miguel Torres company in Chile, where he was free to pursue his own ideas without the constant constraint of parental supervision. But recurring tension between father and son did cause a temporary rift in 1982, and Miguel Junior retreated for a year to study the latest winemaking and viticultural techniques at Montpellier University. He returned re-invigorated, and relationships within the family have been improving ever since. In fact, in 1988, Miguel Torres Senior transferred 70 per cent of the company's shares into his childrens' names.

Miguel Torres Junior's ideas have borne fruit, resulting in wines that challenge the classics of France.

Although the Torres family has been dealing in wine for three centuries, the present business was started by Jaime Torres in 1870, after he had struck lucky in the Cuban oil boom a few years earlier. He returned to Catalonia, built a winery, bought ships, and started to export the wines of his native Penedès to Cuba. Jaime's grandson, Miguel Torres Senior, inherited the company when he was only 23. Four years later, the Spanish Civil War broke out, and the business was confiscated by the local Republican workers' committee. Worse was to come, when Franco's forces bombed Vilafranca del Penedès before they advanced to "liberate" the town, and the bombs hit the Torres winery instead of the railway station close by.

Undeterred, Miguel Torres and his wife Margarita set out in 1940 on a massive sales trip around North and South America. Their wines were enthusiastically welcomed in the United States – especially since the neutral Spanish ships were able to cross the Atlantic unmolested by either side, whereas exports of French wines had been stopped by the fighting. The company was saved by its American sales, but Miguel was unstoppable. He hawked his samples as far north as Denmark, expanding the business still further throughout Europe immediately the war had ended.

The next step in the masterplan was for the company to start making its own wines. Up to this point, the Torres company had acted solely as a merchant, buying wines produced by local Catalan growers, blending and selling them. Miguel Senior sent his son to Dijon to learn the sciences of viticulture and winemaking, and, when Miguel Junior returned in 1961, the company started experimenting with different winemaking techniques and producing its own wines. Stainless steel tanks were installed so that fermentation could be carried out at controlled temperatures, a modern laboratory was built, and cool maturation cellars were dug deep into the hillside. The white wines were bottled as soon as possible, to preserve their youthful fruitiness, and the best of the reds spent up to 18 months in small, new oak barrels, just like fine Bordeaux.

But not everything went smoothly at first. In spite of having sent his son to earn the winemaking qualifications no one else in the family possessed, Miguel Senior found it hard to relinquish overall control of any aspect of the business, and there were frequent clashes between father and son about how the wines should be made. One thing they did agree on was the necessity of buying their own vineyards. They both wanted to ensure the highest-quality grapes possible for the new style of wines that Miguel Junior was making. However, if they agreed on the vineyards, they disagreed completely on what should be planted in them. Miguel Junior believed that they could succeed with some of the "international" varieties such as Cabernet Sauvignon, Chardonnay, Pinot Noir, Gewürz-traminer and Riesling, as well as indigenous Spanish grapes; his father did not.

Eventually, Miguel Junior won that particular battle, and in 1962 he planted his first, experimental Cabernet Sauvignon vines. The commercial plantings that followed in 1966, from which he made Gran Coronas Black Label (now called Gran Coronas Mas la Plana), completely vindicated his decision 13 years later. The Gran Coronas 1970 swept all before it in the top Cabernet Sauvignon class at the 1979 Gault-Millau Wine Olympiades in Paris. It was voted the winner by a team of judges that included 27 Frenchmen, beating wines such as Château Latour 1970 and Château La Mission-Haut-Brion 1961. The squeals of indignation from the French wine establishment were predictable, but they were sweet music to Torres' ears, and the event provided better publicity than anything the company could have organized itself.

But the changes that Miguel Torres Junior had put into practice were far more wide-ranging than the successful introduction of foreign grape varieties. Another radical difference in his approach to vineyard plantation was the density with which he planted his vineyards, 5,000 vines to each hectare, as opposed to the normal Penedès density of about half that. This method of plantation evolved in response to two sets of new research – typical of the way in which Miguel keeps abreast of all the latest viticultural information.

Although the rainfall in Penedès is adequate to support a growing vine throughout the year's cycle, the summers are very hot and there is a danger of losing much of the precious moisture by evaporation. The soil structure is obviously crucial, and one of the priorities is to plant new vineyards in sites where the soil contains a certain proportion of clay, which retains moisture well. Traditionally, vines were widely spaced to allow limited water reserves to reach a limited number of vines, but the new research projects indicated that

Torres' success has been threatened regularly by disaster throughout its 300-year history. Now, at last, tradition, courageous innovation and commercial genius are working together - with spectacular results.

planting the vines closer together would actually give vines more water: first, because more closely-planted vines developed more roots, and the more roots vines have, the more nutrients and water they are able to absorb; and second, because roots near the surface are capable of attracting water from only one foot (30 centimetres) or so around them, leaving pockets of precious water unused in sparsely planted sites. In addition, the increased shading from vine foliage reduced the risk of water evaporating in the hot Penedès sun.

The close planting has also improved the quality of the grapes. Densely planted vines have to compete more strongly for the soil's nutrients, which reduces their vigour and, in turn, their yield. However, because of the greater number of plants, the vineyard's overall yield has remained constant in quantity, but the healthy, low-yielding vines produce more flavoursome grapes.

At first, the main problem was that there were no tractors that could work between these narrow rows of vines. Gradually, though, as the new viticultural fashion for closely-spaced rows spread, a new generation of tractors evolved, perched high on long legs that straddle a row of vines, making cultivation between the rows possible. This is an important development for Torres, as more and more vineyard work is carried out mechanically. Over half the pruning, and much of the picking of the red grapes, is done by machine.

In the winery, Miguel Torres Junior has been just as innovative. He was one of the first winemakers in Spain to use cold fermentation for his white wines – and to realize its limitations. Just as most of the rest of Spain's producers were getting round to installing the essential stainless steel and refrigeration equipment, Torres was experimenting with other French and Californian methods such as fermenting Chardonnay in new oak barrels and giving white grape juice longer "skin contact" before fermentation to improve the extraction of important aromatic substances from the skins.

The temperature-controlled red wine fermentation tanks open at the bottom, allowing gravity to do most of the work of removing grape skins and solids from the tank after fermentation; the grape skins shoot out into a press that moves up and down between the tanks on railway lines. But nothing illustrates the winemaking philosophy of Miguel Torres Junior better than this vinification plant: it has a roof but no walls, and could be dismantled in a week. As he says, "I don't want to build permanent installations that might become redundant with technological changes".

Miguel Torres Junior is passionately concerned to keep up to date with the latest advances in the vineyard and winery. The improvement of the Torres range of wines has come about purely because he was aware of the technical changes in the industry and had the courage to bring them home to Penedès. The laboratory at the Torres headquarters in Vilafranca has a staff of three permanently employed on research into grape flavour, oak flavour – anything that might improve the wines still further.

Now he is applying himself once again to the Torres company in Chile, and to the latest Torres project, a Chardonnay vineyard in the Sonoma Valley, California. As in Spain, the Torres vines in California are planted at a density of about 5,000 plants to the hectare. The only other California vineyard with a comparable density is Opus One (see page 190), the celebrated joint venture between Robert Mondavi and Mouton-Rothschild. The Chilean wines are already rated among the country's best and the release of the first California Chardonnay in 1991, and a new Merlot from Penedès, Las Torres, are eagerly awaited. The Merlot will join the select list of top Penedès wines: Gran Coronas Mas la Plana (Black Label), Milmanda Chardonnay and Gran Viña Sol Green Label from the Fransola vineyard, a blend of oak-aged Sauvignon Blanc and Parellada.

New wines and new projects will doubtless emerge soon to excite Miguel Torres Junior, and the world in general. Whether it is a single-vineyard Spanish Pinot Noir, a classic Champagne-grape fizz from the high mountains of Penedès or a new vineyard project in China – anything that Miguel Torres undertakes the wine world ignores at its peril, and the world's wine drinkers usually applaud.

Top red wines at Torres, such as Gran Coronas, are aged in American oak, the wood traditionally used for maturation throughout Spain.

THE DUERO

Vega Sicilia

Baking hot summer days, chilly summer nights and freezing winters make the high Duero plateau one of Spain's most inhospitable and desolate-looking regions. Yet the vine, far from despising these harsh, fluctuating conditions, thrives on them – as Vega Sicilia has ably, and almost single-handedly, demonstrated since the 19th century. The character of the wine, writes **Simon Loftus**, is formed initially in the vineyard and is then shaped by Vega Sicilia's uncompromising, highly individual methods of winemaking.

The Duero winds westward across the high plateau of Castile in northern Spain, heading towards Portugal where it becomes the Douro, river of port. Countless sheep graze the rolling steppes and low hills of this vast landscape, and in the distance there are mountains. The eye is held by solitary figures: a man and his mule, or a shepherd with the traditional cloak slung across his shoulders as he surveys his straggling flock. There may be a line of *piñon* trees, bent by the prevailing wind, and down by the river you can see poplars, their leaves rippling in the golden light – but the overwhelming sensation is of arid emptiness.

Roads degenerate into dusty tracks and the sun bakes the crumbly earth to the colour of cement, mixed with flakes of white from the underlying limestone. Summer days are fiercely hot but at night the temperature drops sharply and in winter it freezes. Breathing the crisp, clean air you are reminded of the altitude, some 2,600 feet (800 metres) above sea level. Curiously enough, such extremes suit the vine. Cold winters kill off potential pests, and the chilly spring and autumn allow for an extended ripening season. This builds acidity and aromatic complexity into the grapes, which would otherwise produce wine characterized by the coarse alcoholic heaviness that results from too much sun. The vines here always flower way behind most other regions of Spain (and, indeed, the rest of Europe) and the vintage may not take place until late October. Frost is a bigger danger than excessive heat; it can, as in 1971, destroy the entire crop.

The harsh climatic conditions were certainly no obstacle to viticulture in the past, when much of the Ribera del Duero was planted with vines to supply the court at Madrid, 80 miles (130 kilometres) to the south. But gradually the farmers switched to less demanding crops, wheat or maize, or abandoned their land to the sheep. Eventually there was only one vineyard left that anyone outside Castile had ever heard of, and that was regarded as an oddity, producing the grandest wine of Spain in total isolation. Vega Sicilia and its fabled,

Conditions are often harsh at Vega Sicilia's vineyards in the limestone hills of the upper Duero valley.

aptly-named Unico achieved a legendary status comparable only to that other unique phenomenon – Australia's Grange Hermitage (see pages 214-18). Both wines were treasured by enthusiasts but ignored by other winemakers as curiosities. Even today, with Australia one of the most exciting wine-producing countries and Ribera del Duero widely recognized as having outstanding potential for great wine, Grange and Unico remain admired but not imitated. Larger than life, they seem like heroes from another age.

Vega Sicilia has had a succession of owners. The vineyards were originally planted in 1864 by a Señor Locanda, who interspersed cuttings of Cabernet Sauvignon, Merlot and Malbec, imported from Bordeaux, with the local varieties Tinto Fino (a variant of Rioja's Tempranillo) and white Albillo. His successor, a Señor Heredos, built the incongruous villa near the original cellars, which has been the infrequently occupied residence of absentee owners ever since. It was Heredos who took the decision in 1912 to sell the estate's wine in bottle, rather than in bulk as hitherto, and perhaps it was he who designed the prototype of the present label, which vies with that of Grange as a pleasingly old-fashioned typographic mess. In 1964 the property was bought by the Neumanns, a family of wealthy Venezuelans, who carried out a major programme of expansion and constructed the new cellars, dug into the side of a hill in the middle of the vineyards. In 1983, the Neumanns sold out to businessman Señor Alvarez Diaz, the present owner.

One man, Don Jesus Anadon, provided continuity throughout most of these changes and established the style that made Vega Sicilia famous. Starting as a young man, he worked his way up to become winemaker in 1950, was given sole charge of the estate in 1964, and only recently retired having handed over to his protegé, the oenologist Mariano Garcia Fernandez, a local man like himself. Pale and preoccupied, with a fringe of black

The most prestigious estate in Spain, Vega Sicilia's powerful wines have become legendary for quality.

beard around his chin, Mariano is reticent about his methods and only gradually unwinds to those who prove their willingness to appreciate his wines as seriously as he does. Though trained in modern techniques, it is clear that he is imbued with the traditions of his mentor and has a comparable sense of local pride.

During his 30 years in charge, Don Jesus is known to have taken only one trip to Bordeaux and has certainly shown no desire to imitate the French. On the contrary, all he learned was assimilated into his own more local traditions and his highly individual techniques. Above all, he developed the lengthy process of oak-ageing his wines into a subtle art – complex variations to achieve a clearly perceived end. For all his enthusiasm for experimentation, this is one thing that Mariano shows little interest in changing. He will show you his testbeds of young vine cuttings grafted onto different rootstocks or the self-emptying stainless steel fermentation *cuves* which he designed himself, but none of the hordes of foreign winemakers who come to visit him are likely to change his mind on the subject of maturation. Each year he experiments, bottling a recent vintage of Unico much younger than has been traditional, but he rejects the results of these trials with a statement of simple certainty: "It develops well in bottle, but it's not Vega Sicilia".

The character of the wine is formed initially in the vineyards. These have been extended in recent years to cover about 320 acres (130 hectares) of the 2,500-acre (1,000-hectare) estate, on north-facing slopes south of the River Duero. The altitude of the hills provides some protection from the sun's glare at the height of summer, but most of the vines are pruned in low bushes to benefit from heat radiated by the soil during the chilly nights. Some more recent patches have been trained on wires, as an experiment, but it is not yet clear whether this will ever become general. Pruning is rigorous, as the unirrigated soil is poor and many of the vines are old. The estate counts itself lucky to achieve a yield of 20 hectolitres per hectare, with a total production of around 20,000 cases a year.

The blend of different grape varieties remains unique to Vega Sicilia: Cabernet Sauvignon brings structure and aromatic intensity; Merlot provides rich fruit; Malbec offers an agreeable rusticity; and the white Albillo adds elegance. Tinto Fino, which accounts for about half the vineyard, is valued for its vigour, alcoholic strength and capacity to age. The actual balance of grape varieties in the final wines varies with the vintage, but in general the three Bordeaux varieties are being slightly increased at the expense of Tinto Fino. In the past, a typical Unico might have contained about 15 per cent Cabernet, five per cent each of Merlot and Malbec, a little Albillo and a lot of Tinto Fino. Nowadays the Bordeaux varieties could account for 40 per cent of the final blend.

But it is not so much the concentration of flavour brought about by low yields, nor even the marriage of different characteristics from an unusual blend of grape varieties, that sets Vega Sicilia apart. It is what happens to the harvest after it arrives at the cellars.

Picked by hand, the grapes are harvested into boxes weighing 90-110 pounds (40-50 kilograms) apiece, to prevent them being crushed by their own weight. The destalked grapes are then fermented in Mariano's stainless steel *cuves* at between 73 and 82°F (23-28°C). It is seldom necessary to exercise much temperature control: the cold days and nights of late October should do the job naturally. This first alcoholic fermentation may take up to three weeks. The new wine is then transferred to thick-walled, epoxy-lined cement *cuves* for the vital malolactic fermentation and thence to large wooden vats made of American oak.

At this stage the final decision is taken as to which vats are destined to become the long-lived Unico (accounting for a third of the crop) and which will be sold as the younger Valbuena. This wine, named after a nearby town, is the produce of the younger vines, the less ripe grapes and the least concentrated vats, and has slightly less of the Bordeaux varieties in the blend – perhaps 30 per cent of the total. In some years there may be no Unico at all. Occasionally it is conceivable that no wine will even be judged worthy to bear the name Valbuena and the entire harvest will be sold off in bulk. Every year the press-wine is rejected, because there is no need for its harsh tannins to stiffen the blend. Added astringency is the last thing that any of the Vega Sicilia wines require by the time they have finished their maturation in oak.

This is the heart of the matter. Vega Sicilia has its own coopers, producing two casks a week to replenish the stock of 4,500 stacked up to five-high in the *bodega*. Most of these casks are made from American oak, which has a strong, direct impact on the wine, but Mariano Garcia has recently introduced some French oak to give greater subtlety. So the permutations of vats and casks of varying sizes, different ages and different oaks allow the winemaker to orchestrate the maturation of Vega Sicilia with great complexity.

In general the progression is from large to small (vat to *barrica*) and from new wood to old. Valbuena might spend a few months – perhaps a year – in vat, followed by six months in relatively new oak and then a period in older casks: a total of two to three years in wood. For Unico the process is much lengthier, lasting up to eight years altogether, and at each stage there is a decision to be made. Does the wine need to pick up more of the harsh tannins of new American oak or the softer, creamier characteristics of French oak; or does it need to rest in the more neutral environment of an older cask? The permutations are endless and test the winemaker's skill to the limit. Mariano Garcia compares the process to cutting a diamond: a series of irrevocable small decisions, gradually shaping and polishing the complex facets of his wine, allowing the acidity to point up and reflect the flavours and aromas which evolve through this elaborate maturation of concentrated fruit.

Oenologist Mariano Garcia Fernandez sticks closely to the local traditions and highly individual techniques practised at Vega Sicilia by his predecessor and mentor, Don Jesus Anadon.

Mariano emphasizes that only through such lengthy ageing in wood (and then in bottle) can Vega Sicilia acquire the multi-dimensional subtlety that sets it apart from the strong but relatively simple tastes of so many modern wines.

During their time in oak the wines are racked (run off their sediment) three times in their first year and every eight months thereafter, great care being taken to avoid oxidation. There is no filtration and only Valbuena is fined before bottling, using the traditional whites of egg. An important characteristic of the *bodega* is that it endeavours to store its wines in bottle after their ageing in cask, and only to release them near the point of maturity. Valbuena is sold at three or five years old, and should be enjoyed relatively soon thereafter. Unico, on the other hand, is often kept for over a decade before release, and its discerning customers will, if they have the patience, cellar it for another decade. Much of the criticism that has been levelled at Unico by modern critics is the result of its being drunk too soon, when it tastes like bottled shoe-leather, rather than when it has been allowed to develop the full splendours of its maturity.

Even at Vega Sicilia, in the company of Mariano Garcia, it was hard for me to extract a fully mature bottle from the cellars. This is not so much meanness as a natural desire to eke out for as long as possible the private reserves of a wine so rare that stocks of the older vintages are counted in bottles, not cases. So we began with the intention of tasting only two recent vintages – the Unico 1986, still in cask, and the Valbuena 1983 – and a private determination on my part to goad Mariano into opening something much older.

The Unico 1986 (a blend of 80 per cent Tinto Fino and 20 per cent Cabernet) had spent a year in large oak vats and the larger-sized casks, six months in new *barricas*, six months in "semi-new" casks and a few weeks in older casks. It tasted utterly delicious: dark, rich, chocolaty and fine, with a lovely balance between fruit and astringency. I wanted it bottled

The old chapel building of the bodega (left) and the medieval castle at Peñafiel (right)
perched, like the vineyards, at an altitude of some 2,600 feet above sea level

straight away, to preserve this potent magnificence, but Mariano was firm: "If we bottled it now it would be like a great French wine, not Vega Sicilia".

The Valbuena 1983, by then five years old, had spent a year in vat, three years in cask and ten months in bottle. Like the Unico it was a rich, deep colour, showing little sign of age, but it lacked the other wine's concentrated fruit, was more elegant and somewhat lighter. The acidity gave a refreshing balance to what was predominantly the product of Tinto Fino, with only five per cent Cabernet, five per cent Merlot and two per cent Malbec. A fine wine, which evolved noticeably in the glass.

There was a pause, mutterings from me about how interesting it would be to taste something a little older, and a few more appreciative sniffs and sips of the younger offerings that we had just opened. Mariano then produced a bottle of the Unico 1973. This, he announced, was composed of 15 per cent Cabernet, five per cent each of Merlot and Malbec and the remainder, Tinto Fino. Evidently more mature, the colour was deep but beginning to turn tawny at the edges and the aroma slightly vegetal, a suggestion of damp ferns. The initial impression on the palate was of acidity and astringency, a sense that the wine had dried out and lost its fruit – but also an awareness of constant shifts of emphasis, of fleeting flavours and subtleties suggesting continuing life. Gradually, over a period of ten to 15 minutes, the wine began to open up in the glass, revealing a long, lingering richness of flavour. It seemed to be getting younger by the moment. Mariano announced that if this wine were kept another ten years it would round out and develop further complexity.

This was my chance, and I challenged him once more to prove his point by demonstrating that Unico really can overcome the mouth-puckering character of its youth and achieve the grandeur associated with its reputation. Mariano explained that he had no access to the stocks of older bottles, but eventually my combination of enthusiasm and scepticism proved sufficiently persuasive and he called for a bottle of the 1962.

It was poured in silence and we admired the wonderful colour, more youthful (deeper and more purple) than the 1973. The bouquet was closed up, ungenerous, and a brief impression of fruit on the palate was followed immediately by an almost overwhelming astringency. I had a panic-stricken moment of disappointment – what on earth was I going to say to mollify Mariano for opening this unappetizing vintage? But before I could express some polite banality I realized that the astringency was fading, the wine enriching itself as it breathed. Mariano suggested we wait for five minutes, so we chatted of this and that, had another taste of the 1973 and eventually returned to contemplate the 1962.

It was a revelation. Over the next quarter of an hour the wine opened up to develop rich aromas of purple fruit and bitter chocolate, a seductive balance of acidity and concentrated richness on the palate, and a quite marvellous persistence – changing, evolving, fascinating and alive. I was reminded of the comparison with the facets of a diamond.

"Tobacco and leather flavours," said Mariano, taking another sniff.

"Chocolate and coffee," said I.

We were both right. Then the astringency came back to refresh the palate before a gentle, almost sweet softness returned again, an autumnal mellowness. This was indeed a unique splendour.

In the lengthy process of oak-ageing, casks of varying size, age and wood all contribute to the wine's complexity.

SHERRY

Miguel Valdespino of Valdespino

Huge modern *bodegas* decked out in the latest high-technology equipment are a familiar sight in Jerez, but the sherry trade's oldest family, Valdespino, does things differently. Miguel Valdespino prefers to keep his computer and stainless steel quotient to a minimum and to rely, instead, on tradition, the human hand and inexhaustible patience. In this way, as **Roger Voss** explains, he makes sherries of great quality and remarkable individuality.

Standing in front of an ancient butt of sherry, Miguel Valdespino wields a *venencia*, the long stick with a tiny silver cup at the end which is used in Jerez to extract wine from a barrel. Deftly he plunges it into the murky depths of the butt and comes up triumphantly with a cupful of dark liquid. The sherry is opaque, deep green in colour, tasting bitter and sweet at the same time, like burnt toffee – almost undrinkable in its concentration. It turns out to be a butt set aside by Don Miguel's father back in 1940. "We have not touched it since because I don't know how we can use it: do we use it for blending, or bottle it as a special wine?"

Miguel Valdespino, owner of the Jerez winery that bears his name, seems more at home considering such questions here in the cool, quiet of the *bodegas* than in his office, with its computer pushed aside into one corner, or describing – with perhaps a hint of distaste – the need to use stainless steel tanks to ferment some of his wines. Unlike the great cathedral buildings that dominate many of the big names of Jerez, Valdespino's *bodegas* are tiny: high-ceilinged, but narrow and short. Running between them are little open alleys, from whence light breezes fan air into the *bodegas*. In spite of the dark, these are fresh-smelling buildings: the aroma of quietly maturing sherry mingles with the moisture from the sandy floor, which is watered to maintain a humid atmosphere.

In the *bodega* that houses Valdespino's most famous wine, the fino Inocente, Don Miguel wields his *venencia* once more. The fino Inocente is a rarity among sherries: a wine made from one vineyard in the best area of Jerez, Macharnudo. Heavier in style than some of the more modern and commercial *finos*, it is good with food. As the *venencia* plunges through the yeast *flor* that covers the *fino*, protects it from air and gives the wine its final yeasty taste, we get a whiff of tangy freshness in the small silver cup.

Once in a glass, the wine smells slightly salty, with the sort of seaside smell an oyster gives just as it is opened. This is *fino* at its freshest, straight from the butt. It is not the finished product, not the Inocente that you will find in the bottle, but wine from a half-way stage in the five-level *solera* ageing process that Valdespino's *fino* passes through before it reaches final blending and bottling. It is easy to forget that, though good *fino* tastes fresh, it is not a young wine.

If you wanted to find tradition in Jerez, you would come to Valdespino. The family is the oldest in the sherry trade, with records in the area that date back to 1264, when Don Miguel's ancestor, Don Alonso, a native of Santander in northern Spain, helped the Castilian king, Alfonso X, to reconquer Jerez from the Moors. His subsequent grant of land in the area set the family on the road to a future in wine.

Valdespino is neither the biggest nor the most public relations oriented of the sherry houses. By comparison with the Domecqs of the industry, it is tiny. Three and a half million bottles are produced each year, compared with Domecq's annual production of 19 million. It is a traditional firm, worlds away from the high technology of the modern *bodegas*

Narrow bodegas house the quietly maturing sherry alongside relics of previous generations.

on the road to Puerto de Santa Maria. Most of the wine here is still fermented in wooden barrels; the stainless steel vats, explains Don Miguel, are used only to contribute an element of lightness to the blend, because "that's what the demand is at present, although I hope fashion returns to a fuller style soon". The aim is quality rather than quantity.

Not that Don Miguel is an out-and-out traditionalist. There are unexpected sides to him: he prefers his BMW sports car and his Harley Davidson motor cycle to horses (of which, unusually for an Andalucian, he is frightened); and he goes deep sea fishing as a member of the crew. He is active, restless, on the move – with only, as he says, "the thought of another glass of *fino* to keep me sitting down".

Don Miguel has known no other life than sherry. "I would not consider any other work," he confesses; "anyway I probably couldn't get a job." He became joint-head of the family firm with his elder brother Rafael on the death of their father; he was then only 22 years old. Now in his fifties, he has run the family-owned company single-handed since his brother retired in 1985.

The *bodegas* are still filled with memories of older generations of Valdespinos. In the *bodega* where the grapes are pressed at harvest time is a row of classic cars, gathering dust but never to be thrown away. Inside each car Don Miguel has locked a case of old sherry, just to see how it ages, and he agonizes about whether he should open them or leave them for his son. Since this is a family *bodega* the attics, traditionally used to store grain, are used as junk rooms. Horse-drawn carriages moulder and decay in one corner. In another large room, there is a rusting brandy still, which, I am assured, could work again and must not, therefore, be dismantled. In a courtyard, a huge water pump still produces water after much heaving by the foreman. In the oldest *bodega*, formerly part of a monastery, there are more relics of the past. Photographs of well-scrubbed schoolchildren line one wall, souvenirs of Don Miguel's education at a school in Bath, to which some 25 years later he sent his son. This explains his almost-too-perfect but idiomatic English.

This *bodega* was the first to be used by Valdespino when the firm went into commercial sherry production in 1740. It is full of tiny little corners where a few "special" barrels gather dust, apparently neglected, though never forgotten. Most sherry *bodegas* are quiet retreats from the world, but this is truly remote; the main courtyard boasts a huge table and some dilapidated chairs that might have served for Rip van Winkle's farewell party. Stand still, and you could be in the heart of the country. Back in the main *bodega*, which was bought by the firm in the 19th century, the chink of the bottling line and the wink of computers remind us that this is the late 20th century.

Valdespino has three *bodegas* in Jerez itself – this one, the old monastery and the press-house across the road – as well as a fourth on the road to the airport, bought for extra storage in 1971. Down towards the sea at Sanlúcar de Barrameda are two more *bodegas* for maturing that town's dry sherries, the *manzanillas*. Sanlúcar is where Don Miguel spends the five hot summer months each year with his family. The small town is cooler than Jerez, and he prefers its slower pace to the frenetic commerce of the city; from there, he can easily drive to his Jerez office each day.

Visitors to Jerez, especially those from northern Europe, are struck by the unusual pattern of the working day. Like all the other sherry *bodegas*, Valdespino opens at seven am, and everybody – from Don Miguel down – works right through until three o'clock in the afternoon, when the whole place closes for the day. Those used to eating around noon would find the extra hours before lunch difficult were it not for the succession of glasses of *fino* sherry and tiny morsels of food (called *tapas*) that find their way in front of you as you sit discussing the sherry world.

This time, though, we have not lingered over *tapas*, as the *bodega* tour has taken us right through to lunchtime. Instead, we go to La Mesa Redonda ("the round table"), a restaurant in Jerez run by Don Miguel's sister. It is time for a *copita* of Valdespino Inocente in its finished state, the perfect antidote to the heat and the white glare outside.

Talk naturally turns to the wine we are drinking and how it is made. Flagship wine it may be, but only 120,000 bottles are produced each year. Valdespino follows the old-fashioned system of classifying the new wine according to its potential. A wine that is destined to become *fino* (or, later, an *amontillado* such as Valdespino's Tio Diego) will show a propensity to develop the yeasty *flor* covering, and the barrel will be marked as such with a strange hieroglyphic. Those that are regarded as unlikely to develop *flor* will be heavily fortified with brandy; these are destined to become *oloroso*, the richer style of sherry. Unlike some sherry houses, there is no suggestion at Valdespino that wines will be "encouraged" to turn into *fino* to meet high demand.

Traditional production is expensive, especially if you don't cut corners, and yet sherry – even Valdespino sherry – is still absurdly under-priced in a market that tends to regard it as a cheap commodity, rather than a great wine. This concerns Don Miguel: he believes that years of cheap sherry have devalued the wine in the public's eye. "It is going to be very difficult in the short term to get a realistic price for sherry. We sell one sherry at £16, but that's 100 years old, so I suppose that is really under-priced as well. In fact, the rarer the sherry, the more ridiculously cheap it is." It helps, perhaps, if your company is both small and family-owned, with no money owing to the banks. Don Miguel believes that the wine trade is one of the few areas of business in which it is still possible for small companies to survive and prosper – "as long as they are quality-conscious".

During the meal we drink red Reserva Rioja, but at the end we return to local produce for a glass of Alfonso, the 25-year-old Valdespino brandy; it is lighter than some of the heavily caramelized versions, and elegantly sophisticated. Unlike many Jerez *bodegas*, for which brandy provides the profits to continue making sherry, Valdespino produces only small quantities.

By now, of course, it is five o'clock. In accordance with Don Miguel's normal after-lunch practice, we then visit the vineyards. The company owns 380 acres (154 hectares) of land, most of it in the Macharnudo region, and the Valdespino family another 370 acres (150 hectares). Indeed, so well established is Valdespino as a landowner here that some maps don't give place names, but simply call vineyards after their Valdespino owners.

It is the end of the harvest. A motley collection of workers are driving around the edge of the vineyard picking up the small plastic boxes of grapes that will go off to the Valdespino *bodega* only ten minutes down the road. Don Miguel is trying to increase *fino* production in the vineyards by planting clones that have a propensity to develop *flor* at fermentation. A deaf-mute, employed by Don Miguel, guards the vineyards – a reminder, even in the midst of these new developments, of the old-family, almost feudal side to Valdespino.

This feeling of age permeates Valdespino. It is hardly surprising: here, after all, is a family that has been established in Jerez for over 600 years. But such permanence does not necessarily lead to great wines. The secret of greatness in wine lies in the affection and care lavished on its production as much as anything else, and Valdespino has both.

On the yellow sandy floor of Don Miguel's *sacristia*, the holy of holies just behind his office, I am offered a glass of superb *palo cortado*, the style of sherry half-way between *amontillado* and *oloroso*. This is followed by a dry *amontillado*, the true "medium" sherry, with its nutty taste and the acidity that comes from an old wine. Here is winemaking of the highest order – the essence of great sherry. But it is not just Miguel Valdespino who deserves congratulation. In accordance with Jerez tradition, the wine comes from a *solera* started way back in the 19th century, to which wine has been added year after year, but which still retains a minute quantity of the original wine. So my congratulations are owed to Valdespino as a family. If this is tradition, long may it flourish.

The chalky albarize soil reflects summer heat onto the low-trained vines.

Portugal

PORTUGAL IS ONE OF THE MOST unsophisticated, intriguing and paradoxical of wine countries. The very concept of controlled *appellation* areas was Portuguese, pioneered as long ago as the mid-18th century when the Douro, home of port, was demarcated by the Marques de Pombal. Yet as recently as 1986, when Portugal joined the EEC, there were still only ten *Regiãos Demarcadas*, or RDs. (At the other extreme the Italians, with unseemly haste, have managed to create hundreds of *Denominaziones di Origine Controllatas*, their equivalent, in under three decades.)

Everywhere the atmosphere is heavy with tradition. But little by little modern ideas and equipment are being introduced, so that the new and the old tend to rub shoulders in curious alliance. In the 1980s the major port houses all invested substantially in advanced technology, in the form of autovinificators to press and ferment their grapes. Yet treading by the primitive, labour-intensive (and therefore expensive) human foot is still favoured by some producers on their finest estates – foremost among them the remarkable Quinta de Vargellas of Taylor, Fladgate & Yeatman.

In the large Vinho Verde region in the north, vines are trained picturesquely up trees and high pergolas – with cabbages, a staple of the Portuguese diet, growing in the shade below the thick, leafy canopy. In other regions, notably the arid expanse of the Alentejo in the south, you can still find wines fermenting in tall clay amphorae, even though stainless steel may glisten in the background. Then again, on the distant Portuguese island of Madeira, the wines are literally cooked, as they have been since the last century, to produce their unique tangy flavour.

Above all, though, what makes Portugal so fascinating in the 1990s is its abundance of idiosyncratic indigenous grape varieties whose potential has scarcely begun to be realized. A smattering of Cabernet Sauvignon and Chardonnay is used to good effect in a tiny handful of wines, but most wines – whether they be historic fortified ports or Madeiras, light commercial pinks, Vinhos Verdes or muscular reds – are made from varieties that no other country grows, and which Portugal is only just beginning to identify and fully appreciate itself. There is enormous potential, not only because the raw material is so unusual but because Portugal is the seventh-largest wine-producing country in the world.

Late September high in the Douro, and Quinta de Vargellas' rich blue-black harvest is ready for the press-house. The best fruit from these vineyards provides the backbone for Taylor's Vintage Port.

PORT

Alistair Robertson of Taylor, Fladgate & Yeatman

Taylor's is the great name of port, and Quinta de Vargellas is its finest estate, but if Alistair Robertson had not agreed to return from England to the country of his birth and take up the reins of the family business in 1967, who knows what might have happened? As it is, writes *Joanna Simon*, Taylor, Fladgate & Yeatman has gone from strength to strength under his leadership and the whole of the port trade has benefited from his vision.

Watching Alistair Robertson dispensing white port and *bonhomie* in equally generous measures high above the River Douro on the terrace of Quinta de Vargellas, it is hard to imagine him saying, a quarter of a century ago, that he never wanted to live in Portugal and work in the port trade. But then it is easy to be seduced by the Douro, the most ruggedly beautiful of rivers. And it is even easier to be thus seduced at Quinta de Vargellas, low, white and glistening in the sun, pinned to the steeply terraced valley sides and surrounded by vines, olives, almonds, vines and yet more vines, with a tiny railway station – Vargellas' own – in the valley below.

Indeed it is all too easy to assume that Vargellas is, and was always, such a paradise. But the reality is somewhat different. It is one of the most remote of *quintas* (literally "farms"), lying high in the upper reaches of the Douro, only 25 miles (40 kilometres) before the river meets the Spanish border and becomes the Duero. The region can be harsh and inhospitable. The terrain is relentlessly hard schist which has to be bulldozed and pickaxed into submission before vines can even be planted, and the climate swings between extremes – baking heat in summer and freezing cold in winter. There are no nearby towns or hamlets, and until a few years ago there were no roads within easy reach, no electricity. Even now, the four-hour train journey from Oporto (where the shippers are based and most port is matured) on the primitive single-gauge railway is preferable to driving to Vargellas, such is the still more primitive quality of many of the roads.

Yet these were really only cosmetic details, compared with the picture of life in the port trade that presented itself to Alistair Robertson in the 1960s. To say that Vargellas was the least of his concerns is not to belittle the estate whose grapes have provided the "backbone" of Taylor's vintage ports for at least 80 years and whose wines, in the years when a Taylor's vintage is not declared, have long been bottled as a single-estate ("single *quinta*") port under the Vargellas label. (As far back as 1828 letters record sales of Vargellas

Alistair and Gillyanne Robertson of Taylors with samples of the Douro's other harvest. Produce from the Vargellas gardens helps stock the kitchens of the hospitable Quinta.

port in London.) But, in the 1960s, the port business was in the doldrums, having never recovered from the decline in the consumption of port-and-lemon as a staple of English pubs which had set in around 1940. Top-quality vintage ports were simply not sought after as they are today and centuries-old British-owned shippers were selling up in droves.

In spite of never wanting to live in Portugal, in spite of the fact that the attractions of the port trade were notable only for their dearth, in spite of the fact that he liked England, had been educated and married there, had established himself successfully in the British wine trade, and by this time had a young family – Alistair Robertson did return to the country and the port company of his birth. On April 1st 1967, at the age of only 29, he took over the running of Taylor, Fladgate & Yeatman (together with Fonseca Guimaraens, which Taylor's had bought in 1948). And neither he nor his wife Gillyanne (who arrived in Portugal pregnant, with two very young children) has regretted the move since.

Perhaps it was the abruptness and the unexpectedness of the move that helped to reduce the agony of making the decision. Alistair's uncle, Dick Yeatman, the sole shareholder who had been running Taylor's for many years, died suddenly in 1966. He had no children and his wife Beryl, finding that she could not manage the firm alone, simply told her nephew that unless he was prepared to come out to Oporto and take over she would have to sell, just as the other British firms were doing. Faced with this ultimatum, Alistair says, "we came to have a go rather than see it sold. We gave ourselves two years to turn it round: it was losing money. Two years was very naive." He pauses – not for effect, but because, behind the relaxed *bonhomie*, the sense of humour, the dashing looks, he is unerringly modest, even slightly diffident – and continues breezily, as though it were hardly worth mentioning, "We made a profit of £10,000 in the first year".

And it is always "we", whether the "we" is Gillyanne, fellow Taylor's partners Huyshe Bower and Bruce Guimaraens, or other members of staff. Yet, as managing director for the last 23 years, it is to Alistair that credit is due for turning the company around and ensuring that Taylor's has remained the foremost name in port. Far more than that, though, he deserves credit for helping to revitalize and reverse the fortunes of the port industry as a whole. Inevitably he makes no such claims for himself, but he does admit to being "very optimistic about the port trade today, because the emphasis is on quality, and people see it as a first-class wine" – a far cry from 1967 when port, he says unequivocally, "was doing terribly badly".

Perhaps Alistair's greatest contribution has been in marketing. Looked at from the perspective of the 1990s, this may sound like the bland, unromantic side of the business in the context of a region as glorious as the Douro and a product as fine as port, but it was both revolutionary and desperately needed in Oporto during the late 1960s and early 1970s. Coming to Portugal from the British wine and brewery trade was a help, for he had experienced the trade from the other side and knew the difficulties faced by those on the receiving end of the multitude of flowery but uninformative names splashed about by the shippers. One of his first moves, therefore, was to sift through the names Taylor's used and throw most of them out. Lovely though the Viceroys, Emperors, Tridents, et cetera sounded, Alistair knew they confused the hotel and restaurant trade – not to mention the consumer. Instead, he went for indications of age on labels, convinced that this was the only logical way to differentiate and draw attention to the various types of port.

He replaced Taylor's "Vintage Reserve", which carried no date, with the now-famous Late-Bottled Vintage (LBV) which does bear a date. He also changed the style of the port from one that threw a crust in bottle and therefore needed decanting to one that is aged longer in cask (five years), is ready for drinking when released for sale and does not need decanting because of the way it is filtered. The relatively light style of LBV has been criticized by other shippers and commentators, as has the nomenclature itself (with its use of the word vintage in conjunction with the year of the vintage, as though it were true vintage port), but there can be no doubt that consumers have taken to Taylor's LBV: it has been a huge success, and copied by almost every other major shipper.

At around the same time Alistair introduced statements of age on Taylor's old tawny ports – ten-year-old, 20-year-old, and so on. The age given is an average, because tawny ports such as these are matured entirely in cask and the casks are topped up and blended together as the port slowly evaporates over the years. (Cheap undated tawnies are another thing altogether: young ruby and white port blended together, with none of the mellow, nutty character of a proper wood-matured tawny.) More recently, Taylor's has reverted to undated port with the introduction of First Estate, which Alistair describes as "a first-class, big, old-fashioned ruby" of the type that was popular in the 1920s and 1930s.

In contrast to his highly-trained and talented winemaking uncle, Alistair also has an instinct for business: "Dick loved his port and his vineyards. He was trained at Montpellier – very unusual in those days. But he was rather reluctant to sell the stuff, that was the difficult thing." Most of the port Dick Yeatman made was sold in bulk to merchants. Taylor's did not even have a bottling line when Alistair arrived – just an old woman with a piece of string round her toe to wind around the tops of the bottles. Now Taylor's bottles most of the port it produces under its own name in Oporto.

To present Alistair Robertson merely as some kind of marketing ace and businessman, however, would be to give a distorted picture. You have only to see Alistair at Vargellas to know that he, too, loves his port and his vineyards. And in recent years, having sorted out the labelling, bottling, styles and identities to produce a coherent (but by no means

*New vines high above the Quinta: the most recent terraces are built by bulldozer and
have earth banks rather than the traditional stone retaining walls.*

unchanging) range of ports, he has allowed himself more time to concentrate on the
vineyards and the vines – something of which Dick would certainly have approved.

As a result of his stint in France, Dick Yeatman took a great interest in grape varieties
and conducted innovative experiments with individual pipes – the traditional 117.5-gallon
(534-litre) barrels – of single-variety ports before the war. But he was an exception. Many
shippers owned an odd *quinta* here and there, but they were not farmers at heart and took no
more interest in the particularity of the vines their managers were cultivating on their own
quintas than they did in the farms from which they bought grapes. This was not an
abnegation of duty. It was simply that they did not recognize the intrinsic character of
individual varieties, except in so far as yields were concerned. They thought that, as long as
they had a good mix in the vineyards, it would ensure the best possible yield year-in, year-
out and, equally, that it would produce a good mix in the final wine.

Port is, after all, a blended wine, whether from a single year and a single *quinta* (Quinta de
Vargellas 1978, for example), or from a blend of years and vineyards (such as old tawny or
crusted port). In fact, the regulations forbid a single-variety port and it is, says Alistair,
"the last thing any of us wants". What Taylor's and other shippers do want nowadays is to

The bowl-shaped contours of the Vargellas estate. New planting here is in single-variety batches.

know what they have in their vineyards. Thanks to Dick Yeatman, Taylor's has a slight head-start in parts of Vargellas, but in general it is difficult and seldom worth anyone's while trying to identify the higgledy-piggledy mass of varieties in the old vineyards. Instead they concentrate on areas being replanted and on new vineyards (of which there have been a lot in the last decade, as the demand for port has increased and grants have been made available). Most concentrate on five or six varieties which, instead of being planted in the previous anonymous jumble, are laid out in batches – just as they would be in any region in the world producing quality wine.

In fact, Alistair is fond of saying that production in the Douro is like winemaking all over Europe. "The difference is that now, here, we measure and control and try to do things more efficiently than we used to." Yet, while the main principles of modern winemaking certainly do apply – fermenting ripe, healthy grapes in a clean, bacteria-free environment under controlled temperatures – one cannot deny the idiosyncrasies of port. Fundamental differences in raw material and procedure make it a quintessentially different kind of wine.

The difference begins with the vineyards themselves. Although all of Vargellas is graded "A", the top grade in the official classification of port vineyards, some vineyards are more equal than others. The best at Vargellas, as Alistair points out, are not the south-east-facing slopes favoured by European convention, but, because of the heat in the upper Douro, those that face north. Then there is the very stuff of the terrain: anyone planting in the Douro has to go to extraordinary lengths to prepare the "soil" – or rather the absence of it – for vine roots to penetrate. Originally the rock was blasted open with dynamite; nowadays bulldozers, pickaxes and muscle-power are usually sufficient to take over where dynamite left off. Terraces also have to be constructed. These used to be so narrow that they often took only a single file of vines, and they were held up by dry stone walls. Now, so that mechanization can be brought into play where possible, the terraces at Quinta de Vargellas are two to four rows wide and there are no stone walls. There are also wider, gently sloping terraces, but these cannot always be worked mechanically and they are harder to keep free of weeds and disease.

In the mid-1980s "up-and-down" (vertical) planting arrived, but it is too soon to know what the long-term effects may be. Certainly there are fears that nutrients may be leached to the bottom of the slope and that in very dry summers, such as 1989, evaporation could be a problem. Certainly Alistair Robertson is cautious about the experimental up-and-down planting at Vargellas, although he thinks it may prove its worth on shallower inclines where tractors can be used.

The port grape varieties themselves are very individual, which in large part explains why "ports" made elsewhere – notably in Australia and California – may be very good fortified wines but don't fool anyone. Taylor's concentrates on five: Touriga Nacional, universally considered the finest port grape, although unpopular with farmers because it is a niggardly producer; Touriga Francesa, an intensely scented, slightly lighter variety, which Dick clearly liked, but to which no special emphasis is given today; Tinta Roriz, the Tempranillo of Rioja and the only classic port grape well-known outside the Douro; Tinto Cão, another low yielder and one that gives complexity and ageing potential to a blend; and Tinta Barroca, a "new variety" (only cultivated in the Douro for about 100 years) which is robust as a plant and as a wine.

There is nothing remarkable about the picking of the vines: it is done by hand, and more attention is paid to the peak-ripeness of individual parcels than used to be. But once inside the winery more peculiarities emerge. True, the vast majority of port is no longer trodden, but there is, Alistair senses, a slight swing back in favour of the human foot. "In the mid- to late 1970s it seemed as though autovinification was the way forward and we'd see the end of treading; it's very expensive. But we were very conservative here. It's not just done for show, although it would be a shame to lose it because it's such fun: it gives better colour and concentration, and in blind tastings it just has the edge – it gives more interesting, subtle results." Maximum colour and concentration are key ingredients of vintage port (the sort of port made at Vargellas whether for a Taylor's declaration or a Quinta de Vargellas), because it needs power to be able to age. But for lesser qualities which will be drunk sooner, less depth is needed, so down-river at Taylor's Salguieral winery, all the wine is fermented in modern autovinification tanks.

Whichever method is used, all port is fortified with grape spirit before it has fermented fully. This stops fermentation dead and keeps the wine sweet, but increases its alcohol to almost double that of most table wines. In the spring following the harvest, port's curious life-cycle involves it in a journey of 150 miles (240 kilometres) or so, depending on where exactly the *quinta* or winery is situated. This is the move down to the shippers' maturation "lodges" in the town of Vila Nova de Gaia, opposite Oporto at the mouth of the Douro. (The regulations have now changed so that it is perfectly legal to mature port in the Douro, but, with the exception of Quinta do Noval, none of the top shippers has taken the plunge, for fear that it will cause "Douro bake", a slightly alarming-sounding affliction which simply means a cooked or burnt taste resulting from excessive heat.)

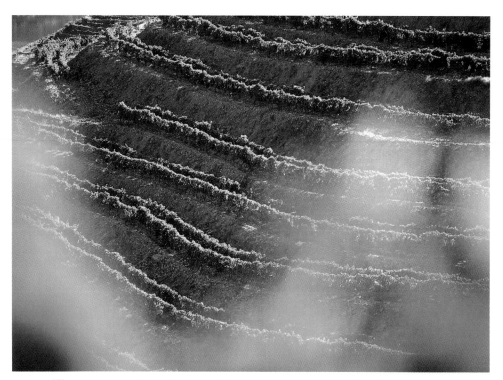

The amount of earth-moving involved in creating new terraces at Vargellas is awesome.

Once in the lodges, the ageing is as eccentric as any: port may rest in the lodges in cask for many years (tawny), or it may be bottled after only two years (vintage) – only to continue its maturation behind glass, which does not breathe, rather than wood, which does. Just to keep the variables going to the last, a shipper releases his main vintage port soon after it has been bottled, so either the wine merchant or the consumer must lay it down for many more years before it is ready (a minimum of ten years from the harvest, and more often 15-20). But he releases his single *quinta* port (such as Vargellas) only when it is ready for drinking, usually at around ten years old.

With so many styles of port, and given the numerous ports that each shipper has ready for drinking at the same time, it is a wonder that any of them can ever decide what to drink. "Oh it's simple," says Alistair: "When we're in Oporto we always drink Taylor's vintages and when we're up here [at Vargellas], we drink Vargellas. I love the 1965, closely followed by the 1967. The 1967 is a more classic vintage-type [interestingly, it was his first vintage]; the 1965 is less classic, but more flowery, more fun. The 1976 is drinking very well now: it's easier and has come round quickly – less flowery, but attractive.

"Vargellas always comes round more quickly – it's lovely at ten or 12 years – but then it goes on a long time. It has a floweriness, a lightness. But it's a funny wine because it has the backbone and can have quite a lot of tannin. Taylor's vintages need the extra time. They have a hardness which has to soften."

So what about Terra Feita, Taylor's other *quinta*, a little further down the Douro, which in a few years' time will be bottled as another single *quinta* vintage port? "Oh that's chunkier, bigger, firmer, fruitier," Alistair says, excited at the prospect of yet another new baby. Ah, but where will they drink it? Perhaps Gillyanne will simply have to turn another run-down farm into the epitome of an English country house, just like Quinta de Vargellas? At this his eyes light up.

MADEIRA

Richard Blandy of Blandy's

Cooked in special ovens to give it the characteristic burnt tang that so shocks beginners and so pleases *aficionados*, Madeira is one of the world's most extraordinary wines. As such, it is hardly surprising that its unusual style was developed during the 19th century more by accident than by design. Richard Blandy's ancestors have been making wine on the Atlantic island of Madeira since that time and he now plays a leading role in both the family firm and the industry as a whole. ***Margaret Rand*** tells the story.

The Blandys have been making Madeira on the island of the same name since 1811, yet Richard Blandy, the current chairman, did not start to drink Madeira until he was 20 or so and living in Scotland. It was certainly available at home – "my mother was French and my parents had a very liberal attitude to introducing us to wine" – but the young Blandy was simply not tempted. "Madeira," he now says, "is not a beginner's wine."

It is true that appreciation of the tangy, burnt flavour characteristic of Madeira is unlikely to be immediate. One who is not already familiar with the range of tastes that grapes can produce is unlikely at first to be quite ready for the distinctive taste. The wine tastes burnt because it is, literally, cooked, being gently heated to 113°F (45°C) in ovens known as *estufas*. It is the only wine in the world to be made this way: a modern winemaker would never in his wildest dreams invent such a method. The process has evolved as a substitute for an almost accidental set of circumstances which reshaped the original wine.

At the beginning of the 19th century, the British in India were beginning to provide an excellent market for Madeira. The producers were quick to respond and it was not long before almost half the island's shipments were crossing the Equator, rounding the Cape and crossing the Equator again to take their cargo to the East Indies as well as the West. The wines, relatively light in their natural state, were fortified with brandy for the long voyage, but it could take six months or more, during which the wine was subjected to the constant rolling motion and stifling Equatorial heat in the ships' holds.

Incredibly, such irreverent treatment did not reduce the wine to an undrinkable stew and instead gave it its familiar piquant edge. Now that the sailing ships are gone, the wine has to acquire the effects of those long, hot journeys without actually moving from dry land, and it does this in the *estufas*. These are built in the wineries (or *loges*) themselves, situated in the capital of Madeira, Funchal.

Sercial 1870, a rare treasure indeed. Only 13 vintages of Madeira have been shipped from the Atlantic island since the last century.

Unlike most of the world's wine-producing areas, on the island of Madeira you either own land and grow grapes (and probably bananas and other crops as well) or you buy grapes and make and ship wine. Most of the shippers own a few vineyards, but these holdings are small and supply only a tiny proportion of their needs. So, come the vintage, truck-loads of grapes arrive in the wineries, ready to be selected and bought.

The shippers hope that as high a proportion as possible of these trucks will contain the classic Madeira varieties – Sercial, Verdelho, Bual and Malmsey. These varieties have lent their names to the four types of Madeira wine: Sercial is the driest; Verdelho is the next-driest; Bual is fairly sweet; and Malmsey is a distinctly sweet after-dinner wine. But in many vineyards the classics have been replaced by the easier-to-grow, but far less exciting, Tinta Negra Mole. Blandy's uses this grape mostly in its Dukes range: Duke of Sussex Sercial, Duke of Cambridge Verdelho, Duke of Cumberland Bual and Duke of Clarence Malmsey. These wines contain a proportion of the noble varieties, but vintage wines, Special Reserves and Reserves are all made from at least 80 per cent of the original strain.

It is common practice to use Tinta Negra Mole as a supplement because, says Blandy, "we don't have enough of the noble varieties to go round. Their availability varies enormously from year to year. Sercial grows high up in the hills, and the harvest depends on the climate. The 1989 crop, for example, was 20-30 per cent down because of mists and rain. But Verdelho is quite a popular grape among the farmers, and grows fairly well locally. Bual is grown mainly in the south and there is plenty of it; the same is true of Malmsey."

One of the problems faced by the shippers, however, is that the easiest of all grapes to grow in Madeira are the dreaded hybrids. These are crosses between European and American varieties, and the grapes they produce are not permitted in any wine calling itself Madeira. They often share vineyard space with pure American strains, known as

The Blandys have been making wine on Madeira since 1811. Richard Blandy, the current chairman,
is determined not to allow the family business "to lose its roots".

"Americano" in Madeira. Their taste – even their smell – is utterly different from that of
any European wine grape. Ripe Americano grapes have a heady May blossom scent, and
this carries through into the wine. Its wine is sold on the island: it is cheap and has no
official designation, but it is pleasant to drink, with a taste much like alcoholic fruit juice.

There are even more complicated issues at stake in the definition of a Madeira than the
grape variety, however. One such debate in which Blandy's has taken a lively part is that
concerning the wines' stated age. The *solera* system, by which a certain amount of wine is
drawn from a cask for bottling, and then topped up with younger wine, is the system used
for ageing sherry in Spain; it used also to be widespread in Madeira. Here, though, says
Blandy, "the *solera* system was used and abused so much that we abandoned it. I believe that
you have to be honest with yourself and with the consumer: I see nothing to be gained by
selling a *solera* wine with a date from the last century on the label. We felt it was more honest
to call our wines Reserves instead."

So now the age attributed to Blandys' Reserves is the age of the youngest drop of wine in
the bottle, as is the case with Scotch whisky. A "ten-year-old" Madeira, for example, will
contain ten-year-old wines, some older and some considerably older, but none younger
than ten. "This definition was our choice," says Blandy, "and was adopted by the Madeira
Wine Institute. It was fairly controversial at the time, because some shippers thought that
the age on the label should refer to the average age of the wine", as indeed is the case with
port. The reason why a decision of Blandys' should carry such weight is that the company is
not just a shipper with its own wines, but also forms the greater part of the Madeira Wine
Company, an association of shippers formed originally so that they could show a united
face, while maintaining their independence within the association.

In 1913, when Madeira's wine industry had been hit first by oidium and then by
phylloxera, two vine diseases which between them almost succeeded in wiping fine wines

off the Madeiran map, there was a deep recession. The wine shippers formed the Madeira Wine Association, an umbrella company under which they could buy grapes at vintage time and vinify and store their wines, while still allowing their member companies to retain their own links with the trade and, crucially, maintain their own individual style and flavour. Blandys' style can be summed up as elegant: full of concentration but clean-tasting and well-balanced, but Blandys' Bual does not, and should not, taste the same as, say, Cossart Gordon's Bual, any more than the claret from Château X should taste the same as that of its Bordelais neighbour, Château Y. The purpose of the Association was to enable the shippers who bought the grapes to present a united front to those who grew them, and to control the running of the trade.

The Portuguese Revolution was in 1974, and Richard Blandy had moved to Madeira in 1972, following some years working as an accountant in London. "I went to work at Blandy Bros then," he says, "in order to have a couple of years working for my father before he retired." But he admits that he has often wondered why he chose that particular side of the company – located on the island – at such a difficult time. "It needed to be done, I suppose. It would have been awful to allow a family business to lose its roots, so I slightly perversely decided to take it on. I don't regret it for a moment."

There are, its seems, great advantages to living on the beautiful island, and Richard Blandy now considers himself a confirmed Madeiran. Even at the height of the revolution, he says, he never seriously contemplated leaving. "We avoided the worst excesses here. There were no mass arrests without warrants, and no major expropriations. Blandy's was under the eye of those who held power, but we continued to run the company, nobody left the island, and we had a clean set of books. They balked at expropriating companies simply because they were foreign, although at one stage it was a possibility. We were a big fish in a small pond and, having been there since 1811, neither my cousin Adam (who was chairman) nor I could see any reason not to stay."

Nevertheless, the old arrangement of the Madeira Wine Association did have to change. As things stood Blandy's owned 33 per cent of the MWA, Leacocks owned 33 per cent and the remaining shares were distributed among the other shippers. For the sake of expediency in dealing with the industry's difficulties, one of the major shareholders needed to be in firm control. So Blandy bought the Leacock shares in the Association, which eventually changed its name to the Madeira Wine Company. From 1988 the Symington group of port shippers (which owns such names as Dow's, Graham's and Warre's) accumulated a 45 per cent share in the Madeira Wine Company, but it still operates in the same way, with Blandys' wines retaining their name and style, just as Leacocks, Cossart Gordon and the rest retain theirs.

So, having ridden the storm, will Richard Blandy be the last of the family to run the company? "My brother and I are both in Blandy's," he explains, "and I am chairman, though not full-time, of the MWC. According to tradition a family member gets as far in the company as his abilities allow him, but no further." So it is up to Richard's son Andrew, who is just 12, but "loves to shove his nose in a glass and pronounce on the merits of a wine. I don't think he actually likes it, though. He thinks it terribly funny that people drink it." But then he is, after all, only a beginner, and like his father, it may take him another decade to appreciate fully that Madeira is not a beginner's wine.

THE ALENTEJO

Domingos Soares Franco of J S Rosado Fernandes

Glistening stainless steel and fast-moving modern machinery form an incongruous-looking alliance with the traditional Portuguese amphorae and stone *lagares* at the J S Rosado Fernandes *adego* in the Alentejo, but this mingling of old and new is at the very heart of the operation. Domingos Soares Franco, trained in the latest wine techniques of California, but wedded to the unique flavours of Portugal's indigenous grapes, is the guiding light of the company, as **Charles Metcalfe** explains.

There can be few better examples of winemaking going back to its roots than the small *adega* of J S Rosado Fernandes in the Alentejo region to the south-east of Lisbon. Walking into the cool of the winery off the sizzling streets of Reguengos de Monsaraz, you glimpse shadowy *lagares*, open stone troughs in which Portuguese grapes have been fermented for as long as wine has been made here, and the dim shapes of huge clay amphorae in serried ranks. It is only when you see the gleaming stainless steel tanks and modern grape-crushing and de-stemming machines that you realize you are standing in anything other than a very primitive winery. Otherwise, the Rosado Fernandes *adega* is typical of many throughout the Alentejo.

Then you meet Domingos Soares Franco, the guiding light behind the *adega* and its wines. Senhor Soares Franco is clearly no backward son of the soil, but an articulate and informed winemaker. His faintly American accent was acquired in California, at the university's renowned winemaking school at Davis where he completed his formal training. So what is a technically qualified winemaker like Domingos Soares Franco doing making wines in a place like this? And why the mixture of old and new winemaking equipment at the *adega*?

Domingos Soares Franco and his brother Antonio are the latest of several generations who have worked for the family wine firm, José Maria da Fonseca Successores. It was started in 1834 by José Maria da Fonseca, who came to manage his family's estates at Azeitão, just south of Lisbon across the Tagus estuary. Fascinated by the winemaking side of the business, he devoted himself to improving the quality of the wines from the family vineyards. At a time when almost all wine was exported in barrel, Fonseca was so sure of his own wines' superiority that he insisted on exporting them in bottle, a relatively expensive form of container in the mid-19th century. He also pioneered the planting of specific grape varieties (whether native Portuguese or imported from France), and was one of the first wine producers in the area to use ploughs to cultivate his vineyards. In the 1850s, he installed bottle-filling machinery, imported from France and Britain as it was not available in Portugal. The new technology, which enabled him to fill 1,800 bottles of wine a day, prompted articles in newspapers. Nowadays, the company has a bottling line capable of processing 6,000 bottles an *hour*.

Fonseca's wines were exported world-wide – from London to Leningrad, San Francisco to Singapore and Berlin to Buenos Aires. After his death, the running of the company passed through other branches of the family until, in 1912, Antonio Soares Franco Junior took over and a new era of expansion began. He started to deal in wines from other regions, as well as the company's own Moscatel de Setúbal and red wine from Palmela. The firm's reputation grew through succeeding generations and by the mid-1980s the family were looking for something else to buy. José Maria da Fonseca was acknowledged to be one of

Traditional clay amphorae, discarded elsewhere in favour of more modern fermentation vessels, line the walls of the cool adega.

Portugal's leading wine producers, its reputation chiefly established by various brands of red wine such as Pasmados, Periquita and Camarate, and by Moscatel de Setúbal.

That is where the estate of J S Rosado Fernandes came in. José de Sousa Rosado Fernandes founded his winery at Reguengos de Monsaraz in the 1880s. Reguengos was already reputed to be one of the best wine areas in the Alentejo, and the fame of the Rosado Fernandes winery was firmly established in the period between 1940 and 1970. In 1976, the owner died and the property passed to his wife's family, who, not wanting the responsibility of running a fine wine estate, resolved to sell it to the people best capable of upholding its leading reputation.

When the 150-acre (60-hectare) estate and its winery were offered to the Soares Franco family, they "nearly died of surprise", as Domingos Soares Franco puts it. It was exactly the kind of investment they wanted to make, and they accepted in May 1986. Faced with the choice between ripping out all the old equipment and turning the winery into a high-tech slice of California, or preserving the picturesque *adega* as it was, they decided to take the traditional path. Having bought one of the few table wine estates in the country with an outstanding reputation – the Portuguese equivalent of a Bordeaux first growth – they wanted to see if they could recreate the kind of red wines that had made it famous 50 years ago. Even though Domingos Soares Franco was equipped with all sorts of technical expertise, he resolved to make the wines with a minimum of modern paraphernalia. Senhor Arlindo, who had made the wines at the *adega* for 30 years, stayed on to advise on the traditional methods.

Domingos Soares Franco set about re-equipping the winery along traditional lines. The old stone *lagares* were still there, but the *adega* was short of the large clay amphorae for fermenting the wines. Throughout the region, people were discarding their amphorae in favour of more modern fermentation vessels, and as there were no new ones to be had he started to buy them second-hand. At first the price was a reasonable 500 escudos, but when word got round the asking price shot up, and he soon found himself having to pay up to 50 times as much for an amphora.

In 1986, the first vintage under new ownership, half the grapes were wiped out by a late frost. The rest, however, were excellent, so he decided to take an ultra-traditional approach and make a *garrafeira* with the resulting wine. By law, a *garrafeira* is a wine considered outstanding by the winemaker, which is aged for two years before bottling and a further year prior to sale. The grapes were trodden in small *lagares* for a few hours, together with some of the stalks, and then removed to the clay amphorae for fermentation. After fermentation, about one-tenth of the wine was aged in new oak barrels. Traditionally, it would have been aged in old oak barrels or vats; the hint of new oak was Soares Franco's dash of 20th-century character. The result is powerful, very tannic red wine, with a tremendous concentration of dark, minty, almost tarry fruit which will take years to come round, and will probably not be released until 1992.

The process of fermentation in narrow-necked clay amphorae is not without problems. One such problem is preventing the wine from overheating during fermentation. This was achieved by the simple expedient of spraying cold water onto the clay pots. The inside of each amphora is sealed with a natural resin (which gives the wine an almost imperceptible hint of pine) so the water soaks the outside of the pot without penetrating as far as the wine. As the fermenting wine heats up, the water evaporates from the outside, cooling the amphora – and the wine inside. The build-up of gas presents another problem. As the juice ferments, all the solid matter such as grape skins, pips and stalks rises to the top of the amphora, where it forms a solid cap. The cap has to be broken up three or four times a day, or else the pressure of the carbon dioxide created by the fermentation inside could cause an explosion. This, in fact, occurred in the middle of the night during the 1987 vintage, when one of the clay amphorae shattered under the pressure of the gas build-up inside.

In 1988, stainless steel tanks were installed to replace the large *lagares* (in which there is no way of cooling the fermentation if it gets out of hand). They were not actually used until the 1989 vintage, as there was enough space in the clay amphorae to ferment the rather small 1988 vintage. But the limited quantity of *garrafeira* made each year still sees no modern machinery except an electric pump to move it from the clay pots into the new oak barrels after fermentation.

The J S Rosado Fernandes wine is already being sold by José Maria da Fonseca from stocks inherited when it bought the property, but the wines available hitherto were made under the previous owners. The wine to look for is the Vinho Tinto Velho 1986, the first vintage made by Domingos Soares Franco – to understand how this cross between 20th-century California science and age-old Portuguese winemaking can really work.

ENGLAND

David Carr Taylor of Carr Taylor Vineyard

The fickle English climate, notwithstanding the possibility of a future "greenhouse effect", is not kind to the country's determined band of vine-growers. Most grape varieties will not even ripen. Yet, as David Carr Taylor has proved in Kent, if the varieties are selected with care, planted in favoured spots and trained in such a way that they are protected from both spring frosts and excessive rain, England can produce wines of a surprisingly distinctive flavour every year. ***Kathryn McWhirter*** describes how.

David Carr Taylor, smilingly brisk and sensible, looks more like the marketing director of a large international company than one of England's most successful winemakers. Ask him why he turned over the 20 acres (eight hectares) surrounding his Kentish family home to vines, installing a winery in the old farm buildings, and his answer sticks firmly along the lines of "creating, pioneering ... the challenge of getting the economics right ... producing the sort of wines the market needs ... bringing my engineering skills to bear on the mechanical handling of grapes ...". No misty images for him of rolling vineyards and dusty cellars, or so it seems. Yet panel after panel of tasters have praised his wines, and in the 1989 English Wine of the Year Competition he scooped two of the three trophies, as well as the only gold medal of the competition, one silver and two bronze awards.

It is no easy matter to produce good, flavoursome, well-balanced wines in the English climate, and it is even harder to make a profit doing so. Carr Taylor Vineyard must be among the most profitable of England's 380 commercial vineyards. At a time in the early 1970s when would-be winemakers were planting vineyards of three to six acres (one to 2.5 hectares) and hoping to make a living from them, David Carr Taylor planned ahead: "In ten years there was no way I'd be surviving on four acres," he explains. "I planted 20 acres straight away, and if I could start again today I'd do it on a bigger scale. After all, you need the same machinery and the same labour for four acres as for 80."

Before planting, David and his wife Linda had their soil tested every 30 yards (27 metres) in a grid pattern to check its suitability for growing vines. Apart from one hopeless patch of solid clay, it proved to be ideal, with thin topsoil but a varied understructure of Hastings iron ore, Tunbridge Wells sandstone and Wadhurst clay. Since money was short, they decided to convert the family farmhouse into luxury flats, which they sold, building a new house for themselves near the old farm buildings, and spending the difference, together

Without the luxury of a foundation in tradition, David Carr Taylor has built up an impressive business with an impressive product – in spite of the vagaries of the English climate.

with income from the family engineering business, on vines and equipment. They were able to economize on the vineyard posts and trellises by buying them second-hand from Guinness' hop-gardens.

There were no savings where the vines were concerned, however. The Carr Taylors went for "the best stock on the market", from the German wine institute of Geisenheim. Germany was the natural source for them as for other English growers, since it, too, has a cool climate. Lying at the very northern limit of vine-growing, southern England must choose its grapes carefully: most varieties would never ripen there. Even Riesling, Germany's finest grape, cannot cope with a traditionally murky English summer. But viticultural institutes such as Geisenheim have developed a whole range of crosses between different varieties, designed to ripen better in cooler climates. It was from these that the Carr Taylors selected their vines, with the advice of Geisenheim's guru Professor Helmut Becker. In 1973 and 1974, they planted seven acres (two hectares) of Reichensteiner and four acres (1.5 hectares) each of Schönburger, Gutenborner and Kerner, with a few odd rows of other varieties.

Carr Taylor Vineyard is not the expanse of trim, neat trellises you might expect. Two great waving canopies of vine branches trail down either side of the widely-spaced rows from five-foot (1.5-metre) wires. To begin with, the Carr Taylors experimented with several different training systems. They finally chose this "Geneva Double Curtain" system, with young buds 4.5 feet (1.4 metres) or more off the ground, because the vines trained this way proved to be unaffected by spring frosts. There are other advantages, too: the open canopy of leaves at the top of the vine gives good exposure to sunlight; the vineyard is cheaper to maintain and cheaper to plant because the vines are so widely spaced;

and the canopy also protects the flowers from the typical bucketing rain of July. Even in the poor summers from 1985 to 1988, when other local vineyards lost much of their crop because the flowers failed to set into fruit, Carr Taylor consistently managed to harvest four tons per acre.

Today, the Carr Taylors' 20 acres are no longer sufficient to cover projected sales. Rather than acquiring more land or buying grapes on the open market, they have persuaded friends and friends of friends to plant up their land with vines on a 12-year contract, providing advice on viticultural techniques and buying the produce. At present, there are 18 of these "satellites", with over 200 acres (80 hectares) under vine. Depending on the soil, they are predominantly planted with the spicy Schönburger, with some Reichensteiner and Würzer; the red grape varieties, Spätburgunder and Müllerrebe (German cool-climate versions of Champagne's Pinot Noir and Pinot Meunier), are also grown to pink up the still and sparkling rosé wines.

Red wines never previously appeared on the Carr Taylor programme, since red grapes seldom ripen properly in Britain. But the hot summer of 1989 was one of the rare occasions when red grapes could ripen, and there will be a red Carr Taylor 1989. The bestselling wines are the medium whites: aromatic Reichensteiner and Gutenborner; "Hastings", a blend of the estate's grapes; and "Sussex County", a blend made from the grapes of 15 or 16 local vineyards. There is also a dry, spicy Schönburger, a Kerner and a Huxelrebe, as well as some very good dry white and rosé sparkling wine, made by the Champagne method.

David Carr Taylor had no formal training in winemaking. He simply read all the textbooks he could lay his hands on and was guided by an English analytical wine chemist. Today he oversees the winemaking, hiring two employees in the cellar for an average vintage – four for the bumper harvest of 1989. He is also an active promoter. One out of every five bottles is sold "over the farm gate", many to the coach-loads of tourists visiting the vineyards in the summer. In recent years, as much as a third of Carr Taylor wine was exported – much of it to France, where it is sold in several supermarkets.

Can English wine compete on an international level? Can an English grower aspire to perfection? "I'm more and more convinced," says Carr Taylor, "that we have some of the finest raw materials. Our grapes don't get the excessive sun to bleach out the fruity flavour. And the spicy, aromatic style is just what the market needs now."

Careful trellising of special vine strains developed at Geisenheim defies even the most unhelpful conditions to produce a consistent harvest.

SWITZERLAND

Château de Trévelin

The golden Chasselas is one of the few grape varieties that is as pleasing to eat fresh as it is to consume in its fermented form. Delicately aromatic, with a gentle *goût de terroir* and a refreshing *pétillance*, it is, writes **Ian Jamieson MW**, one of Switzerland's best-kept secrets. At Château de Trévelin in the foothills of the Jura the grape's natural qualities are brought out by a rigorous restriction on yields and a little judicious irrigation from the Trévelin stream.

Switzerland has long enjoyed a self-imposed isolation, and much of its attraction lies in the feeling you have as you sip your two decilitres of wine by Lake Geneva, that here everything is under control, dependable and unchanging. Since the Congress of Vienna established the country's neutrality in 1815, Swiss winemaking has followed a steady course, supported by a flourishing home market that makes exports not only unnecessary but almost impossible. Now, however, as pressure from the single European market impinges on its island economy, we should expect to see – and taste – more of the delicate, aromatic wines that the Swiss have for so long been keeping to themselves.

One of Switzerland's best-kept secrets is a charming white wine made at the 16th-century Château de Trévelin, in the foothills of the Jura Mountains some 12 miles (19 kilometres) west of Lausanne. The La Côte region in which it is situated bears a noticeable resemblance to that other Côte in Burgundy, both in the layout of the vineyards and in the structure of the local wine trade. In 1959, the château was acquired by Monsieur Agostino Soldati, the Swiss ambassador to Paris, and it is now the home of his daughter, Madame Chamorel. She and her husband Pierre leave the running of the vineyards and the winemaking to Monsieur Brocard of Hammel SA and his son, who trained at the local viticultural college at Changins.

The ripe golden Chasselas grapes grown on the estate produce a fresh, clean-tasting wine gentle in acidity, which gives a slight prickling sensation on the tongue. At the harvest the grape juice usually promises an alcohol level of about ten degrees, which is then raised by a further half degree or so through the addition of a little sugar. Trévelin's aim is to allow the wine to retain the naturally neutral flavour of the grape, enhanced by a *goût de terroir*, an additional flavour from the soil. When so many of the world's producers are trying to make dry wine with high acidity, Château de Trévelin has all the freshness without any of the hard flavour that comes from unripe malic acid: not only *flatteur*, but also very *digestible*.

The clean precision of the Swiss — and of their wines — seems reflected in the regular symmetry of the pretty château and its neat patchwork of vineyards. Lake Geneva, in the middle distance, provides an essential tempering effect on the climate.

It is often suggested that Chasselas should be drunk within two years of the vintage, advice that may encourage a quick turnover but that is not always accurate. The Château de Trévelin 1976 still retained its characteristic *pétillance* in 1989, and even a wine from the 1969 vintage seemed set for a few more years.

Wrought-iron gates lead from an avenue of plane trees into the château courtyard, its walls covered with virginia creepers and punctuated with the herring-bone patterns of shuttered windows. From the courtyard at the rear you pass directly through the house to a large lawn overlooking the sloping vineyards and Lake Geneva in the middle distance. Situated on the edge of the Roman Via Strata, the estate's 13 acres (five hectares) of vineyard pre-date the château itself by perhaps a thousand years. Sadly, details of their origin were lost during an uprising in 1802, when the château's archives were burnt.

The Chasselas grape has been grown in Switzerland since the 18th century, and suits the table as well as it does the wine press. Unrestrained, it will supply up to 150 hectolitres per hectare of grape juice, stretching the wine well beyond its means. To counteract this exuberance and balance the wine, excessive bunches of grapes are removed in early summer, on as many as three separate occasions in some years. Exceptionally, the estate also has permission from the local authorities to irrigate its vineyards from the nearby Trévelin stream after which the château is named. The oldest vines – some of them aged 25 years or so – can look after themselves but, in the hot July of 1989, this special dispensation proved very helpful to the young vines whose roots had not yet had time to reach deep into the sub-soil for moisture. Lake Geneva's tempering effect on the climate is essential: without it, the cultivation of Chasselas here at 1,480 feet (450 metres) above sea level would be virtually impossible.

The press-house is at the far end of the vineyards, a few hundred metres from the château. Here the grapes are crushed, the juice passing from the Vaslin press into vats in the brown-tiled cellar below, where any vineyard dirt is deposited by gravity. After the alcoholic and malolactic fermentations, the wine is transferred to the Hammel cellars at nearby Rolle for its *élevage* until it is ready for bottling.

Château de Trévelin is starting to win prizes in international competitions, where it appears in the category of "Chardonnay and other rich wines". Truth to tell, this wine's strength lies not in the weight and fullness of flavour characteristic of Chardonnay, but in its refreshing, clean-tasting *pétillance* and freshness. Although it may never rank as one of the truly great wines of the world, it will always be counted among the best – and therein lies the reason for its success.

AUSTRIA

Erich Saloman of Weingut Undhof

Austria has a long wine tradition, and until quite recently it was a distinguished one, in which the ripe, aromatic, dry whites made from the unique Grüner Veltliner grape and the rich dessert wines from Burgenland were especially valued. The wine scandal of 1985 turned that reputation upside down, but since then much has changed and new laws now govern production. Erich Saloman is one of a new generation of wine entrepreneurs, but one who brings the best of the past with him, as **Margaret Rand** explains.

Erich Saloman is something of a contradiction – that, at least, is how he appears to the visitor: a combination of sophisticate and farmer, of entrepreneurial determination and unwillingness to monopolize the limelight. For a man seeking returns on a 22 million-schilling investment, he is remarkably reserved.

Saloman owns 35 acres (14 hectares) of vineyards, planted with Austria's favourite white grape, Grüner Veltliner, as well as Riesling, Pinot Blanc, Traminer and Riesling/Silvaner. This is a decent-sized holding by Austrian standards, and his wines are remarkable for their elegance and depth. But it is not *his* wines that he is most anxious to show: it is everyone else's. Turn up at his large, solidly-built farmhouse, and you will promptly be shown out – into a 17th-century Capuchin monastery.

This is his huge investment. Saloman and his partner, Herr Alt, saved it from demolition in 1985 during the Austrian wine scandal, when sales of the country's wines were plummeting world-wide. Impressed with the French approach to marketing wine by linking wine appreciation with wider aspects of the country's culture, they decided to adopt a similar approach to the crisis-ridden Austrian wine industry and chose the monastery as a starting point.

The idea was to provide a showcase for wines from all over the country, where people could wander and taste as many different Austrian wines as they wanted in a setting typical of Austrian culture. The baroque monastery, with its plain, monastic lines, soaring heights, frescoed walls and vaulted cellars, was ideal. There was even, in the best fairy-tale tradition, a well of healing water. It is supposed to cure skin diseases, says Saloman. "The architect who was working with us had a skin complaint on his arm," he adds, and shrugs. "He tried the water – well, why not, he thought – and he was cured."

Samples of well water are not, however, on offer. Instead there are roughly 135 wines, and for the price of the entrance fee visitors can pick up a metal *tastevin*, a small tasting cup, and sample as wide a selection of Austrian wines as their palates will allow. All the charm of an old, underground wine cellar is there, without the damp chill that can creep into the bones and take the edge off one's interest. In spite of its size, the range is not intimidating. Wines are laid out clearly region by region, with information on each estate. Saloman's own wines are there with other wines from the Wachau, but they are given no greater prominence than those of any other producer.

When you're tired of tasting wine, you can look at the collection of vinous antiques on loan from Vienna or eat a meal in the restaurant. The monastery, which took ten months to restore, is also used as a venue for fashion shows, business meetings, and even balls: this is Austria, after all, and you can't go very far without falling over a waltz or two. You could even, assuming you can decide what you want, buy the wines.

Should Saloman's own wines take your fancy, simply walk the short distance to the farmhouse, where his family have lived for seven generations, and buy at the cellar door.

Saloman displays his wines in the vaulted cellars of a Baroque monastery.

The white wines made from Grüner Veltliner are light and dry, of the sort drunk by the quarter-litre mug in urban bars and country *buschenschanken*, or inns, all over Austria. Indeed, the noticeable thing about Austrian wines in general is this dryness. The labels are, of course, written in German and the grape varieties are often the same as those found in Germany, but the taste is distinctly different. Austrian Riesling, particularly when vinified by the likes of Erich Saloman, is frequently riper than its German counterpart, but elegant, with a firm structure and plenty of depth. The phrase "lovely refinement" crops up in my tasting notes time and again – a refinement achieved, he says, by traditional winemaking; "I am not a magician," he grins.

Saloman's winemaking techniques are those his father taught him. He eschews cultivated yeasts and additives of any sort; nor does he go in for the small barrels of new oak that some Austrian winemakers are experimenting with. Instead he keeps his wines in large old wooden vats that have been used for generations, and keeps them scrupulously clean. The wines are bottled between six months and a year after the vintage.

There was one occasion, however, when his father returned bottled wine to barrel – simply by filling the barrel with bottles. And he was very glad that he did: in 1945 soldiers from the visiting Russian army tapped the barrel and thought it was empty. As a result, among all those new wines at Kloster Und, there are still just a few much older ones; but these are not, sadly, available for tasting – not even for visiting Russians.

HUNGARY

Tokay

Clinging autumn mists are as crucial to the production of the fabled Hungarian sweet wines of Tokay as they are to Sauternes. They bring with them a benevolent fungus, a "noble rot", which shrivels the grapes, concentrating the juice and sugars within. But, as **Stephen Brook** explains, there is far more to Tokay than this. A highly unusual process of vinification follows, which gives to the wines their rare, honeyed, somewhat sherry-like flavour.

Had you been in the habit of dining at the Tsarist court a century or two ago, you might well have concluded your banquet with a glass or two of intensely sweet, syrupy Hungarian Tokay. The wine was so highly prized by Peter the Great and his successors that the Tsars set up a Commission for Hungarian Wines at St Petersburg to ensure regular supplies. That the wines of Tokay are now remarkably affordable has more to do with fluctuations in taste than with declining quality.

We don't know exactly what Tokay tasted like then, although there are priceless ancient bottles still in existence guarding the secret. Before the outbreak of phylloxera in the 19th century, which came close to destroying the vineyards of Europe, the wine was made from dozens of different grape varieties; today it is made from only three – Furmint, Hárslevelü and Muscat Lunel. Not all Tokay is sweet: the two principal varieties grown in the Tokaj-Hegyalja region, Furmint and Hárslevelü, produce wonderfully fat and full-flavoured dry wines too. But the slopes of the Carpathian Mountains on which the vineyards are located face the floodplain of the River Bodrog, and in the autumn the mists creep up from the plain and, as often as not, infect the grapes with *Botrytis cinerea*, or "noble rot" This fungus shrivels the grapes, concentrating the juice and intensifying the sugar content. The grapes are picked as late as possible, by hand, to give the noble rot every opportunity to attack the grapes. Despite the easterly location of the vineyards close to the Czech and Soviet borders, frost is rarely a problem before December.

It is the vinification that gives Tokay its distinctive sweet, honeyed, slightly sherry-like flavour. After harvesting, the *aszú* (botrytized) grapes are taken to the press-house. Traditionally, they would have arrived in 55-pound (25-kilogram) batches, in baskets known as *puttonyos*; today these are usually buckets. The contents of each *puttony* are crushed into a mash, which is then added to a 129-gallon (586-litre) cask of wine made from healthy grapes. The information on each bottle of Tokay as to the number of *puttonyos*

The mould in Tokay's tunnel cellars maintains a heavy humidity that helps preserve the wine almost indefinitely.

contained in the wine refers to the ratio of mash to wine. The higher the *puttonyos*, the richer the wine. Thus a four-*puttonyos* Tokay has a ratio of 220 pounds (100 kilograms) of mash to 129 gallons of wine. Wines with three, four or five *puttonyos* are the most common; six-*puttonyos* Tokay is produced in exceptional years.

Adding the mash to dry wine extracts flavour and tannin from the botrytized grapes and induces a second fermentation which boosts the alcoholic level by one to two degrees. This second fermentation can take years. *Aszú* wines are aged for a minimum of five years, in barrels stacked along the ancient tunnels bored into the Tokay hills. The cellars are an amazing sight, covered everywhere – walls, casks and bottles alike – with a furry black mould that does wonders for the humidity, thus preserving the wines and their corks virtually indefinitely.

Long ageing in casks that are not always topped up gives Tokay its unmistakable oxidized flavour. But this is only one element in a very complex wine: the flavour of the grapes, the high alcohol and the richness of extract all combine to create, when the wine is at its best, a burly yet voluptuous magnificence unique to Tokay. The region's vineyards are on volcanic soil, so the extraction of minerals is formidable. This accounts for the wine's reputation as a life-enhancing elixir and suggests there may be some justification to claims made for its restorative properties; whatever the truth, the wine is better appreciated as a drink than as a medicine.

The co-operative system of agriculture in Hungary, together with technological advances, has brought some changes to these artisanal methods of vinification and ageing; the wine's richness, for example, is now regulated by formula. The ageing of the wine in cask remains utterly traditional, however, although nowadays the wine is filtered and

*Ripe grapes are crushed into a mash in buckets known as puttonyos. The mash is simply
added to the cask wine – the more puttonyos, the richer the resulting taste.*

blended before bottling. There are private growers in the region, but the great majority of
growers take their grapes to the state farms for vinification, bottling and marketing.
Industrial winemaking rarely produces quality wines, yet most dispassionate tasters would
agree that the quality of Tokay remains extremely high.

In mediocre years, when noble rot is patchy or non-existent, no selection of *aszú* grapes is
made. Botrytized and healthy grapes are vinified together and the resulting wine is called
Szamorodni, which means "as it comes". This can be sweet or dry, and although not as rich
as Aszú, the sweet version can age splendidly. During intervals at the Budapest Opera,
sweet Szamorodni is served in the bars, and a most alluring drink it is too.

In exceptional years, ultra-rich wines are made that are roughly equivalent to what used
to be marketed as six-*puttonyos* Tokay; these are sold for high prices as Aszú Essencia. Very
occasionally, bottles of pure Essencia are released. This consists of the free-run must that
oozes from the botrytized grapes before crushing. In very great years small quantities of
this must are vinified separately. So rich in sugar is the must that fermentation staggers up
to only a few degrees, leaving an incredibly rich, syrupy, concentrated wine. Since a half-
litre bottle of the vintage currently on sale, 1947, will set you back around £500, you are
unlikely to encounter Essencia very often. Most Essencia is not sold but is employed as a
kind of concentrate to improve less exalted wines.

Although Tokay is ready to drink on release, even the most humble bottles repay
keeping. I still have a few bottles of Szamorodni 1969 that are drinking beautifully, and
Aszú from the excellent 1975 and 1976 vintages will easily keep for another 20 years. The
powerful, honeyed, slightly maderized, almost burnt, flavour of good Tokay makes the
wine difficult to match with food, and it is best enjoyed on its own at the end of the meal, or
alternatively as an apéritif in place of sherry.

GREECE

John Carras of Domaine Porto Carras

To transform a hilly wilderness in a neglected part of Mediterranean Greece into an estate renowned for wines of character and quality, the late John Carras needed vision, tenacity, deep patriotism and an appreciation of fine wine. He took no short cuts – hiring a Bordeaux university professor to supervise trials of many French and Greek grape varieties, and carefully identifying the most suitable hillside microclimate for each. But his perseverance and dedication paid off, as *Maggie McNie MW* relates.

The vineyards of Domaine Porto Carras, growing in among the pine-trees and olive groves on the steep slopes of Mount Meliton in the Sithonian Peninsula of Halkidiki, must be some of the loveliest in Europe. That they exist at all is due to the vision of one man, John Carras.

It was in 1963, while visiting the region for the millennium of Mount Athos, that John Carras first set eyes on the wilderness that he was to acquire from the Church later that year. An intensely patriotic man, Carras had invested heavily in Greek industry from the proceeds of his shipping company. And, being also a lover of good wine, he had long been convinced that Greece offered an enormous, untapped potential for winemaking. He used his latest purchase to initiate an experiment that led to the establishment of Domaine Porto Carras, one of Greece's premier vineyards.

Wine, however, was not the only aspect of John Carras' interest in the huge estate he had acquired. Anxious to increase prosperity in a much neglected area of Greece, he drained the marshy land lying between the hills and the sea, and built a large hotel and leisure complex. He also built a home, Château Carras, which gives its name to the estate's finest wines.

At the beginning, he sought the help of Professor Emile Peynaud of Bordeaux University, adviser to many of the finest Bordeaux châteaux. Between 1964 and 1967, Peynaud supervised the experimental planting of many French and Greek grape varieties. The resulting test batches of wine were carefully assessed and 27 varieties selected as suitable for the production of fine wines. The first vintage was in 1971.

Taking the vineyard route high into the hills, small parcels of vines lie on either side, interspersed with pine-trees and olive plantations, from which the estate produces its own olives and olive oil. The vines, many of them planted in rows following the contours of the slopes, are very carefully sited: the imported French grape varieties lie on the cooler side of the hills, at relatively high altitudes; the Greek varieties, accustomed to heat, occupy the hotter aspects. Cabernet Sauvignon is by far the most widely-planted red grape, followed by Cabernet Franc and the native Limnio, with small amounts of Merlot, Grenache and Cinsaut. White wines are made from the Assyrtiko, Athiri and Rhoditis grapes, with the addition of imported Sauvignon Blanc and Ugni Blanc.

The oenologist, Evanghelos Gerovassiliou, is an enthusiast whose youthful looks belie his experience and long service at Domaine Porto Carras. After training at Thessaloniki, he studied for two years in Bordeaux with Professors Peynaud, Pascal and Ribereau-Gayon. He spent a short time working in France and then returned to Greece in 1976 to work at Porto Carras. Since 1977 he has been the oenologist in charge. Evanghelos Gerovassiliou is particularly proud that, alone among Greek wine producers, the Domaine relies exclusively on grapes from its own vineyard. About 180 local people are hired to harvest the vintage, bringing in the Sauvignon Blanc first, then the Cabernet Sauvignon and other French varieties, and finally the Greek grapes.

In the modern, purpose-built winery at the foot of the vineyard slopes, fermentation temperatures are carefully controlled, giving the wines plenty of fruit and aroma. The red wines, though not the whites, undergo malolactic fermentation as early as possible; in 1989 this process was well advanced by the end of September. All red wines also spend about 18 months in small casks of Limousin or Nevers oak before being bottled and laid down. It is a rule of the Domaine not to release a wine until it is ready for drinking.

The range consists of just eight wines, all made to a high standard. Outstanding among the dry, elegant white and rosé wines, which are made for early drinking, are the white Carras Reserve and the Carras Rosé Special. These, along with the red Cava Carras, are only produced in small quantities in the best years and can be difficult to obtain.

The principal red wines are Domaine Carras, a blend of Limnio and Cabernet Sauvignon, and Château Carras itself, the flagship wine of the estate. It is made from Cabernet Sauvignon and Cabernet Franc with a little Merlot added, aged in oak for 18-20 months, and then laid down until Evanghelos Gerovassiliou feels it is ready. Like any other fine wine, different vintages age at different speeds. The 1975 is now ready, the 1981 nearly all sold, and the 1978 just released; Gerovassiliou believes the 1980 still needs some years, so it remains maturing in the cellar.

Sadly, after years of failing health, John Carras died in June 1989. Yet, to the perceptive visitor, his personality and his goals still pervade the atmosphere at Porto Carras. Inevitably, this will change. However, the entire Domaine will always stand as a monument to his breadth of vision, and the wines, most particularly Château Carras, are a testament to his conviction that Greece can, and does, produce fine wine.

Greek vines are traditionally grown among other crops.

LEBANON

Serge Hochar of Château Musar

It takes a courageous man to make wine in the Lebanon, and an exceptional one to remain cheerful and continually strive to improve upon his already notable achievements. For years Serge Hochar's unique red wines – the product of an unlikely-seeming blend of French grape varieties, grown on one side of the battle lines and vinified on the other – have astonished and pleased the world's fine wine drinkers. *Joanna Simon* tells the story.

Serge Hochar is one of the jolliest winemakers you could hope to meet. If you knew no better, you would surely imagine this beaming dynamo of a man producing vintage after vintage of his Château Musar in some favoured locale in the peaceful vineyards of France – concerned about his wines, certainly, but not over-anxious about them.

But we do know better. Serge Hochar has a greater cause for anxiety than any other winemaker in the world: anxiety not so much about the outcome of each year's harvest, the state of his vineyards or of his winery, but about body and soul, his family, his staff, his whole country. For Serge Hochar makes wine in the Lebanon, a country which is hardly ever referred to without the qualification "war-torn". And each year, as other wine producers around the world indulge in their habitual rote of preaching doom and disaster because of frost, hail, rain, drought, tropical heat, arctic cold, vine disease or whatever, Serge Hochar cannot even afford the luxury of predicting a vintage. The simple fact is that it might not happen.

In 1984 it did not. Although there were grapes and it was possible to pick them in good condition, it was not possible to get them from the vineyards to the winery 30 miles (48 kilometres) away. The distance in itself was not a problem – in Australia grapes are "trucked" hundreds of miles without mishap – but Hochar's vineyards lie in Muslim territory high up in the Beka'a Valley and the winery is in the mountains at Ghazir, a Christian zone overlooking the bay of Jounié 20 miles (32 kilometres) north of Beirut. Between the two lies the front line of the civil war – and with it barriers, blockades and constant bitter battles. In some years grape-laden Musar trucks have reached the winery, their cargo still intact after lengthy detours to the north, but in 1984 they were besieged in the Beka'a Valley and no Château Musar was made.

In 1989, the situation in the Lebanon was even worse, yet miraculously trucks came through the firing line and Musar was made. "I did not believe it would happen. It is the vintage that was not supposed to be. It was Hell," says Hochar, without a hint of melodrama. "I never thought I would make it through to the vintage. Not a single piece of property was not hit." The winery was hit by shelling, the offices were hit, Serge's apartment was hit and his brother Ronald's house was completely destroyed; Serge's hair is a good deal greyer now.

Yet, after three challenging, painful, but ultimately satisfying decades, he has no intention of giving up making wine here. He was born into it. His father Gaston founded Château Musar more than 50 years ago and Serge trained in Bordeaux, studying under the famous Professor Emile Peynaud and working for the late Ronald Barton (after whom Serge's brother is named) at his two classed-growth châteaux in St-Julien, Léoville-Barton and Langoa-Barton. More important, the red wine he has been making for the last three decades in the Lebanon is unique: no other wine tastes quite the same. It shares something of the character of Bordeaux and something more of the Rhône; some vintages are more like one than the other, yet they are never really very similar to either. There is always an elusive wild, spicy-smoky element in Château Musar; sometimes it lies behind the rich, ripe, velvety fruit and sometimes it overlays it; sometimes it starts one way and then develops in the other direction.

It is this unpredictable character that makes Musar so exciting for both winemaker and wine drinker, together with the fact that the wine continues to develop for a very long time. "All the wines I've produced since 1959 are still developing," Serge says, and he does not even release any of them onto the market until they are seven years old. At seven years they are gloriously drinkable but, according to Serge, "they don't show what they can do: Musar has to be drunk at 15 years ... I aim to make a wine that is good to drink at three years, but better in 30."

Quite what it is that gives Musar its unusual character is not clear, partly because there is so little with which to compare it (there are a handful of other Lebanese wines, but none has made the impact of Musar) and partly because, though many people have had the good fortune to enjoy Serge Hochar's company, few have visited him on his home ground. Probably, as so often is the case with wine, it is the particular combination of conditions and circumstances exploited by an imaginative and talented winemaker.

Viticulturally speaking, there is nothing extraordinary about the Beka'a Valley, although it is certainly a good place to grow wine grapes. There is plenty of sun, and both frost and disease are rare in the vineyards. The grapes Hochar uses are more unusual. He starts with the ubiquitous Cabernet Sauvignon but, instead of blending it with its classic Bordeaux partners, he combines it with two quite different French varieties – the rather ill-regarded Cinsault of the south, and the far more noble Syrah of the northern Rhône. The proportions of each vary from year to year: in 1982 there was about 40 per cent Cinsault, but more often than not there is approximately 75 per cent Cabernet, 20 per cent Cinsault and five per cent Syrah.

There are no set rules for the vinification and ageing processes. In principle, Hochar follows Bordeaux precepts, ageing wines in Alliers oak *barriques* like many good Bordeaux, but his overriding philosophy is not to copy anyone slavishly and not to establish a rigid Musar formula: "I still play it by ear every year. I don't try to imitate what I did the year before." Using 1989 as an example, he explains that the Cinsault grapes that year had an exceptional fruit character – "raspberry- and strawberry-like" – and, wanting to develop that aspect, he left the skins with the fermenting and fermented liquid for between five and six weeks, until the colour was nearly black. Yet the tannin, even after six weeks, remained smooth without a trace of harshness. The Cabernet, on the other hand, needed to be racked off its skins after two to three weeks so that it did not develop an aggressive hardness.

Pickers in eastern dress add an exotic note to the vineyards of Château Musar.
Vines here are trained low in the classic Mediterranean manner.

He does not know how the 1989s will turn out in the end. He says he never does know early on, but of one thing he is sure – that each vintage should develop something unique from its year. A Musar that failed to do so would be a disappointment to him. So far, happily, he has rarely been disappointed. "Every time I see a wine that was disappointing to me, like the 1967, I see it do well in tastings, so I don't complain. It's because there's a Musar for everyone: you don't get consensus like you do with Bordeaux vintages. The 1978 was a worry at one stage. When I made it, I thought I'd done something wrong – probably I had – but now it's unique. It has a marvellous velvet and fragrance."

Although he makes each vintage according to the particular characteristics he perceives at the time, Hochar does admit to discernible broad trends in his winemaking over the years. The first half of the 1960s and 1969 saw big, powerful wines with great ageing potential, among them the 1964 which, when pressed, he admits is his all-time favourite: "it's so wild". Then in the second half of the decade, after his time in Bordeaux, he moved – above all with the 1967 – towards a lighter, more Médocain style. With the 1970, 1972 and 1977, he switched back to something a little more powerful: "more St-Emilion, Pomerol, Côtes-du-Rhône". And now he is going back to wines of greater power – big, spicy, full wines, with lots of *matière* and great ageing ability: "what people expect of Musar".

What people certainly do not expect of Musar is Hochar's latest project, a white wine. But I doubt anyone will complain, for this looks set to be as unusual in its own way as the red. It is a blend – one would not really expect Hochar to be content with a varietal – and it is predominantly Chardonnay, but its other component is Sauvignon Blanc. Both varieties are highly fashionable and both take well to blending, but no winemaker has yet coaxed the two of them into the same blending vat and therein persuaded them that they should take well to each other. If anyone can, I am willing to believe it is Serge Hochar.

ISRAEL

Golan Heights Winery

A startling diversity of soil types, microclimates and vines roll out across the Golan Heights, where local *kibbutzim* grow grapes for a winery built by the enterprising Shimshon Welner. Vinification methods are highly sophisticated, but harvesting and handling are subject to the strict religious precepts that regulate the production of kosher wines. Today, as ***Stephen Brook*** explains, Golan Heights wines are ranked alongside some of the world's best.

Israelis do not drink much wine – only about half a gallon (2.5 litres) per capita annually – so it is hardly surprising that the average quality of the country's wines is uninspiring. However, there is a substantial demand for Israeli kosher wines, which form the bulk of production, among Orthodox Jewish communities outside Israel. Recent improvements in quality owe more, I suspect, to the demand in export markets for better wines than to any internal rebellion against the standard mediocre fare of baked, oxidized reds and flat, flabby whites.

It was this demand that prompted astute *kibbutzim* in the Golan Heights to plant vineyards with the aim of producing top-quality kosher wines. Shimshon Welner, the highly successful apple packer who was asked to co-ordinate the scheme, had the foresight to build an ultra-modern winery and to hire expert winemakers from California. Since the release of the first vintage, a 1983 Sauvignon Blanc, the Golan winery has made an impact on both export and domestic markets with its range of 19 wines.

Most Israeli vineyards are situated near the coastal plain, where summertime temperatures can be savage, but Welner built his winery high up on the Golan Heights a few miles from the Syrian border and he buys his grapes from the vineyards of local *kibbutzim*. The vineyards are scattered throughout the region, varying in height from 1,300 to 3,900 feet (400-1,200 metres) and containing a startling range of soil types and microclimates, not to mention grape varieties. Early plantings of less exalted varieties such as French Colombard and Emerald Riesling are now being phased out in favour of "international" varieties: Cabernet Sauvignon, Merlot, and Sauvignon Blanc. Yields are low, again in contrast to the coastal vineyards, and drainage is usually good – excellent on the volcanic soil. Despite the relative youth of the vines, most of which were planted after 1979, the quality of the fruit is excellent, and the long cool growing season is producing Cabernet and Merlot of increasingly impressive stature.

The Golan vineyards are among the most unusual I have ever visited. Although there have been no hostilities between Israelis and Syrians in the region for many years, vast areas of the Golan are still strewn with minefields. Before planting could begin, dozens of wrecked tanks and armoured cars had to be hauled away. Cuttings were imported from California and there has since been very little disease, other than mildew, among the vines. The winery markets three ranges of wines: Yarden, Gamla and Golan. Gamla and Golan are often hard to distinguish from each other, and it is the high-priced Yarden wines that have enjoyed international acclaim.

The production of kosher wines imposes very specific demands on the winery. Young vines cannot be harvested until their fifth year, and once in every seven years a vineyard must lie fallow. Drip irrigation and mechanical harvesting are permitted, but the vineyards and wineries cannot employ just anyone: once the grapes have been crushed only Orthodox Jews may handle the must and the vinification equipment, and religious law forbids women from having any contact with the product until it has been corked. Twice a week, a rabbi visits the winery to ensure that there are no infringements of religious law: if there were, the entire batch of wine would have to be discarded.

Realizing, however, that Israeli winemakers had neither the training nor the knowledge to produce wines that could compete on the international market, Welner hired cellarmasters from California. Like his predecessor, Golan's current winemaker Jim Klein is Jewish but not Orthodox. "I'm not allowed to touch the hoses or tanks, or perform any act that will move the wine," he explains. "If I want to taste from a barrel, I have to ask one of the Orthodox winery workers to get the sample for me. I also have to keep away from the bottling line."

The vinification, as one would expect from California oenology graduates, is highly sophisticated. Golan practises skin contact for white wines, uses pneumatic presses and ferments at low temperatures. Bottles as well as casks are imported from France, as Israeli bottles are not of high enough quality for the export market. Not surprisingly the wines are expensive, but the overall standard of Golan wines is remarkably high – and not only in comparison with other Israeli wines. Even the most commercial wines in the Golan range are clean and well-made, and at the top end of the range the results are exciting.

The most successful white wine, Sauvignon Blanc, is given a short period of wood-ageing to create a style closer to white Graves than Sancerre. Early vintages of Sauvignon were aged in new wood as a way of breaking in the barrels before using them for red wines. Chardonnay will soon be playing a greater part in the Golan range, and Klein hopes to ferment this variety in barrel. Cabernet spends up to 18 months in oak and Merlot about 12 months. Of the other red varieties, Syrah is blended into the popular Mount Hermon brand, but at present Pinot Noir is used only in the sparkling wine blend. Klein is particularly excited by the potential for Merlot, although the tough, concentrated, spicy Cabernet Sauvignon remains Golan's best wine.

It would be a brave taster who could identify these wines as unmistakably Israeli: like many New World wines they lack specific local character. Since, however, the local character of Israeli wines was fairly disgusting, this may be no bad thing. For the first time, Orthodox Jews can enjoy distinguished wines with their meals. Other wine lovers will keep a careful eye on developments in the Golan, for Klein and his associates have every intention of making the most of the distinctive climates and soils of this ancient and long-neglected winemaking region.

The Americas

—

It is surprising how few North American states do not make wine nowadays. Yet, to most consumers, American wine means California wine. California's high profile may be inevitable in view of its sheer output when compared with the other states of the USA (although it is does not begin to approach that of Argentina), but even without volume on its side, it seems certain that California would have established itself as pre-eminent in the Americas – as France is in Europe.

That is not to denigrate the blossoming achievements of regions such as Oregon, Washington State or Chile, but there is no disputing that, in America, California produces the largest quantity of world-class wine. Within North America that will always be the case, because the amount of suitable viticultural land is so much greater there than in other states. Texas, for example, has plenty of space, but not so much of it under ideal conditions. And Oregon, while revealing some exciting territory for the elusive Pinot Noir, has not much of it to reveal.

Ultimately, depending on political and economic developments, the wineries of California may find themselves more seriously challenged in the quality league by Chile and Argentina. Argentina undoubtedly has considerable natural resources, but its wine industry is backward and oriented to quantity rather than quality, so there will need to be radical progress before it begins to fulfill its potential. Chile, on the other hand – frequently referred to as a "viticultural paradise" because of its climate and its phylloxera-free environment – is beginning to realize some of its considerable potential. And this has not passed unnoticed at the grandest levels; why else would Château Lafite-Rothschild have decided in 1988 to invest in Chile's Los Vascos winery?

But for the time being, California reigns supreme, having achieved in less than a quarter of a century the quality that it took Europe hundreds, even thousands of years to achieve. In terms of technology, California's lead is global. The Australians run a very close second – indeed, they may now be neck and neck – but California certainly got there first. It was California that brought the world supremely ripe fruity "varietal" wines, above all Cabernet Sauvignon and Chardonnay. And it was California that recognized the importance of hygienic winery conditions, made a science out of microclimate, and put

Oregon (top) and California, the two best-known of the many states now making wine. Uninhibited by tradition and unafraid of technological experiment, American winemaking is already equal to the European challenge.

everything under the microscope – clones, rootstocks, vine crossings, phylloxera, yeasts, *Botrytis*, lees, oak and anything else you care to mention.

The Californians simply had no winemaking heritage to speak of, but instead of allowing this to be a handicap, they turned it to their advantage. They let Europe serve as a model, but had no preconceptions about what they could grow where on their own soil; they just went out and planted. Although they are now increasingly defining specific viticultural regions, these are not restrictive in the way of French *appellations contrôllées*. California winemakers do not even allow nature to defeat them: if it rains during the harvest, they blow-dry the vines from helicopters.

All this may sound gimmicky, and the Old World certainly looked askance at first, but by 1987 it was taking its lead from the New: Châteaux Mouton-Rothschild and Pétrus blew-dry their vines; Robert Drouhin bought land in Oregon; a growing number of Champagne houses invested in land and wineries to make sparkling wine; and there were two prestigious California-Bordeaux liaisons under the unmistakably ambitious names of Opus One and Dominus. The Old World was not only following but joining the New.

*With vines literally on the doorstep, this Oregon farmer can keep
a close eye on his crop almost without stepping outside.*

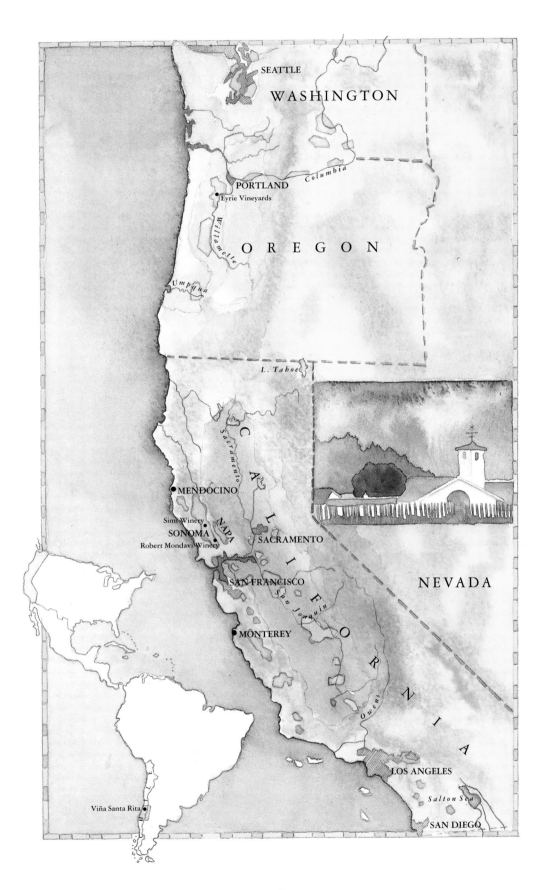

NAPA VALLEY

Robert Mondavi

Robert Mondavi's list of ingredients for successful winemaking contains no surprises: climate, soil and grape varieties, in the right place with the right facilities. In California's Napa Valley he has had no difficulty combining those various elements. But there is more to a recipe than its ingredients. Robert Mondavi's winning formula, explains **Bob Thompson**, includes a blend of irrepressible enthusiasm and attention to detail with considerable business acumen — and a seemingly endless willingness to experiment.

Early in their acquaintance, author Hugh Johnson and Robert Mondavi were seatmates on a flight to San Francisco after a wine hullabaloo in San Diego. "The flight lasted more than an hour, but Bob's speech was only 20 minutes," Johnson said afterwards: "I heard it three times."

Once, during her ten years of winemaking at Robert Mondavi Winery, Zelma Long, now President of Simi Winery (see pages 194-98), was listening to one of Robert Mondavi's set pieces. She interrupted to say "you know, Bob, we could record this and you wouldn't have to come up to the laboratory".

Tim Mondavi, Bob's younger son and winemaker, took his newly-wed bride, Dorothy, to several family dinners. "She was always seated next to my father ... she was a new person for his *Wines of the World* speech, 1-A; also for 1-B and 1-C – *The Potential of California* and *The Future of The Robert Mondavi Winery*."

There is, however, more to Robert Gerald Mondavi – Bob to thousands who know him and tens of thousands who do not – than his extraordinarily vocal enthusiasm for wine. He and his wife, Margrit Biever, are grand patrons of the arts and generous members of their community. But it is his single-minded devotion to wine that explains how both the man and his wares have become ubiquitous in California and in every other part of the globe where the pleasures of the table matter. As Bob barrels through his late seventies – he was born in 1913 in Victoria, Minnesota – he is the untempered outgrowth of the high school footballer who gained two yards when his team needed one, four when it needed three, to keep marching goalwards.

Anyone who wants to know the paths Mondavi has followed need only listen to The Speeches, particularly *Napa is World-Class* and *We've Just Begun to Scratch the Surface*. But the one that bedevils hard-core traditionalists most is *Better Big Than Little*. "I've believed from the beginning," Bob told a writer in 1981, "we could go to a million cases and keep

Robert Mondavi has achieved premium quality wine on an
industrial scale – but is still striving to improve.

improving." The Robert Mondavi Winery produced 20,000 cases in its first vintage, 1966. Within 20 years its annual volume had reached 500,000 cases, perhaps more (the company is not keen on giving out precise business figures).

The Mondavian list of ingredients for success contains no revelations: climate, soil and grape varieties properly matched to location, and proper facilities. Add to these "dedication, desire, the will to train people, and ... you can duplicate what the smallest producers can do. In fact," Mondavi told a writer in 1977, "I believe that once I get a group of people with me ... I can do not only as good a job, but possibly a better job. There's no reason we can't do it."

On a rational, managerial level Mondavi's reason for doing it goes back well before his own winery. He came to the wine business in 1936 with a freshly minted economics degree from Stanford University. Then, or soon after, he concluded that the only way a wine business could prosper was to offer reliable quality at a large enough volume to be important to the clients who look for that quality. Seeing no room to compete at the low end of the price scale, he aimed for the top.

Mondavi's uncompromising ambition is echoed by the dramatic and confident lines of the winery itself.

On an earthier plane, Robert Mondavi wants to have the best and be the best. He credits his mother Rosa with instilling that drive in him during his early childhood. While her husband Cesare ran a working man's bar in Minnesota she operated a rooming house, saving enough to give her family the finest food and clothing, and letting them know what they were getting.

Visitors to Mondavi's California mission-style cellars at Oakville come away dazed, especially if their reference point is quaintly Burgundian. "Where," asked Pierre-Marie Doutrelant of *Le Nouvel Observateur*, as he wandered among stainless steel fermenting tanks, centrifuges, and other ultra-modern, hospital-clean equipment, "are the spiders of Burgundian cellars, the mossy dampnesses of Bordelais *chais*?" Mondavi, who overlooks nothing, probably had his technical staff check the possible benefits of spiders and moss; a decade later, the winery has a minimum of the former and none of the latter. The stainless steel screw that starts the grapes on their way to the crushers, meanwhile, has acquired an edgecover. When the staff suspected that its rough-milled edge might be grinding unwanted tannins out of skins and seeds, a bead of Teflon swiftly covered it.

Producing the right grapes in the right sun and soil remains the most elusive factor in Mondavi's formula for success. Within the tight confines of the Côte d'Or are enough sainted vineyards to produce a million cases of *premier cru* and better. However, one firm gaining control of them all is only the first impossibility in that eternally redividing region. The Mondavis have not rounded up anything like a million cases worth of land yet, but, in far less settled Napa, they have been able to acquire 1,500 acres (607 hectares) of prime vineyards in two decades.

The biggest patch, called ToKalon, surrounds the winery at Oakville, touching the famous Beaulieu No. 2 (source of Georges Delatour Cabernet Sauvignon) at one point, the yet more famous Martha's Vineyard at another. Not surprisingly to those familiar with

Checking the fermentation of a tank of Mondavi Chenin Blanc.

California, this 650-acre (263-hectare) property yields the heart of Mondavi's Cabernet Sauvignons. A second piece, the 400-acre (162-hectare) Oak Knoll vineyard, lies at one edge of the Stag's Leap district south-east of Yountville; lower, in heavier soil than the best-known Cabernet vineyards there, much of it is planted to Sauvignon Blanc and other white varieties. The newest Mondavi vineyard consists of 425 acres (172 hectares) in fog-cooled Carneros, acquired in 1989 expressly for Pinot Noir and Chardonnay.

Mondavi's evaluations of these properties – or at least their potential – are central to his second perennial lecture, *Napa is World-Class*. He never claims Napa to be best, never contends that its wines must finish first. In fact the winery generally avoids outright win-or-lose competitions. But Bob insists that everyone recognize Napa's right to sit in company with the traditional greats, particularly Bordeaux and Burgundy.

While Bob will point to the impressive performance of Napa wines in such formal evaluations as the Gault-Millau Wine Olympiades, he much prefers first-hand proof for his audience of the moment. To this end he endlessly pits his own wines against the rest of the world for influential visitors to the winery. Any writer on wine with rat-pack tendencies can pull out old, middle-aged and young notes on Robert Mondavi Napa Valley Cabernet Sauvignon tasted blind with classed growths from Bordeaux, or Robert Mondavi Napa Valley Chardonnay shown with whites from Burgundy's top drawer. Even Frenchmen are not exempt from these demonstrations. In 1979 the afore-mentioned Doutrelant faced up to a comparison of Mondavi Reserve Cabernet Sauvignons 1968 and 1970 with Château Giscours 1967 and Château La Mission-Haut-Brion 1966. He ranked the Mondavi 1970 right at the shoulder of the Mission-Haut-Brion.

Bob's greatest single stroke on behalf of Napa may well turn out to be another winery in which he is only half-owner, Opus One. The other half-owner at the founding in 1979 was Baron Philipe de Rothschild, the only man ever to have the 1855 Classification of Bordeaux

The exquisite velvet bloom of healthy Napa Cabernet Sauvignon.

changed to his benefit. As Opus moves toward estate status, Baroness Philippine de Rothschild is the Baron's heir and the Mondavis' active new partner. But getting the original stamp of approval on Napa Valley from the owner of Mouton-Rothschild ranks high on Bob's list of his own achievements.

Bob Mondavi stands by his claims for Napa – and for California in general – in other, subtler ways, more surprising for someone as competitive as he. After a San Francisco socialite came to him in 1979 to propose a charity wine auction, Bob embellished the idea and took it to his colleagues in the Napa Valley Vintners Association. The charities became Napa Valley hospitals and clinics while the auction itself became a four-day showcase for the valley's wines and wineries. Mondavi stepped back to let others direct the event as soon as the idea was adopted.

In 1980 he and aides began working with executives of the Hilton-International hotel chain to broaden the hotels' selection of California wines. Two years later Mondavi and the hoteliers invited a dozen or so of Mondavi's competitors to join in blind tastings that would select a core list of California wines for the hotels. The Robert Mondavi Winery hosted the first; since then the annual tastings have been co-hosted by several participating Napa and Sonoma firms, Mondavi included. The Mondavi winery was also the catalyst for a similar set of tastings for the Westin Hotels group.

Mondavi regularly extends a helping hand to other wineries, winemakers and growers in the valley. Miljenko Grgich of Grgich Hills and Warren Winiarski of Stag's Leap Wine Cellars served apprenticeships at Mondavi. When Michael and Arlene Bernstein were trying to get their Mt Veeder Winery off the ground, Mondavi hired them as tour guides so they would have some income as well as a technical resource. Tulocay Vineyards owner Bill Cadman works as a guide for Mondavi now. In this Bob is only following a tradition from which he has benefited himself. As a newcomer to the valley and a rookie winemaker in 1936, he sought and got unstinting counsel from André Tchelistcheff, Louis M Martini and others he saw as the titans of the valley.

Cyril Ray was particularly taken by Mondavi's friendliness towards his competitors. In his *Robert Mondavi of the Napa Valley*, Ray writes that he habitually asks interview subjects whose wines they drink when they can't get their own. French respondents usually named only one wine; Mondavi gave him a roll-call that included almost every Napa winery the author had ever heard mentioned. Mondavi's own explanation is that nobody will take his winery seriously unless high standards prevail in its home territory.

More often than not *Napa is World-Class* segues straight into *We've Just Begun to Scratch the Surface*. The claims mix contradiction and hyperbole. Interviews with Mondavi are full of his slight but persistent dissatisfaction with his wines. They also report again and again that he believes the major parts of any one puzzle to be in place, but that the last few pieces require a little more knowledge. For his son Tim this is vintage Bob: "He has always been very positive but demanding. The whole time we were growing up, it was 'this is great – but'; and there was always a but."

Bob's most succinct description of the state of wine in Napa and the rest of California came in a 1977 interview. "We're compressing our history. The French have inherited their traditions through centuries; we're developing ours through experimentation. It will get more feverish." His willingness to experiment with well-received wines awes his staff, and his readiness to change the methods behind them sometimes staggers employees. "Once," Zelma Long recalled from the perspective of 1989, "I had to say to him, 'Bob, we can do anything, but we can't do everything at once'." Tim, meanwhile, remembers that early era as much less experimental than now, probably because his father was moving cautiously with partners he has since bought out.

During the late 1970s and early 1980s, the winery conducted a series of Harvest Seminars in an effort to educate writers about the ins and outs of style. The sessions were veritable blizzards of information about grape maturity, fermentation temperature curves, fining agents, coopering techniques, the role of lees – all accompanied by tastings to show off the differences. If fining was the discussion of the day, participants tasted samples of a wine fined with bentonite, egg whites, casein, gelatin and isinglass, and assorted combinations thereof. If it was oak-ageing, each set of samples showed barrels from the oaks of different forests prepared with steam (short-lived), with varying levels of toasting or steam, or a combination of the two. Every major cooperage was represented by as many different techniques as it offered. Threaded through was the sub-text: we used to do it this way, but now we are on a new course.

This is not inside stuff. The general public got and still gets boiled-down, updated versions of these seminars in dozens if not scores of cities every year, and competing winemakers are welcome guests at Oakville.

It is easy to be seduced by these ceaseless explorations into thinking that every year at Robert Mondavi Winery is another revolution. Notes from dozens of tastings, many blind, suggest that such is not the case, that there is a coherent path. Long, who became one of the state's most celebrated oenologists before stepping up to the presidency of Simi Winery, ranks her old boss high for his willingness to keep hunting for a better way, perhaps higher still for his unwavering sense of style.

Until Tim Mondavi settled in as winemaker, Bob had the final vote at tastings. During the harvest he tasted every fermenting lot daily. In other seasons he tasted at all of the blending trials, as often as four days a week. He was never autocratic, says Long, but the staff never left a tasting with any doubt about which direction to take with any of the wines. Mondavi has a knack of boiling down what he wants to one or two words: "middle-body" was a favourite for a while; the current codeword is "sculpted"; and the invariable tag is "accessible". Almost all of these codewords deal with the whole wine, and especially its tactile qualities. One rarely catches Bob at the fruit and vegetable bins or spice shelves that are so beloved of wine writers.

Most of Mondavi's attention is devoted to four varietal wines: Cabernet Sauvignon, Chardonnay, Pinot Noir and Fumé Blanc (made from Sauvignon Blanc); off-dry Chenin Blanc, Johannisberg Riesling and Muscat Blanc round out the roster. In this, as in almost every other California winery, the big two are Cabernet Sauvignon and Chardonnay. Fumé Blanc and Pinot Noir, meanwhile, may be more instructive examples of how Mondavi wines keep evolving toward a fixed goal.

Sauvignon Blanc was languishing as a varietal wine everywhere in California when Mondavi gave it the new name of Fumé Blanc in 1971. Lord knows what echo "Fumé" struck in American wine drinkers that Sauvignon could not, but it caused them to start buying the wine. Bob, meanwhile, remained dissatisfied with what he was tasting. For him, the flavours smacked too much of grass and the textures felt too sharp.

Early vintages included a proportion of Sémillon in the blend. Sauvignon's old running-mate for Graves filled out the textures but blunted the flavours of Sauvignon more than the proprietor wanted. A couple of vintages later Sémillon began to dwindle as a presence. Barrel fermentation of riper Sauvignon grapes replaced it as the source of enriched textures and the wines became poor man's Chardonnays. At about the same time, a long string of experiments with fining materials ended with two being chosen because no single one would knock all of the characteristic sharpness out of the variety. Barrel fermentation followed Sémillon onto the scrapheap in 1983, when DFF – "Direct From Fermenters" – became the buzzword. What it means is fermenting Sauvignon in stainless steel, then racking the still-cloudy new wine to casks or barrels to age on its light lees. The result was enriched textures and intact Sauvignon flavours. DFF still is the basic technique. Reserve Fumé Blancs are a bit richer and riper than the regular bottlings, primarily through vineyard selection.

Pinot Noir has been a more consuming, more complicated project. Making great wine from the great black grape of France's Côte d'Or is one of the toughest of challenges. Even the Burgundians have trouble getting it right. None of this daunts Mondavi, though the wine has kept his staff up more nights than any other plotting new ways to attack the problems. What Bob has always sought is the lush, even velvety textures of great Burgundians, and flavours as subtle as theirs.

The first great effort was ageing the wine in French oak barrels. After they did not answer as fully as they had for Chardonnay, Bob came back from Beaune with the idea of leaving a proportion of stems in the fermenting tanks with the grapes. When stems did not produce everything he was seeking, much riper grapes and considerably warmer fermentation temperatures joined barrels and stems. Mondavi was sure they had caught lightning with the 1978. The reedy, almost saxophonic voice (up-tempo Ben Webster) still rings in the ears of those who heard his impassioned explanation of how extra ripeness was the key that had finally unlocked the door. The wine, alas, never did quite ring on the palate; Mondavi and his staff have backed away from all the extremes though they have not abandoned any of the general ideas. But something new is in the works. The 1984 and 1985 Reserve Pinot Noir bottlings show promise their forebears never did.

New ideas have come and still do come from everywhere. A relentless globe-trotter (trotter does not begin to express Mondavi's velocity), Bob hauls himself and his staff from Oakville to Beaune, Pauillac, Torgiano, the Yarra Valley – wherever – in search of more ways to put another scratch in the surface.

Robert Mondavi did not become a household word until his name went on his own labels, but nothing he has done with his own winery should have come as a surprise to anyone who knew of him from his Charles Krug days. He started scratching the various surfaces in 1936, when he began managing what is now Sunny St Helena as a bulk winery for his father, Cesare. Cesare had singled out Napa Valley as having the best vineyards for dry table wines when he was shipping fresh grapes to home winemakers from Lodi during Prohibition, and he had sensed that the market for such wines would come.

Bob returned the favour in 1943, convincing his father that the bottled rather than the bulk market was where Napa's future lay, and then convincing him to buy the old Charles Krug property. By that time Bob had enough confidence in his bulk wines to bring them along for bottling at Krug, under the modest CK-Mondavi label.

By 1947 the Mondavis were ready to sell varietal wines under the restored Charles Krug label. From then until 1966 Bob managed Krug increasingly in the ways he would come to run his own company. A few parallels stand out in particular. During the Krug years Bob somehow divined that Americans apathetic to a dry white called White Pinot would somehow flock to a sweeter one called Chenin Blanc by renaming it Fumé Blanc. When Chardonnay began to blossom in California, he recognized what Brad Webb had achieved using French oak barrels at Hanzell and brought them to Krug in time for the 1963s – years ahead of Napa's other sizeable wineries. He kept CK-Mondavi as a less expensive alternative label to Charles Krug, roughly the equivalent of today's Robert Mondavi-Woodbridge line.

In general, Bob's methods of operation were too adventurous for his mother Rosa and brother Peter. After Cesare died in 1959 what had been rumbles of discontent turned into family warfare, though Bob did not leave until Rosa told him, in 1965, that there would be no place at Krug for Bob's eldest son, Robert Michael, now president of Robert Mondavi Winery. Bob had to sue his mother and brother to get payment for his quarter-ownership of Charles Krug. While the case dragged on, he found himself required to make a complex exchange of half-interest partners in order to raise capital for the new Robert Mondavi Winery. It is testimony to his business acumen that he never seems to have parted with any of the votes. Once the suit was settled he gained complete ownership in 1978, and he has not looked back since.

The only part of him that ever slowed down was his knees. After they began giving him more grief than he wanted he had them surgically rebuilt in the summer of 1989. "I went in a couple of days after the operation," his son Tim said some months afterward, "and my father told me, 'The first day and a half was terrible, but I'm doing great now'. A week later it was 'Last week was really awful, but I'm doing great now'. Then it was 'Last month was really bad, but I'm doing great now'."

Bob underwent the operations at the end of July. On September 28th he took off to lead a wine tour of Europe. "When he gets back he'll be all charged up," said Tim: "He'll have a whole new programme for getting to Nirvana. Every time he goes anywhere he comes back with a whole new programme for getting to Nirvana."

SONOMA COUNTY

Zelma Long of Simi Winery

Robert Mondavi once confessed that, of the many promising winemakers to have passed through his winery, he hated losing Zelma Long, his erstwhile understudy, the most. Long, too, found it difficult to leave the Mondavi winery, but she went on to even greater things. At Simi Winery in Sonoma County, of which she is now president, she has made some of the world's finest Chardonnay wines and, predicts **James Laube**, the best is yet to come.

Side by side they look like perfect companions: Zelma Long's smiling face framed by short-cropped, yellow-golden locks, next to a glass of Simi Reserve Chardonnay, its brilliant hues mirroring the colour of her hair. In a high-profile decade of winemaking, 46-year-old Zelma Long has made her mark in California wine with richly flavoured, deep, complex Chardonnays. Both at Simi Winery in Sonoma County, where she is president and was until recently winemaker, and at Long Vineyards in Napa Valley, where she is co-owner with her former husband Bob, Long has crafted the kind of creamy, buttery, elegantly-styled Chardonnays that make you pause and ponder for a moment if a glass of wine can really taste much better.

Under Long's tenure, Simi Winery has moved to the forefront of the fast-paced, ever-changing California wine scene. Tall, cool and confident, she has emerged as one of the industry's leaders, recognized for her talents both as a winemaker and as a grape-grower. Her Simi Chardonnays have gradually risen to the top of their class in California, and by many critical accounts, they now rank among the élite in the world of fine wine – which is no small achievement. For most of its 114-year history, Simi had been best known for its red wines, such as Cabernet Sauvignon and Zinfandel. When Long took over, those who knew her well never doubted her ability to create magnificent wines, and now she is making prophets of those who cast her as one of wine's rising stars.

The simple truth about Long is that she is fascinated by every aspect of winemaking, from analyzing soils, microclimates and grape varieties to vine-pruning, training methods and fermentation temperatures; from analyzing a wine's character when aged in French oak barrels to its texture and feel in the mouth when consumed. She respects wine's traditions, and has travelled extensively to the fine wine regions of the world in search of greater knowledge and understanding about the art of winemaking and the essence of grape-growing. Yet she loves to experiment with innovative techniques – a trait that is

Zelma Long's rejuvenation programme at Simi was comprehensive: not only with new technology in the winery but with important new plantings in key regions throughout Sonoma County.

linked both to her personality and education, and to her work as an understudy of Robert Mondavi. In short, she is quietly driven to perfection. Underneath her warm, articulate nature is a woman who might just be the most talented winemaker in America today.

Long never planned to be a winemaker, but her educational background proved beneficial in understanding the chemistry of wine. A native of The Dalles, Oregon, a small town on the Columbia River, Long attended Oregon State University, majoring in chemistry and microbiology and minoring in nutrition. After college she worked as a professional dietician in the San Francisco Bay Area, before marrying and moving to Napa Valley where her husband's parents had bought land in the narrow hills east of the valley and planted a vineyard. Living in wine country gave Long greater exposure to winemaking and she reasoned that with a family-owned vineyard it might be fun to try her hand at the centuries-old practice of turning grapes into wine.

With that incentive, she enrolled at the prestigious oenology school of the University of California at Davis, about 50 miles (80 kilometres) from her Napa home, and began working on her master's degree. Then one day, out of the blue, she received a telephone query from a winemaker named Miljenko Grgich at Robert Mondavi Winery (see pages 186-93). He asked her if she would like to work part-time as a lab assistant. Her college credentials were ideal, and in 1970 she began her winemaking career.

Robert Mondavi surrounds himself with highly talented and highly motivated people, and few are more gifted than Long's first mentor, "Mike" Grgich, the day-to-day winemaker at Mondavi. If anyone in Napa Valley deserves the title of Mr Chardonnay, it is perhaps Grgich. While he introduced Long to the excitement and possibilities of winemaking, Grgich moved on and increased his mastery of the Chardonnay grape with monumental Chardonnays, first at Chateau Montelena and then at his own winery, Grgich Hills Cellar. When he left in 1972, Long replaced him as head oenologist and, had it not been for the fact that Robert Mondavi's talented son Tim was the heir apparent as winemaker, Long might still be making wine for Mondavi.

On an autumn day in 1979, Michael Dixon, then President of Simi Winery and now its Chairman, ended his search for a new winemaker. He offered the job to Long and she accepted. "It was a difficult decision to leave Mondavi," she said at the time, but the challenge of rejuvenating Simi proved too tempting. Robert Mondavi confided that, of his many fine employees, he hated losing Long the most, for she displayed an almost unlimited talent combined with a desire for precision and self-improvement.

At Simi came new challenges, with the opportunity to shape the future of this historic old winery, not only through modernizing the winemaking facilities, but also – and perhaps more importantly – through the planting of new vineyards in key regions

The stone-built barn at Simi has seen the historic old winery expand and develop to meet the challenge of the 1990s.

throughout Sonoma County. Simi's wines were always good and well made, but in the 1970s, when fine wine came of age in the United States, it was time for change and a step up in quality. Dixon believed Simi could do better, and after interviewing a field of potential candidates he chose Long. With wine it always takes time to effect change and measure results, but now, a full decade after Long took over at the helm at Simi, Dixon looks like the brilliant futurist who could see all along that Long had the right stuff.

Today Simi's wines have never been better, and if the truth be know, the best is yet to come. For while Long has given the Simi Chardonnays brilliant polish, silky-smooth texture and tiers of honey, butter, pear and spice flavours that glide across the palate, the next quantum leap for Long and Simi will come with another of the world's noble grapes, Cabernet Sauvignon. Long's progress with Cabernet through the 1980s has helped Simi reach new highs. A succession of excellent vintages, from 1984 to 1988, gave her the fruit from which great wines are made. Where others might make excellent wines, Long's are dramatic – offering uncommon richness, depth, balance and flavour, with the kind of gentle, soft tannins that make them delicious to drink tonight, but also offer the promise that moves you to lay a few bottles down in your cellar for future enjoyment.

The decade of the 1980s was a time of change at Simi. As American wine tastes increasingly shifted from reds and sweet-styled wines to dry whites, Simi had plenty of room for improvement. Under Long's direction, Simi's whites – Chenin Blanc, Sauvignon

Blanc and Chardonnay – almost immediately showed fresher, crisper, fruitier flavours. The Chenin is tart and lively with apple and spice notes, the Sauvignon Blanc crisp with fig and melon notes and a smooth texture. The Chardonnays became more complex and Long began to focus as much on their texture and feel in the mouth as on pure varietal character. She began to use malolactic fermentation and successfully blended parcels of grapes from different regions, taking for instance Chardonnay fruit from Sonoma and Mendocino County to the north and blending them together – piece by piece creating and refining Simi's style to achieve wines of complexity, grace and delicacy. She designed a new fermentation cellar and implemented a renovation programme for the winery. When she was done, she had in effect built a new winery within the winery.

Sonoma County's diversity of geography, climate and soil produces a number of distinct wine grape characteristics and also allows for flexibility with winemaking styles. More than 30,000 acres (12,140 hectares) are planted to vineyards and there is considerable room for more acreage. The climate in particular is shaped by the Pacific Ocean to the west, whose cold coastal waters provide a cooling effect with afternoon breezes and chilly morning and overnight temperatures, and by the moderating influence of the cool marine air from San Pablo Bay to the south.

The areas from which Long can select grapes vary greatly. In the southernmost region of Carneros, the Chardonnay fruit provides bracing acidity along with full, ripe, opulent flavours that echo pineapple, pear and spice notes. Fruit from the Russian River Valley, to the west of the winery, is also crisp and lively, with depth and concentration. The area is so well suited to white grape varieties that Simi, acting on Long's advice, has planted nearly 100 acres (40 hectares) of its own vines there. In fact, says Long, Chardonnay grows well in many of Sonoma's districts. Cabernet is another matter: it is more selective in its need for proper soils and climate. Cabernet in California needs warmth to ripen, but it also needs moderate temperatures so it does not overripen or ripen too quickly. When it does overripen, it can taste jammy and alcoholic; when it ripens too quickly, grapes can lose acidity, which affects the crispness and structure of the wine.

For Long, Cabernet is the greatest red wine produced in California. The vine yields tiny berries that are deeply coloured, with rich, concentrated fruit flavours echoing currant, plum, black cherry and anise notes. By its nature a rugged vine, Cabernet is also tannic, providing that puckerish sensation in youth which marks it out as one of the world's longest-lived red wines. Through experimentation with different vinification techniques, Long is finding that she can produce wines with ample tannins for long ageing and complexity, but soft and supple, without an astringent edge. Like most California winemakers, she prefers to age her wines in French oak barrels while rounding out some of the rough edges, as well as giving a wine structure and complexity through the toasty vanillin flavours imparted by the wood. Oak is used as a seasoning element for the wine; her wines are never overly oaky.

Alexander Valley Cabernets are often distinguished by their softer tannins and their herb and bell pepper notes. The best-known Cabernets are produced by Silver Oak (a Napa Valley winery with vineyards in southern Alexander Valley), Jordan, Alexander Valley Vineyards and Lyeth. The allure of Alexander Valley Cabernets is the smooth, polished texture that allows the wines to be enjoyed early on in their lives. The most recent Simi Reserve Cabernets, which are produced from the best lots of Cabernet, show a greater concentration of fruit, more richness and breadth of flavour and rounder, smoother tannins, but also less of the herb and bell pepper flavours.

The next decade at Simi is dedicated to improving the vineyards, as the winery concentrates on bringing its new vineyards into full production and its output begins to level off at 130,000 cases. In the 1980s, scientific and technological progress by Californian winemakers inside the wineries led to significant advances in the control of fermentation temperatures, as well as virtually eliminating bacterial problems. Now the focus is on growing grapes so that they achieve optimum ripeness, denser flavours, lower levels of alcohol and better balance, and ultimately produce more sophisticated wines.

Simi's now owns more than 100 acres (40 hectares) of Cabernet Sauvignon, Merlot, Cabernet Franc and Petit Verdot vines in the southern Alexander Valley area, a site Long selected as one of the best cooler areas of the valley. In the Simi vineyard, Long and her staff are conducting experiments with different grape clones, to determine which training techniques work best for which grape varieties. For instance, some vines have their leaf canopies trimmed to allow greater exposure to sunlight; others are pruned to reduce excessive growth, which can detract from the quality of the fruit the vine is producing and lead to undesirable crop levels of inferior-quality fruit. This kind of research takes several vintages, at best, to ascertain which approach yields the optimum-quality fruit, but it is a step that is essential to the production of quality wines. While the Simi Reserve Cabernets 1985 and 1986 are the finest produced in winery history, early signs are that with the 1987 and 1988 vintages, Simi is on the verge of producing even finer wines. With its own vineyards, the winery is ensured of greater quality control from vine to wine; Long's eyes light up with proud enthusiasm when tasting the new wines from her vineyards.

Success has its own rewards, but now Moët-Hennessy, the French parent firm that owns Simi, has promoted Long to president of the winery, and she is gradually easing herself out of the day-to-day, hands-on winemaking duties, allowing her assistant Paul Hobbs to take on more responsibility as winemaker. Long still takes the bottom-line decisions concerning winemaking style and quality, but also now oversees all other aspects of the winery – from public relations and marketing to grape-grower relations. To enhance her administrative skills, she has taken a management course at Stanford University. She is also still active at Long Vineyards in Napa Valley, where, in a California-style divorce, she continues to make wine with her former husband. On Sundays, her day off at Simi, she drives there from her home in Alexander Valley to taste the Riesling, Chardonnay and Cabernet they produce. Long is now engaged to Phil Freese, a vineyard manager for Robert Mondavi Winery, and is planning to remarry.

Zelma Long, says Richard Armstrong, President of Moët-Hennessy US Corp, is "the heart and soul" of Simi, and she intends to remain active in key winemaking decisions. "They can take Zelma Long out of the lab, but they can't take the lab out of Zelma," jokes one of her winemaker colleagues: "She will always be interested in winemaking." The biggest change is that as president she will now be responsible for steering the company in new directions, shouldering new duties such as personnel management and achieving sales goals. It's a challenge that is well suited to the curious, energetic, perfectionist figure of Zelma Long. She is one step closer to realizing her dream of leading Simi Winery to the top, from the vineyards up.

OREGON

David Lett of The Eyrie Vineyards

The grapes in cool, undulating Oregon take six weeks longer to ripen than those in sunny California. For David Lett, pioneer of the Pinot Noir grape here, these nail-biting weeks are what bring quality to the crop. And this quality, allied to Lett's dogged pursuit of perfection, has led to his wine being judged the equal of Burgundy's finest. The story of David Lett's extraordinary success at Eyrie Vineyards is also the story of the wine boom in the Pacific north-west, as *Gerald Asher* explains.

In 1964, armed with a viticulture degree and letters of introduction, David Lett left California for Europe. For almost a year he wandered from research station to research station and from grower to grower. It was a trip, Lett says, that both enhanced and qualified what he had learned at the University of California's Department of Viticulture and Enology at Davis. But it left him convinced that the best wines are made from grapes grown in marginal climates, where full grape maturity cannot be taken for granted.

This stimulated his interest in Pinot Noir, the great red grape of Burgundy. Unlike Cabernet Sauvignon, Pinot Noir grapes tear and bruise easily. Wine made from them is tender and blooms while still young; it owes less to the art of the winemaker than to his or her skill at preserving the fragrance, flavour and texture intrinsic to the variety. The extent of that fragrance and flavour depends on a well-tempered climate – a climate which, by definition, entails risk. In the uncertainty of such conditions Pinot Noir can be capricious, even in regions where it has long been established.

In California in the early 1960s it was farmers, by and large, who grew the grapes and winemakers who turned them into wine. Lett, however, had completed the required winemaking courses at Davis while taking his degree in viticulture. He saw no dividing line between vineyard and cellar. He was also preoccupied with Pinot Noir at least in part because of the challenge of making a wine dependent to a large extent on his skill in the vineyard. Harold Berg, one of his professors at Davis, had said that there was nowhere in the state cool enough for Pinot Noir, and so Lett decided to take his search for a marginal climate to Oregon.

He headed north to the Willamette Valley, a region already well-known for the intense flavour of its varied fruit crops. Opening to the Columbia River, Oregon's northern border, the Willamette Valley stretches south about half-way down the state. Though shielded from the Pacific by the Coast Range Mountains, it has an essentially maritime climate. Extremes of hot or cold, deluge or drought, are rare. Oregon was a destination for settlers from the east before California, and the valley's undulating landscape of ploughed field and pasture, woods and orchard, still wears a decidedly old-fashioned air.

In 1966, Lett bought 20 acres (eight hectares) of land in the Dundee Hills on the western side of the valley. The land was well-drained and had a sunny exposure at an elevation ranging from 250 to 450 feet (76-137 metres), high enough to protect the vines from frosty air trapped on the valley floor. He and his wife Diana called it The Eyrie Vineyards after the eyrie of red-tailed hawks they found there. In the first year they planted vines on four acres (1.5 hectares), in the second on three more acres (one hectare) – and so on, a few acres at a time, in each succeeding year.

The slow pace was dictated partly by a lack of funds to take on help and partly by the shortage of appropriate vine material. Pinot Noir is notoriously unstable, with scores – possibly hundreds – of clone variants. In fact, the conclusion drawn from most recent research is that the multiplicity of clones within mature Burgundian vineyards contributes to the depth of the flavour in wine produced there. United States' plant quarantine regulations hold back new material for years, however, and Lett was obliged to forgo the use of a range of clones from overseas and take what was available from California. He drew cuttings of one clone from Davis and of another from the Wente Bros ranch at Arroyo Seco in Monterey County; his Pinot Gris and Pinot Meunier cuttings came from Davis. He managed to obtain just 160 cuttings of each, and had to propagate successive generations of cuttings from these.

As other clones of Pinot Noir have become available over the years through a programme of Oregon State University, Lett has been able to enrich the mix of his vineyards. His one regret, though, is that he did not take steps at the beginning to put into quarantine all the Burgundian clones he could have mustered. Today they would be mature vines. He shrugs: "to be young is to be impatient ...".

It was also to be indefatigable. Photographs show him in those early years smiling contentedly at mud, wheelbarrows and heaps of pruned cuttings. The labour in establishing the vines, which sometimes obliged the Letts and their two children to camp for weeks at a time in the vineyard itself, must have been as rigorous as that of any earlier pioneer in the West.

Since purchasing that first vineyard, the Letts – on their own and with partners – have bought more land and planted more vineyards, none more than a mile from the others.

Eyrie's Stonehenge vineyard is in the Willamette Valley, in the cool north-west of the state where the climate is essentially maritime.

David Lett, Oregon's most celebrated winemaker. Having studied viticulture and winemaking in depth,
he knew that finding an appropriate site for the capricious Pinot Noir would not be easy.

With their partners, they have in production six acres (two hectares) of Pinot Noir, 16 acres
(six hectares) of Pinot Gris, four acres (1.5 hectares) of Chardonnay, and lesser acreages of
Pinot Meunier and Muscat Ottonel. Further plantings of Pinot Gris and Pinot Noir will be
bearing grapes within a year or two.

The Eyrie Vineyard produces 6,000-7,000 cases of wine a year, about half of it Pinot
Gris. In Oregon, Pinot Gris makes a wine that combines the unbridled aroma typical of
Alsace and the plumpness we expect of a white Burgundy. Its naturally full texture needs
no oak-ageing, yet in bottle an Oregon Pinot Gris can develop both bouquet and flavour of
an unexpected complexity. Pinot Meunier, a black grape grown in Champagne for limited
use in some *cuvées*, is not usually produced commercially as a red wine. Lett's limited
production of it is unique. Pinot Meunier lacks the refinement of Pinot Noir; its wine is a
little more tannic and its fruitiness more obvious, more rustic.

But it is with Pinot Noir – the focus of his efforts from the start – that David Lett, The
Eyrie Vineyards and Oregon itself have earned world-wide respect. Lett succinctly
accounts for the state's success with Pinot Noir thus: "In Oregon, Pinot Noir achieves fruit
maturity about six weeks later than in California, reaching a satisfactory sugar level just at
the end of the growing season. The grapes have ripened slowly in the cool and even
temperatures that Pinot Noir requires to develop its fullest potentials of flavour. Although
these extra six weeks are nerve-racking for the grower, they are essential in achieving the
finest wines possible from this variety."

Without the benefit of such advice himself, Lett had to unlearn much of what he had
been taught at Davis, so different were the conditions in Oregon. In California, for
example, ripening grapes are at least partially leaf-shaded to avoid sunburn. Not so in
Oregon, where shoots are trained high and summer leaves pulled away to keep foliage

from ripening bunches. The freer circulation of air helps prevent rot by allowing bunches to dry more quickly, an unnecessary precaution in the dry summers of California.

Since Lett planted his first cutting 25 years ago, more than 200 other vineyards have been established in the Willamette Valley. His first few acres planted there have swollen to more than 3,000 acres (1,214 hectares), of which well over a third are bearing Pinot Noir.

Though he takes into account the quality of Burgundy's wines, Lett has always insisted that Oregon Pinot Noir does not have to taste like, nor be mistaken for, European Pinot Noir to be legitimate. Nevertheless, 13 years of struggle, often in the face of dismissive indifference, seemed vindicated when a tasting panel of the 1979 Gault-Millau Wine Olympiades in Paris placed The Eyrie Vineyards' Pinot Noir 1975 third in a range of wines that included distinguished Burgundian competition.

Robert Drouhin, the Beaune grower and *négociant* (see pages 42-49), was dismayed at that much-publicized result, and suggested that it would have been quite otherwise had the competing Burgundies been of appropriate quality. In the following year, therefore, he assembled a jury composed essentially of European professionals in the thousand-year-old Hall of Justice of the former Dukes of Burgundy. They tasted blind a dozen wines including The Eyrie Vineyards' Pinot Noir 1975, six assorted Drouhin Burgundies (among them a Chambertin Clos-de-Bèze 1961, a Beaune Clos des Mouches 1978 and a Chambolle-Musigny 1959) as well as Pinot Noirs from other countries. The assumption was that this more carefully constructed, and meticulously conducted, tasting would reverse the findings of the Gault-Millau Olympiades. But, although the wine with the highest combined score of 70.0 was Drouhin's Chambolle-Musigny, in second place by only a fifth of a point was The Eyrie Vineyards' Pinot Noir. And more than three points behind, in third place, was Drouhin's Chambertin Clos-de-Bèze.

David Lett, at least outwardly, made light of the fact that his wine was placed virtually equal first with the best that a top Burgundian producer could put forward to defeat him. Robert Drouhin, on the other hand, reacted in a way that no one would have foreseen. He selected and bought 100 acres (40 hectares) of vineyard land in the Dundee Hills, quite close to the Letts' Eyrie Vineyards and adopted the admirably pragmatic philosophy – if you can't beat them, join them.

Robert Drouhin of Burgundy was so impressed by Lett's success that he bought 100 acres in the Dundee Hills nearby.

CHILE

Viña Santa Rita

Like many other Chilean wine producers, Viña Santa Rita has spared no money buying vineyards in the country's favoured Central Valley and equipping its two wineries with all the machinery any modern winemaker could want. But, in its determination to put quality before quantity, Santa Rita is tapping more fully than any other firm Chile's fund of natural resources. *Maggie McNie MW* describes how it is done in this rare phylloxera-free country.

In 1814, four years after the people of Chile rose in revolt against Spanish rule, the native Chilean forces commanded by General Bernardo O'Higgins were heavily defeated by the Spanish at the Battle of Rancagua. The defeated general, together with 120 of his men, took refuge on an estate at Buin, near Santiago, where the lady of the house, Dona Paula Jaraquemada, hid them in the cellars. From there O'Higgins succeeded in escaping to Argentina and joined forces with the Argentinian general, San Martin. The combined armies, now known as the Army of the Andes, made an epic crossing of the mountains, finally defeating the Spaniards and liberating Chile in 1820. O'Higgins became the first president of Chile – but the estate on which he took refuge has another claim to fame, for it was here that Viña Santa Rita was founded in 1880, and today its most famous brand bears the name "120" in memory of the events of 1814.

Viña Santa Rita is situated in the Central Valley, the home of Chile's finest wines. Strictly speaking, the Central Valley is not a valley at all, but a plateau stretching between the Andes and the Coastal Cordilleras, a lesser range of mountains bordering the Pacific Ocean. The plateau is crossed by five major rivers flowing from the Andes to the Pacific which, in late winter and spring, are fast-flowing torrents capable of sweeping away bridges. By vintage time, however, much of the water in these rivers has been channelled into Chile's vital agricultural irrigation systems, and the torrents have dwindled to tiny streams within large stony expanses of dry river bed.

The estate was originally owned by the Garcia Huidobro family, and it remained in their hands until 1978. After changing hands twice, Viña Santa Rita was bought in 1980 by Ricardo Claro, an industrialist and steel magnate, who also controls Viña Carmen and the largest bottle-manufacturing plant in Chile. Since Claro's acquisition of Santa Rita. its wines have become steadily finer. It is a thoroughly modern firm and, on current production figures, appears to be the fastest-growing wine company in Chile. It is also an

Chile's Central Valley, a huge, well-irrigated plateau stretching between the Andes and the coastal Cordilleras mountains, is now producing premium wines for an international market.

adventurous firm, at least as far as export wines are concerned. In many countries with a long history of winemaking – and, according to tradition, Chile has been making wine since 1548 – there can be a significant difference between local taste and that of the export markets; this is certainly the case in Chile.

The company's 555 acres (225 hectares) of vineyards lie within sight of the Andes, snow-capped for much of the year and bathed in the most wonderful light; grapes are also bought in from other independent growers on long-term contract. Most of production is taken up by Cabernet Sauvignon – indeed, it is often said that Chile has only one wine, Cabernet Sauvignon – but Santa Rita also grows and makes Chardonnay, Sauvignon Blanc and Riesling, a recent addition.

Viña Santa Rita has two wineries, one situated to the south in the Lontue Valley and the other at Buin in the Maipo Valley. Close by the Buin winery lies the historic old house and its park, one of the most beautiful estates in a country renowned for lavish growth and lush parkland. The house, with its wooden floors, large echoing rooms and famous private chapel (where Cardinal Giuseppe Sarto, later Pope Pius X, once celebrated mass), is shaded from the heat by huge trees and surrounded by a profusion of roses, plumbago, jasmine, hydrangeas and other plants, in a riot of colour and scent.

Claro and his oenologist/winemaker, Ignacio Recabarren, share an unusual approach to the question of quality versus quantity. Like many other Chilean companies, Viña Santa Rita has spared no expense in investing heavily in new vineyard holdings and modern equipment. But Recabarren is alone among the country's oenologists in attempting to concentrate his wine and improve quality by reducing the high yields that are so easily obtained in this climate with the aid of irrigation. At Santa Rita new vine plantings are much denser, and pruning far harder, than is usual in Chile. Coupled with a significant reduction in the use of fertilizer and irrigation, which makes the vine struggle to produce its fruit, this results in a much-reduced yield; in some instances yields have dropped by nearly 50 per cent.

At the winery, the reception, crushing and pressing of newly-picked grapes takes place under cover in the open. Red grapes, which suffer less than white grapes from the intense heat, are picked throughout the day, and fermented in large old "Rauli" tanks. Rauli is a local wood, often referred to as "redwood", but probably a local species of beech. The wine is then transferred into small oak *barriques* for up to 12 months before laying down in bottle for a year. Great emphasis is placed on oak-ageing, and Recabarren is at present experimenting with several different types of oak – French, American and Yugoslavian. There are three cellars at Santa Rita: a modern cellar filled with barrels stacked on pallets; a 200-year old cellar for the Cabernet Reserva wines, and a third separate cellar for ageing the Medalla Real Cabernet.

White grapes are harvested from early morning until just after midday, in order to avoid the afternoon heat. There is no shortage of cheap labour, so the grapes can be picked by hand. Most white wines are cool-fermented in stainless steel to preserve the fruit and aromas. An exception is the Chardonnay, part of which is barrel-fermented using French oak, and then left on its lees for a short while, before being blended with wine fermented in stainless steel. The eventual aim is to have sufficient wood of different types to ferment 75 per cent of the Chardonnay in barrel.

Recabarren is now experimenting with malolactic fermentation on a percentage of his Chardonnay, a process rarely used for white wines in hot climates, since one result is a fall in the wine's overall acidity. He feels, however, that the extra complexity created by the malolactic is an asset, and that if necessary the acid levels of the wine can be adjusted. Red wines, too, are the subject of experimentation, with a new Cabernet wine being made, not by traditional methods with long skin contact, but by *macération carbonique*.

That these methods have improved the quality of the wines is borne out by the number of awards Santa Rita has won lately in international wine shows, often against stiff competition. Most notable among these was the first place awarded at the 1987 Gault-Millau Wine Olympiades held in Paris, when a Santa Rita Medalla Real Cabernet Sauvignon 1984 was awarded higher marks than many distinguished Cabernet-based wines from Australia, the United States and France, including Domaine de Chevalier, Châteaux Lynch-Bages and Cos d'Estournel.

The energetic export manager, Rodrigo Buzeta, plainly feels that there is a great market for Santa Rita wines both in the United States and in the Western European markets, particularly for the premium Chardonnay and Cabernet Sauvignon wines. On current showing, who could contradict him?

Australia and New Zealand

How fast Australia has moved in the world of wine is evident from a single fact: the first quality Chardonnays were made scarcely 20 years ago, in 1973. And when you consider that Australia only really started to make table wines, as opposed to heavy fortified wines, in the last 30 years, you begin to realize what aptitude for winemaking the Australians have shown and what natural resources this Brobdingnagian country must have.

In fact, because of its latitude, only a small proportion of the country is cool enough for viticulture. The wine regions are thus almost all confined to the south (the area furthest from the Equator); indeed, with the exception of an important outcrop around the southern tip of Western Australia and a handful of maverick wineries in the north, they are restricted to the south-east corner. These are, nonetheless, generous expanses compared with the vineyards of Europe. The harvest starts at the end of January in the Upper Hunter and continues through a succession of regions, finishing in May; Europe's pickers are seldom out before the beginning of September or after the end of October.

Overall, Australia can fairly be classed as having a warm climate for wine, but with many climatic and geological subdivisions which yield wines of distinct regional character. The Chardonnay of Leeuwin Estate in Western Australia's Margaret River region will always be more restrained, more refined than the full, ripe Hunter Valley style epitomized by The Rothbury Estate in New South Wales. Both have their own substantial merits. The *terra rossa* (red earth) of the Coonawarra region, for example, is legendary and undoubtedly a factor behind the excellent Coonawarra Cabernet Sauvignons.

The variations are also increasing, as winemakers go in search of cooler, more "European" hill-sites where lower temperatures prolong the growing season to give more profound flavour to the grapes and greater finesse to their wines – areas such as the Adelaide Hills in South Australia, the Yarra Valley in Victoria and northern Tasmania. This dynamism is invigorating and fruitful, but there is a potential hazard. If Australia were to proceed overwhelmingly in favour of subtler wines, we could lose the massive, rich, vigorous style of red wine that Max Schubert created and perfected in Penfolds

The modern buildings of The Rothbury Estate in New South Wales and, at the other end of the country, the new vineyards of Leeuwin Estate among the Margaret River hills in Western Australia.

Grange Hermitage and for which there is certainly no easing of demand: quite the contrary, for it has become a cult wine world-wide.

Stylistically, there could be no more vivid contrast than New Zealand's Cloudy Bay, a vibrant, aromatic Sauvignon Blanc, made at the northern tip of the South Island in that much cooler, wetter country hundreds of miles south-east across the Tasman Sea. But Cloudy Bay, like Grange, has become a cult wine – and for one of the same reasons. It is quintessentially a wine of its country, a perfect expression of the intense, but elegant fruit and the electrifying freshness that characterize New Zealand wines.

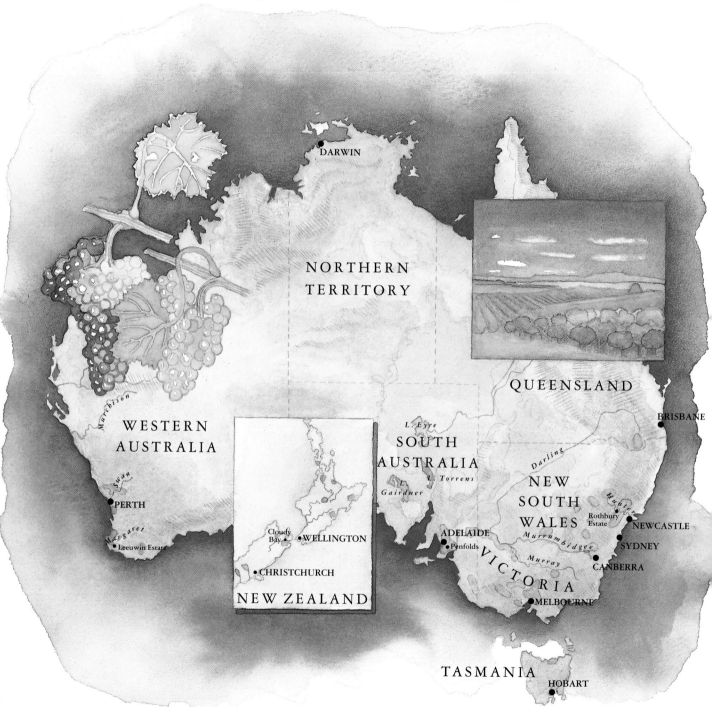

THE HUNTER VALLEY

Len Evans of The Rothbury Estate

The list of Len Evans' contributions to the Australian wine industry makes remarkable reading. As a wine judge, promoter, writer and critic, he has done perhaps more for the wines of his adopted country than any other single person. But his greatest pride is The Rothbury Estate in the Hunter Valley, where he set himself the challenge of making the finest Semillon and Shiraz of the region. *James Halliday* explains how he has achieved so much.

"Leonard Paul Evans, OBE. Born 1930 in Suffolk, England, but conceived in Wales; arrived in Australia 1956. Australia's most senior wine judge, co-founder and Chairman of The Rothbury Estate, Chairman of Petaluma, author, wine columnist and restaurateur; former professional golfer, television and radio satirical scriptwriter and hotelier; other interests include fly-fishing, fine food and female company. Hopes he will be remembered for the buildings he has helped restore, design and/or build, but will most probably be remembered as the single most important contributor to the Australian wine industry in the second half of the 20th century."

Thus might an entry read in a somewhat liberated *Who's Who*, and it might give some insight into a man whose prodigious energy, sheer tenacity and exceptional intellect have propelled him through life at a pace that would leave most mortals gasping. In best Australian tradition it has also led to the statutory number of petty critics, those who seek to chop tall poppies down to size. They are fewer these days than they once were, for Evans' achievements are as compelling as is his full-fronted, no-holds-barred approach to life and to all the enjoyable things it has to offer.

By the time Evans arrived in Australia he had abandoned a public school scholarship and an intended university degree in architecture in favour of professional golf. This, too, had gone by the wayside when, in his words, "I discovered there was a world of difference between being a professional golfer and a golf professional". He had also served as a national serviceman in Germany for nine months, and stopped off on the way to Australia to spend two years as a timber cutter and deer culler in New Zealand.

His pace did not slacken once he arrived in Australia. His first stop, from 1956 to 1958, was in Mount Isa, a bustling mining town in north-western Queensland, where he held three jobs (simultaneously) and met his wife-to-be Trish; thence to Sydney to try his hand (successfully) as a scriptwriter for radio and television; and to graduate from pub glasswasher to Food and Beverage Manager of Sydney's newest hotel, The Chevron, in charge of 350 staff including 80 cooks and apprentices.

It was here that his life-long love affair with wine (and, if you wish, women and song) blossomed. He was responsible for building up a wine cellar that had no equal in Australia, and he formed close links with most of the leading wine companies. He soon became Australia's first regular wine columnist, and it was this that led to his employment (on January 1st 1965) by the Australian Wine Board as its first National Promotions Executive, a strange title for what was a strange position – no real job description, no superiors and no particular objectives. Evans being Evans, this presented no difficulty, and within three years the Australian Wine Bureau was up and running, with employees in all states.

Len Evans, a vigorous and apparently inexhaustible campaigner, has played an unparalleled role in shaping the Australian wine industry.

By the end of 1967 the red wine boom was well and truly under way in Australia, and it was time for Evans to move on. He set himself up as a consultant, with Tooth & Co, Qantas, The Summit Restaurant, The Coachman Restaurant and The Travelodge as his first clients. 1968 was a momentous year: he earned three times as much as he had received as Director of the Wine Bureau; he started Bulletin Place, his wonderful retail wine shop-cum-restaurant complex in Sydney, and he founded The Rothbury Estate. Of distinctly lesser moment, he met me as a patron of Bulletin Place: some years before, I had attended one of his wine courses, but I had been just another face in a room full of bashful acolytes.

Bulletin Place was of enormous importance to Evans, and to me: it was here that our friendship was forged and here that my wine knowledge grew week by week as the Monday Table and the Options game developed. The Tasting Room, the first of the two restaurants to be developed (the Beef Room came later, upstairs) was a Mecca for wine lovers from all parts of the globe. All the great names came there at one time or another, some many times. It was also the venue for the early Single Bottle Club dinners. But Bulletin Place was essentially an indulgence: when it made money (which wasn't always) it was almost always in spite of Evans's best efforts to the contrary. Evans was never a wine merchant: he was a consumer, not a seller. His motivation in running Bulletin Place was to provide fine food and great wine in the wonderful ambience of the 1816 warehouse in which Bulletin Place operated and which Evans had painstakingly transformed from shabby anonymity to one of the most beautiful old buildings in Sydney. It was not to make money, much to the chagrin of a series of its long-suffering managers.

The original protagonists involved in the founding of The Rothbury Estate were Evans and long-term Hunter *vigneron* and identity Murray Tyrrell, with Hungarian-born Sydney art dealer and bon vivant-cum-wine judge Rudy Komon providing his unique kind of spice. The other eight in the founding syndicate were an assortment of accountants, orthodontists, radiologists, department store owners, broadcasters, dentists and surgeons. Each was relatively affluent, and each wanted to be part of the wine boom which was then

The stark, jutting silhouette of the Rothbury winery bears witness to Len Evans' skills as a designer.

sweeping Australia. The Hunter Valley was the logical, indeed the only, location for a Sydney-based syndicate. For Evans, the challenge was to produce two great estate-grown, -made and -bottled wines: one from Semillon, which is the Hunter Valley's greatest claim to international recognition as a wine style, the other from Hermitage (or, more correctly, Shiraz – the grape known in France as Syrah).

These were heady times: table wine consumption (principally red) was increasing in leaps and bounds. Five years earlier (in 1963) Sydney surgeon and wine writer Max Lake had opened the lid of Pandora's box when he founded Lake's Folly, the first of many hundreds of weekend wine operations which were intended to provide a relaxing hobby for their busy and successful professional owners, but which in the fullness of time often consumed their creators, body, soul and bank balance.

In any event, the syndicate planted hundreds of acres on the Herlstone, Homestead Hill, Brokenback and Rothbury blocks. Keith Cottier, even then a leading Sydney architect, was asked to design the winery according to concepts provided by Evans. It was duly erected just in time for the 1971 vintage (the worst for the Hunter in living memory). Gerry Sissingh was lured away from Lindemans to become winemaker, and the greatest show on earth was on the road.

The winery was, is, and always will be, a splendid building, beautifully sited on the slope of a gentle hill. It received a major architectural design award, and deserved many others. Evans has always regarded it as at least half his, and rests comfortably in the sure knowledge that it will be admired for centuries to come. It is both functionally and

Yields vary widely in the Hunter Valley, where high temperatures and irregular rainfall make it almost impossible to produce a consistent harvest and so to predict a wine's success.

aesthetically pleasing, and, while it has since been much extended (most recently the 1989 multi-million dollar administration block, air-conditioned warehouse and barrel store facility), the integrity of the original design has never been challenged. Ignoring the experimental wines of 1971 (the vineyards produced only a tiny crop in any event), right from the outset Gerry Sissingh produced quite magical Semillon.

Rothbury's financial future is, by now, secure, and it cannot be long before its long-suffering shareholders receive their maiden dividend. In the intervening 20 years there was little financial joy for any of the players, however significant the role of Rothbury in producing and promoting fine Hunter Valley wine. This is not a financial *post mortem*, but Evans has summarized the problems this way: "At the time of the red wine boom we planted too much Shiraz, not foreseeing the end to the demand for it; we planted too many vines on soils that could not sustain an appropriate yield; we had faith in the true estate concept of 'from own vineyards to bottle', and too many other estates' buying material from anywhere ruined the name. We were the wrong size, being too big for a boutique and too small to compete with the major wineries; we suffered badly from the drought of 1980-83, the vineyards sometimes yielding less than a tonne per hectare; and we were affected by the wages explosion of the mid-1970s, making it necessary to plan loss years and to re-finance the company." Job could not have endured more.

That Rothbury has survived and at last prospered is due entirely to Len Evans. Through his sheer persistence (I prefer to forget the squash match in which I led him 9-1, 9-3, 7-2 – but did not win), his courage and his burning conviction that Rothbury was fundamentally right, he variously bullied and seduced a succession of bankers and investors into providing financial support when all seemed lost. The outcome is that Rothbury has emerged as the foremost producer of Semillon in the Hunter Valley since 1972: its wines of that year, for example, will live for another decade at least if properly corked and cellared. In an ironical twist of fate, much of its present prosperity turns on its opulent Chardonnays, produced principally from its Cowra vineyards but also from the Hunter Valley. It is these wines that have attracted such praise overseas – in the United States in particular. The Rothbury Estate Reserve Chardonnay 1986 was the *Wine Spectator's* highest-pointed Australian wine in 1987, and was chosen as *Decanter's* top Australian Chardonnay in the magazine's world tasting of 1988.

I say ironical, because Chardonnay is such a compliant mistress, giving luxuriantly of her charms quickly and with little persuasion. Great Semillon eschews oak, shows almost nothing other than a slightly sour, faintly herbaceous and distinctly thin taste when young, and only reluctantly starts to reveal its charms with a minimum of five years in bottle, often requiring ten or 15 years to give of its best. Hunter Semillon then assumes its rightful position as one of the great wine styles of the world, uniquely Australian yet international in its sheer class. Time and again I have seen distinguished wine men and women start in amazement when told that this honeyed wine, with its flavours of butter on toast and sundry nuts, with its almost creamy texture, has never been near oak and has no Chardonnay in its make-up. The Rothbury Semillons in my cellar from 1972, 1973, 1974 and 1979 give me as much pleasure as any Australian wine.

The Rothbury red wines have never given me as much pleasure; I am sure that part of the problem was a combination of young vines and young wines. Hunter Valley Hermitage is as surprising in its way as is Semillon. It can appear light-bodied and soft when young, seemingly denying it has any particular future. Yet 20 years can bring a similar transformation, unveiling an immensely complex, soft, velvety, gently earthy wine with an almost ethereal bouquet and aftertaste.

The one thing Evans and I do not see eye-to-eye on is the future for Pinot Noir. Rothbury makes a distinctive carbonic maceration style of wine which says much about the making technique when it is young and much about the district when it is old, but at no time does it say anything about the flavour and structure of Pinot Noir as it appears in Burgundy. We get onto treacherous ground here, with a debate that can go on indefinitely, so I shall say no more, knowing Evans will strongly disagree with me in any event.

There is, of course, much more to the story of Len Evans' involvement with wine: his one-time ownership of Château Rahoul in Graves, Château Padouen in Sauternes, the Silverado vineyard in Napa Valley and his continuing involvement in Petaluma, the highly-regarded winery in South Australia. No less important has been his lifelong mission of spreading knowledge of great wine and his tireless work for charities. Finally, there is Loggerheads, that extraordinary house (a pale and inadequate word if ever there was one) on the hill behind Rothbury in which he and Trish and an endless stream of friends from around the world now live.

SOUTH AUSTRALIA

Max Schubert and Grange Hermitage

A visit to Bordeaux by a young Australian winemaker 40 years ago was to change not only his own life, but the direction of the entire Australian wine industry. When Max Schubert returned home to Australia from his study-tour of three European wine regions, he was flushed with the idea of making a dry red table wine in the Bordeaux manner. The result was Grange Hermitage, Australia's greatest wine. *James Halliday* tells the story.

The story of Max Schubert and Grange Hermitage is a fairy-tale on a grand scale. The hero arises from obscurity, with neither family, wealth nor education to assist him. He conceives a vision that is not only long in advance of its time, but that no one else is able to share. His masterpieces are derided and ignored, and he is formally directed to cease their creation. Eventually, their brilliance is recognized, and his wine becomes famous, but only grudging credit is given to its creator. He retires, and might well have lived his remaining days in relative obscurity, honoured by his peers but otherwise the forgotten man. Once again, it is the sheer magnificence of his creations that is his saviour, and that belatedly brings him the fame he so richly deserves.

It is also a particularly Australian fairy-tale: it is a national characteristic to "have a go". It derives from our early days when we faced a vast and often inhospitable continent, accepting physical challenges that now seem incomprehensible or impossible. There really wasn't any choice: you either had a go or accepted failure before you even tried. Max Schubert was born in the hamlet of Moculta in the East Barossa Ranges in 1915, one of six children of the village blacksmith. Before long the Schuberts moved to Nuriootpa, and it was here in the heart of the Barossa Valley that Schubert went to school.

In 1931, at the age of 16, he left school and joined Penfolds Nuriootpa winery as a messenger boy. Within one year, he had been seconded to help the newly appointed (and first) wine chemist. Schubert was a willing student and soon enrolled at night-school to learn more about chemistry. By this time Leslie Penfold Hyland had, in a somewhat eccentric fashion, adopted Schubert and moved him to Magill, where in due course he became a cellar-hand and, in 1940, assistant winemaker.

In 1949 Schubert's big opportunity came: he was sent to Jerez for a month to learn more about sherry; thence to the Douro for a fortnight at the height of vintage; and, almost as an afterthought, to Bordeaux. Here his host was Christian Cruse, and 40 years later, Max

Max Schubert, the humble genius whose career took him from winery messenger boy to creator of the brilliant Grange Hermitage, the famed "first growth" of the Southern Hemisphere.

Schubert's voice still rings with emotion as he recalls his time with Cruse. "Mr Cruse showed me magnificent old French wines, some 60-70 years old, but which still had so much life in them. I have never forgotten those wines, and I don't think I have ever tasted wines like them since."

When Schubert returned to Australia in 1950, he did so with a dream of emulating the great red wines of Bordeaux that Christian Cruse had revealed to him. In this day and age that might seem a perfectly normal, if laudable, ambition. In 1950 it was not. Max Schubert was, and is, a dyed-in-the-wool company man, deeply conscious of the opportunities that Penfolds had given him and all too aware of his own humble family circumstances. His loyalty to the Penfold Hylands was absolute. At the time, and for the 50 years previously, Australia was almost exclusively a producer of fortified wine: precise figures are hard to come by, but over 90 per cent of all wine produced was sherry (of every imaginable shape and hue), tawny port and vintage port. Penfolds was no less a fortified winemaker; it was fortified wine that Schubert had spent the previous 20 years learning about; and it was sherry and port that had prompted his trip to Europe.

Australia had been a significant producer of fine table wine in the 19th century: Victoria had been nicknamed "John Bull's vineyard", and in 1890 produced over 50 per cent of all Australian wine – much of it from cool-climate areas such as Geelong, the Yarra Valley, Metropolitan Melbourne and Bendigo. It is a little-known fact that between 1928 and 1938 Australia exported more wine than France to the United Kingdom – and 95 per cent of this was fortified wine. Much of it, incidentally, was of appalling quality, with bacterial activity that Schubert and his superiors (most notably among them John Fornachon) were finally to understand and conquer.

So when Max Schubert set about making his first experimental red wine in 1951, utilizing his Bordeaux experience, it was in an almost alien world. Dry red table wine was made, of course, but it enjoyed a tiny market – a handful of doctors, lawyers and professionals (many of whom had gained their knowledge overseas) and the winemakers themselves. The wine itself was made from Grenache, Mataro and – at the premium end – Shiraz. Pinot Noir did not exist, and even at the end of the 1950s the entire Australian crush of Cabernet Sauvignon amounted to 200 tonnes. Wine was fermented in concrete vats (sometimes upright wooden vats) without cooling, with subsequent maturation in ancient 330-gallon (1,500-litre) and 495-gallon (2,250-litre) casks.

Wine writers and winemakers from overseas took home with them an indelible impression of Australian table wine: hot, roasted, alcoholic and tannic red wines, which tasted much the same whatever part of Australia they were made in (with the possible exception of the Hunter Valley) and irrespective of the grape variety used. This was not an unfair view, and it is indeed fundamental to understanding the reaction that was accorded to Grange Hermitage when it was ultimately shown to the public.

In the meantime, Schubert had had to make a number of key decisions in planning his first vintage. The first was the choice of oak: French was virtually unobtainable; American was scarce but available (and cheaper). So, without any great science, American was chosen, almost unwittingly setting a style path that Penfolds follows to this day across the broad spectrum of its top wines.

The second choice was of grape variety. Max Schubert remembers it this way: "The grape material used in Bordeaux consisted of four basic varieties – namely, Cabernet Sauvignon, Cabernet Franc, Merlot and Malbec. Only Cabernet Sauvignon and Malbec were available in South Australia at the time, but a survey showed that they were in such short supply as to make them impracticable commercially. I elected to use Hermitage (or Shiraz) only, which was in plentiful supply, knowing full well that if I was careful enough in the choice of area and vineyard, and coupled with the correct production procedure, I would be able to make the type and style of wine I wanted."

Schubert had observed that in Bordeaux the wines finished with 11.5-12 degrees of alcohol, and that they were seldom taken off skins and pressed in under 12 days. Denied chaptalization in Australia, he implemented a number of other finely balanced technical measures which were calculated to achieve a similar effect.

Once again, Schubert had made a control wine, using the same base but in the conventional large old oak fermentation vessels. He then observed the development of both wines, and even after a month was convinced his experiment was a success. "After 12 months, both wines were crystal clear, with superb dark, full, rich colour and body – but there the similarity ended. The experimental wine was bigger in all respects. It was a big wine in bouquet, flavour and balance. The raw wood was not so apparent, but the fruit characteristics had become more pronounced and defined, with more than a faint suggestion of cranberry. It was almost as if the new wood had acted as a catalyst to release previously unsuspected flavours and aromas from the Hermitage grape."

The 1952 vintage followed; then the 1953 (and a brief, though very successful, experiment with Cabernet Sauvignon, a wine that Schubert still regards as one of the best); then the 1954, 1955 and 1956. Both Schubert and Penfolds' head office felt the time had come for the wine to be unveiled: Schubert, because the 1951 and 1952 were starting to show all he was hoping for; and head office, because it wanted to see some return on its by now very considerable investment. The company had seen the end of beer-rationing (a wartime measure) and the beginning of a 30-year period of change in which table wine production and sales would rise from ten to 90 per cent of total wine sales.

Vines were first planted at Penfolds' Magill estate to the east of Adelaide in 1844. Since the 1950s it has been the heart of Grange Hermitage.

A grand unveiling was arranged in Sydney to which all the leading wine trade figures were invited. No wine writers were asked, because there were none. Schubert reminisces: "The result was absolutely disastrous. Simply, no one liked Grange Hermitage". Tastings were hurriedly arranged in Adelaide, with the same (or worse) results. Some of the comments were burned on Max Schubert's soul and he can recall them to this day: "A concoction of wild fruits and sundry berries, with crushed ants predominating," said one well-known wine man. "Schubert, I congratulate you. A very good dry port which no one in their right mind will buy, let alone drink," said another. Yet another, remembers Schubert, "wanted to buy it and use it as an aphrodisiac. His theory was that the wine was like bull's blood in all respects and would raise his blood count to twice the norm when the occasion demanded."

Shortly before the 1957 vintage, Schubert received written instructions from the company's head office in Sydney to discontinue production of Grange. With the support of all of the winery staff at Magill, and with a broad wink from Jeffrey Penfold Hyland, Schubert continued to make small quantities of Grange, but was denied his all-important supplies of new oak. The resulting wines are collector's items, notable for their rarity rather than their quality.

But the wine in the bottle continued to blossom, and slowly the whisper went around. A few wise men – George Fairbrother, Max Lake and Douglas Lamb among them – had supported the wine from the start, and the older Granges started to sell. Shortly before the 1960 vintage, Schubert received official instructions to start making Grange again.

In February 1962, Penfolds decided to re-enter the all-important Australian wine show system after a long absence. The Grange 1955 was entered at the Sydney Show and won a gold medal, the first of 50 the wine would win before its retirement in 1977, when it carried off the trophy for best red wine of the show at Melbourne. It was not that the wine was past its peak: it was just that Penfolds decided it was time to let some of the younger Granges have their chance. Grange is, in fact, no longer entered in the show system – it is beyond it – but collectively the wines amassed 27 trophies, 117 gold medals, 63 silver medals and 34 bronze medals by the time Penfolds called game, set and match.

The Penfold Hyland family sold the company to Tooths in 1976, the year after Max Schubert retired as executive winemaker, although he was retained as a consultant. For the next five years he was welcomed by the winemaking staff, tolerated by management and ignored by the marketing department. Then, in the twilight of his life, Penfolds realized he was a living treasure, and he has been a centrepiece of the Penfolds' promotion and marketing programme ever since. If you detect a note of minor disapproval in my voice, you are right, but only because the company took so long to give him his due.

And what of Grange, his masterpiece? Well, I have participated in a number of vertical tastings over the years, and I have participated in countless individual bottles. Here I will add a few comments and explanations of my own. Most importantly, Grange continues to be made as it always has been, give or take a few minor pieces of fine-tuning, reflecting increasing technical knowledge. First Don Ditter, and now John Duval, are willing and sympathetic guardians of a priceless inheritance. Indeed, I see no small measure of Max Schubert's humility in the make-up of each, but that is a story for another day.

At the core of his continuum are the grapes, all coming from very old, low-yielding, unirrigated vines. The basic formula, too, has remained the same, and here an element of controversy emerges even now. Quite apart from significant use of additional tannin (added as red tannin in powdered form) Schubert deliberately engineered high levels of volatile acidity, varying between 0.8 and 1.2 grammes per litre. His belief was that a wine with such massive flavour needed the lift of some volatility, an approach with which I whole-heartedly agree, but which has not always endeared itself to some of the more technical and literal judges in Australia.

The other feature of Grange is its longevity. The three greatest Granges (ignoring the magnificent experimental wines of 1951, 1952 and 1953) are the 1955, the 1962 and the 1971 (with a host of challengers from the 1980s waiting to go on the list as the 21st century arrives). Over the past decade I have drunk these wines (usually as part of a group) at least once a year, and – if the gods have been kind to me – more than once. On November 30th 1988, I attended a retrospective tasting of the 1978-88 vintages, at the conclusion of which we had the 1971, 1966 and 1955 as a kind of vinous bonne-bouche. One of the great truisms is that there are no great old wines, only great old bottles, but once again the 1955 was a great old bottle. The bouquet was fragrant – but it was that of an old wine; the palate, however, promised eternal youth. It was wonderfully rich, with ripe berry fruit and tannin still there in abundance.

André Tchelistcheff, the great American winemaker, first tasted a bottle of Bin 60A 1962 (a show wine made by Schubert in the manner of Grange) in the presence of a distinguished group of winemakers and judges. He leapt to his feet and commanded, "Gentlemen, you will please stand in the presence of such a wine". Anyone who understands red wine would also stand in the presence of Max Schubert.

WESTERN AUSTRALIA

Denis Horgan and Bob Cartwright of Leeuwin Estate

The wines of Western Australia, though less well-known than those of the eastern states, are rapidly gaining a reputation for quality – and it is in the mild, maritime climate of the Margaret River region that they are achieving their greatest stature. At Leeuwin Estate, where millionaire Denis Horgan has spared no expense in his avowed "pursuit of excellence", winemaker Bob Cartwright makes Chardonnay and Cabernet Sauvignon wines that are winning world-wide respect, as **Charles Metcalfe** explains.

The Leeuwin Estate vineyard came into being almost by accident. In 1973, Robert Mondavi (see pages 186-93) was prospecting in Australia for an ideal site for a new winery. After a careful study of soil types, geology, climate and other factors, he settled on the Margaret River, a promising region where there were only a handful of experimental winemakers at the time. The best virgin site he found was on land used for grazing cattle, just outside the little town of Margaret River, where the Leeuwin Estate vineyard now stands. The only problem was that it was owned by Denis Horgan, a millionaire in no hurry to sell – not even to California's most famous winemaker.

Horgan, though, was never a man to miss a heaven-sent business opportunity. Encouraged by this expert interest, and with some advice from Mondavi, he planted a vineyard there himself in 1974. The vineyard and winery now occupy a fifth of the property – some 220 acres (89 hectares) out of a total 4,700 acres (1,900 hectares). Leeuwin Farms, which manages the rest, has 800 head of beef cattle and a dairy herd of 150, as well as a lot of sheep "to keep the scrub down".

Denis Horgan has described his objective at Leeuwin Estate as "the pursuit of excellence", and visitors soon realize that no expense has been spared to help him realize it. The winery is not only a supremely functional building, filled with state-of-the-art winemaking machinery, but also an important contributor to Denis Horgan's public relations machinery. The entrance is imposing, dominated by a structure that suggests a bell-tower, with an ornamental waterfall running down carefully landscaped rocks to one side. Inside the visitor reception area are a tasting room and restaurant, built mainly from local wood, notably the rich, red *jarrah*.

The restaurant, which serves the best food for miles around, is decorated with the originals of the paintings by distinguished Australian artists that adorn the labels of top Leeuwin Estate wines. The view outside over wide lawns to majestic *karri* trees is the

Specially-planted trees provide a windbreak, as well as an alternative source of food for wildlife.

setting for annual summer concerts, which have become important events in Western Australia's social and cultural calendar. Since the concerts started in 1985, they have featured such diverse talents as the London Philharmonic Orchestra, the Berlin State Orchestra, the Royal Danish Orchestra, Ray Charles, Dionne Warwick, Kiri Te Kanawa and James Galway. The ambience and the glittering social events all contribute to the success of the estate, but none of it would be possible had the Leeuwin wines not already gained a considerable reputation.

"You cannot make any compromises when you're looking for quality. You either do the whole thing, or forget about it." This is the single-minded way in which winemaker Bob Cartwright articulates the estate's winemaking philosophy. The Margaret River's mild climate is near-ideal for the classic varieties of both Bordeaux and Burgundy, and irrigation is unnecessary as there is ample rain in the winter months to sustain the vines through the growing season. However, Leeuwin's position, only a few miles from the western coast of Australia on the Indian Ocean, posed a potential hazard to vines in the form of salt spray brought by on-shore winds. The short-term solution was to plant rye between every second row of vines. This grew to the same height as the vines and protected them from the worst of the winds. The long-term solution was a tree-planting programme on the seaward side of the vineyards to provide shelter in the years to come.

The attractive, and active, bird life of the region also presented problems: it seems there is nothing parrots likes better than ripe, juicy grapes. The rye grain windbreak between the vines helps to distract some marauding birds from the grapes; others are tempted by patches of sunflowers or flowering trees that are specially grown to offer alternative food sources. Every effort is made to protect the precious grapes without harming wildlife, and no insecticides or herbicides are used in the vineyards.

The "bell-tower" and ornamental waterfall which greet the many welcome visitors to Leeuwin Estate.

All the grapes at Leeuwin Estate are hand-picked, again for reasons of quality control. Machine-harvesting makes for huge savings, but is inevitably less selective than a team of human pickers. When the job is done by hand, rotten or unripe grapes can be discarded before the grapes return to the winery, and a winemaker can brief his pickers to include higher proportions of ripe or less ripe grapes if the weather conditions have yielded fruit too high or low in acidity. Yields are kept deliberately low – at around 55 hectolitres per hectare for Cabernet Sauvignon, 37 for Chardonnay, and even less for Pinot Noir – because Bob Cartwright believes that low-yielding vines make better-quality wines. Not all the vines originally planted have been kept in production, as certain varieties have proved better suited to Margaret River conditions than others – but time and money are saved by grafting new vines onto old. When the estate managers decided to stop growing Shiraz, rather than ripping out the vines and having to start all over again, buds of Sauvignon Blanc were grafted onto the old Shiraz vines. The vines immediately started to produce Sauvignon Blanc grapes, and three years of lost production were avoided. The next vines to disappear from the estate may be the limited plantings of Gewürztraminer.

Bob Cartwright is particularly proud of the Leeuwin Estate Chardonnay. He is obviously in love with the grape: "Chardonnay is a variety you can work with. You can sculpture it, you can form it. Chardonnay's not just a drink: it should be an experience." While the other white grapes – Riesling, Sauvignon Blanc and Gewürztraminer – run the full gamut of modern, scientific winemaking, Chardonnay gets very different treatment. After the grapes have been lightly crushed, they are left in contact with the skins for a few hours to pick up extra flavour, unlike the other white varieties which are pressed immediately. Instead of being fermented in temperature-controlled stainless steel tanks, 80 per cent of the Chardonnay is fermented in new French oak barrels.

Australian winemakers like Cartwright are beginning to realize that old French techniques were not necessarily just lazy winemaking, but essential to the complexity of the finished wine, and they are rediscovering the winemaking tricks of regions like Burgundy. As he puts it: "The first thing they taught us in winemaking college was that when a white wine has finished its fermentation, we should get it off the lees. We were naive young students, and we believed them. Then, about ten years ago, the penny dropped." At Leeuwin Estate, he leaves the Chardonnay on its lees to gain extra, rich, yeasty flavours and gives the contents of the barrel an occasional stir. In 1989, for the first time, he bottled the Chardonnay without filtering it. Now he is wondering whether to do the same with his Cabernet. The reason is simple, and bluntly expressed: "filtration buggers up the wine".

The oak barrels for the Chardonnay have to be new every year, and now about half the Sauvignon Blanc is fermented in new oak barrels as well. But whereas the Chardonnay stays in the barrels for nine months to a year before being bottled, the Sauvignon Blanc has only a couple of months. In both cases, the barrel-fermented wine is blended with wine fermented in stainless steel tanks for further complexity.

The fermentation of the red wines, with their skins, lasts four to five days, and then the new wine is left in contact with the skins for about another ten days, soaking up the extra tannin that will enable it to last and develop. After spending the winter in stainless steel tanks to clear, the wines age for one to two years in new oak barrels. As Leeuwin Estate is dedicated to producing wine of the highest quality, the Cabernet Sauvignons are then kept until they are deemed ready to be drunk: the wines currently available are the 1979 and 1984. They are very different wines, the 1979 lean and mintily austere and the 1984 spicily blackcurranty, with a firm, tannic backbone.

However, Leeuwin Estate is best known for its Chardonnays. The Chardonnay 1985 is Cartwright's favourite yet, although it was the 1982 that was judged the world's finest Chardonnay by a tasting panel for *Decanter* magazine in London in 1984. Cartwright calls his 1985 "the seducer. It doesn't seem much at first, then sucks you in and seduces you. And the more you taste it, the better it gets."

With the meticulous care that goes into the vineyards and winemaking at Leeuwin Estate, its wines should continue to improve. At the moment, as Cartwright says, "we're trying to make first-growth wines out of young vines". By the time those vineyards are 30 years old, Leeuwin's wines may be some of the best in Australia, or even the world. After all, Robert Mondavi was prepared to put money on the possibility.

NEW ZEALAND

David Hohnen of Cloudy Bay

Determination to make a top-class white wine that would be the equal of his award-winning reds led Australian David Hohnen across the Tasman Sea to New Zealand. There, having identified the Marlborough/Blenheim region of the South Island as best-suited to growing Sauvignon Blanc, he bought land and hired the winemaker whose Sauvignon he most admired. Since then, as *James Halliday* explains, his Cloudy Bay wines have gone from strength to strength.

At the ripe old age of 40, David Hohnen seems to have achieved everything possible in a normal lifetime. His Margaret River winery, Cape Mentelle, produces Australia's most highly-decorated small winery Cabernet Sauvignon, while his Marlborough winery produces New Zealand's world-famous Cloudy Bay Sauvignon Blanc. Yet he still peers somewhat suspiciously out on the world. He is a complex man, shy and reserved, yet with a great sense of humour; he suffers fools badly, yet is sensitive and, one suspects, somewhat introspective.

Visually and temperamentally he is as different from elder brother Mark Hohnen as any two brothers could be. Mark Hohnen is the mover and shaker, one of those entrepreneurial men from Western Australia who have prospered mightily and not hesitated to take on the eastern states establishment. Robert Holmes à Court and Alan Bond have flown higher, but like Icarus before them, have learned what it is to fall. Mark Hohnen has a more earthly perspective; David Hohnen a more earthy one. Between them, they formed a potent financial, production and marketing team. Twenty years ago they put Cape Mentelle Vineyards Limited on a precisely-determined course, and this course has not wavered an inch since day one.

For no one should doubt that everything David Hohnen does is the product of meticulous planning. He cares deeply about the wines he makes, and has keenly felt any criticism of them. Indeed, that criticism has meant more to him than the astonishing record he set of winning two Jimmy Watson Trophies in succession with his 1982 and 1983 vintage Cape Mentelle Cabernet Sauvignons. Astonishing, because this most eagerly sought-after trophy of the entire Australian wine show system is usually the preserve of the big wine companies and of Coonawarra, Australia's premium red wine district. To win it once was a hundred-to-one long shot, estimated to be worth $1 million in retail sales value. Hohnen could have written his own ticket on the odds against winning it twice in a row.

Having dazzled Australia with his Cabernet Sauvignon, Hohnen looked for a new challenge.
He found it in New Zealand's South Island, a region ideal for making top-class Sauvignon Blanc.

So a lesser mortal would have been content to sit back and bask in the reflected glory of his achievements. Not Hohnen: there remained the challenge of making a top-class white wine, and with typical lack of sentimentality (the one characteristic I would never accuse him of) he decided to look outside the Margaret River region for the site. It was almost coincidentally that he made a marketing trip (for Cape Mentelle) to New Zealand in 1983, but the impact was immediate.

He soon identified the Marlborough/Blenheim region in the north of the New Zealand's South Island – a region pioneered by Montana – as the district in which to grow and make Sauvignon Blanc. It is typical of Hohnen that he barely considers it worth mentioning in casual conversation (and certainly never in promotional material) that to achieve his objective he became the first non-resident ever to buy rural land in New Zealand, promoting a major change in New Zealand's investment laws in so doing.

Having surmounted that small hurdle, and having chosen a site, he set about finding himself a winemaker. Once again the hard-nosed realist in Hohnen came to the fore. A lesser man would have chosen a puppet, a reasonably skilled and experienced winemaker who would have been content to live in Hohnen's shadow, do Hohnen's bidding and allow Hohnen to take all the glory. What is more, such a winemaker would have had to be recruited in Australia. Instead, he went to the winemaker who had been responsible for producing what Hohnen believed to be the best Sauvignon Blanc he had tasted in New Zealand. The winemaker was Kevin Judd, who had lifted Selaks to the top rank of New Zealand white wine producers. It just so happened that Judd was an Australian who had served his apprenticeship with Geoff Merrill at Chateau Reynella in South Australia, by then part of the Thomas Hardy group.

Right from the outset, David Hohnen was content to let Judd make many of the decisions and receive his due share of the credit. Indeed, in recent years the Cloudy Bay

Clever marketing has helped to focus the wine world's attention on Cloudy Bay. The central image, the evocative and graphically brilliant label, has made it an internationally recognized brand.

team has come to Cape Mentelle to help with the latter's white wines – with great effect, I should add. But Kevin Judd would be the first to admit that Hohnen's experience, creative ability and (above all else) vision have been absolutely critical to the success of Cloudy Bay. At the core of that success lies the truly exceptional marketing effort that made Cloudy Bay an internationally recognized brand overnight. It is one thing to make an outstanding wine; it is an altogether different thing to have it recognized as such. The most immediately obvious symbol of that success is the evocative and graphically brilliant label, in large part the work of David Hohnen's sister. There is no such thing as the definitive label (unless it be linked to a centuries-old tradition such as that of Château Lafite) but the Cloudy Bay label comes as close as any designed in the past decade.

The other feature of Cloudy Bay's drive into the market-place was that (exceptionally in the case of Australia and New Zealand) it was a single wine, and a singularly striking one at that. It was not necessary to know that it was a Sauvignon Blanc, nor to delve into the arcane differentiation (or lack of it) between Sauvignon Blanc and "Fumé Blanc". Even more importantly, it eliminated the agonizing – and for some terminally intimidating – choice between various wines under the one label. It is well understood that among the problems wine faces are domineering *sommeliers*, seas of brands and labels in the better retail shops, and underneath it all, the fear of making a fool of oneself, of making the wrong choice. Create a mono-*cru* brand and you eliminate all of those worries.

Thus, in smart café society from Auckland to Sydney to London, it became the fashionable thing to order "Cloudy Bay". One never added "Sauvignon Blanc" because it was not necessary to do so. It was for all of these reasons, indeed, that I was critical of the much later decision to extend the Cloudy Bay range to Chardonnay and Cabernet-Merlot. Time will prove who was right: I suspect, as ever, it will be Hohnen; if so, I will simply point to three things. First, the time lag (almost five years) before the introduction of the additional wines. Second, their quality (very good), and third, the continued emphasis on Sauvignon Blanc as the major project.

What is more, notwithstanding the rapturous response to the first and every succeeding vintage of Cloudy Bay (and from here on when referring to Cloudy Bay I am talking of its Sauvignon Blanc and excluding the secondary wines), Hohnen and Judd have actively sought to improve and refine the quality of the wine.

As ever, these efforts have started in the vineyard. Initially, all the grapes were contract-grown by growers using traditional New Zealand viticultural methods. Cloudy Bay now has 100 acres (40 hectares) of its own vines to supplement its continuing contract purchases, and all the vineyards are under the control of viticulturist Ivan Sutherland, with consultancy advice and input from the internationally renowned Dr Richard Smart. The result has been a radical change in trellising (the adoption of the Scott Henry two-level trellis) designed to maximize fruit exposure and eliminate the jungle-like jumble of flavours which lesser New Zealand Sauvignon Blanc can exhibit.

In the winery, the practice of barrel-fermenting 15-20 per cent of the wine has been refined, and better fruit quality has eliminated the earlier need for a touch of residual sugar; the 1989 wine is the first completely dry wine under the label. To describe Cloudy Bay is not easy: the pungent, smoky-gooseberry aroma, the flavours of gooseberry and green melon, with a haunting touch of grapefruit, and the crisp, tingling acid to finish are easy enough. What is harder to describe is the intensity of the flavour, an intensity achieved without sacrificing elegance. All I can suggest is that you experience it for yourself.

Finally, I would not like it to be thought that Cloudy Bay is some form of superior conjuror's marketing trick. Sauvignon Blanc has its detractors the world over: Hugh Johnson of England (see pages 231-38) and Len Evans of Australia (see pages 209-13) are among those who either actively dislike it or barely tolerate it. For such judges, Sauvignon will never make a great wine, but then Hohnen did not necessarily set out to achieve that.

What he has made is a wine that the best producers in Sancerre and Pouilly-Fumé will immediately acknowledge to be of the highest quality. He has produced a wine that matches a wide range of food with flair and *élan*, but that is particularly satisfying with all types of seafood. And he has produced a wine that in a recent vertical tasting of the first five vintages (1985-89) showed it had the ability to age with considerable grace, even if 95 per cent of it is destined to be consumed within weeks of its purchase.

Kevin Judd's impressive track record – especially his previous success with Sauvignon Blanc – made him the ideal winemaker for Cloudy Bay.

SOUTH AFRICA

Tim Hamilton-Russell of Hamilton-Russell Vineyards

By virtue of its climate and soil, South Africa has the potential to make wines comparable with any in the New World (and even perhaps the Old), but it has been held back by its international isolation and its wine industry's own inflexible structure. Amid all the turbulence, Tim Hamilton-Russell has emerged as a leading reformer and a great wine producer, who has used his expertise in climatology to discover the perfect spot for growing Pinot Noir and Chardonnay, as *Joanna Simon* explains.

It is a cruel irony that the world's most spectacularly beautiful vine-growing country should harbour such sadness, injustice and cruelty that it is seldom visited or appreciated. And it is doubly ironic when you consider that in this haunting landscape lies the climatic and soil potential to make world-class wines – but wines that many people, through their own choice or that of their government, will never taste.

Thank Heavens, then, for the chairman of one of South Africa's leading advertising agencies, Tim Hamilton-Russell of J Walter Thompson. It is everybody's good fortune within and without the country that this thoughtful man, who speaks out bravely but whose remarks are always tempered by humility, should have taken up wine. Not for him the easy way out – running his farm in accordance with his own enlightened principles in relative isolation from the rest of the industry. Instead, he has set out to improve conditions throughout this most primitive of all South African agricultural sectors.

This brings him into frequent conflict with the authorities – notably those in the KWV, the government-created co-operative which has legislative control over the wine industry. But it has also resulted in the Winelands Commitment, a declaration by a group of Cape wine producers rejecting apartheid, calling for the unconditional opening of land and vineyard ownership to all races and urging reforms in employment practices (such as a minimum wage and the banning of the "Dop" system of paying wages in wine).

So far there are only four signatories – Simon Barlow of Rustenberg Wines, John Platter of Clos du Ciel, Peter Younghusband of Haute Provence Vineyards and Hamilton-Russell himself – but their importance far outweighs their number. This rebellious quartet represents four of South Africa's finest estates. Hamilton-Russell Vineyards Chardonnay and Pinot Noir not only excel in the South African arena, but stand comparison with their models in Burgundy and the best wines of California, Oregon and Australia. That top wines can go hand in hand with humane ideals and practices is cause for hope.

Hamilton-Russell's wine successes are considerable, still more so when viewed in the context of their brief history. He was not born into the wine business (very few English-speaking South Africans own wine estates; most are Afrikaans). True, he specialized in climatology and geology as an undergraduate at Oxford in the 1950s, where he developed and was able to indulge an interest in wine at the same time, and he also spent many years visiting wine regions around the world, but he did not buy the impoverished farm which was to become Hamilton-Russell Vineyards until 1975; and it was another six years before he saw his first vintage. But then, it was just a short wait before his wines began winning blind tastings – somewhat to the chagrin of the authorities for whom Hamilton-Russell was already proving a thorn.

Behind this meteoric rise there were, however, years of painstaking research and reconnaissance. Having decided that he wanted to grow the two great grapes of the Côte d'Or, Pinot Noir and Chardonnay, to produce "better than ordinary wine – wine of international quality that could match up to any in blind tastings", he spent no less than ten years looking for the perfect site. "Starting symbolically at the southernmost spot", he went in search of a cooler climate where long, warm summer days would never become excessively hot. "Hot summer months destroy the flavour and bouquet in wines and they lack complexity." Beaune, at the heart of the Côte d'Or, Hamilton-Russell frequently reminded himself, is 47° north of the Equator, but South Africa extends no further from the Equator than 35° south, so he sought "a microclimate to compensate". Eventually, he discovered a steep-sided valley called Hemel-en-Aarde ("Heaven and Earth" in Afrikaans) at 34° 35' S, close to the village of Hermanus in the Walker Bay area.

The site is less than two miles (three kilometres) from the Atlantic, and on summer afternoons, as hot air rises in the valley, convection draws cool breezes in from the sea and up across the 124 acres (50 hectares) of Hamilton-Russell vines, making this South Africa's coolest wine region. The shale soils have sufficient clay to retain moisture, but not so much as to waterlog the vineyard; and that, says Hamilton-Russell the geologist, is all that is required. "Too much mystique is attached to soil as a contributor to the flavour constituents of wine ... it is the physical properties [of soil] in relation to the microclimate that are so important."

Having found the ideal location, Hamilton-Russell's real problems were only just beginning. He had great difficulty getting hold of the vines he wanted (and does not elaborate on how he managed it), because the Viticultural Research Institute was the only legal importer of vines. And even when he had overcome that hurdle and was making wine, he was without a wine quota, because the farm's previous owner had owned little more than a few pigs and goats. As Walker Bay was not an established vine-growing area, there were no wine quotas on other farms either.

For the first few vintages, this meant that Hamilton-Russell labels were not allowed to mention either the grape variety, the area of origin or the vintage date. To know that something labelled "Grand Vin Noir 4" from Hamilton-Russell Vineyards was an estate-bottled 1984 Pinot Noir from the Cape's most southerly vineyard, you needed to be rather well-informed: few people were. But then in 1985 the regulations were changed so that quotas could be transferred from one farm to another. Hamilton-Russell acquired a quota and since 1986 his wine labels have carried the vintage date, the area of origin, the grape variety and an official wine seal.

During all these legal changes, Hamilton-Russell was getting on with the business of producing wine. Peter Finlayson, a University of Stellenbosch oenology graduate who also studied at Geisenheim in Germany, and in Burgundy and California, actually carried out the operations – and Tim is the first to give him credit. "I made wine in the Transvaal when

*Tim Hamilton-Russell (left) and his creative winemaker Peter Finlayson. It took ten years to find
the right combination of soil and microclimate, but even then the struggle had just begun.*

I lived in Johannesburg, but it was terrible, so I thought I'd better get a winemaker," says
Tim (omitting to point out that being Chairman of J Walter Thompson and preparing the
Winelands Commitment hardly left him much time to be his own "hands-on" winemaker
as well). In spite of his impressive academic and science credentials, Finlayson is a
"creative winemaker" according to Tim, and this is very much in keeping with the
Hamilton-Russell philosophy of winemaking as "more an art than a science ... The
winemaker must hand-craft each wine."

When Finlayson arrived in 1979 there was no question of hand-crafting the wine: there
was none. Although there were vines planted in parcels, each named after a different
Burgundy village, there was no equipment in which to turn grapes into wine. Finlayson's
first project, therefore, was a study tour of California to help him plan his cellar, and the
purchase of equipment in time for the first (1981) vintage.

The two key ingredients in the Hamilton-Russell *batterie de vin* remain efficient
temperature-controlled fermentation tanks and small French oak barrels, replaced after
four years when they no longer yield any oak flavour. The Chardonnay – rich, lemony and
vanilla-toned – is aged for about nine months in these *barriques*, mainly in the new and
second-year ones. The elegant, silky Pinot Noir matures for about 18 months, mainly in
second, third and fourth-year *barriques*.

There is nothing extraordinary about any of this when compared with the rest of the
wine world, but the South African industry has long been geared to quantity rather than
quality, and has kept its distance from developments in the New World. The emphasis on
quantity has meant dedication to high-yielding workhorse varieties such as Chenin Blanc,
Colombard and Cinsault. Tim Hamilton-Russell's Chardonnay and Pinot Noir vines,
planted close together and heavily pruned to produce very low yields, are exceptional.
With them he makes exceptional wines – a fitting tribute to an exceptional man.

Getting the best out of the bottle

No matter how fine a wine, no matter how much effort, expertise and expense has been yielded in its creation, once it has left the producer's own cellars, the winemaker very rarely has the opportunity to control its final destiny. It is up to the wine drinker, therefore, to reward those who pursue excellence in winemaking by treating their endeavours with the care and the appreciation that they so richly deserve.

There is no one more eloquent than **Hugh Johnson** on the subject of cellaring, serving and enjoying wine. From the vantage point of his two cellars and two decades of experience, he talks to *Joanna Simon* about its pleasures and occasional pitfalls.

Michael Broadbent MW has probably tasted more of the wine world's great rarities than anyone else. He describes below some of the exceptional tastings that he has attended and the extraordinary wines that he has encountered there.

Anthony Rose, wine enthusiast and alert but modest collector, concludes the section by weighing up the pros and cons both of buying young wine *en primeur*, while it is still in cask, and of bidding for mature wine at auction.

HUGH JOHNSON IN HIS CELLAR

An Interview with Joanna Simon

It was not the 1699 façade, the 16th-century interior, the ample 12 acres (five hectares) of grounds, nor even the five healthy vines that Hugh Johnson really fell in love with. It was the cellar – underneath the Elizabethan house in Essex in which he has now lived for nearly two decades.

In 1971, still in his early thirties, Hugh had already written his bestselling book *Wine* and just completed *The World Atlas of Wine*, a book whose research had taken him all over the world and which was to become still more successful than *Wine*, yet he had no proper wine cellar in his Islington house. This was by no means his only reason for selling up and moving to the country – his growing family was something of an incentive – but when he saw the cellar in Essex it suddenly became a particularly potent reason. As fortune would have it he was to discover, some time after moving in, a door in a garage that led under the cool north-east-facing wing of the house to another cellar, larger and still better-appointed than the original one that had convinced him he should buy the house.

The pleasures of a cellar

Now, of course, Hugh cannot imagine life without two cellars. He uses the smaller (though by no means small) one that descends from the stairwell in the centre of the house for old wines and bin ends: "Old claret, Burgundies, German wines, strange old bottles, Champagne, port, English wine ... By the way, have you ever tried this?", he asks suddenly, with the irrepressible excitement that has enthused millions of wine drinkers and readers over a quarter of a century, as he pulls out a bottle of Yearlston Riesling 1987 from a rack. "It really is Riesling – marvellous. It's going to take years." Then, as suddenly, he picks up where he left off: "I also use this cellar for unpacking things that I've got to taste – it's sort of the drinks cupboard – unless it's for a massive tasting, in which case I do it in the other cellar where there's more room."

The larger cellar, then, is mainly used for laying down young wines and for storing other wines in any quantity. It is also the venue for the Johnsons' bottling parties, variations on the bring-a-bottle theme, where guests bring empty bottles to have them filled up. It all started in the 1970s when, somewhat ahead of the times as usual, Hugh "discovered" Chilean Cabernet Sauvignon – in Chile rather than on an English high street – and imported his own hogshead. Since then, whenever the fancy has taken him, he has bought wine in barrel – a white Burgundy quite recently – and, with the help of a small hand machine and a party of friends, held special Essex bottlings. As far as Hugh is concerned, that part of the *raison d'être* of a cellar is to derive enjoyment from the place itself.

"If you are lucky enough to have a cellar, you multiply the pleasure of wine. The cellar itself becomes part of the pleasure: going down to the cellar, anticipating, wondering about when to open, and the range of possibilities it gives you. Ideally, I suppose, you have a cellar book which is up-to-date and you don't have to pop down to the cellar at all. You just look at the list and see exactly what there is. I don't, though. It gets out of control, it's perpetually out of date and giving me the wrong information! I think most people are in that state. So in practice, when I'm going to choose a wine I always go down, see how the bottles look, how they feel, hold them up to the light and things like that. If we're having a dinner party, as soon as Judy [Mrs Johnson, an excellent cook] tells me what food we're having, I go down and just potter around. I enjoy doing it, and you get ideas about wines that might go well in sequence.

"I think very much about who's coming: wines for people is as important a consideration as wines for food – well, almost. You get to know your friends' particular likes and dislikes, and you can have fun giving them a treat, or giving them a surprise, or pulling their leg. If there is someone who would expect a terrific bottle of vintage Champagne, I might pull their leg by giving them a bottle of Omar Khayam [Indian sparkling wine]: nobody can believe it isn't French. Or you can educate them – not pompously, but usefully, by showing them a wine that is like something they like, but perhaps cheaper. Think how many people are still wandering around in a daze saying, 'but isn't it amazing Australian wine is so good?'.

"Also I like proselytizing about some things, German wines for example, which I just happen to adore and can be quite boring about – how they improve with age, et cetera. And I've often found that things like Saar Rieslings go stunningly well with a variety of foods that no one expects, particularly cold meat. Curiously, cold meat has such a powerful flavour that what's thought of as conventional – full-bodied red – often doesn't work. So you come back to the piquancy of a wine with really good acidity and you find it transforms what is otherwise a very boring dish of cold lamb. But you can rarely serve German wine all through a meal. Most people feel somewhere along the line that they'd rather have a mouthful of red."

Important as he considers planning wine and food together, Hugh is not convinced by the current fad for trying to divine by laborious tastings a list of supposedly definitive partnerships. "Except in certain well-known examples, it's an unproven hypothesis that one and one makes three in cases of food and wine. I think the conventional things that have been around for years may not be adventurous but they don't actually trip you up, and it's better to find a good bottle of wine and a bad dish than try to find some magic formula to put the two together. If the meat is tender and the wine is good, you'll enjoy it.

"The other day we had a small first course and I hadn't thought about having any white wine. We'd just had some Champagne and we were going to have some red Burgundy. So, at the last moment, I opened a bottle of Manzanilla and passed it around the table, as one does port after dinner, and said, 'Give yourself a splash of this – in your Champagne glass'. It was incredible. Everybody raved about it: it was very appetizing, and it was so effortless. Much easier than fiddling about with a couple of bottles of Chardonnay."

In spite of his taste for proselytizing and gentle leg-pulling, Hugh doesn't believe in putting his guests through punishing blind-tasting exercises unless they volunteer. "But you can certainly enhance some people's pleasure by delaying telling them what the wine is. I'd rather not be told what the wine is before I've begun because I'd rather ask myself the fundamental questions, get myself interested, in tune. By the time I get round to saying 'what a lovely claret this is', they'll say 'actually it's Burgundy'. Timing's very important!"

At this point, perhaps I should make it clear to those who do not possess a cellar – let alone two – that Hugh Johnson believes it is perfectly possible to be serious about wine without one. You can, he says, buy mature wines at reasonable and realistic prices, preferably by thinking a little ahead. "You can't get everything, but you can get an awful lot. Wine merchants cover the ground amazingly well. Recently I wanted some Château Haut-Brion for a particular friend who was intrigued by its history, and very quickly someone had found about half a dozen mature vintages for me.

"I think the old-fashioned axiom that somehow you've got to contrive to lay down wine yourself if you want to be able to drink it at its best is a counsel of perfection. And if the whole thing is a great agony, as awkward as hell, then I think one might as well look at realistic ways to avoid it." Renting storage with a wine merchant or warehouse is an obvious solution for the cellarless who want to buy young wines to lay down.

If you are lucky enough to have the space in your house, then the bare essentials, says Hugh, are somewhere as remote and insulated as possible (which rules out most garages and sheds). "The thing that is going to affect the progress of wine most is temperature. If you're going to keep a long-maturing wine for a lifetime, it's probably unwise to think about keeping it in makeshift conditions, because over the years the random temperatures matter more than they do over a short period." An ideal cellar temperature is between 45 and 55°F (7-13°C), but anything from a couple of degrees above freezing to almost 70°F (21°C) may be acceptable, as long as the temperature is constant and not fluctuating. Humidity is also vitally important, so that corks do not dry out. (It is a simple matter to preserve any labels that begin to disintegrate in ideally humid conditions, using the Johnson trick of spraying with hair lacquer or painting with varnish.)

Although Hugh admits that his cellar can let him down ("I'd be a fraud if I pretended I could find everything"), on the whole it works admirably well. A simple formula is used for coding each bottle-space with a number and a letter: letters run vertically down the left-hand side of each rack; numbers run horizontally along the bottom from the left. Thus in space E8 the cellar book might identify the Yearlston Riesling 1987. If the bottle were pushed some way back in the space Hugh would know there was only one, whereas if the bottle were prominent there would be another of the same wine behind.

Handling

No amount of accomplished organization and military-style cellarbook-keeping will tell you the most important thing, however, and that is when a wine is ready to drink. Hugh has no magic answer, any more than anyone else, but he has guidelines. "You start with the literature. Reading about it is the first way to find out if the wine is ready – in vintage charts and pocket books." (He is too modest to mention his own annual Pocket Wine Book by name, but that is the place to begin.) "But your approach is very different if you have one bottle rather than several. If you have several, then if you're sensible, your object is not to try and catch them all at some mystical moment when they've never been better and will never be as good again. It's to watch progress through a period of time.

"The notion of 'ready' is very much a matter of taste, as we know looking at the French, who like their wines much younger than the English. The French like Bordeaux really to

A simple formula codes each bottle space with a number and letter. If all goes according to plan, the cellar book should lead him straight to his chosen wine.

punch them in the teeth. I cannot see how people can pay the fabulous sums the first growths cost and then drink them young, because the thing that makes the first growths worth a lot of money only happens when they're mature. On their way up they're more concentrated – but less pleasant."

Your approach should also be different if wines have not been kept in the best of conditions. "Mistrust any bottle where the cork has wept – don't accept it – and if it's your own wine, you should try a bottle straight away. Usually it happens because wine has been heated up and got jolly warm at some point. When it gets that warm it tends to oxidize alarmingly fast. I once bought a case of good vintage first growth at two years old, Lafite 1966, in 1968. Nine or ten years later, I opened the case and six bottles had wept. They'd also got a New York importer's label, so they'd crossed the Atlantic twice and obviously cooked, and then been nailed back in a crate with six direct from the château. The only possible moral to that tale is to open every case when you get it." (In fact it is wise to open wooden boxes as a precaution against the possibility, albeit slight, of dry rot.)

Another indication of maturity is colour, but Hugh does not regard this factor as completely reliable. "With red wines you can't usually tell through the glass, and with white Bordeaux, by the time the colour has started to change significantly, it probably wants drinking anyway. And even experience can lead you astray. Some vintages change colour much faster: for example, 1975 Sauternes are very pale – much paler than 1976s because there was less *Botrytis*."

The essential feature to look for in a bottle of red wine is the state of the sediment. This will tell you nothing about the wine's readiness for drinking, but it will indicate whether or not it needs decanting – a decision quite separate from whether or not you think it needs to breathe (although a wine that would improve with breathing should be decanted). "One's got to debunk the notion that just taking the cork out of a bottle somehow aerates it: all it does is commit you to drinking it. If you think the wine will benefit from contact with the air, then a decanter is required." Most wines do benefit, says Hugh, even white wines, "but they don't look good in decanters and you can get the same amount of aeration by pouring them generously [from a height]. In fact, the first five or ten minutes in the glass are probably enough to bring most whites to the point at which they really belong. The first sniff is often disappointing, but that's all.

"A wine with sediment really *has* to be decanted. I once asked the chef in a smart French restaurant in London to decant a bottle of Burgundy and he said no, he'd do it his way, which was in one of those baskets. By the third glass it was muddy, so at the end I said I'd only pay for half the bottle – and I did. He was furious! The restaurant basket is a total abomination. Baskets are useless except for the purpose of decanting, for getting the bottle in the right position, like decanting cradles."

With or without basket or cradle, decanting is something you simply cannot rush, says Hugh; and it can be a difficult operation if either the wine or the glass is very dark, as in the case of vintage port, because you cannot see what you are doing. "Burgundy is the easiest because the wine is palest. A mature Burgundy is bright orange, but a 1961 claret even now is pretty dark. Quite honestly it does take a bit of study and practice." However, you can make things easier for yourself: "It's helpful to have a good look at the bottle first by holding it up against a light. Size up the situation: see where the sediment is and how much there is, and whether it's loose or sticking to the glass. You can help yourself a great deal by encouraging the sediment to be at the bottom rather than the top. It gives you a head start if you stand the bottle up for 24 hours beforehand, preferably for 48. Sometimes wine has been standing on its cork for quite a long time somewhere along the line, and then the sediment can be stuck to the cork; it can be absolutely filthy with sediment. You won't know that unless you look. And it's maddening when the sediment's in the neck of the bottle." (If you do not have time to coax the sediment to the bottom, or the sediment is particularly recalcitrant, a decanting basket or cradle may come into its own.)

"If you've got a bottle that you can hardly see through, take the whole seal off and try to make sure the label and neck label aren't in your eyeline. Then you've got to figure out a good light source; I use a flat torch like a bicycle lamp underneath. With a magnum it's quite hard to get a grip. With a double magnum you almost need two people – one just to steady it, because there's one absolutely fundamental rule for decanting: you can only ever do it in one movement of the hand. Any time you bring it back up from the non-pouring position, you've done exactly what you set out not to do – stir up the sediment."

For the same reason, if you are taking a wine direct from a rack to decant it, you must keep it as near horizontal as possible, even when pulling the cork. This entails wielding the corkscrew with more than usual skill (again, a basket can prove its worth here), and using a reliable corkscrew. "The test of a good corkscrew is that you've got to be able to look into it and up through the spiral," says Hugh, " I don't think anything touches the various forms of Screwpull – above all the Leverpull.

"For very old vintage port – I mean older than, say, 30 years – it sounds quaint, but you need port tongs. You can't pull the cork, because it's wider at the bottom, so you cut off the neck of the bottle – which is very much easier than people think. You just get the tongs really hot on a fire or a gas ring, clamp them tight round the neck of the bottle just above the bottom of the cork, leave them for about 30 seconds, take them away and wipe the bottle with a wet cloth. In my experience it snaps so cleanly that there is no question of there being little bits of broken glass about." Not that Hugh Johnson's uncorking ceremonies have always proceeded without a hitch: "I was once asked to sabre the top off a Champagne bottle in the United States when I was launching a new video label, and someone had the bright idea that I should chop the top off a magnum. Instead of slicing off, the whole thing shattered and left me poised in a cloud of mousse."

On the whole, though, corks and bottles behave as they should *chez* Johnson, and the process of uncorking can teach him something about the wine: "for example, if the cork comes out very easily, I'd be on the alert for oxidation, although it won't tell me anything definite. I once had a bottle of Malescot 1929 without a cork; the cork was lying at the bottom of the bottle. At some point, presumably, the wine had been standing up for so long the cork had dried out and fallen in. Yet the wine was perfect."

Tasting and assessing

How does Hugh Johnson assess a wine? "Look at the colour first. Use something white – a source of light is no good: use white paper or a tablecloth. Tip the glass very close towards it – the easiest way is to hold a piece of paper in one hand – and you can see precisely how the colour grades from the deepest part in the middle of the glass to the shallowest part at the rim. The colour can be both pretty and contain some information which can be compared with your expectations. You're quite likely to think, 'this is paler than I expected', or the other way round. That's all you'll learn and it doesn't take a moment: just a gesture in passing, nothing pretentious. Then, having swirled the glass around, more to wet the glass so there's more surface to volatilize than to aerate the wine, give a long, strong, close-up sniff, nose practically touching the glass.

"Unless you concentrate at that moment there's no point in doing it at all. It actually helps to shut your eyes and not to listen to anything around you. You may get a message: it might be 'I have tasted this wine before and know exactly what it is'; or 'it's perfectly disgusting' because it's vinegary, corky or whatever; or, much more likely, 'this has an in-between quality that is up to my expectations'; or 'this is good value for money'.

"There are all sorts of conclusions you can draw at this stage, depending largely on your expectations. If you've paid a great deal of money and it doesn't smell of anything, you may think you've opened it too soon, or you've got a cold, or you've been conned or made a mistake. But a first growth should have more concentration of all the flavours you expect wine to have. Unless it has more flavour, more perfume, it doesn't justify its higher price.

"Now you've smelt it and either aroused or disappointed your expectations, taste. The first thing to say is that the wine needs a thoroughly good 'chewing'. It's no good just putting it in the middle of your mouth and either swallowing or spitting. You have to treat it as though it were a good piece of steak: it's got to reach and soak every part of the palate and tongue, so that all the pluses and minuses show themselves at the same time.

"If you still haven't got the message, you can turn the volume up a bit. The amplifier you have at your disposal you use to volatize some of the wine in your mouth, by sucking air through it. Everyone who tries this for the first time is quite startled: it's just like turning up the volume on a record player. It accentuates the impressions altogether. You then have all the material at your disposal to judge the wine. And what you're saying is: 'how much do I like this, how much am I surprised by it, does it conform to what I'm looking for?'.

"This is before you start getting analytical about what the components of the flavour might be. It's another business saying, 'can I smell oak, am I smelling Cabernet?'. You're purely taking it at its face value, as the whole complex of whatever it is. Once you start breaking it down, you've gone past the amateur appreciation stage – although it does help to enjoy things if you can remember them, and it helps to remember them if you label them, whether it's flowers in the garden or whatever. So from that point of view there's a good reason for ticking off components and getting to know grape varieties.

Beautiful glass adds further aesthetic pleasure to the enjoyment of fine wine, and can enhance taste and aroma. The shape of a glass is critical in directing the bouquet and its clarity aids the appreciation of a wine's colour.

"Whenever the flavour ends, it should end with a cleanness and a slight sweetness, but not a sugary sweetness. A wine that ends in pure sharpness or is very dry, musty or bitter can't rate very high. Quite a lot of Italian wines do end very distinctly bitter, but even those must have a sweetness to back them up.

"The more you pay, the longer you expect the flavour to last and the louder it should be, although length and volume aren't directly related. You can have a very subtle flavour that's lingering. A wine that deserves to be described as short is definitely disappointing. I think the French system of counting the number of seconds the flavour persists, though it sounds ridiculous and pedantic, in practice works remarkably well, so that any wine that lasts more than half a minute in flavour is quite something.

"But there is a difference between tasting and drinking: they're two different functions. At a dinner table, you're drinking and enjoying it – supposed to be. Some people get so serious about wine, they give themselves a hell of a hassle. I do think having attractive glasses is terribly important, but I think you can re-use glasses at the table (not at a wine tasting, of course). I regularly pour white Burgundy into Champagne glasses. Although it gives the first little sip the slight smell of Champagne, so what? – that's what's happening in your mouth. The question of whether or not it has traces of another related wine isn't nearly as important as having a well-designed glass to drink out of, one that you really like – I prefer simple designs – and I hate washing up!"

There are, nonetheless, a few practical Johnson ground rules for choosing glasses: "A glass's job is to be simple, graceful, like all other good design. The bowl should be narrower at the top than in its middle because you're going to move the wine around in it, swill it, and you don't want the aromas to dissipate into the room. The size of the glass is important. I hate very big glasses where the wine is a little trace in the bottom: the maximum size is something you can hold very easily in the palm of your hand and not feel that you're picking up a great big vase. And I hate glasses that are very small. In practice we tend to use the same size glass for just about everything."

Hugh has some equally practical thoughts on serving temperatures: charts can be a useful guideline, but the key points are to recognize that room temperature should be taken to mean storage temperature ("room temperature is too warm for any wine") and that the first thing to take into account is the weather. "In a way the season matters more than the wine. Cool claret is lovely in summer and an abomination in winter – so you can relate it to your metabolism." If you do need to warm a wine that has emerged from a chilly winter cellar, simply put it in a bucket of warm water at about 70°F (21°C) for a few minutes. "It's the only efficient way. The idea of putting wine by the side of a fire horrifies me. Nothing spoils red wine more than a good stew by the fire."

Like all Hugh's advice, it is straightforward and unpretentious, yet polished. Wine, you can never forget in his company, is for enjoying. Should you ever find yourself beginning to develop too reverential an attitude to it, remember that the maestro would probably accuse you of indulging in "codswallop", and remind yourself of some of his refreshingly non-conformist views – on the disposal of left-over wine, for example:

"I can see no conceivable reason for not making a blend of left-over bottles, certainly among wines that are just ordinary and have been blended along the way anyway. There's a sort of unwritten law, certainly among professionals, that you never add one wine to another – as though there was something sacrosanct about the wine in the bottle. I think that's absolute codswallop, especially if it has no singular interest. You might well get a better drink by putting two bottles together. Be your own blender if you think they're compatible or just of interest. I wouldn't recommend blending claret and Burgundy, but if you put some Rhône wine into some claret you might have a great 18th-century experience!" And great experiences – be they 18th-, 19th- or 20th-century – are what fine wine is all about.

GREAT TASTINGS

by Michael Broadbent MW

MY MOVE TO CHRISTIE'S IN 1966 was well timed. The wine market was fragmented and, in starting a brand new wine department, the company immediately tapped a rich vein, unearthing – almost literally – cellars of old wine to satisfy an increasingly international demand. "Collectors", as they are called somewhat pejoratively by those who are not of their bent, soon started acquiring great classics hitherto denied them and about which they had only read. At first these classic wines were consumed at wine-orientated dinners; soon after, when a sufficiently large range of châteaux and vintages had been accumulated, comparative tastings were organized.

Apart from trade tastings of young vintages, the concept of serious, often spectacular, tastings of great wines and vintages organized by amateurs did not really exist before the mid-1970s. The first really memorable "vertical" tasting (comparing several vintages of the same wine) was of 47 vintages of Château Latour. Organized by Marvin Overton, a neurosurgeon, at his home in Fort Worth, Texas, it was a black tie evening event. Representing France, and Latour, was Henri Martin, a director of the château, and at the other end of the specially-made vast oval table, behind the British flag, was myself, "moderator" and commentator.

This was in May 1976. Three years later Dr Overton hosted a "modest" tasting of Château Lafite, just 30 vintages, but chosen to represent every decade from the 1960s back to the 1790s. This time Baron Elie de Rothschild, who had brought from the château some of the oldest wines, sat opposite, and Hugh Johnson and Cyril Ray supplemented the English contingent. The rest of Dr Overton's guests included wine producers Robert Mondavi (see pages 186-93) and John Parducci; the doyen of Napa Valley winemakers, André Tschelistcheff, and a mixture of American wine merchants and amateur enthusiasts. As at the Latour tasting, the wines were served in descending vintage order, that is to say starting with the youngest and ending with the oldest. This has a certain logic, but one tends to spend time and energy on the young and relatively tannic wines so that, nearing midnight, when the "golden oldies" appear, one's taste-buds are flagging. Nevertheless, it was both fascinating and instructive. The wines were noted in a beautifully bound tasting book which was illustrated with hand-painted portraits of the leading tasters. In an equally substantial, hand-tooled, cowhide slip case was a matching bound copy of the Christie edition of Ray's "Lafite". It was quite an evening.

What motivated the good doctor? Not self-aggrandisement, but a rather American determination – aided by a large dose of Texan hospitality – to do something spectacularly well, and to provide a marvellous opportunity for his guests, selected for their tasting abilities and seriousness, to share his enthusiasm and to assess legendary vintages.

The first notable "horizontal" tasting (several different châteaux of one vintage) took place in a small country town in Holland in May 1978. Planned and executed by a local doctor, it was a horizontal of 19 top Bordeaux châteaux of the 1961 vintage. Dr John Taam's aim, quite simply, was to see whether the reputation of the vintage was justified and to decide which châteaux held the most promise. He had invited a dozen or so friends and one or two professionals such as myself to be judge and jury. The wines were tasted blind to avoid bias. It was a very pleasant and instructive day.

Soon other collectors followed suit. The nucleus of wines was generally from their own cellars, with guests chipping in to fill the gaps, delivering bottles well in advance of the scheduled tasting to give the wine time to settle. Typically, to celebrate and assess their 20th anniversary, the modest, unassuming and generous Dr Louis Skinner hosted a horizontal tasting of 1961 clarets in 1981. It was for this tasting that he and I devised the system of serving wines in "flights" at precise and quite speedy intervals, with review breaks in between. To avoid fatigue the tasting was in three sessions: Saturday morning, Saturday afternoon and Sunday morning. A similar programme was emulated by Robert Paul, Dr Skinner's neighbour in Coral Gables, Florida, at more recent tastings. First he held a horizontal of 1978 red Bordeaux and, the following year, an equally instructive horizontal of 96 châteaux from St-Emilion and Pomerol, all of the 1982 vintage. At the Skinner and Paul tastings, by serving two bottles of each wine and pouring alternately, bottle variation – which is encountered not infrequently, even with comparatively young vintages – can be more easily detected. Another recent and welcome development has been the presence of châteaux proprietors, for whom these tastings are a revelation as they have no parallel in France.

There are also semi-commercial tastings, the sort organized by Bipin Desai, a physicist, in Los Angeles. Desai purchases the wines over a long period and invites paying guests. I tend to sing for my supper at these events, acting as co-ordinator and commentator, and find them invaluable. Perhaps the most notable have been the verticals of Châteaux Margaux and La Mission-Haut-Brion, both attended by their respective proprietors, who found the comparison of a large number of vintages most instructive.

Over the past few years German collectors have entered the field, and in their company I have encountered some of the very finest wines. Happily, as I speak no German, I can concentrate on tasting without distraction. Undoubtedly, "the host with the most" is Hardy Rodenstock. I forget the date of the first of his annual tastings I attended, though everything else I remember all too well. It took place in a German country inn and guests assembled, in black ties, at 11.30 am for a welcoming glass (or two) of Champagne. We sat down at 12 noon and, 72 wines and a six-course meal later, with only a short mid-afternoon break, arose at 12 midnight. I had a splitting headache and was very ill that night. The misery was not improved by having to get up at six am the following morning to catch an early flight from Dusseldorf to London to conduct a wine auction held "at 11 am precisely". The following year I took my own spittoon and, between wines, avoiding the rich food, consumed mainly bread and water!

Rodenstock's next spectacular was an all-day affair held at Château d'Yquem. The guests included the proprietor, Comte Alexandre de Lur Saluces, and several other French notables, and my customary solitary English representation was augmented by Jancis Robinson. Then came two weekend spectaculars, both held at a luxurious ski-resort hotel near the top of a pass in Austria. The entire hotel had been commandeered, and Rodenstock's guests were overwhelmed with a vast array of rare, often magnificent, and it must be admitted, one or two disappointing, aged wines. Each event, which takes Rodenstock nearly a year to organize, is a treasured experience.

My preference is for instructive verticals and I shall try to describe two. The first, a spectacular 116 vintages of Château Lafite from 1985 back to 1784, plus 11 old vintages of Carruades, was held in New Orleans in October 1988. This monumental tasting was given by Lloyd Flatt who, incidentally, was one of the guests at Dr Overton's original Lafite tasting. Lloyd's method is original and sensible. To avoid fatigue, his tastings are held in five sessions over three days. Each session consists of a "flight" or group averaging six vintages, and, more significantly, these flights are arranged in related vintages and in such an order as to ensure that the greatest wines are served at a stage when our senses are most alert and palates least fatigued. For example, on the first morning, to get ourselves attuned, flight one consisted of the 1954, 1953, 1952, 1951 and 1950 vintages, 1953 naturally being the touchstone. Next was a leap into the past with a group of vintages rarely seen and therefore particularly interesting: 1902, 1903, 1904, 1905, 1906, 1907 and 1908, including the Carruades of Château Lafite 1902. There were some surprises here, particularly the 1905 and 1906, though the (single) bottles of 1903 and 1908 were sadly oxidized. For flight three, Flatt served the first group of the great pre-phylloxeras: 1868, 1869, 1870 and 1872. The rarely-seen 1868 was rich but dry; the 1869, a reliably big vintage, still magnificent; and the legendary 1870 as perfect, rich, and beautifully balanced as its reputation.

Even if I had the space, it would be tedious to describe all the flights. Suffice to say that during the course of this marathon event we tasted every vintage between 1864 and 1985, with the exception of 1866 and 1867, 1871 and 1873, 1884 and 1885, 1901, 1909, 1915, 1930, 1932, 1935 and 1936. For good measure, we also tasted the 1844, 1846 and 1848, a marvellous trio; then the 1832 and 1806, both bought at Christie's and, happily, in superb condition, the latter light, elegant and delicious, the 1832 magnificent, and sound as a bell. Alas, the *pièce de résistance*, the 1787, recumbent in a Lear jet between Malibu and New Orleans, had half its contents syphoned out. All that remained was a most beautifully perfumed, intense, rich vinegar. A great pity, because the Mouton 1787 from the same cellar, opened a year or so previously at the château, had been incredibly good.

Château d'Yquem has been the subject of quite a few remarkable tastings, the most memorable that I have been connected with taking place in Chicago the day before a big Christie's wine auction. Just over 50 vintages were assembled by a private collector, Bud Moon. Between us we combined the two methods of tasting. There were eight flights, the first four in the afternoon, each of six vintages from 1983 back to 1956. The evening session opened with a flight of relatively poor vintages (1946, 1940, 1931, 1919, 1913 and 1912) followed by one of the very best (1949, 1947, 1945, 1937, 1929 and 1921) – each with its own character and all absolutely magnificent. The penultimate flight was of 19th-century vintages: 1892 oxidized, 1875 acetic, 1871 remarkably good. But the 1825 was the surprise of the day: a rich amber-tawny colour with a pronounced green rim, incredible fragrance, like ambrosial fruit salad; still sweet, concentrated and fig-like, with marvellous acidity and fabulous aftertaste. The 1900 was good but overshadowed; the 1847, alas, a poor bottle. At a previous Rodenstock weekend I had rated the Yquem 1847 the most marvellous wine I had *ever* tasted. But that's the challenge of old wine. Some you win, some you lose.

Do tasters ever drink? Yes, of course, but it is foolish to drink through a long tasting – though I notice that the Germans never spit out. I make copious notes. As soon as the wine is put before me, I give it a twirl to coat the whole of the inside surface. Next, noting the precise time, assess the initial impact of the bouquet. Then back to the appearance, observing its colour, depth, and the gradation revealing the signs of maturity at the rim. I nose it again, and taste. After I have tasted and noted the entire flight, I look at the development of the bouquet in the glass through to its eventual fading. Why? Because for me the hallmark of a fine – a great – wine, is the way the bouquet evolves, blossoms and is retained over a period of time, and how its concentration, finesse and length develop on the palate. But I never lose sight of the principal purpose of the tasting, which is to assess the quality and stage of development of a wine of a particular vintage, making due allowance for bottle variation and the fallibility of corks.

For me, every tasting is a voyage of discovery.

BUYING WINE EN PRIMEUR

by Anthony Rose

IN THIS "LIVE NOW, PAY LATER" ERA, it takes some doing to stand the idea on its head and ask the customer to pay now and live later, but that is precisely what buying *en primeur* (or buying futures as it is known in the United States) is about: paying for wine now, to enjoy it at some unspecified time in the future. Instead of buying wine in bottle in the usual way, the customer pays for it shortly after the vintage when the wine is still in cask, and then takes delivery as soon as it is bottled and shipped, normally two years later.

If this sounds like a brilliant coup on the part of the wine trade, that's exactly what it is. By getting its cash early for a product the consumer has not yet even tasted, it shifts the burden of financing the stock to the consumer when the wine is delivered. Instead of the wine trade performing its traditional role and sitting on stock until it is released, the consumer becomes the hen, waiting patiently for the golden egg to hatch. It doesn't take Holmesian powers of deduction to work out that buying *en primeur* has more than a little to do with accountants working behind the scenes.

This is not to say that the whole thing is just one big confidence trick perpetrated on the innocent consumer. In a buyer's market, buying *en primeur* can be an excellent way of building up a cellar – the acceptable face of speculation to accumulate. The ultimate test is this, however. When inflation and other financial calculations are taken into account, have you paid a price that leaves you with a wine significantly cheaper than one bought subsequently through traditional wine merchant channels?

Price is important, but it is not the sole consideration. As wine merchants become increasingly reluctant to fulfil the traditional role of storing wines, storage conditions become a relevant issue. Fine Bordeaux, the major currency of the *en primeur* market, requires between ten and 20 years of cellaring. Buying in advance offers an opportunity to control the storage of your wine at the earliest possible stage. Wine is a living micro-organic product, sensitive to heat, light and vibration, so the control that a cellar or some other reliable means of storage can provide is an important bonus. An additional advantage of buying *en primeur* is the "first come, first served" principle. In a top vintage, limited quantities of highly-prized wines tend to get snapped up. Buying *en primeur* is a way of securing your allocation in advance.

It would be nice, of course, to think that sweet reason is the driving force behind the *en primeur* market, that in all cases the customer carefully weighs the pros and cons before taking a leap into the dark. In fact, the speculative side of buying wine *en primeur* can be every bit as irresistible as a flutter on the Grand National. And for many people, the secret thrill of gambling on fine wine is enhanced by the idea that they could be sitting on liquid gold. If you don't make money, you can always drink the stuff. So the theory goes.

Wine lovers now sitting on their 1982 Bordeaux (or any good vintage before it) are certainly entitled to a little smile of satisfaction. Until 1983, conditions were particularly favourable for this form of advance buying. It was almost impossible to go wrong. But changing economic conditions and a poor Bordeaux vintage in 1984, coupled with foolish price rises, have taken the Midas touch out of buying wine *en primeur*.

For this kind of speculation to be worthwhile, at least four conditions have to be met. First, it is obviously essential to buy a vintage that will increase in value – at the very least a good one, preferably a great one; the cachet of a great vintage adds value to every purchase. Secondly, only buy the wine of a good property, ideally one that is under-valued in relation to its true quality; this might be a recently-acquired château where new investment is under way. Thirdly, only buy if the asking price is reasonable: too high a base leaves little or no room to set a gap between the price you pay and the future market price. Finally, buy only wines that are capable of ageing, preferably with a minimum lifespan of ten years.

The heady days when speculation threatened the price and availability of the best wines are over, at least for the time being. Plentiful harvests and bulging cellars have helped to restore equilibrium. But where supply is limited and demand increasing, scarcity value will always push up prices. The art of *en primeur* buying will be to predict which properties are under-valued and where prices are likely to rise – and to get in there before everyone else. Bordeaux, thanks to its ready market, remains the yardstick. But don't overlook well-chosen Côte d'Or red Burgundy, northern Rhône wines, top-quality vintage Champagne, Barolo from Piedmont or fine California Cabernet Sauvignon as possible candidates for *en primeur* buying in the 1990s.

INSIDE THE AUCTION ROOMS

by Anthony Rose

AS THE 300-BOTTLE BARREL of Beaune Hugues et Louis Bétault came up for auction, a hush descended on the packed market hall in medieval Beaune. No one knew who he was, but every time André Boisseaux, a merchant who always likes to get his way, put in a bid, the mystery bidder raised the stakes. The crowd roared approval like spectators at a Wimbledon final. The previous record for a barrel of wine, 500,000 francs, was passed to a huge roar. Eventually, after 17 minutes of competitive bidding, the barrel went under the hammer: a new auction record of 605,000 francs was set. Further applause was this time accompanied by the traditional Burgundian drinking song. And, after frantic behind-the-scenes activity to establish the credit-worthiness of the mystery bidder, the auction resumed its snail-like pace.

As wine auctions go, the annual charity auction at the Hospices de Beaune – the centrepiece of three days of glorious gluttony known appropriately as "Les Trois Glorieuses" – is the world's most famous. The *bons bourgeois* of Beaune have orchestrated this set-piece event, every third weekend in November, as a way of banging the drum for the new vintage. Prices tend to be unrealistically high, but for the patrician heads of Burgundy's most illustrious wine merchant firms, the opportunity to be magnanimous in public is not one to be missed. For the rest of the world, yearly differences in the final prices paid act as a useful barometer for the average price of the new vintage.

Publicity can repay even the most outrageous bid. A new auction record for a bottle of wine was set in 1985 at Christie's in London, when Christopher Forbes, the American magazine magnate, successfully bid £105,000 for a bottle of Château Lafite 1787, wheel-engraved with the initials Th J. The controversy as to whether or not it had belonged to the Francophile American revolutionary Thomas Jefferson, author of the American Declaration of Independence, generated enormous publicity – fanned by the auctioneers themselves. "I would have been infinitely better off if Jefferson had drunk the damned thing," remarked Forbes Senior ruefully, after hearing that the cork had crumbled into the ill-fated bottle under the heat of the Forbes Gallery display lights. With this postscript itself attracting yet more publicity, the issue of provenance rather lost its relevance.

Not every collector's motives are publicity-orientated. The following year, I attended the sale in London of a bottle of Château d'Yquem 1784, reputedly from the same bricked-up cellar. When it was knocked down to an unknown buyer for £36,000, a new record for a white wine, the press mobbed the buyer who claimed to be buying it for a shy but wealthy industrialist who didn't wish to be named. Stories to that effect duly appeared in the newspapers, with speculation rife as to who the mystery buyer might be. The true story didn't emerge until long after. It was an elaborate ruse to get the press off his back: in reality he was buying it for his own cellar.

The scarcity value of rarities and collectors' items gives the saleroom an aura of fashionable respectability. Château Mouton-Rothschild became an instant collector's item when the late Baron Philippe de Rothschild had the bright idea of commissioning a new label from a different artist each year from 1945 onwards. Quinta do Noval Nacional 1931 is a valuable rarity because it comes from a small plot of vines not grafted onto American rootstock like other vineyards throughout Europe. Tokay Essencia (see pages 172-74), elixir of the pre-revolutionary Tsars of Russia, fetches high prices thanks to its legendary longevity and romantic origins.

Much of the credit for establishing the commercial link between fine wine and culture must go to Michael Broadbent MW (see pages 239-41), who turned Christie's occasional sales into a regular feature in the mid-1960s. Perhaps more importantly, he started filling the saleroom with regular stocks of a consistent standard – whether bankrupt or surplus stock, the realization of a speculative investment or the liquid assets of a deceased wine lover. With stock as good as any wine merchant's, the buzz of the saleroom, beneath the discreet town or country club façade, is frequently the sound of the wine trade fighting it out for a share of the action. From whatever source, the saleroom provides an opportunity to purchase certain kinds of wine not otherwise available. Claret's unique combination of longevity and availability ensures that there is always a ready market; vintage port, too, finds a ready, if more specialized market. These are the bread-and-butter wines of the fine wine stock exchange. The specialist magazine *Decanter* even runs its own claret and port index based on the most important sales.

The London salerooms tend to be dominated by the wine trade, whose nod-and-wink familiarity can unnerve newcomers. It needn't however: the saleroom is open to anyone who cares to walk in off the street, whether buying or not. Bargains may be few and far between these days, but the saleroom offers a chance to buy unusual wines and mature vintages that are not commercially available. If you know your wines, fine German wines, Burgundy and lesser vintages of red Bordeaux (1976, 1979, 1980, 1981) or port (1975, 1980), can still be snapped up at near-bargain prices. And buying this way – if you have an ounce of competitiveness in you – can be fun.

A word of caution to anyone contemplating buying by auction. Two words, actually: *caveat emptor*. The saleroom is a consumer no-man's-land. Buying at auction does not entitle you to the statutory guarantee of merchantable quality normally available to consumers, and inspection of the goods is not normally practicable. Even if you do get the opportunity to inspect, it is not always possible to detect whether a wine is faulty or not.

If you are serious about buying at auction, it's a good idea to go with one or two like-minded friends; apart from anything else, it will expand your purchasing power. Pick up a catalogue a few days before the sale and familiarize yourself with the standard

Some of the world's finest and most venerable bottles are auctioned at Christie's. The atmosphere can be intimidating, but the saleroom is open to anyone who walks in off the street.

abbreviations. They can be expensive: a buyer's premium of ten per cent is now standard (though not universal) practice; add on tax, duties and delivery, depending on where the wine is lying, and the extras can mount up alarmingly.

The key to safe bidding is to give yourself a budget and stick to it; it is easy to get carried away in the heat of the moment. Bidding itself, however, is straightforward. Scratching an ear is unlikely to land you with an unwanted lot: any such lot can be returned to the auction if you notify the auctioneer's assistant before the end. If anything the reverse is true, although the job of attracting the auctioneer's attention has been made easier since the introduction of numbered "paddles". When the excitement is over, pay the invoice promptly on receipt to avoid storage charges and knock off any delivery charge if you are collecting the wine yourself. Finally, check for any damage or omissions to ensure that your precious 1978s are not 1977s, your Piesporter Goldtröpfchen not Piesporter Michelsberg, or that for any other reason your wine is not mutton dressed as Mouton.

Great Cellars of the World

A great cellar offers more than just the traditional classics. As winemaking flourishes around the world and wine drinkers themselves are increasingly well informed, good cellar management becomes ever more vital.

To have one's own cellar is perhaps the ultimate luxury for any wine lover. Yet however extensive a personal cellar might be, it is no substitute for choosing from time to time from the outstanding and lavish stocks of the world's top restaurants and wine stores.

Joanna Simon, **Nick Lander**, **Steven Spurrier**, **Gerald Asher** and **Claus Arius** examine the people, the philosophies and the intricacies behind some of the best cellars and wine lists across the globe, from Wiesbaden to San Francisco.

HARRODS WINE DEPARTMENT, LONDON

by Joanna Simon

"WE FIND A STOCK ASSORTED TO SUIT THE TASTES of all opponents of total abstinence. There are clarets from 'ordinaire' to high-class château productions, ports of the vintages sacred to those who have no dread of the gout, and selected from the best shipments of Cockburn, Kopke, Graham, Morgan and others. Champagnes from that bearing the very broad description 'superior' up to such luxurious drinks as Giesler, Mumm, Perinet, Piper or Pommery, while for those of smaller means or semi-abstainers there are the exhilarating but somewhat saccharine liquors that owe their origin to fruits grown on British soil. Then there are spirits called not 'from the vasty deep' – for water is a matter that when Gin, Brandy, Rum or whisky are concerned Mr Harrod prefers to leave to the discretion of his customers – but there are those of the mineral class from soda to the medicinal Carlsbad, Schlossbunnen, Taunas and some which are surely bottled for the fair sex namely, Mesdames and Celestines."

Times have changed somewhat since the description in the *Chelsea Herald*, dated August 30th 1884, of the newly reopened Harrods Wine Department in the store rebuilt after the devastating fire of December 1883: the idea that port is a prime cause of gout is, happily, discredited; some of the brand names are unfamiliar (who ever heard of the "luxurious" Perinet Champagne?); there are rather fewer "saccharine liquors" made from "fruits grown on British soil" – least of all, one suspects, in Harrods; and, while mineral water may be one of the boom drinks of the end of this century, just as it was at the end of the 19th, claims made about its "medicinal" value are extremely limited.

Yet there is a flavour evoked by this report that is not out of place in the Harrods Wine Department of the 1990s. If you leave aside the period prose, omit some of the brand names, liquors and waters, you are left with a range of products to suit all palates and various sizes of pocket, from clarets for everyday drinking to the top classed growths, vintage ports from the leading shippers and a broad spectrum of Champagnes.

All of which is exactly what you would find in Harrods today. The difference is that you would find a great deal more as well. Champagne, claret, port – as well as white Burgundy, whisky, brandy, exotic liqueurs and other classics of the traditional fine wine merchant – continue to be the mainstays, lavishly stocked and equally lavishly bought by customers. But in the last few years, wines from other parts of the world have appeared on the shelves and in the twice-yearly list. This is a reflection not only of the greater knowledge and interest in wine among Harrods' cosmopolitan shoppers, but also of the sound instincts of the store's new wine buyer, Hugh Cochrane MW, who joined the company in 1987.

His own tastes, he is quite clear, are "very conservative: white Burgundy, Champagne, claret. I'm a straightforward traditionalist, but I've been increasingly impressed by other, new areas. I haven't changed most of the French areas dramatically, though I've plugged some gaps, such as an own-label Beaujolais-Villages." Most of his buying, therefore, has concentrated on lesser-known areas. The number of "Other French Wines" has swelled

Twenty years ago, Harrods bottled much wine themselves.

and includes unusual *vins de pays*, organic wines, dessert Muscats, rosés – among them inexpensive wines, together with more expensive limited-production wines. Fashionable New World areas such as Australia, New Zealand and Chile have been embraced, but fashion alone is not a criterion here; there are East European and South American countries whose wine quality has not yet merited inclusion. On the other hand, Cochrane is not afraid to list an expensive, avant-garde wine if he feels the quality justifies it. The oddly-named Geheimrat 'J' Riesling Spätlese Trocken (from the firm of Wegeler-Deinhard) – one of the new breed of bone-dry German wines – is a case in point.

Another area of expansion is that of Champagne and sparkling wines, and no wonder – they account for 20 per cent of turnover. Champagne itself was well covered prior to Cochrane's arrival (although the rosé section has been augmented), but the sparkling wine range seemed a little cautious. So now there are German sparklers, a Crémant d'Alsace, two Australian sparkling wines and one from New Zealand, not to mention examples from Spain, California, Italy, the Loire and Limoux.

The main list runs to a staggering 1,400 wines, about 50 of which account for 65-70 per cent of volume. These are Harrods' phenomenally popular own-label wines and spirits. It would be easy for the store to abuse its success by fixing the Harrods label to all sorts of products, but it would go strictly against the grain, so numbers – and of course quality – are tightly regulated. In many ways the quality control aspect is more complicated than it was until the early 1970s, when the wine department carried out much of its own bottling in the basement cellars. But equally, bottling by wine producers is infinitely more sophisticated and reliable than it was 20 years ago.

The 1,400 wines are complemented by another 600 or so rare items which are available in small quantities only. These appear on the constantly changing *Fine and Rare Wines* list, where you might find 1945 and 1959 first-growth clarets, jeroboams and imperials of Château Pétrus (see pages 30-36), venerable vintages of Château d'Yquem, Tokay Essencia (see pages 172-74), La Tache and Richebourg from Domaine de la Romanée-Conti, Vega Sicilia (see pages 137-43), old Champagnes, vintage ports dating back to the 1920s, rare bottlings of malt whiskies, and vintage Cognacs and Armagnacs. And that is only a taste of what it holds. For the full flavour, you will need the Harrods list. Or, better still, wend your way through the store's Food Halls or the Fine Jewellery Department until you come across an Aladdin's cave of fine bottles: I defy you not to feel like a child in a sweet shop.

TAILLEVENT, PARIS

by Nick Lander

WHEN AND WHERE DID ORSON WELLES drink Margaux 1900, the Duke and Duchess of Windsor La Mission-Haut-Brion 1947, John McEnroe Domaine de la Romanée-Conti Montrachet 1967 and Richard Nixon Léoville-Las Cases 1934? Not surprisingly, the occasions were different – 1954, 1963, 1985 and 1986 respectively – but the location was always the same: the famous restaurant of Taillevent in Paris.

It took no great detective work to discover this: the empty bottles stand in the Caves Taillevent, the wine shop that Jean-Claude Vrinat opened in November 1987, just around the corner from his three-star restaurant. The shop, together with Taillevent's cellars and various Taillevent Champagnes and brandies, forms the basis on which Jean-Claude leads his passionate crusade to bring the very best wine to his customers.

Taillevent itself was started by Jean-Claude's father, André, after the Second World War. André had initially been persuaded against a career as a restaurateur by his parents, and for 20 years he was an engineer. But in the 1930s he finally abandoned engineering to embark on his chosen career – and thereafter pursued it with fearsome determination. He met Raymond Baudoin, one of the founders of the *Revue des Vins de France* and one of the rescuers of the Burgundian vineyards after 1945, who became his "wine teacher".

Vrinat *père* was a highly disciplined man who, when not working in his restaurant, was visiting vineyards, and Jean-Claude realized at a tender age that if he wanted to keep up with his father he ought to begin learning about wine. He visited his first vineyard when he was 13 years old but did not begin to taste wine, even with water, until he was 16. When he did, however, he soon understood the fascination that wine can inspire, and its elemental importance in the context of the restaurant. Wine has remained a passion ever since, as has devotion to the restaurant. Even in France, such a combination of expertise is rare.

Taillevent represents a dedicated family business. It is open for lunch and dinner Monday to Friday, and Jean-Claude is there for every service. The only exception was in June 1989 when he took a Monday off – to visit Vinexpo, the biennial wine exhibition in Bordeaux. Weekends and holidays are invariably spent in the vineyards; Jean-Claude's wife is, luckily, equally enthusiastic about wine and a redoubtable taster. Although he feels he missed watching his daughter grow up, he can now enjoy working with her: she helps him run Les Caves Taillevent.

In wine terms, Jean-Claude has a great deal to show for all his hard work. His cellars in Paris house 350,000 bottles: 200,000 lie in a large cellar on the outskirts of Paris, a disused chalk cave, where he has joined forces with another three-star chef, Joel Robuchon of Jamin, to hold stocks; there are two other fully air-conditioned cellars, each holding 50,000 bottles; and the shop and restaurant each hold another 25,000.

This does not include Jean-Claude's own Champagne stock. Ten years ago he began the selection and *assemblage* of his own-label Champagne in order to control quality. This has progressed to the stage where he is a partner in a *négociant/manipulant* business which makes a Champagne to his own specification – 70 per cent Chardonnay, 30 per cent Pinot Noir. There are 250,000 more bottles housed in the company's 17th-century cellar – ample stock to cover annual sales of 60,000. Some are exported as far afield as Los Angeles. It is a revealing exercise to view these huge stocks against the restaurant's actual annual wine consumption. In a year, the restaurant serves a mere 25,000 bottles: around 12,500 Bordeaux, 5,000 white Burgundy and 3,000 red Burgundy. There is enough existing stock to cover the restaurant's requirements for the next 12 years!

Wherever possible, Jean-Claude buys directly from the producer. To guarantee quality and to ensure that the wine has not been shipped out of France and then back again, he will now buy only *en primeur* from Bordeaux (see pages 242-43). He will not buy any wines from Burgundy *négociants*, and his list reads like a roll-call of the good and great "small producers" – Henri Jayer, Lafarge and Gouges for reds; Coche Dury, Raveneau (see pages 50-55) and Niellon for whites – with vintages dating back to 1961.

The choice of wine is seen as such an integral part of Taillevent's style that there is no separate wine list. The menu, which is changed every two months, is printed as a four-page,

It is a matter of family pride to ensure that the
wine list meets the same exacting standards as the menu.

large-format sheet of parchment with the menu on the outside and the wine list in the middle. Everyone therefore receives a copy – there is no chance of the host hogging it – and everyone can see what is available. Nor are there any *sommeliers*: Jean-Claude believes that he has done his very best in selecting the wines, and that from then on the customers should be free to choose what they want without any added pressure.

In order to pass the rigorous Vrinat selection process and make its way onto the Taillevent wine list, a wine must fulfil two vital conditions. The first is that it must represent the very best of its type; Jean-Claude takes at least as much care over the quality of his wines as he does over the quality of the produce for his three-star kitchen. His second objective is to seek out the small producers of top-quality wines and spirits, and where they measure up to his exacting standards, to endorse them by including them in his prestigious list. In this way, he has helped to popularize some of the lesser wine regions of France, and he has now begun to import the wines of Niebaum Coppola from California's Napa Valley as well as a wonderful range of digestifs from around the world, particularly port and malt whisky. He does see the day when more wines from outside France will be on his restaurant list, particularly after a tasting this summer when he mistook a Chalone Pinot Noir 1978 from California for a Henri Jayer red Burgundy.

It is little wonder that Robert Parker dedicated his first *Wine Buyers' Guide* to Jean-Claude Vrinat, calling him a true oenophile – a man who combines knowledge and enthusiasm with a remarkable passion for wine.

THE PEAT INN, FIFE

by Nick Lander

DAVID WILSON IS NOT ONLY CHEF and proprietor of The Peat Inn, Fife, but also a very canny Scot whose hobby happens to be wine. He is therefore able to offer, on almost every page of his thoughtfully compiled wine list, the wines that most appeal to him, that best complement his cooking and that represent real value for money.

The principles behind the list have stayed the same since The Peat Inn opened for business in 1972 because, while proud both of his wines and of his cooking, David Wilson sees them as only part of what he has to offer. As a chef he appreciates that running a restaurant involves far more than simply providing good food: its success depends on the careful orchestration of the ambience, the service, the meal and the wines.

While The Peat Inn's list reflects David's determination to offer his customers the very best, it also reveals his own enduring interest in and love of wine. When I asked about his particular favourites, he confessed that he adores the uncomplicated tastes of California and other New World wines, though for him Champagne has no substitute. He also belongs to the very small minority who are under the spell of old Chenin Blanc wines, such as Bonnezeaux, and he loves the marvellous fruit flavours of Alsace. For his own pleasure he would drink Burgundy; he currently offers white Burgundies from 1972 onwards and reds dating back to 1962.

Reaffirming the Auld Alliance between France and Scotland, David has very strong feelings about Bordeaux. Claret, for him, is the wine above all others – a wine to drink with friends, to discuss, to analyze and to compare. From the great 1945 vintage there are Pétrus (see pages 30-36) and Latour; vintages of Grand-Puy-Lacoste and Palmer date back to 1970, Léoville-Las Cases to 1959; and seven vintages of his particular favourite, Château Pichon-Longueville Lalande, are available, from 1961 to 1981.

The list balances this apparent classicism with a liberal dash of iconoclasm. There are two pages devoted to Chardonnays from around the world, four vintages of Stag's Leap Cabernet dating back to 1977, and a particularly *outré* Cabernet Sauvignon from Yeringberg in Australia's Yarra Valley (whose total production is only 950 cases). Three years ago, David Wilson was visited by a small bearded man who introduced himself as Philip Togni. He had heard of David's interest in wine and had brought a sample; David tasted it, liked it, and Philip Togni's Sauvignon Blanc has been on the list ever since.

David Wilson would have made an excellent wine merchant. He believes that constructing a first-class wine list follows the same basic principles as constructing a mouthwatering menu. The essential ingredients are quality, balance, some unusual wines and some of especially good value, and the confidence to buy and to list the wines that he likes. If there are any wines missing from his list, he maintains, it is because he has yet to discover them, or because he has actually bought them but they are not yet mature.

The Peat Inn's list is not only easy to read but it is also cleverly and helpfully presented. White wines are listed on white sheets, red wines on pink; there are two pages of half-bottles of white wines and one of red, and each wine area is preceded by a perspicacious introduction. His list of Chablis is, unusually, broken down into those producers who use

One of only two Michelin-starred restaurants in Scotland, the Peat Inn has an awesome reputation to maintain. David Wilson knows that success depends on more than a mouthwatering menu.

oak and those who use stainless steel; his descriptions of Alsace grape varieties are precise and he astutely recommends his range of German wines as being low in alcohol.

This is a wine list that is not only the result of a great deal of patience but also one designed to give as much pleasure to the customer as to the proprietor. David admits that as both chef and wine-buyer he might have to work twice as hard, but on the other hand he does earn twice the satisfaction.

Naturally modest, he is quick to point out that he has had sterling support from the better wine merchants. As The Peat Inn is one of only two Michelin-starred restaurants in the whole of Scotland, its wine list obviously attracts a great deal of attention. But, located as it is so far from the London tasting circuit, David says he would not have been able to compile such an impressive selection without his trusted suppliers offering him allocations of the rare finds and small parcels of fine wine.

Above all, he claims, David Wilson owes his thanks to Patricia, his sympathetic wife, who has not objected to his reading wine lists in bed these past 17 years.

GIDLEIGH PARK, DEVON

by Nick Lander

GIDLEIGH PARK OPENED IN 1977. Since then, there have been three major factors behind the success of this outstanding restaurant and its equally outstanding wine list. The first is Paul Henderson's passion for wine, and his uncompromising determination to serve only the wines he likes. The second is a characteristic Paul developed during his years at McKinseys, the management consultants, where he learnt to accept only the very best regardless of cost. And the third is his unswerving resolve to take the long-term view in his decision-making – whether it concerns the acquisition of Burgundy, California Cabernet, or another croquet lawn.

Paul did not grow up with wine – discovering it only when he was posted to Amsterdam in the late 1960s. There, a friend introduced him to his father's cellar, which contained 100 cases of Cheval Blanc 1955 – and Paul was smitten. From Amsterdam Paul and his wife Kay, a wonderful cook who ran the Gidleigh Park kitchens for the first ten years – toured the vineyards of France, reading Hugh Johnson's *Wine* and Alexis Lichine's *The Wines of France* diligently every night before the following day's excursion.

It was on these trips that Paul began to buy wine seriously. During the crash of 1974, in the wake of the oil crisis, which followed two boom years for wine, the price of fine wines – and especially of Bordeaux – slumped. Happily, Paul was able to take advantage of the fall in prices to begin building up his cellar in earnest, starting with 30 cases of Château Ducru-Beaucaillou 1970 at £34 per case. By the time he and Kay decided to buy Gidleigh Park in 1977, his personal cellar was worth some £30,000 and it was this that formed the basis of the hotel's wine list.

Realizing, nevertheless, that his own wines did not offer a sufficiently comprehensive range for the hotel, Paul decided to consult an expert. Knowing nothing of German wines, he went to the late Anthony Goldthorp of O W Loeb. He sold some wines that were surplus to requirements and, reinvesting as directed, acquired Rhine and Mosel from the lovely 1976 and 1971 vintages. Goldthorpe's guidance also led to Paul's buying other wines, most notably the wonderful Hermitage La Chapelle 1978.

At about this time, Paul heard of a new wine merchant called Geoffrey Roberts who was about to ship some of California's best wines to London for the first time. Having swiftly consulted a San Franciscan friend to find out in advance what was being shipped, he astutely placed an order for most of this first shipment. Gidleigh Park soon became the proud owner of a number of California Cabernets from the acclaimed 1973, 1974 and 1975 vintages, and began to gain a reputation as the place to drink them. Many of these wines are still available: there are eight from the 1974 vintage and six from 1973 – and most at prices lower than those in any American restaurant.

The strength of Gidleigh's wine list has proved a very powerful marketing tool. The two most influential reviews of the hotel – in *Gourmet* magazine in early 1981 and in *The New York Times* later that year – both stressed its unique qualities. Paul cleverly held Wine Weekends to fill the quieter months of those early years. Trade is now so brisk that these weekends have been squeezed out, but there are other annual highlights. In the winter of

1989 for example, there were three Saturdays devoted to lunches and vertical tastings of Château Latour, Sassicaia and Vega Sicilia (see pages 137-43).

In the 12 years since the restaurant was founded, the criteria for any wine's appearance on the list have not changed. First and foremost every wine should be good and ready to drink regardless of price. This makes Paul a major buyer of wines that have to be snapped up when they are offered, like Burgundy and California wines – but not of *en primeur* claret, because of the large trading market for such wines in Britain. He believes in holding large stocks: in 1989 his total stock was valued at £150,000, while the annual turnover of the hotel was just over £1 million.

Paul will not list any wines that he would not drink himself: there is no place for Liebfraumilch, Mateus Rosé or even English wines, but the stocks he does hold are carefully controlled on computer. He also has a strict pricing policy which offers an extra inducement to drink the list's better wines such as Salon Le Mesnil Champagne, old Châteauneuf-du-Pape Les Cèdres from Jaboulet and mature red Burgundy.

But, however exciting the present list, Paul Henderson has no intention of resting on his laurels. He has bought £25,000-worth of 1985 red Burgundies (of which only a third are on the list) and has already invested in the 1988s. But it is when Italy is mentioned that his eyes really light up. It is his intention to have the best (not the most comprehensive, he stresses) list of modern Italian red wines in Britain by the early 1990s.

Together with his great friend Bill Baker from Reid Wines he has already bought £10,000-worth of Italian red wines, mainly from the 1985 vintage, and most are unlisted. At the moment you could drink the wines of Maurizio Zanella, Gaja (see pages 102-107), Lungarotti and Sassicaia, but many more will follow. As long, Paul adds quickly, as his bank manager permits.

SPARK'S STEAK HOUSE, NEW YORK

by Steven Spurrier

"OURS IS PROBABLY THE ONLY *REAL* CELLAR in New York, not just an impressive list with 'one to show and one to go'." So speaks the ebullient Pat Cetta, co-founder with his brother of Spark's Steak House and its amazing wine list.

The list comes with the menu – or perhaps it is the other way around. The menu itself, which offers the best steak and shellfish from around New York, plainly prepared and simply but beautifully served, takes up just the outside of a huge folder of heavy white paper; inside are the wines. As if the selection of 354 wines (mostly from California, France and Italy) were not enough, there is a separate dessert menu with 19 Sauternes, 12 late harvest selections from California, nine from Germany and 18 vintage ports. And all this at prices 30-50 per cent lower than other establishments. Spark's list is a labour of love, from which the producers, the consumers and the Cetta brothers benefit equally.

For Pat Cetta, a cellar means mature wines. He likes continuity from vintage to vintage, but won't buy "off-vintages" and won't generally support prestigious labels that do not perform to their best. An exception was his decision to list the rather light Sonoma Cutrer Chardonnay 1986: "not a good vintage for them, but I bought a little anyway because Bill Bonetti's a friend and I admire him". As an admirer myself, I had already chosen this wine – priced at $29 as against the $45 I saw quoted in Florida later that week – before Cetta came over and replaced it with a rich, weighty Balverne Vineyards Chardonnay 1981, reminiscent of Batard-Montrachet. Not many cellars in the world list eight-year-old

Pat Cetta, co-founder of Sparks Steak House

Sonoma Chardonnay in perfect condition, nor do they list a dozen 1970 clarets. Knowing that fine wine – white or red – may hold up for many years after "maturity" if properly looked after, Cetta doesn't push these rarities. Through the sense of excitement that his list creates and the confidence that fills the restaurant, such wines sell themselves. Asked to recommend a claret, he went immediately for Château Giscours 1978 at $48: "perfect with our steaks, perfect to drink now; we still have 80 cases".

There is no specialized *sommelier* at Spark's – just as there is none *chez* Taillevent in Paris (see pages 249-50) – for both Pat Cetta and Jean-Claude Vrinat have their lists at their fingertips. Like Vrinat, Cetta acts both as buyer and as a *sommelier* of the old school, believing that the overall happiness of the client is the important thing. "Once I begin to see bottle variation, I no longer sell the wine again; nothing is worse than a customer having that bad taste, having to send a bottle back if he knows about wine, at any rate spoiling the meal."

Cetta is a true wine man, with an innate feeling for what is right – a creator, rather than a follower of trends. He buys with his instinct for the market, anticipating investment potential, but not driven by it. His 1978 clarets, all classed growths or equivalents in quality, and all ready to drink, are very fairly priced at $44-50. Prices could be a lot higher, but with 60,000 bottles of good wine drunk at Spark's every year, both Cetta and his customers are happy with things as they are.

For special occasions, there are large bottles: magnums of course, but also double-magnums (four bottles) and imperials (eight bottles). An imperial of Château Lafite-Rothschild 1971, just reaching its peak now, is good value at $725, or under $100 a bottle. And how about the perfect Château d'Yquem 1975 at $175, less than the current price at auction? "When such wines are ordered, especially the large bottles, there is an immediate sense of fête in the restaurant. My waiters are excited, tables nearby feel the thrill of those who are drinking it. I never serve great wines to tables who are just showing off, so there is no jealousy at all." Vintage ports date back to 1945: "I always knew that vintage port was better than money in the bank, but now people are really drinking it".

The Spark's cellar running through the basements is controlled to a temperature of 58°F (14.5°C). Cold rooms and large storage facilities provide a good day cellar. Every wine is correctly stored: wines in wood in their original cases, the rest binned. It is one of the most extraordinary cellars I have been in, a living Aladdin's cave. Surveying a large pile of Castello di Volpaia (see pages 114-19) – he believes that the next trend will be in Sangiovese-Cabernet blends from Tuscany – Cetta described it as "a working cellar".

"You do seem to have just about everything," I said.

"Yes," replied Cetta with a grin, "we're supposed to."

ZUNI CAFE, SAN FRANCISCO

by Gerald Asher

IN WINE, AS IN FOOD, Billy West and his Zuni Cafe partners Vince Calcagno and Judy Rodgers believe the world turns on an honest, comforting table. In February 1979, Billy West opened his restaurant at a simple store front on what was then a sad section of San Francisco's Market Street. He himself was cook until 1982, and there were excellent cooks to follow him. I do not mean to disparage any of them when I say, nonetheless, that Zuni entered its golden age when Judy Rodgers took over the kitchen in 1987.

As a Missouri high-school exchange student in France, Judy Rodgers had found herself delivered by a benevolent fate to the kitchen door of the Jean Troisgros family home in Roanne. She took to pan and spatula with aplomb, and after putting in her time at Stanford University returned to France and Italy to improve her cooking skills. To me her food is a deliciously Italianate version of rural French, but she and Billy West describe it as essentially an abstraction of Elizabeth David's Mediterranean. Whatever the label, the warmth of Judy Rodgers' cooking quickly attracted such a following that since her arrival tables have spread into the adjoining premises, into the next again, upstairs, downstairs and, at lunch-time, out onto the pavement where great mounds of clams and oysters from east and west coasts wait on beds of crushed ice to be shucked to order. Though the restaurant has become a light and airy warren, no one ever seems to be far from the busy open kitchen flanked by its brick-built wood-burning oven and grill, with a reassuringly high stack of split logs always ready.

An energetic young French woman is responsible for matching wines to Zuni's food. The daughter of small restaurateurs on the Cap d'Antibes, Sylvie Darr first broadened her professional experience at Orsi in Lyon (a darling of Gault-Millau presently wearing two Michelin rosettes), where an interest in wine soon earned her responsibility for keeping the cellar stocked. An extended trip to California to learn about the wines of the New World brought her marriage, a job in the wine and food programme at the Robert Mondavi Winery (see pages 186-93), and now a key role at Zuni.

The greatest contrast with Lyon, she found, was the availability of a greater variety of wine in San Francisco, and the more eclectic tastes and expectations of customers. "Nevertheless," she told me, "first and foremost I must buy wines that follow the kitchen, fit the ambience of Zuni, and please the broad spectrum of our customers – not just those with a special interest. And the choice must be manageable from all points of view, so every wine must count – no window dressing."

A good wine list, in any event, is not constructed: it evolves. It need not be long – how many wines does one have time to consider when ordering in a restaurant? – but it should, for a start, inspire confidence by what is not there as much as by what is. It should reflect a point of view and a familiarity with what the market offers; it should throw in a surprise or two and coax interest in a few unknowns; its older vintages should be approachably priced – not mere gilding – and clearly the result of forethought rather than of an earlier misplaced enthusiasm. Even the best of lists have limits, but I would no more trust a wine list that tried to cover the world than I would a menu that attempted to offer all things to all men.

Zuni's list starts with a dozen Champagnes and sparkling wines, ranging form Roederer Cristal to the Scharffenberger Brut from Mendocino's Anderson Valley. About 100 wines follow, fairly evenly divided between reds and whites, with roughly equal proportions of imported, and what Zuni refers to quaintly as "domestic", wines. A separate list of dessert wines available by the glass and half-bottle, as well as brandies, Cognacs, Armagnacs, grappas, Calvados and aged rums, arrives with the cheese and dessert menu. With an occasional exception from Oregon, the American wines are from California. Among the imported wines the only exceptions to the dominion of France and Italy are high-quality sherries, and late-bottled and vintage ports.

Changing constantly – sometimes between lunch and dinner – a half-dozen wines are available by the glass. "They are rarely from the main list," Sylvie Darr says. "We sell by the glass wines that are unfamiliar – a Cahors, perhaps, a Nebbiolo delle Langhe, a Cabernet Sauvignon from a new winery we think has promise. I have to be sure an unusual wine is typical of its region or I shall mislead customers who buy it for the experience. I must watch that wines sold by the glass remain in perfect condition or I can damage a new winery's reputation as well as our own. Of course sometimes I sell a wine by the glass just to clear a few remnant bottles after a list or vintage change, but that is peripheral."

Not unexpectedly, the list is strong in California Chardonnays, but it also has an intelligently chosen selection of white Burgundies, with a greater emphasis on wines like de Villaine's Bourgogne Aligoté de Bouzeron, Faiveley's Mercurey Clos des Rochettes and Leflaive's white St-Aubin Premier Cru than on a multiplication of Meursault and Pouilly-Fuissé. Red Bordeaux offered are *cru bourgeois* rather than classed growths. "Few restaurants now can make the investment of laying down classed growths, but we can afford to put aside some good *bourgeois*. Our customers will get a better idea of what Bordeaux is about by drinking the *bourgeois* growths we are maturing for them than by drinking a newly released, raw classed growth, no matter how grand its vintage.

"We age some of our California Cabernet Sauvignons, too. But each time I revise the list I seem to pick up more Zinfandel and Pinot Noir at the expense of Cabernet. There are really exciting Pinot Noirs available now, and Zinfandels have shaken free of the 'big wine' syndrome. They are approachable and comforting to drink. Our customers like that."

DIE ENTE VOM LEHEL, WIESBADEN

by Claus Arius

HANS-PETER WODARZ, WHOSE EXCEPTIONAL all-round culinary talents have earned him the sobriquet "the German Bocuse", is perhaps the most famous of Germany's specialists in *haute cuisine*. No one has done more for the reputation of German gastronomy over the last few years than the imaginative "HPW".

Wodarz's first restaurant, which he opened after serving his apprenticeship as a cook and travelling for several years, was in the Lehel district of Munich. And later, when he found a new domain at the Nassauer Hof in Wiesbaden (one of the best hotels in the world), he named it "Die Ente vom Lehel" – The Lehel Duck – in memory of this successful start in Munich. That was 11 years ago. Today, Die Ente is a celebrated institution.

The emphasis from the start was on providing not only first-class food and excellent service, but also fine wine. Every year, without fail, months of hard work are spent updating the restaurant's wine list. And, as Wodarz and his *sommeliers* discover interesting new offerings to include, the regular customers continue to cling to their favourite wines – so the choice grows ever wider. There are already more than 40 vintages of Châteaux Palmer, Mouton-Rothschild and d'Yquem in the cellar, and the wine list has now assumed record proportions. Indeed, the 1990 edition lists almost 1,990 offerings, each chosen by a skilful and exhaustive process of tasting, selection and purchase, and each matured with the greatest of care. There is more than enough work here for one person.

The design of the wine list rivals its contents. A hefty 19 × 13 inches (48 × 33 centimetres) in size, it is a pleasure to the eye and a sheer delight for any wine connoisseur. Wines are arranged by country and region, and are colour-coded: black type for white wines, red for red wines, and pink for rosés. The list itself is a collector's item, and over 500 copies are sold to enthusiasts every year.

In the restaurant time is of no importance, though the diners are never neglected. Those who know what they are about choose at their leisure, while those who don't can follow the advice of Die Ente's experienced waiters. It is a restaurant sensitive to the size of your purse, with a comprehensive menu to suit every customer.

Wodarz's approach is to offer top-quality wines from a dozen countries, the important châteaux appearing alongside a host of less well-known discoveries, exotic *cuvées* and personal recommendations. German wines, of course, are strongly represented. There are hundreds listed, from every one of the country's 11 vine-growing regions, and the choice is agonizing. Wodarz professes a conviction that German white wines are gradually making headway against French whites, as customers increasingly show a preference for wines with a lower alcohol content. Many of the best German wines on the list come from the Bodensee, from the Ahr, and above all from the nearby Rheingau. There are even a handful of wines from the environs of Wiesbaden itself, as well as a couple more from East Germany. Neglected for many years, these wines are now much in demand.

Prices are not excessive – though, as one would expect, classic rare vintages such as 1961 Bordeaux do not come cheap. There is a wealth of interesting tastes to discover, with one or two particular bargains hidden away among the rest, unobtrusively awaiting recognition. The *sommelier* gives nothing away, and Wodarz delights in watching to see how many of his customers will pick them out. Those who do are recognized as true connoisseurs – for the wines here are chosen lovingly, and never mechanically.

Wiesbaden is the capital of *Sekt* (German sparkling wine) and, as you would expect, every major producer is represented on the wine list, together with the competing wines of Champagne, for which there is a considerable demand from the international clientele. Die Ente's customers come from every part of the world and from a variety of professions; the visitors' book is littered with some of the most famous names of our time – politicians, artists, businessmen and sportsmen alike. All 70 seats in the main restaurant are taken every evening, but further space is available in the bistro and "Duck Bar".

Many a Bacchanalian tasting session has been held at Die Ente. A wealthy wine collector might, for example, invite a dozen or so friends for a day-long appraisal, first horizontal and then vertical, of the world's finest wines – Latour, perhaps, or d'Yquem, or pre-phylloxera claret. The restaurant is, not surprisingly, a popular venue for such occasions, and this is largely due to Hans-Peter Wodarz himself, for, as well as being a great expert on wine, he is an accomplished conversationalist.

Vintage charts

These charts are general guides to the wines of the major regions in any given year. Like other vintage charts they are not definitive indications of any producer's wines, but taken in conjunction with the profiles and introductory sections in this book, they give a good indication of what you might reasonably expect in each relevant year.

It has been said many times before, but it is worth reiterating, that good, possibly great, wines may be made by skilled winemakers in apparently poor years, while no amount of excellent weather will overcome sloppy vineyard practices or winemaking. Equally relevant is microclimate: the more individual microclimates are sought out by producers, the more variations there are to the general pattern.

New World countries do not suffer the climatic extremes of Europe, so vintage variation is less pronounced and disasters are rare. Nonetheless it is a significant factor, particularly for those producers seeking cooler microclimates.

FRANCE

Red Bordeaux

1989 A very, very promising finale to a fine decade and certainly one of the best of the 1980s. Whether or not it will turn out to be the vintage of the decade is too soon to say, but it looks as though quality will bear comparison with the best of the century so far – **1929**, **1945**, **1961** and **1982**. All three main grape varieties were very healthy, with high sugar levels, concentrated, ripe tannin, powerful aromas and medium acid levels. Thus, both Left Bank (Cabernet-dominated Médoc) and Right Bank (Merlot-dominated Pomerol and St-Emilion) seem to have been equally highly favoured.

1988 A large crop of good to very good wines: the Médocs are dark-coloured, firm and quite tannic (though not as tannic as the **1986s**); the Pomerols and St-Emilions are harder and more tannic than usual, but with ripe fruit.

1987 After heavy harvest-time rain this vintage was initially dismissed as dilute and lean, but many wines have turned out utterly charming, light and fragrant.

1986 An extremely good, concentrated vintage with very high tannins that will need many years to soften. Very much a Cabernet Sauvignon (Médoc) year; particularly fine in the northern Haut-Médoc communes and Graves.

1985 Hailed as a great year initially, particularly for Merlot, but many top wines are already so soft, supple and forward that there must be doubts about their long-term ageing. Many St-Emilions are disappointing.

1984 An abnormal year in which there was almost no Merlot; many perfectly sound, if lean, Cabernet-style wines were made, but they were initially over-priced.

1983 Classic claret: as simple as that. The wines will not be as long-lived as the extraordinary **1982s**, which continue to overshadow them, but they are classically well-balanced – and the Margaux are superb.

1982 Exceptional – an early, hot harvest of grapes massively rich in sugar. Opulent, concentrated wines with dense, ripe tannins. Most top growths should not be broached before the second half of the 1990s.

1981 Quite good, elegant, but not very intense wines; most at their peak in 1990

1980 Light wines, most of which should be drunk before 1991-92.

1979 A very pleasing vintage. At first the large crop seemed to lack depth, but the wines evolved beautifully during the 1980s; most top wines are reaching their peak in 1990, but will stay there for several years.

1978 Dark, concentrated, ripe, tannic wines that will last a long time; most are just beginning to approach their peak period in 1990.

1975 At the time, this was greeted as a great vintage of full-bodied, tannic wines, but many of the wines have turned out to be too hard, dry and tannic – ie unbalanced.

1970 Gloriously ripe, rounded wines; now mature

1966 Turned out more austere and less opulent than expected, but the best wines are drinking well in 1990.

1961 Magnificent: top wines will remain so for years.

Dry White Bordeaux

1989 was a fine year. Early on there were fears that the grapes had ripened too far, producing high alcohol with too little acidity, but the wines are beautifully aromatic with well-concentrated fruit.

Except for a few top Graves (most of them in Pessac-Léognan), white Bordeaux is best drunk within a couple of years of the vintage. For laying down, **1988**, **1987** and **1986** were all good, as was **1985**.

Sweet White Bordeaux

1989 was another great Sauternes year with higher sugar concentrations even than **1988**. The 1980s saw a comeback for Sauternes. Even before the 1989 result there had been three superb vintages – **1988**, **1986** and **1983**. Previous great years for drinking in the early 1990s are **1976**, **1975**, **1971**, **1970**, **1967** and **1962**.

Red Burgundy

1989 An early harvest with good, but not outstanding results. Sugar levels were good, acid was a bit low and in general concentration was weaker than **1988** and **1985**. The wines seem likely to turn out soft, supple and for relatively early drinking.

1988 A great vintage: well-coloured, ripe, tannic and with a good acid structure. The wines are not quite as fat as **1985**, but they may live longer.

1987 An unfashionable, underrated vintage: the wines are perfumed, very elegant and well-balanced.

1986 Lean and relatively early-maturing, the Côte de Nuits having the edge over the Côte de Beaune.

1985 An outstanding vintage with opulent, ripe, supple and very perfumed fruit; good tannin and structure, but not as firm as **1988**.

1984 Adequate wines, even the best of which should be drunk by the early 1990s.

1983 A controversial vintage with an erratic outcome. There are a few big, ripe tannic wines for the long haul, but most were spoiled by rot and are unbalanced.

1982 Soft, rather dilute wines

1981-1979 Undistinguished: need drinking up.

1978 Generally excellent with richness and power; the wines are now mature.

1972-1969 All good vintages, but in need of drinking.

White Burgundy

1989 Words like "perfect" have been used to describe the grapes harvested in both the Côte d'Or and Chablis. Sugar levels were very high and in Chablis there is the aroma and acidity for great wine. The Côte d'Or wines will be very opulent, but the question-mark over their balance means they may not be as stylish as the **1986s**.

1988 A good, almost very good, year throughout the Côte d'Or and Chablis.

1987 Sound wines in a light, fairly lean style

1986 Very good in Chablis and the Côte d'Or. The wines have concentrated fruit and good acid backbone, giving depth but also elegance.

1985 Full-flavoured, powerful, alcoholic wines but with lower acidity than **1986**. The best should be excellent quality, but there is inconsistency.

1984 Lean wines: only the best are still holding up.

1983 As controversial in white as in red, with the same problems of rot, clumsiness and erratic results. There is some excellent heavyweight Côte d'Or, but not much. *Grands crus* Chablis, though very fine, need drinking up.

1982 Attractive, soft, fruity Côte d'Or wines now need to be drunk. Chablis wines are over the hill.

1981 Better than **1980**, but the wines have been rather unyielding; drink now.

1979-1978 The **1979s** turned out nearly as well as the more concentrated **1978s** and both are now delightful.

Champagne

1989 Absolutely outstanding and sure to be declared as a vintage by most houses. The grapes were said to be perfectly balanced ("better even than **1947** and **1959**") and this applied equally to Chardonnay and Pinot Noir. The quantity was generous, too.

1988 Good, well-balanced wines widely expected to be made into vintage Champagne, but now that the **1989** has come along some shippers may blend their **1988s**.

1987 Miserable quality except for a little good Pinot; it is unlikely there will be any vintage Champagne.

1986 Fair quality but not special enough to warrant a vintage declaration.

1985 Very good, ripe, balanced vintage Champagnes

1984 Very poor

1983 Large crop of very good wines, most of which were declared.

1982 Superbly rich, creamy Champagnes which were very forward; the best show staying power.

Among the older vintages, **1979**, **1976**, **1975** and **1971** were very good, but only the best Champagnes keep much beyond ten years.

Alsace

1989 An exceptional vintage, comparable to **1976**, with good volume as well. The two late harvest styles – *Vendange Tardive* and *Sélection des Grains Nobles* – were certainly produced in well-above-average quantities.

1988 Last-minute rain diluted quality and dashed hopes of a great vintage, but there are some very good wines from producers who left their grapes to dry after the rain. Otherwise quality is sound but unexciting.

1987 Light, but balanced and pleasant – and better than expected after a rainy year

1986 Good *Vendanges Tardives* and *Botrytis*-affected *Sélection des Grains Nobles*, but otherwise dilute wines

1985 Gloriously fruity wines with good concentration, though not as fat as **1983**; a large proportion of late harvest wines, and these will last well.

1984 Generally poor and not worth keeping

1983 The best vintage since **1976** and **1971**; immensely ripe at all levels and the top wines will keep well.

1982-1977 Except for the top wines, these vintages are now generally past their best. **1979** and **1981** are the best bet; **1980** and **1977** the worst.

1976 Fabulously rich wines, many late-picked; some are still not ready.

Of the older vintages, the best **1971s** and **1967s** are still holding up well.

Loire

There seems to be reasonable justification for declaring **1989** one of the vintages of the century; it certainly stands comparison with **1976**. Exceptionally, just about all grape varieties did well, so there are good dry whites, reds and rosés, and fine sweet, semi-sweet and sparkling wines. But some Sancerres and Pouilly-Fumés may suffer from low acidity.

Except for the great sweet wines of Coteaux du Layon and Vouvray, and the extraordinary dry white Savennières – all made from the Chenin Blanc grape – Loire wines are basically for drinking fresh and young. That said, **1988**, **1987**, **1986** and **1985** were all good years for dry wines. **1988**, **1985**, **1983**, **1976**, **1969** and **1964** were outstanding for Chenin Blanc.

Rhône

1989 A severe drought reduced yields throughout the region. The harvested grapes were, nonetheless, in a healthy condition, with good alcohol and tannin. Acidity tended to be rather low, but quality-conscious producers had a superb vintage.

1988 Deep-coloured, tannic, solid, concentrated reds in both the north and the south – wines for long cellaring. Powerful, aromatic whites

1987 Respectable northern Rhônes, but very weak wines from Châteauneuf-du-Pape and the rest of the south. Good whites

1986 A difficult vintage because of rain, but some very good Châteauneuf that will age well. Quite good whites

1985 Excellent rich, ripe northern Rhônes – especially Cornas, Côte Rôtie and (white) Condrieu. Seductively fruity Châteauneuf

1984 Generally meagre wines, although Châteauneuf developed well and many wines now have a most attractive perfumed fruit character. Some very good whites

1983 Outstanding northern reds – the best since **1978**, although not quite as rich. Very good Châteauneuf

1982 A very hot year which gave full-bodied but low-acid, early-maturing northern reds and soft, fragile southern reds. Whites were short of acid.

1981 Often excellent, powerful Châteauneuf, but fairly lean astringent northern reds

1980 Good, medium-weight red wines throughout the region. Underrated and attractive now.

1979 Excellent reds with richness and density, both north and south. Now mature, but the best will last. Good northern whites

1978 The best since **1961**; fabulously ripe, concentrated reds which are still not fully mature.

Older red Rhône vintages to look for include **1971**, **1970**, **1969** and, of course, **1961**.

GERMANY

1989 A superb vintage on the Rhine – the best of the decade and in many cases the best since **1971**. Sugar and acid are beautifully balanced and wines have been made at all quality levels right up to *Trockenbeerenauslese*. For the Mosel, too, an outstanding year – the second in a row, but with more *Botrytis* than in **1988**, so more sweet wines.

1988 An outstanding year for the Middle Mosel, with supremely elegant wines. Rhine regions fared less well, especially the Rheingau, but on the whole the wines are good. Some very good Rheinhessen were made.

1987 A maligned vintage. There was a high proportion of *Kabinett* wines, but very fine ones in the Rheingau, Middle Mosel and Rheinpfalz. Worth seeking out.

1986 Fair quality overall. Least good in the Mosel because of rain; balanced, quite forward Rheingau

1985 Some excellent ripe, age-worthy Middle Mosels and very good wines from the Rheinpfalz. The Rheingau had unique problems (associated with use of a pesticide); those who avoided it made good rather than great wines.

1984 Small crop of light wines. The best Mosels will age quite well.

1983 Not as good as originally thought, but a very good year, above all in the Mosel-Saar-Ruwer and Rheingau.

1982 Enormous crop of rather dilute wines

1981 Similar to **1987**. Best in the Mosel. Drink soon.

1980 Basically poor, although there are exceptions.

1979 A good vintage, especially on the Mosel; now needs drinking.

1976 A superb, ripe vintage, but with a tendency to low acidity. Most should be drunk soon.

ITALY

Piedmont

1989 Piedmont seemed to be favoured with Tuscany's quota of sun. Barolos and Barbarescos both look very promising – ripe, concentrated and well-structured.

1988 Because of harvest-time rain, not the great Barolo vintage that the fine summer originally promised, but good all the same, and good to very good for Barbaresco.

1987 Rain was a problem. Less good than the **1988**s; quite attractive for drinking in the short to medium term

1986 A small crop of good wines in Barolo; some very good Barbaresco

1985 Superb – one of the all-time greats; intensely fruity, beautifully balanced wines

1984 Erratic – some very fine Barolo and Barbaresco, but some very meagre wines too

1983 Though there are some good wines, this is not the great vintage it was said to be.

1982 A magnificent vintage: voluptuously perfumed, fruity wines; however, low acidity could limit the long-term ageing potential.

1981 Weak

1980-1979 Both quite good, but should be drunk soon.

1978 Seemed superb at first, but may never quite live up to expectations.

Of the older vintages, **1971** was superb and the wines are now fully mature.

Valpolicella

1989 was a sorry tale of summer storm damage, low yields and erratic quality.

Only the *Recioti* wines (sweet and dry) are for ageing here, but in the great years – **1986**, **1985**, **1983**, **1981**, **1977**, **1974**, **1971**, **1970** – the best wines can live 20 years.

Tuscany

1989 In comparison with much of the rest of Europe and with Piedmont, a disappointment. Chianti simply did not get the sun. The wines will be lightweight.

1988   An outstanding vintage. Ripe, succulent wines with ageing potential

1987   A rain-soaked vintage: generally light wines as a result, but the best have charm; others are too lean.

1986   Averagely good, medium-bodied, supple wines for drinking within the next few years

1985   A splendid year – superb wines; but a few do have a slightly baked taste because of over-hot fermentations.

1984   Poor

1983   A tough, tannic year, but the wines are now developing attractively.

1982   Opinions are divided as to how good these wines are: although rich and ripe, their low acidity is not encouraging for the future.

1981-1977   All quite good vintages, but they now need drinking, as do the very good **1975s**.

SPAIN

Rioja
1989 was good, slightly above average in quality and quantities – a great relief after the previous few years. **1988** was erratic: quality varies from below-average to very good. **1987**, **1985**, and **1983**, were all good years. **1981** was very good and **1982** was outstanding. The **1986s** are largely sound but lacking intensity. **1978** *Gran Reservas* are very good, as, still, are a few from **1976**, **1973** and **1970**.

Penedès
In **1989** massive summer storms badly affected the native white grapes. But the French varietals were largely unaffected, as were the native red varieties with the exception of Garnacha, and quality should be sound.

Most wines are made for fairly early consumption, but the 1980s (except for **1989**) was a good decade for the wines made for maturing; **1987** was outstanding.

Duero
1989 was good to very good in quality but there was not much of it because of drought. **1988** was disastrous and **1987** was not much more than adequate. **1986** was reasonably good. **1985**, **1983**, **1979**, **1977**, **1976**, **1975** and **1973** were all good years. **1982** and **1981** were very good, and **1970** was excellent, but so far only Vega Sicilia Unico has the track record of ageing ten years or more.

PORTUGAL

Port
1989   An early harvest, producing healthy, above-average-quality grapes. Yields, however, were low. It is too soon to say whether a vintage will be declared, but shippers will be taking into account the fact that there have already been three from the 1980s.

1988   Unlikely to be declared, though quality looks promising, because such a small crop was harvested.

1985   Universally declared; very fine

1983/1982   Shippers declared one or other of these vintages, not both: the **1983s** are bigger and will last longer; some of the **1982s** are ready for drinking.

1980   Elegant, nicely structured wines

1977   One of the great post-war classics, along with the **1963** and **1945**

1975   A light year, ready now

1970   A rich ripe year; can be drunk, but still evolving.

1966   Silky, but firm wines, ready now

1963   Superb and still developing

Table wines
At this stage in Portugal's modern table wine career, climatic conditions are still a great deal less important than the producer. That said, **1985**, **1983** and **1980** stand out as above average.

CALIFORNIA

1989   The most difficult harvest since **1972** because of torrential rain mid-harvest. This does not mean that overall quality is poor, but it is mixed. It took vineyard management and winemakers to make good wine.

1988   Creditable quality but reduced quantity from a very difficult year; Chardonnay and Pinot Noir emerged from the climatic assaults best of all.

1987   A very good vintage for all main varieties, with the Cabernets in particular promising to be long-lived.

1986   A very good all-round vintage, though without the benefit of the acidity and structure of **1985**.

1985   Outstanding: the vintage of the decade

1984   A very good year, though overshadowed by **1985**. The rich, ripe red wines still have life in them.

Previous vintages of the 1980s were not exciting and are now generally past their best. The best vintages of the 1970s (for reds) were **1978**, **1974** and **1970**; the best wines still have life in them.

AUSTRALIA

1989   A problematic year with patchy results, but not the disaster some initially thought. Barossa, Clare and Padthaway all produced good quality, although volumes were varied. Coonawarra and the Hunter Valley were more erratic and the Yarra Valley was hard hit. Western Australia fared quite well overall.

1988   A good vintage in most regions, except for the rain-buffeted Hunter Valley

1987   The fourth successive cool year. Excellent quality, if small quantity, for all South Australia except Coonawarra; good elsewhere

1986   Another cool year and an extremely good one

1985   Consistently good, and particularly fine in the Margaret River

1984   The first of the cool years. Especially good reds, though slightly less so in the Hunter Valley and Victoria

1983   Very successful in the Hunter Valley, but not so good elsewhere

1982   An excellent vintage, holding up well

1981   Never very good and now past it

1980   Highly-regarded reds from Barossa, Victoria, Clare and Coonawarra, the best still showing very well.

Glossary

Adega Portuguese term for a winery or wine cellar

Alberello Bush-style method of training vines used in southern Italy

Amontillado Dry, nutty style of sherry that develops naturally from **fino** when the **flor** dies; can also be made by adding alcohol to *fino* sherry and leaving the wine to mature further

Appellation Contrôlée (AC) Official regional designation in France, guaranteeing source, grape varieties, yields, alcohol level and production method of wine

Assemblage French term for the blending of wines

Aszú Hungarian term for the **botrytized** grapes used to make Tokay

Auslese Official German term for quality wine (**QmP**) made from selected grapes, often with a natural sweetness caused by **Botrytis**

Barrica Spanish term for **barrique**

Barrique Standard barrel of 49.5 gallons (225 litres) in Bordeaux or 45 gallons (205 litres) in Burgundy, made of oak and used to store maturing wine

Beerenauslese Official German term for intensely sweet top-quality wine (**QmP**) made from individually selected overripe grapes

Biodynamism System of cultivation using only organic fertilizers and no synthetic chemical treatments

Bodega Spanish term for a winery, wine cellar or wine-producing firm

Botrytis cinerea "Noble rot" which shrivels grapes and concentrates the sugar, making possible the production of opulent, naturally sweet white wines

Botrytized Affected by the **Botrytis** fungus

Botte Large oak cask in which wine is matured in Italy

Carbonic maceration See **macération carbonique**

Centrifuge Machine used for separating the solids from new wine

Cépage French term for grape variety

Chai, chais French term for an overground wine store

Chapeau French term for the mass of grape skins, stalks and pips that rises to the surface of the juice during fermentation, forming a "cap"

Chaptalization The addition of sugar during fermentation to increase the alcohol level of wine

Chef de cave French term for the person in charge of a winemaking establishment

Classed growth See **cru classé**

Climat Burgundian term for an individual vineyard

Clonal selection Vineyard programme of selecting the best or most suitable vine **clones** for planting

Clone One of a group of plants reproduced asexually from a single sexually-produced plant

Cooper Maker of barrels, casks, etc

Copita Glass used in Jerez for sherry

Cru French term for a "growth" – a wine-producing estate or vineyard

Cru bourgeois Bordeaux château which meets criteria set by a *syndicat*; below **crus classés**, above *petits châteaux*

Cru classé Classed growth – in particular a Bordeaux château ranked under the 1855 Classification of the Médoc as a *premier*, *deuxième*, *troisième*, *quatrième* or *cinquième cru* (first, second, third, fourth or fifth growth)

Cuvaison French term for the fermentation of wine on the grape skins

Cuve French term for a vat

Cuvée French term for a (specially selected) blend of different wines

Cuverie French term for a winery

Demijohn Large glass bottle with a wide body and narrow neck

Deutscher Tafelwein (DTW) Official German designation for basic table wine, below **QbA** in the eyes of the law, though not necessarily in quality

Diatomaceous earth A fossiliferous earth used for filtering wine

Denominazione di Origine Controllata (DOC) An official regional designation in Italy, guaranteeing source, grape varieties, yields, alcohol levels and production methods of wine

Denominazione di Origine Controllata e Garantita (DOCG) Stricter version of **DOC**, awarded to a smaller number of regions in Italy, regulating and guaranteeing the above

Drip-irrigation Technique of providing water to vines via a slow trickle of water from hoses

Eiswein Official German term for rare and highly concentrated quality wine (**QmP**), of equal or greater ripeness to **Beerenauselese**

Elevage Ageing of a wine in the period between fermentation and bottling

Enology See **oenology**

Estufa Special oven used to heat Madeira

Exclusivity Exclusive right to sell the wines of a given vineyard or château

Extract Tasting term referring to the amount of body and flavour in a wine

Fining The addition of material (eg egg whites) to a wine during vinification to attract particles in suspension and thus clarify the wine

Fino Style of sherry produced by the action of **flor**

First growth See **cru classé**

Flash-freezing The rapid chilling of wine in order to precipitate **tartrates**

Flatteur Tasting term, meaning literally "flattering"

Flor Yeast which forms on the surface of newly-fermented sherry, protecting it from oxidation, and which produces the taste of **fino**

Foudre French term for a large cask

Fût French term for a cask (smaller than a **foudre**)

Garrafeira Portuguese term for a matured vintage wine; often a merchant's special selection, and by implication superior wine

Goût de terroir French term for the wine taste attributable to a particular vineyard: "the taste of the soil"

Grand cru   In Burgundy, a vineyard in the top classification; elsewhere in France, a less specific term for a superior wine

Hogshead   Wine, beer or spirit cask of varying size

Horizontal tasting   Tasting of different wines of the same vintage; see also **vertical tasting**

Kabinett   German term for the most basic category of quality (**QmP**) wine

Lees   Wine sediment

Lieux-dit   French term for a specific vineyard or site

Loge   Madeiran term for a winery

Macération carbonique   The fermentation of whole bunches of unbroken grapes in an atmosphere saturated with carbon dioxide; traditional in Beaujolais

Malic acid   Raw, "appley" acid in underripe grapes

Malolactic fermentation   Secondary fermentation of wine in which harsh malic acids are converted into softer lactic acids

Manzanilla   Type of **fino** sherry produced at Sanlúcar in the Jerez region, with a salty tang

Marc   Residue of grape stems, pips and skins left after crushing; also the distilled spirit made from this

Microclimate   Climate prevailing in a small area such as a vineyard, possibly untypical of the region as a whole in which it is situated

Micropore filtering   Very fine filtering to remove micro-organisms from wine

Mise en bouteille   French term meaning "bottled"

Must   Unfermented grape juice

Master of Wine (MW)   Formerly British, now international, distinction earned by wine professionals passing a rigorous examination

Négociant   French term for a wine merchant

Négociant/manipulant   French term for a company that both makes and sells wine (usually found in the context of Champagne)

Oak-ageing   Process of maturing wine in oak casks for complexity and extra flavour

Oenologist   Practicioner of **oenology**

Oenology   Science of winemaking

Oidium   A fungal disease of vines, also known as powdery mildew

Oloroso   Full-bodied style of sherry, heavier and richer than **fino** and **amontillado** because it has never developed much **flor**

Oxidation   Chemical process triggered in wine by its exposure to air

Palo cortado   Unusual style of sherry that starts as **fino** and develops into **oloroso**

Pétillant   Slightly sparkling

Phylloxera   Vine pest which infects roots, causing the death of the plant: responsible for destroying most of the vineyards of Europe in the late 19th century; cured by grafting vines onto immune American rootstocks

Pneumatic press   Type of grape-press which is worked by air pressure

Premier cru   In Bordeaux, a vineyard in the top classification (see **cru classé**); in Burgundy, the second rank after **grand cru**

Puttony   Hungarian term measuring sweetness in Tokay, from three (medium sweet) to six (very sweet)

Qualitätswein bestimmter Anbaugebiete (QbA)   Official German designation for quality wine from a specific region, made from authorized grapes; between **DTW** and **QmP** in quality

Qualitätswein mit Prädikat (QmP)   Official German designation for "quality wine with distinction", made from grapes with enough natural sweetness not to need **chaptalization**; the highest category of German wine, ranging from **Kabinett** to **Trockenbeerenauslese**

Quinta   Portuguese term for a winemaking estate

Racking   Process of transferring wine from one container to another to separate a wine from its **lees**

Régisseur   French term for the manager of a property

Rootstock   Rooting part of a grafted vine

Sekt   German word for sparkling wine

Sélection des Grains Nobles   Alsatian term for the individual selection of **botrytized** grapes

Solera   A collection of sherry butts; also the term for the blending process used particularly in Jerez, whereby butts containing young wine are topped up with progressively older wines

Sommelier   Wine-waiter

Spätlese   Official German term for quality wine (**QmP**) made from selected grapes picked late in the harvest

Tannin   Astringent substance in the skins, pips and stems of grapes – also in wood – which is essential in a wine that is to be aged

Tartaric acid   The most important grape acid

Tartrates   Solid crystalline matter appearing in wine when **tartaric acid** forms crystals

Trockenbeerenauslese   The top category of German quality (**QmP**) wine, made from selected withered grapes, thus very sweet

Vanillin   The substance that gives vanilla its smell

Vendange   French term for the grape harvest

Vendange Tardive   Alsatian term for late harvest, equivalent to the German term **Auslese**

Vertical tasting   Tasting of several vintages of the same wine; see also **horizontal tasting**

Vigneron   French term for a grower of vines

Vin de Pays   Category of French wines of the junior rank (below **AC**), regulated as to origin, grape variety and production process

Vin de Table   Standard French table wine, *not* regulated as to origin, grape variety or production process

Vinification   Winemaking

Vino da Tavola   Italian term for basic "table wine" below **DOC**, which now includes some prestige wines made using methods or grape varieties that do not conform to **DOC** rules

Viticulture   Grape-growing

Contributors' biographies

Joanna Simon

Joanna Simon, the General Editor, is Wine Correspondent of *The Sunday Times*. She was already interested in wine when she went up to university, where she was a leading light in the wine society's blind-tasting team. After a year as a trainee wine buyer, she joined *Wine & Spirit* magazine, becoming Editor in 1984. In 1986-87, she was Editor of *Wine* magazine, for which she remains the Contributing Editor. She edited *The Sunday Times Handbook of Wine* in 1988 and gives bulletins on *Guidelines*, the newspaper's telephone advice service.

As well as travelling extensively around the wine regions of the world, Joanna Simon has tasted and written for a wide range of publications and has made appearances as a wine expert on British and Australian television. She is also Consultant Editor on a series of books on the wines of France, Spain and Portugal, Italy and the Americas, published by Salamander Books.

Burton Anderson

A native of Minnesota, Burton Anderson has spent most of his adult life in Europe, working first as a reporter. In 1977 he left newspapers to write a book, *Vino, the Wines and Winemakers of Italy*, which won him the Glenfiddich Award in 1981 and established him in a new career as a wine writer. He has followed up this success with *The Mitchell Beazley Pocket Guide to Italian Wines* (1982), now in its third edition, and *The Wine Atlas of Italy* (1990), also published by Mitchell Beazley.

Burton Anderson's articles have been published in numerous English language publications, as well as in Italian journals. He lives with his wife and two teenaged children in a restored 16th-century farmhouse on the edge of Chianti in Tuscany.

Claus Arius

Claus Arius has written about wine for many years. After a long career as an advertising manager for wine, he is now a freelance journalist specializing in food, drink and gastronomy. His extensive library of 4,000 books includes a whole row of his own works on wine, cocktails and cookery. He has also contributed many articles on the subject to trade journals and consumer publications.

Wine is still his first love. His frequent travels have taken him from his native West Germany to the world's most prominent wine-producing regions, providing him with wide first-hand experience of wine production and countless wine tastings.

Gerald Asher

Born and educated in the United Kingdom, Gerald Asher trained in the wine trade there and in Europe before moving to the United States in 1970. He was decorated by the French Government in 1974 with the star and ribbon of the *Mérite Agricole* for his contribution to French agriculture, and remained actively involved in many aspects of the wine trade until 1987.

A contributor to books, periodicals and newspapers on both sides of the Atlantic, Gerald Asher has served as a guest lecturer in the wine marketing programme of the University of San Francisco and in the Department of Viticulture and Enology of the University of California. In 1984 he was awarded the *Wines and Vines* Perpetual Award for Wine Writing. He is currently Wine Editor of *Gourmet* magazine.

Michael Broadbent MW

Director of Christie's, President of the International Wine & Food Society, past-Chairman of the Institute of Masters of Wine, painter and pianist, Michael Broadbent has also been honoured by the French: in 1979 he was dubbed *Chevalier dans l'Ordre National du Mérite* and, more recently, he was a recipient of the highest award of the City of Paris, *La Grande Medaille de Vermeil*.

For over 30 years a regular wine columnist and lecturer, he is author of the seminal work *Wine Tasting*, first published in 1968, and *The Great Vintage Wine Book*, published by Mitchell Beazley in 1980. Both books won the annual Glenfiddich Award and the *Grand Prix de L'Académie Internationale du Vin*. Married, with a son in the port trade and a barrister daughter, Michael Broadbent spends his time between a flat in London, a house near Bath and flights to far away places.

Stephen Brook

Stephen Brook was born in London in 1947. After graduating from Cambridge, he worked for many years in publishing on both sides of the Atlantic before becoming a full-time writer. For two years he wrote a monthly column on wine for the *New Statesman*, and since 1988 he has contributed a wine column to *Vogue*.

Author of *Liquid Gold: Dessert Wines of the World*, published by Constable in 1987, which won the André Simon Memorial Prize, Stephen Brook is currently working on a guide to the grape varieties Sauvignon Blanc and Sémillon. He is also the author of numerous travel books, including *New York Days, New York Nights, Honktonk Gelato, Maple Leaf Rag* and *The Double Eagle*, and of the widely acclaimed book *The Club: The Jews of Modern Britain*.

David Gleave MW

Born and educated in Toronto, David Gleave came to England in 1978 and, apart from the two years that he spent in Dublin during the early 1980s, he has lived in London ever since. He became a Master of Wine in 1986.

A specialist in Italian wines, David Gleave buys them for the London-based firm Winecellars, one of the leading Italian wine importers in the United Kingdom, writes about them for such periodicals as *Wine, Decanter* and *Wine & Spirit*, and lectures on them for the Wine and Spirit Trust. His book *The Wines of Italy* was published by Salamander Books in 1989, and he is currently writing a guide to the wines of Tuscany to be published in 1991.

James Halliday

James Halliday is one of Australia's most respected wine experts. In 1970, after several years of writing on wine, he founded Brokenwood Winery in the Hunter Valley with two colleagues from his Sydney law firm. From 1971 to 1983, he helped to run the winery in his spare time and also gained vintage experience in Bordeaux and Burgundy. In 1985, he established Coldstream Hills in Victoria's Yarra Valley, which is now among the country's most highly-regarded wineries.

As well as writing on wine and food for a variety of periodicals, James Halliday is a wine consultant, a regular judge at wine shows, and the author of 14 books on Australian wines, including *The Australian Wine Compendium* (1985). He makes annual trips to the wine regions of Europe and has an extensive cellar dating back to 1850.

Ian Jamieson MW

After serving in the British Parachute Regiment, Ian Jamieson studied hotel management at the Ecole Hôtelière in Lausanne, where he became interested in wine. He worked in the wine trade in France and London, eventually specializing in German wines with Deinhard & Company, and became a Master of Wine in 1970. He has written and contributed to a number of wine books, including the German section of André Simon's *Wines of the World* (1981) and *The Mitchell Beazley Pocket Guide to German Wines* (1984).

Lecturing engagements have taken Ian Jamieson to the United States, Germany, Holland and Japan, and he contributes frequently to British, German, American and Scandinavian periodicals. He is currently writing a book on German wines, his special interest. He works as a full-time freelance writer and lives with his wife Ulla in the United Kingdom.

Hugh Johnson

Described by Jancis Robinson MW as "the wine writer with the magic pen", Hugh Johnson is the world's bestselling author of wine books. Twenty-four years after the publication of his seminal book *Wine* (1966), international sales of his books total some seven million copies. Among his most notable successes as a wine writer are the classic *World Atlas of Wine* (1971), now in its third edition, *The Wine Companion* (1983) and his widely acclaimed *Story of Wine* (1989), all published by Mitchell Beazley. His

Pocket Wine Book, updated annually since 1977, is unrivalled and rarely off the bestseller lists.

Hugh Johnson and his family live in a 16th-century farmhouse in Essex, where his other great passions for gardening and trees have led to the publication of his *Principles of Gardening* and *Encyclopaedia of Trees*. His wife Judy is a graphic designer.

Nick Lander

Educated at Manchester Grammar School and Cambridge, Nick Lander was initially in the textile business and later worked as a commodity trader. His interest in wine and food grew in the early 1980s when he re-opened L'Escargot, the restaurant in Soho, and married the wine writer Jancis Robinson MW. Although the restaurant prospered his health did not, and in 1988 he sold it.

Since 1989, Nick Lander has been Restaurant Correspondent for *The Financial Times*. With his wife he has produced *Matters of Taste*, the first of a documentary series for television on what, and how, we eat and drink, dealing with the life and influence of Elizabeth David. Together they are working on the first ever *Oxford Companion to Wine*.

James Laube

James Laube is a senior editor and columnist for *The Wine Spectator*, America's leading wine consumer publication, and author of *California's Great Cabernets*. A native of Chicago, Illinois, he has lived most of his life in California. He is a graduate of San Diego State University and holds a master's degree in history.

He began writing about wine in 1978, and during the 1980s he has travelled to and written regularly on the wines of France, Portugal, Germany, Italy, Spain, Australia, the United States and Mexico. James Laube lives in Napa, California with his wife and two children, and is currently writing a book on California Chardonnay. He tastes nearly 5,000 wines a year.

Simon Loftus

Simon Loftus is a wine merchant, hotelier, restaurateur and writer. His annual wine lists for Adnams of Southwold, the British wine merchants, provide compulsive reading for customers and rivals throughout the world.

He is the author of two books, *Anatomy of the Wine Trade* and *A Pike in the Basement*, and Editor of a recent series of *Regional Guides to the Wines of*

France published by Octopus. As well as writing for *Country Life* as Wine Correspondent, Simon Loftus is a regular contributor to numerous other publications. When not travelling the world in search of good wines, he lives in Suffolk with his wife and daughter.

Maggie McNie MW

Maggie McNie trained and worked as an actress and singer. Her wine career began at International Distillers & Vintners, and continued at British Transport Hotels. A growing interest in wine led to her taking the examinations of the Wine & Spirit Trust. After the privatization of BTH, she worked in turn for a City wine merchant and for Arthur Rackham's Vintner Wine Club.

Since passing the Master of Wine examination in 1986, Maggie McNie has spent much time teaching and lecturing about wine throughout the United Kingdom and in Ireland. She has written on a freelance basis for wine magazines and glossies such as *House and Garden* and *Country Homes and Interiors*.

Kathryn McWhirter

After a brief spell in the wine trade, Kathryn McWhirter worked for five years on the trade magazine *Wine & Spirit*, for four years as Editor of the magazine. In 1985-86 she edited the Consumers' Association's *Which? Wine Guide*. She also edited the *Good Wine Bar Guide* in 1986, as well as the monthly newsletter, *Which? Wine Monthly*.

Kathryn McWhirter has written for many publications, including *The Observer*, and she is now Drinks Correspondent of *The Independent on Sunday*. Together with her husband, Charles Metcalfe, she has written *The Wines of Spain and Portugal*, published by Salamander Books, which won the Glenfiddich Wine Book of the Year Award in 1989, and Marks & Spencer's *Quick and Easy Guide to Choosing Wine with Food*.

Charles Metcalfe

Trained as an opera singer, Charles Metcalfe developed an interest in wine writing after four years on the *Evening Standard* wine-tasting team. He was a co-founder of *Wine* magazine, and is now Associate Editor, as well as contributing a monthly drinks page to *Homes & Gardens*. Together with his wife, Kathryn McWhirter, he has had two books published, *The Wines of Spain and Portugal*, winner of the 1989

Glenfiddich Award, and *The Quick and Easy Guide to Choosing Wine with Food* for Marks & Spencer.

Charles Metcalfe has been the drinks presenter for *This Morning*, the popular mid-morning television show, since its start in 1988. He and his wife live in Sussex with two daughters, two cats, three sheep, 25 chickens and about 50,000 bees.

Robert M Parker Jr

Robert Parker was born in Baltimore, Maryland. His interest in wine began in 1967, when he spent a month at the University of Alsace. In addition to writing for *The Wine Advocate*, he is a contributing editor for *Food and Wine* magazine and the main wine writer for *Connoisseur* magazine.

His first book, *Bordeaux*, published in 1985, was followed in 1987 by *Parker's Wine Buyer's Guide* and *The Wines of the Rhône Valley and Provence*, which won the 1989 Tastemaker's Award in the United States and the Wine Guild's Wine Book of the Year Award in the United Kingdom. His second *Wine Buyer's Guide* (1989) will be followed by the forthcoming *Wines of Burgundy*. Robert Parker lives in Maryland with his wife Patricia, his young daughter Maia and various basset hounds.

David Peppercorn MW

David Peppercorn has been a member of the British wine trade for over 30 years. During the 1960s, he was Wine Buyer for Peter Dominic and IDV. Since 1974, he has acted as an independent consultant and agent. A Master of Wine since 1962, he represented the United Kingdom on the Technical Committee of the *Office Internationale des Vins et des Vignes* for several years and was British judge at the *Concours Mondial* in 1972.

David Peppercorn has written and lectured extensively on wine. He is the author of *Bordeaux*, published by Faber in 1982, and the *Pocket Guide to the Wines of Bordeaux*, published by Mitchell Beazley in 1986. He is a Director of the Wine Standards Board. In 1988, he was created a *Chevalier dans l'Ordre des Arts et des Lettres* by the French Government for his writing and research on French wines.

Margaret Rand

Margaret Rand began her career in book publishing, when she first became interested in wine. She was formerly Editor of *Wine & Spirit*, for which she still writes, and is currently Editor of *Wine* magazine. As well as contributing to a number of periodicals on wine-related topics, she is the author of *The Red Wines of France*, published by Salamander Books in 1987.

When not busy writing and editing, Margaret Rand spends much of her time tasting wines and travelling to vineyards all over the world. She lives in London.

Anthony Rose

Anthony Rose worked as a full-time lawyer until 1986. Law began to take a back seat after he won the New Wine Writer Award sponsored by *The Observer* and Peter Dominic in 1985, when he became Wine Correspondent of *The Independent*. Since 1986 he has contributed a weekly column to the Food and Drinks page, which won the Glenfiddich Award in 1989.

In 1988 and 1989, Anthony Rose won the Wine Journalist of the Year Award, presented by the Wine Guild of the United Kingdom. He is also a regular contributor to *House and Garden*, *Decanter*, *Wine* and *Wine & Spirit* magazines.

Steven Spurrier

Educated at Rugby School and the London School of Economics, Steven Spurrier joined Christopher & Co, the wine merchants, as a trainee cellarman. After four years in the London trade, he moved to France and in 1971 bought the Caves de la Madeleine, a small wine shop that he was to turn into one of the best and best-known outlets in Paris.

In 1973 Steven Spurrier created L'Académie du Vin, the first wine-tasting school in Paris, which now has branches in London (with Christie's), Canada, Switzerland and Japan. His publications include *French Country Wines*, *French Fine Wines* and *The Académie du Vin Wine Course*. In 1989 he was named *Personalité de l'Année – Oenologie* for his services to oenology. He divides his time between Paris and London.

Serena Sutcliffe MW

Serena Sutcliffe is a Master of Wine and an international wine consultant. She is the author of five books on wine. Her most recent *oeuvres*, both published by Mitchell Beazley, are the *Pocket Guide to the Wines of Burgundy* (1986) and *A Celebration of Champagne* (1988). *Le Monde* described her as "franco-anglaise dans l'âme", and *A Celebration of Champagne* as "l'un des plus intéressants ouvrages connus sur le champagne".

In 1988, Serena Sutcliffe was made a *Chevalier dans l'Ordre des Arts et des Lettres* by the French Government for her writing and research into French wines. She divides her time between the vineyards of the world and more exotic travel in the Far East. While wine will always remain a consuming passion, she intends to return to where her published writing began in her teens, short stories.

Bob Thompson

Bob Thompson is a freelance editor, a writer and an expert on the wines of California. He is the author of eight books on wine, including *California Wine Country* (1968), *American Wine & Wine Cooking* (1973), *The California Wine Book* (1976), with Hugh Johnson, and *The Pocket Encyclopaedia of California Wines*, first published by Mitchell Beazley in 1980.

For many years he has written a newspaper column on wine for the *San Francisco Examiner*, and he is currently also a wine columnist for the *Sacramento Bee*. As well as contributing to a wide range of American and British wine periodicals, Bob Thompson appears as a professional wine judge at many national wine competitions in the United States. He lives in California.

Roger Voss

Roger Voss has been a wine writer for ten years, as Drinks Writer for the catering trade magazine *Caterer and Hotelkeeper*, Wine Correspondent of *The Daily Telegraph*, and more recently Editor of the annual *Which? Wine Guide* and joint Editor of *Which? Wine Monthly*. He has written two books in the Mitchell Beazley pocket wine series, *French Regional Wines* (1987) and *Fortified and Dessert Wines*, published in 1989.

Roger Voss is currently working on two Mitchell Beazley pocket guides to Chardonnay and Cabernet Sauvignon. His interest in sherry is long-standing, inspired both by the almost perfect combination of a glass of *fino* and *tapas* on a warm day in Andalusia, and by the pleasure of an *amontillado* and fresh roasted almonds on a winter's day in England.

Index

Page numbers in **bold type** refer to principal entries; those in *italics* refer to illustrations.

PICTURE CREDITS

Abbreviations: Jean-Luc Barde/Scope – JLB/S; Jaques
Guillard/Scope – JG/S; Michel Guillard/Scope – MG/S; Mick
Rock/Cephas Picture Library – MR/C; Jean-Daniel Sudres/
Scope – JDS/S; Alan Williams – AW; Mitchell Beazley
Publishers – MB.

Key: left – L; right – R; top – T; bottom – B

Specially commissioned photography by Jaques Guillard, Jean-
Daniel Sudres, Alan Williams and Mick Rock.

Cover: MB/Photo: Stephen Haywood

P. 5, 9, 11 MG/S; 13L JG/S; 13R MG/S; 15L Patrick Eagar;
15R Jon Wyand; 17, 18L/R MR/C; 19, 20, 25 JDS/S; 26, 27L/
R, 28 MG/S; 31L/R, 32, 33, 35, 36 JDS/S; 38 MG/S; 39
Patrick Eagar; 40 MG/S; 43L/R, 44, 47L/R, 48, 51, 52, 53 JG/
S; 54, 57 AW; 59 Nic Barlow; 61L/R, 62 AW; 64T/B, 66 JG/S;
68, 69, 71, 72 JDS/S; 74, 76, 79, 81, 82 JG/S; 83L/R AW; 84,
86, 90, 91, 95L/R, 97 JG/S; 98 MR/C; 100, 103, 105, 107, 109,
111, 112 AW; 113 Janet Price; 115, 117, 118T/B, 121, 122 AW;
124 JLB/S; 128, 129, 130, 131L/R JG/S; 133, 135L/R, 136
JLB/S; 138, 139, 141, 142L/R, 143 JG/S; 145 Jon Wyand; 147
JLB/S; 148, 151, 153, 156 John Heseltine; 158 The Madeira
Wine Company, SA; 159 Jon Wyand/The Madeira Wine
Company, SA; 162 Jan Read; 165, 166 MR/C; 168T/B Rolaz
and Company; 171 JG/S; 173, 174L/R MG/S; 176 Porto
Carras; 179 Wines from Lebanon, Château Musar UK Ltd.;
182T MR/C; 182B Adina Amsel Tovy/Horizon; 184 Janet
Price; 187 Robert Mondavi Winery; 188 Jon Wyand; 189
Michael Freeman; 190 Jon Wyand; 195, 196 Simi Winery; 200,
201L MR/C; 201R Janet Price; 202 MR/C; 204 Jan Read;
206T/B, 210 MR/C; 211 Australian Picture Library; 212 Heidi
Ecker/Horizon; 215, 217, 220, 221L MR/C; 221R Janet Price;
222 Patrick Eagar; 224 Janet Price; 225L Rodney Laredo; 225R
Janet Price; 226 Patrick Eager; 229L/R Nan Melville; 231, 234,
237 MB; 245 Christie's; 246 JG/S; 248 Harrod's; 250 A. de
Roll/Taillevent; 252 Martin Brigdale; 255 Sparks Steak House.